Business Ethics
in America

Business Ethics in America

George C.S. Benson
Salvatori Center,
Claremont McKenna College

LexingtonBooks
D.C. Heath and Company
Lexington, Massachusetts
Toronto

Library of Congress Cataloging in Publication Data

Benson, George Charles Sumner, 1908-
   Business ethics in America.

   Bibliography: p.
   Includes index.
   1. Business ethics. I. Title.
HF5387.B46   174′.4′0973   81-48392
ISBN 0-669-05353-8   AACR2

Published simultaneously in Canada

Printed in the United States of America

International Standard Book Number: 0-669-05353-8

Library of Congress Catalog Card Number: 81-48392

Contents

	Preface	xi
	Introduction	xiii
Chapter 1	**America's Heritage of Business Ethics**	1
Chapter 2	**Ethics of Businessmen**	5
	Studies of Businessmen's Ethics	5
	There is a Big Problem	8
	Executives Who Let It Happen	9
	Business Interests Are Most Important	10
	Pressures of Competitive Business	12
	Influence of Business Associates	14
	Stealing from Corporations Is OK	16
	Youthful Viewpoints	17
	Reduction of Employee Thefts	18
	Ethical Education	20
	Higher Education and the Ethics of Businessmen	21
	Religion and Business Ethics	22
	Conclusions	23
Chapter 3	**The Morality of the Corporation**	27
	Ethical and Historical Background	27
	Is Corporate Organization Moral?	30
	Effect of the Corporation on Individuals	31
	Does a Corporation Have Rights?	33
	Corporate Citizenship	34
	Corporate Political Power	36
	Conflict of Interest	37
	Corporate Codes	42
	Industry Codes	44
	Conclusions	48
Chapter 4	**Business Relations with Employees**	51
	Ethical History	51
	Ethics of Compensation	52
	"Blowing the Whistle"	54
	Safeguards of Employee Rights	57

Company Policy toward Dishonest Employees 58
Ethics of Union Relationships: One Bad Turn
    Deserves Another 60
Nonunion Firms 62
Union Attitudes toward Supervision 63
Seniority 64
Must Employees Accept Union Attitudes? 64
Closed Shop 65
Unions and Organized Crime 65
Strikes 68
Responsibility for Health and Safety of
    Employees 69
Conclusions 72

Chapter 5   **Does Supervision Require Subordination?** 77

Slow Evolution of Western Ethics 77
Mechanisms for Better Supervision 78
Psychological-Ethical Techniques of Supervision 79
Participation in Work Planning 80
Quality of Working Life 81
Japanese Management Methods 82
American Industrial-Psychological Theories of
    Supervision 85
Conclusions 87

Chapter 6   **The Social Responsibilities of Business** 89

Ethical Background of Corporate Social
    Responsibility 89
Does a Corporation Have the Charitable
    Responsibilities of an Individual? 90
Affirmative Action 92
Psychological Adjustment 95
Treatment of the Environment 97
Business Policy and Social Standards 100
Welfare and Social Betterment Activities 102
Conclusions 104

Chapter 7   **Business and Consumers** 107

Ethical Traditions 107
Historical Sketch 108

Consumer Health Problems   109
Consumer Fraud   112
Legal Difficulties of Consumer Debt   113
Consumer Complaints   114
Business Self-Regulation   115
State and Local Regulation   116
Improvement of Laws of Consumer Relations   122
Federal Action   123
Conclusions   124

Chapter 8   **Investment in Land or Securities**   127

Ethics and History of Land Sales   127
Real-Estate Investment Trusts   128
History of Security Sales   130
Marketing of Securities   132
Watered Stock and Unethical Stock Transfers   133
Holding Companies and Investment Trusts   134
"Corners" and "Bears"   136
Legislative Control of Investment Banking   136
"Boiler Rooms"   137
Troubles on the Stock Exchange   138
Conflicts of Interest in the Securities Business   140
Is Disclosure of Corporate Finance an Ethical
    Necessity?   143
Insider Information   145
Conclusions   147

Chapter 9   **Is There an Antitrust Ethic?**   151

Judaic and Roman Law   151
Anglo-American Legislation against Monopoly   151
Early Antitrust Administrative and Legal
    Problems   155
Later Antitrust Legislation   156
The Electrical Manufacturers' Case   156
Antitrust Problems Continue   159
Antitrust Laws and Politics   160
A Critical Look at Conglomerate Mergers   163
The Case for Conglomerate Mergers   164
The Case against Conglomerates   165
Conclusions   168

Chapter 10   **The Ethics of Government Regulation**   171

Ethical and Historical Background   171
Detailed Regulations of the Twentieth Century   172
Regulation for Health and Safety of Employees
    and the Public   174
Regulation of Industry Rates and Services   176
Regulations Affecting All Businesses   179
Is There an Ethical Responsibility to Obey
    Excessive Regulations?   182
The General Problem of Enforcement of
    Regulations   183
Conclusions   186

Chapter 11   **The Ethics of Accounting**   189

History of Accounting   189
American Accounting Standards   193
When Accounting Has Not Worked   196
The Looseness of Generally Accepted
    Accounting Principles   199
Conclusion: The Courts Prescribe Accounting
    Ethics   201

Chapter 12   **The Pros and Cons of Advertising**   205

Ethical Principles   205
Historical Background   205
Caveat Emptor   206
The Slow Reform of Advertising   208
Is Advertising Necessary?   212
Objections to Advertising and Some Answers   213
Enforcement of Advertising Ethics   218
Control by State and Local Governments   219
Federal-Government Regulation   220
Criticisms of FTC Control of Advertising   222
Corrective Advertising   225
Comparative Advertising   227
Conclusions   227

Chapter 13   **Product Liability and Related Problems**   233

Ethical and Legal History   233
Did Business Deserve This?   237

Business Resistance to New Ethics of Product
    Liability   239
Legal Resistance to New Ethical Standards   242
A Note on Repair of Complex Consumer
    Products   243
Conclusions   244

Chapter 14   **The Ethics of International Corporations**   247

Ethical Background of Multinational
    Corporations   248
Bribes or Extortion   249
What Do International Bribes Tell Us about
    American Business Ethics?   252
American Unions and Multinational Corporations   253
Labor Abroad and Multinational Corporations   254
Economic Ethics of Multinational Corporations   255
Balance-of-Trade Problems   258
Mixing Politics and Economics   258
Conclusions   259

Chapter 15   **Conclusions**   263

Overall Obligations   267
Commercial Obligations   268
Business Operations   269

Bibliography   273

Index   285

About the Author   295

Business Resistance to New Ethics of Product
    Liability   239
Legal Resistance to New Ethical Standards   242
A Note on Repair of Complex Consumer
    Products   243
Conclusions   244

Chapter 14   **The Ethics of International Corporations**   247

Ethical Background of Multinational
    Corporations   248
Bribes or Extortion   249
What Do International Bribes Tell Us about
    American Business Ethics?   252
American Unions and Multinational Corporations   253
Labor Abroad and Multinational Corporations   254
Economic Ethics of Multinational Corporations   255
Balance-of-Trade Problems   258
Mixing Politics and Economics   258
Conclusions   259

Chapter 15   **Conclusions**   263

Overall Obligations   267
Commercial Obligations   268
Business Operations   269

Bibliography   273

Index   285

About the Author   295

Preface

This book is a product of the Henry Salvatori Center for the Study of Individual Freedom in the Modern World, located at Claremont McKenna College. It is part of a series of books on applied ethics supported by the Center. The college joins me in expressing gratitude to Mr. Salvatori for the opportunity to undertake these studies.

Gratitude should also be expressed to the Tuohy Foundation, which has financed much of my time for the last several years, and to Harris Seed who offered many excellent suggestions.

Mrs. Mavis Thompson has been helpful and conscientious in preparing the manuscript; she has won my special admiration through her mastery of word-processing equipment. Thanks are due to Mrs. Donna Marleau who typed most of the original drafts. The assistance of several students—Lollie Collins, Terry Marpert, and Pat Brenny—is much appreciated. My colleagues, Professors George Gibbs, John Rae, James Taylor, Colin Wright, and especially Roger Ransom, have read and made useful criticisms of the manuscript. Charles Lofgren and John Niven contributed many useful suggestions about historical materials. I also thank Robert Bartz for his assistance.

The mistakes are all mine.

Introduction

This book is part of my effort to study the field of applied ethics in America following the suggestion made by Henry Salvatori a decade ago that ethics is one of the conditions of a free society. In addition, I have written *Amoral America* (with Thomas S. Engeman) and *Political Corruption in America* (with Alan Heslop and Steve Maaranen). All three books concern aspects of the problem that the United States, despite its wealth and education and ideals, has real evidence of a lower level of applied ethics than that in other modern democracies. Its records of violent crime and political corruption are poorer than those of other modern democracies. Its record of business ethics is no better overall, and is probably worse in some respects. The naturally resulting questions are "Why?" and "What can we do about it?", questions this book attempts to answer.

The book is not intended to be an attack on business, although some aspects of some businesses are sharply criticized. I am a moderate conservative, believing strongly that a system of economic freedom is essential to the continuance and development of all freedom, but also believing that civic forces and government are responsible for establishing a legal and ethical framework for economic operations. I agree with almost all of chapters 1 and 2 of Milton Friedman's *Capitalism and Freedom*, which emphasize the free market but recognize the necessity of some functions of government. Although I have worked primarily in government and education, not business, I have had many connections with business. Through these connections my opinion of business is generally high. This book talks more of the vices of business than its virtues only because the vices raise more ethical problems.

Literature on Business Ethics

There is a large but fragmentary literature on business ethics. Raymond Baumhart has produced a thoughtful book on businessmen's answers to a careful questionnaire[1]; several others have made follow-up studies. Dozens of reporters and free-lance writers have written books that criticize or describe a firm, an industry, or business practice: less than half of these "describe"; the majority criticize. The books written by Ralph Nader and his associates vary from sketchy criticism to well-thought-out analyses of specific problems. Others have written what they think business ethics should be. More-recent books of readings compiled by professors of philosophy are more objective than those of the free-lance writers, but are spotty in their coverage of ethical problems. None of these books seems to give the general (though far from complete) coverage of American business ethics that is the purpose of this book.

What are Business Ethics?

•Business ethics are those principles, or aspirations toward principles, that guide businessmen in their commercial connections with suppliers, customers, workers, or others. Business ethics are normally part of and consistent with general ethics. They may prescribe certain actions, forbid others, or urge one to do jobs such as auditing more carefully or bill collecting more humanely.•There are also questions of the social responsibility of corporations discussed in chapter 6; some are questions of charity rather than justice, and must be discussed separately.

Business ethics may range from the general injunction against stealing (which is in the Ten Commandments and appears in all legal codes) to prohibitions on unfair trade practices in industry codes. There are rules that have been developed by stock exchanges, or by merchants' associations or other trade groups; some of these rules have been given the force of law by inclusion in statutes or judicial decisions. There are other ethical rules of theological or philosophical origin that have been accepted by ethically minded men. For example, an ethical man does not deliberately deceive a customer or a client. He often, but not always, believes that he should not force a competitor or supplier into bankruptcy, a feeling derived not from law but from the Golden Rule or the injunction to love one's neighbor as oneself. Ethical rules may be rigid legal precepts, customs or mores, or aspirations for better human relations or harmonious economic or political relationships. Judges and philosophers and theologians and lawyers have worked out some degree of logical relationship between these ethical rules and aspirations; often a study of aspirations will indicate that a new ethical rule is needed.

General Ethics are a Basis of Business Ethics

How are business ethics determined? Philosophers and theologians have a claim to authorship. Most of their writing on ethics consists of commendable efforts to determine a basis on which individuals can calculate their own ethical approaches. The Eighth Commandment tells us not to steal. Both Judaism and Christianity suggest the doctrine of "love thy neighbor." Immanual Kant suggests categorical imperatives: to act as if your action were a result of universal law and to act as if every individual were an end in himself. The utilitarians suggest that you act in accordance with the greatest

good for the greatest number. The egoists suggest that you act to promote
your own long-term interests. The situation ethicists argue that a moral action
is one that produces the greatest amount of Christian love. The Golden Rule
asks that we do unto others as we wish they would do unto us. John Rawles
has suggested that ethical decisions should give each participant an equal right
to the greatest liberty that agrees with an equal liberty for all and inequality
only insofar as it serves each person's advantage and arises under conditions
of equal opportunity. Alan Gewirth, in *Reason and Morality*, writes that
ethics should be built under a Principle of Generic Consistency.[2] Some of
these general principles furnish a basis for reasoning in business ethics but
they are not always helpful. There are obvious inconsistencies among them.
Several are so generally phrased that their meaning is far from clear. Some
may prove to be unworkable. There is a substantial gap between their
generality and the specific rules which are needed in business practice.

Some economists believe that the market can generate its own ethics; it
can, but only in part. Business ethics usually attempt to remain consistent
with general ethics. General principles, like the philosophic rules cited and
each of their many subdivisions and corollaries, may serve a useful purpose
in helping an inquiring mind.

One example of the push for general ethical consistency is labor legislation in the nineteenth-century United States. Legal ethics moved sharply
toward greater rights for labor and labor associations during the century; it
is highly probable that the "natural rights" philosophy that was popular in
the first half of the century contributed to labor-law development. Another
example is that some businessmen have made major financial sacrifices to
help our government in wartime; they may have been trying to follow a
utilitarian rule, or to love their neighbors; but they were clearly following an
ethic other than that of the market.

Many economists recognize the relationship of business ethics to general
ethics. Adam Smith, *The Wealth of Nations,* commented that each man
should be free to act independently in economic matters "so long as he does
not violate the laws of justice."[3] John Stuart Mill pointed out in *On Liberty*
that the free market requires ethics as a means of enforcing decisions and
assuring competitive conditions. Ethics are as important to the business
world as to other parts of society. Since the law-enforcement machinery applies to all parts of society, ethical-legal principles applying to business cannot vary greatly from general ethics. Business ethics will be more specific
than general ethics but should be consistent with them.

Business-Generated Ethics

A large proportion of business ethics does come from the needs of the
marketplace. Stockbrokers will honor an oral commitment involving many

thousands of dollars of loss because they must keep the confidence of other brokers if trade is to continue. Bernard Baruch gives several examples in his autobiography of capitalist speculators who honored damaging promises to each other, in large part to secure cooperation with each other in the future. Friedrich A. von Hayek believes that the first man to claim private property contributed to the ethics of exchange.[4]

Different situations lead to different sources of ethics. A businessman who attacks and kills his competitor runs counter to the stricture in all societies against murder; no stockbroker-made rule is needed to punish him. On the other hand, brokers may develop their own interactive ethics in order to keep the stock-exchange mechanism functioning. Grocery stores often develop very generous attitudes toward customers in order to keep their patronage, but the salesman of an automobile firm who will not see a customer again for seven years is not as likely to develop a high ethical relationship with him. As a result of the market's failures to create adequate ethics, legislatures and courts have established procedures for warranties and other aspects of the sale of motor vehicles or other complex equipment.

The doctrine of *caveat emptor* ("buyer beware"), discussed in several chapters of this book, is an example of a temporary difference and later reconciliation between societal ethics and business-generated ethics. The general rule of the Western world, found in Mosaic law, the Code of Hammurabi, Roman law, civil law, and common law, is that a seller should not deceive a buyer as to the quality of the product sold. That rule, following a general ethic in favor of truth, has been preserved without legal change for over three thousand years. A shift away from this rule came when lawyers, perhaps seeking to expedite business transactions, persuaded common-law courts in both England and the United States to adopt the very different rule of *caveat emptor*. Businessmen in the early nineteenth century supported the new doctrine. However, it often resulted in injustice, and by the early twentieth century businessmen and others persuaded courts and legislatures to return to the earlier, more general ethic of truth that is once again the rule of Anglo-American law.

Society Needs Business Ethics and General Ethics

Business ethics must be aligned with general ethics. But what are general ethics striving for? It seems to me that ethics, whether pronounced by a representative of the Deity, by a learned man, by a court, or by a legislative body, are an effort to find the rules under which society can operate with reasonable harmony, implying some degree of justice for all its members. Business must devise rules that are in accord with requirements of justice, but in our modern, intricate society, it must extend the more general work of the prophet or the sage to develop more detailed ethical rules for itself. If market competition and business leadership cannot enforce these rules, and to some extent U.S. legal principles keep business from enforcing them, then business may cooperate with government in enacting and administering the legislation that will accomplish the desired ethical result without unduly handicapping business operations. This statement of business responsibility for cooperation with ethically necessary legislation is made with full agreement that much of the governmental regulation of recent decades is too detailed, and hence, not ethically helpful.

Roger Ransom comments that the adversarial environment between business and labor and between business and government, both noted in this book, may have affected ethical codes. He is quite right; much of the slowness of American progress in the ethics of labor-management and government-business relations is a result of an unfortunate history of conflict.

Legal Approach to Ethics

Laws are documentary proof of efforts to establish ethical principles. Laws add certainty and breadth to developing ethics.

Do laws help build accepted ethical principles? Yes, in some cases. Saul Engelbourg gives examples of American businessmen who indicated that price discrimination, monopoly, and conflict of interest became ethically less acceptable after relevant federal statutes were enacted.[5] The Securities Acts of the 1930s made many businessmen conscious of the ethical difficulties of conflict of interest. But before generalizing that laws help establish ethical practices, it must be remembered that American Prohibition failed, and that antitrust laws have had constant difficulties.

Both Roman law and common law seem to have developed greater recognition of some individual rights; Jewish law moved earlier in the same direction. But common law also developed what must be viewed as an unfriendly attitude toward labor, and as noted, in the nineteenth century adopted the aberrant attitude of *caveat emptor*. It has, however, subsequently reversed its course. Common law is flexible; judges change their minds as popular beliefs shift direction.

Are legal systems fundamentally ethical? The answer is "partly." Lawyers at least talk more about ethics and justice than do other professions. Both civil and common law were surely intended to bring more justice. But both have tended to operate against poorer people because of the great expense of fighting a case in the legal system, and because of the nineteenth-century judges' bias in favor of the mercantile classes. Richard Posner says the common law is based on economics; it is an effort to adjust values between disputing parties. But he also suggests that common law can be viewed as an effort to attach costs to the violation of moral principles.[6] Both views tend toward a recognition of the ethical basis of law.

Do Ethics Change?

Legal, economic, physical, financial, or psychological attitudes sometimes enter into the determination of a business ethic. In addition to business rules, families, churches, schools, courts, and legislatures may contribute to business ethics. Since any one of these attitudes or agencies may change, Roger Ransom has suggested that ethical standards themselves may change over time. The point is a good one, and raises a pertinent question about the generalizations found in this book, especially in the final chapter about rising or declining standards. Judged by the standards of its time, including Social Darwinism, the last half of the nineteenth century may not have been as unethical as it seems today. I have modified some references to improving or declining ethics in partial agreement with Ransom. In particular, I have tried to confine such terms to particular industries. But there do seem to be some ethical standards that have survived and developed over the centuries; business practices contrary to those general ethics are likely to cause dissension in society to the detriment of all business.

Notes

1. Raymond Baumhart, *Ethics in Business*.
2. Alan Gewirth, *Reason and Morality*, p. 135.
3. Adam Smith, *The Wealth of Nations* (Vol. 2), p. 180.
4. Conversation with Friedrich A. von Hayek, American Enterprise Institute, 1979.
5. Saul Engelbourg, *Power and Morality*, pp. 65-71.
6. Richard A. Posner, *Economic Analysis of Law*, p. 180.

1 America's Heritage of Business Ethics

America at the time of her independence had inherited a number of ethical traditions from a variety of sources. Most recent and most important was the English common law that was at least partly recognized in all the colonies. Almost equally important was the Judaic-Christian ethical tradition. Some rules in the Code of Hammurabi and some Egyptian writings were similar to the Old Testament Greek and Roman law, chiefly the latter, had real influence on common law, and on the canon or church law that ruled some British activities into the nineteenth century. Saint Thomas Aquinas (1225-1274) wrote out many ethical precepts that were repeated in canon and in common law; he drew his maxims principally from Old and New Testaments, from Roman law, and from Aristotle.

The principles presented here are drawn from one or more of the above sources. They are somewhat arbitrarily selected; space limitations make it impossible to present specific sources. Some of the principles were not enforced; they were more aspirations than rules. There have also clearly been regressive movements. No rigid classification of the principles outlined here is possible. An effort has been made to group them into three categories:

I. *Overall Obligations of Business.* In general the Western ethical tradition seemed at the beginning of the Republic to recognize various public obligations of business. These range from real legal requirements to general ethical responsibilities.
1. *Salus populi suprema lex est.* ("Public health and safety is the supreme law").
2. *Sic utere tuo ut alienium non laedas.* "So use your property that it does not damage others").
3. Manufacturers and artisans should maintain the quality of products.
4. Prices may be controlled by governments under special circumstances.
5. There should be some generally accepted currency or means of exchange with banks or other agencies to facilitate trade.
6. "Love thy neighbor as thyself" (every individual should be respected as a person).
7. Business has some responsibility for charitable giving.
8. The law should be obeyed.

II. *Commercial Obligations.* A half-dozen precepts of legal and ethical obligation govern a myriad of types of business activity.

1. Stealing is forbidden.
2. Commercial transactions should be conducted without deception. This rule is the opposite of *caveat emptor.*
3. Reporting of truth must be systematic; weights and measures and accounting are two systems toward that end.
4. The obligation of contracts must be respected, although there are many legal idiosyncrasies in the way of doing this.
5. Interest on loans is now generally legal.
6. Trusts are a useful device that require much legal scrutiny.
7. Leasing and hiring have proved to be important means of doing business.
8. The consumer's needs are paramount.

III. *Business Operations.* Operations within business organizations or between them involve a number of complex ethical legal problems.

1. The right to hold property, subject to overriding public use, is generally accepted.
2. Recognition of employee rights was limited until recently.
3. Mid-nineteenth-century America developed a genuine "work ethic," a belief that workers should try hard for successful performance of tasks. By the early twentieth century, this ethic was slackening.
4. Corporations, a useful economic mechanism, raised many unsolved ethical problems at the beginning of the Republic.
5. Conflicts of interest, both within and outside of corporations, present many unsolved ethical problems. The only known precedents forbade bribing of judges and some public officials.
6. In the United States, most business actions that create monopoly are illegal, although the laws were not enforced until after federal action in the Sherman Act of 1890.
7. Patents have been recognized as a legal monopoly, intended to encourage inventions, since Roman law.

There have been major changes in the observance of these principles in the two centuries since American independence. The principle of *Sic utere tuo* for example was neglected during much of the nineteenth century, but has come back strongly with the environmental movement in the twentieth century. "Love thy neighbor as thyself," easily the vaguest of the principles, was opposed by Social Darwinists in the nineteenth century. It has been followed more in the twentieth century, although it is still far from ubiquitous. Business interest in charitable contributions was almost negligible in the nineteenth century but is slowly growing in the twentieth century.

Obedience to the law by businesses was variable in the nineteenth century; is followed much more often in this century.

In regard to commercial obligations, reputable firms in both centuries followed the prohibition against stealing. There is a great deal of stealing in the United States and some businessmen are part of it, but the commandment is generally recognized. The spread of the doctrine of *caveat emptor* in the eighteenth and nineteenth centuries was a clear departure of the United States and Great Britain from the Western ethic against deceiving the buyer. Both countries have moved back to the Western ethic in this century; but in America the heritage of *caveat emptor* is still to be found in some business crimes, especially in fraudulent or near-fraudulent sales to poorer customers.

Weights and measures were used, at least in commercial centers, throughout the history of the United States. Accounting developed more slowly in America than in Western Europe, but by the end of the nineteenth century it had begun to be accepted in America. Today it is a multibillion-dollar industry, in general making more honest business, though it has some weaknesses resulting partly from accountants' desire to keep clients.

The obligation of contracts has been threatened only in deflationary periods when it seemed to be especially tough for farmers to pay, and legislative moratoria on mortgages were passed in many states. Interest rates have been subjected to intermittent legislative controls but interest is a generally recognized commercial necessity. Trusts have been employed quite successfully, especially in the twentieth century. Leasing and hiring continue to be useful.

Within business operations, ethical rules have developed as the American business structure has expanded. There has been no major change in the right to hold property, although condemnation of property for public purposes and regulation of it for social purposes has greatly increased, especially in the twentieth century.

Treatment of workers has improved greatly in both centuries, but especially in the twentieth century. There is some question in 1981 as to whether some employee organizations have too much power. Corporations, now the major mechanism of commerce, have, especially in the twentieth century, been brought under numerous controlling laws; these laws are often too detailed and complex but some are necessary. Conflicts of interest began to disappear as courts and legislatures worked out principles that opposed such conflicts. There are still many examples, and there is still need for more definition of unethical conflicts.

The ethical tradition in America against monopoly had deep roots in English, Roman, and Judaic law. But it had difficulty establishing itself on a firm basis in the United States. A federal antitrust law was passed in 1890 but now almost a century later it is only partially enforced.

In succeeding chapters on specific problems, an early section will usually review the ethical history of that area. The final chapter includes a brief review of the history of American business ethics.

Business ethics have been defined as those principles, or aspirations toward principles, that guided most or at least some businessmen in their commercial connections. Some economists believe that the market itself creates adequate ethics. It is clear that not all the rules cited earlier are created by the market. Courts, legislatures, theologians, and philosophies have helped create some of them; although in business, ethics are probably more likely to come from market operations or from the government. Adam Smith commented that each man should be free to act, "so long as he does not violate the laws of justice." The laws of justice are what some leading businessmen and politicians are trying to discover and express clearly. The market alone has often succeeded in legalizing the commitment of one broker to another, or of an established retail store to its regular customers. But buyers of securities are not so well protected as brokers because they know less about what they are receiving.

Promises or warranties to buyers of equipment that will be used for several years apparently require some governmental supervision if justice is to be achieved. More regulation costs more money; less regulation may impair the consumer's confidence in the American economy and result in more burdensome regulation. Where pollution of the environment is concerned, damage may be so heavy that governmental intervention is needed, but costs may be so high that government needs to think carefully about how to regulate. An economically burdensome regulation is undesirable, if not unethical, unless it is very necessary.

In some fields of employment, unions and business have fallen into an antagonistic relationship that probably does not produce the best result for either side. Here, the ethical problem is for each side to find ways of dealing with the other side which help to create an ethic of cooperation.

2 Ethics of Businessmen

Studies of Businessmen's Ethics

A few studies help give a general picture of the ethical level of American business leaders. These studies clearly indicate important gaps in their ethical education; however, these gaps may be in part a result of weakness of the questionnaire method. A majority of the respondents appear to be men who wish to be honest, but are not very sure what honesty in business means.

Most important of the studies is that by Raymond Baumhart, now president of Loyola University, Chicago. Baumhart arranged for interviews of 100 businessmen attending executive development programs at Harvard; secured returns to a questionnaire by 1,512 subscribers to *Harvard Business Review*; and then arranged further interviews with another 100 businessmen. The questionnaire and interviews occurred chiefly in the early 1960s.[1] Later studies support many of Baumhart's findings.

The businessmen seemed unclear about the nature of their ethics. Of the second 100 interviewed, 58 chose "What my feelings tell me is right" as first or second out of 9 proposed bases for ethics. Another large group, 25, chose "in accordance with my religious beliefs" and 18 thought they conformed to the Golden Rule. None of these are clear-cut bases of ethics.

Of the 1,500 business executives, 43 percent indicated that they would use confidential corporate information for private financial gain. Fifteen percent indicated they would tell a friend about the possibility. Almost 66 percent answered that there were generally accepted unethical practices in the industry with which they were associated. Price discrimination, unfair pricing, price collusion, bribes and gifts, and dishonest advertising made up the bulk of the answers to the question of which practice they would most like to see eliminated. Most thought their firm was better than the rest of the industry.

The business executives showed a sincere desire to treat others well in their discussion of personnel problems. Closing a plant, a major layoff, even firing of an individual, caused distress to many managers. This is not surprising in view of the American educational emphasis on relations with other people. Over half of the 100 interviewees gave examples of decisions "made on principle" and 28 others gave examples of those which may not have been made on principle. The examples in both groups were fairly convincing; the result of the decisions were good in many cases.

5

Businessmen's reasons for acting ethically are almost as cloudy as their bases of ethics. With a ranking of 1 as most influential and 5 as least influential, the highest ranking of 1.5 was "a man's personal code of behavior"; formal company policy and behavior of superiors were both ranked 2.8; ethical climate of the industry ranked 3.8, and the behavior of equals 4.0. In regard to the question of what makes unethical decisions, the behavior of superiors ranked first at 1.8; ethical climate of the industry second at 2.6; followed by behavior of a man's equals, lack of company policy, and personal financial needs. Almost all respondents agreed that good ethics is good business, although a number cited examples in which bad ethics had succeeded. Several, however, offered examples of cases in which bad ethics had bad results. A majority agreed that good ethics was good business for customers, repeat sales, employees, union relations, low turnover of personnel, good reputation, and consistent behavior. Expanding on these questions, several managers stated the nature of the conscience that kept them ethical. Some believed that conscience could change and ethical standards could improve with age. Some found a divine basis for conscience, or a desire for a place in heaven; others had family reputations or good records in the wartime armed forces to maintain. All felt a major responsibility to keep their businesses solvent, which may operate against ethical standards. Most felt that making money should be ethical.

Personal ethical influences were predominantly the father or both parents, the "boss" (10 out of 100), teacher or clergy, and then wife. Thirty percent believed that the "typical businessman" had different ethical standards for home and office. Baumhart infers from the answers of 100 men that "though environment and generally accepted practices are frequently not conducive to ethical behavior, the manager with a well defined personal code and good motivation can still act ethically."[2]

Older businessmen were more likely to be ethical according to Baumhart's surveys; the usual reason being that experience teaches that it is better to be ethical, though a few cynics felt that older people were more tired of fighting. Others felt that the younger and less ethical managers simply reflected the ethics of their time. Discussing "The Long Shadow of the Boss," Baumhart found that many more businessmen recalled penalties for bad ethics than rewards for good ethics. Several other writers agree that the example of the boss had a far-reaching effect. There are different temptations at differing levels of the hierarchy. It was disappointing to find that higher managerial levels did not have higher ethics. Persons in accounting and engineering were more likely to be ethical than those in sales and purchasing (for fairly obvious reasons).

Indirect evidence suggests that ethical standards do vary among companies. Respondents from large companies seemed to be more ethical than those from small companies, though Baumhart came to the opposite conclusion from his own experience. Of 1,459 respondents to the questionnaire, 70 percent acknowledged that there were unethical practices in their industries. Banking, investment, and insurance were more likely to be viewed as ethical; advertising, construction, and garment industries as unethical. Competition makes for less-ethical industries. Forty-two managers expressed opinions as to whether government regulation made business more ethical; 64 percent thought it did. Fifty percent of 1,471 respondents favored industry codes of ethics strongly; 21 percent favored them somewhat. Men from construction, consumer services, and advertising were more favorably disposed toward industry codes.

There is little evidence that formal education in ethics or moral philosophy affects ethical attitudes; this is not surprising because few had much real ethical training. Executive-development programs have a small effect on ethical standards. Similarly religion has had less influence on business ethics than might be expected. Replies from the religiously affiliated and the unaffiliated show only slight variation. Differences between Protestants, Catholics, and Jews were not great. Only 17 percent of 1,505 respondents thought the church gave the right amount of ethical guidance.

Steven N. Brenner and Earl A. Molander reported on a follow-up survey in 1977 of 1,227 business executives.[3] Fifty-seven percent of the respondents had experienced a conflict between expected managerial conduct and ethical expectations. This was 19 percent less than in the 1960 surveys; Brenner and Molander speculate that this may be because of lower ethical standards. Personnel problems appeared to be less troublesome than in the 1960s. Pressure from superiors was apparently greater. Sixty-six percent of the executives in 1977 indicated that unethical practices existed in their industries; whereas 80 percent so believed in 1962. The practices that executives would have liked to see eliminated in 1976 were similar to those in 1961—gifts, kickbacks, and misrepresentation to customers.

Sixty-five percent of those who returned the Brenner-Molander survey believed that society, not business, had the responsibility for teaching ethics. (In other books, I have indicated my belief that there are national or regional or local ethical standards and that these standards tend to be similar in business and in government; facts which seem to support the desirability of a societal responsibility for teaching ethics.)[4] As in 1962, almost half the executives believed that the American executive is more concerned with gain than with applying ethical laws. Respondents of 1976 also tended to be cynical about the ethical standards of other businesses in their industries.

A survey of about one hundred executives in a UCLA management-training program in the early 1960s attempted to secure their judgment of certain ethical situations. A substantial majority strongly disapproved of the actions of the electrical-manufacturing executives in the antitrust conspiracy of the early 1950s. However, almost half approved the use of insider information to profit from a stock transaction in a case where the profit is urgently needed. Forty percent would pirate a competitor's employee to learn a trade secret. Forty percent approved of sending expensive Christmas gifts to customers, but 86 percent disapproved of sharp practices in used-car sales. Over 90 percent disapproved of making a low bid with the intention of using inferior materials. Ninety percent disapproved of concealing a planned plant shutdown from employees.[5]

It is interesting that a poll of 288 young business managers taken by Archie B. Carroll of the University of Georgia indicated that 60 percent would have gone along with their bosses in a cover-up like that of Watergate. Sixty-five percent felt that they were under pressure to compromise personal standards to achieve company goals. A majority felt, however, that business ethics were improving.[6]

These surveys, and there are others with somewhat similar results, seem to give pessimistic views of American business ethics. Most business executives are honest, or at least want to be honest. But many, perhaps a quarter or more, are unclear as to both the basis and the context of their ethics. Many do not have an adequate sense of responsibility for shareholders. Many are cynical about their peers. Their ethical attitudes reflect national ethical attitudes.

There is a Big Problem

America suffers from a great deal of crime within or closely associated with business. A U.S. Chamber of Commerce report on white-collar crime in 1974 estimated losses from such crimes, usually including embezzlement, consumer fraud, illegal competition, and deceptive practices, at $40 billion a year. Other estimates indicate this figure is increasing despite larger FBI attention.[7] Almost $4 billion a year is lost in security crimes.[8] Norman Jaspan estimated that in 1960 employees stole more than $5 billion (now probably $10 billion) a year; and that kickback payments amounted to $5 billion a year.[9] Jaspan's own statistics, based on 200 clients listed on the New York Stock Exchange and others, showed the most financially important dishonesty was on the part of supervisory and executive personnel. Women in positions of trust are as likely as men to be dishonest, according to Jaspan.

A more recent estimate is that half the nation's work force does some stealing from businesses, at a cost of $15 billion a year.[10] National Retail Merchant Association figures for 1957 indicated shortages (mostly thefts) of 1.2 percent of sales for stores between $20 million and $50 million of business. Profits for those stores were only 2.6 percent of sales, so the amount of "shortages" was significant. Current losses would be much larger.

There is evidence of the existence of a substantial proportion of criminals in white-collar groups. Large retail chains believe that thefts by their own employees exceed those by outsiders. Edwin H. Sutherland, writing in 1940, reported that lie-detector tests, usually supported by confessions, indicated thefts by 20 percent of employees of certain banks.[11] Jaspan notes that one turn of dishonesty is soon followed by another.[12] The most trusted employee may be the one who is conspiring to steal from the company. A company that was very sure of its outside guard service learned that the night sergeant of the guards had made arrangements to deliver company goods to the routeman servicing the food-vending machine. A perpetual inventory system was defeated by several employees who put empty shoe boxes back on the shelf, ready for surprise checks. "People bent on collusion can beat any system." Jaspan gives many examples of kickbacks, mostly from his own practice. Kickbacks may come as loans, consulting fees, false invoices, stockbroker accounts, yearly auto rentals, use of credit cards, paid vacations, golf tournaments with lavish prizes, country-club dues, gift certificates, and even works of art. The next few sections will review some possible reasons for business crime.

Executives Who Let It Happen

Business, like government, is full of men who may suspect something is wrongly handled but will not take the time or trouble to investigate the situation. From the late 1950s until the crisis in 1962, the Board of Directors of the American Stock Exchange was just such a group.[13] In the early 1930s the "establishment" of the New York Stock Exchange similarly ignored ethical analysis until Richard Whitney's troubles made them realize the weakness of their position. Most outside directors probably are not aware of the difficulties of business management. Outside members of the Board of Directors of Penn-Central were quite uninformed until the bankruptcy was inevitable. So were the directors of Equity Funding. Too many such directors are people who "let it happen."

Chris Welles quotes an attorney who specialized in New York "derivative" suits against some mismanaged mutual funds:

> The law requires that at least 40 percent of the fund's directors have to be "unaffiliated," unconnected with the fund. They are supposed to be the watchdogs. They are supposed to watch the manager, who is always struggling between his own greed and his fiduciary duty. . . . But history reports that these watchdogs have been asleep. . . . They never fire the managers for performance, even when they have been lousy advisors and the performance is bottom of the barrel.[14]

The general counsel of Gulf Oil from 1961 until early 1969 knew of some of Gulf's illegal political contributions, preferred alternative procedures, but did not tell his subordinate to stop making such contributions. He told his superiors about his misgivings about the contributions. The executive vice president of Gulf Oil probably knew something of the political arrangements. The evidence is conflicting. The controller did not make adequate inquiries into the purposes of the political fund.[15]

Senator William Proxmire, testifying before the U.S. Senate Committee on Banking, Housing, and Urban Affairs, said about the former president of Gulf, "Mr. Dorsey, whom as you know is connected with Gulf Oil and was dismissed from Gulf Oil, indicated how helpful this kind of law would have been for him. He said, such a statute on our books would make it easier to resist the very intense pressures which are placed on corporate officials from time to time. If they could cite our law which says we just may not do it, they would be in a better position to resist those pressures and refuse these payments."[16]

Those who have administered a large or even medium-sized organization know that they cannot be aware of everything done in the organization. Rarely do executives make honesty the major goal of their administration. The minimum program to assure honesty would be to appoint honest subordinates, which most executives do, and to urge them to follow up on the honesty of their employees, which most executives shrink from doing. The trouble may be the failure to stress honesty in American education; it may be embarrassment about talking too "moralistically" in stressing honesty; it may be other factors or a combination of factors.

Business Interests Are Most Important

Marshall B. Clinard, in an interesting study of the Office of Price Administration (OPA) violations in World War II, explored the motivation of a group of law-breaking businessmen. Most of the OPA violators were like the antitrust violators to be discussed in chapter 9, men of little or no previous criminal record. Many also expressed a lack of knowledge of the purpose of the laws they were violating. There seemed little doubt that most of the lawbreakers knew they were offenders. However, many of the offenders did not view themselves as criminals and thought they should not be treated as criminals. This attitude was curious since in many cases they were violating other laws as well as that of price control.[17]

Many black-market operators advanced the theory that the rights of free enterprise meant that government had no right to pass a price-control law. There appeared to be a thought that business could select the laws it would follow. There were other businessmen who believed it was all right to disobey the law if one could get away with it. Clinard also cites evidence that an overly materialist selfishness motivated some violators.[18]

In the case of high-ranking corporate wrongdoers, there is always the possibility that they might be operating on a business interpretation of the doctrine of *raison d' état* ("reason of state"). As business executives think of the scores of thousands of employees dependent on the corporation and the scores of thousands of shareholders who are partly dependent on it, they may conclude that the corporation's welfare as they see it demands lies, cheating, or bribery. For example: the president of Westinghouse made vague and evasive answers to the Kefauver Committee investigating the electrical manufacturers' violation of the antitrust laws in 1961. Was he primarily concerned about how Westinghouse was doing in a poor sales period? The president of Northrop Corporation made an illegal $100,000 contribution to the Committee for the Reelection of the President (CREP) in 1976; he was clearly worried about Northrop securing a government contract. An executive of Lockheed turned over $25 million in illegal bribes to Japanese political figures, in order to secure a much needed sales contract. The same argument probably could be applied to the action of President Nixon and his staff in connection with Watergate. Their theory may have been that it was so important to keep themselves in power that the cover-up of the Watergate break-in was justified.

Another explanation of ethical attitudes is psychological. In a widely read book, Michael Maccoby, a psychoanalyst, has attempted to classify types of corporate managers. The craftsman type is motivated by the challenge of the work itself. Craftsmen enjoy inventing, like their home life, and are often classified as gentle. They probably have the greatest sense of moral constraint; they seldom reach the top corporate job. The "jungle fighter," including the so-called robber-baron of the Civil War period, was primarily interested in advancing himself, was especially successful in highly competitive industries, and likely to foment hostility in his company. Sometimes he is hired for the express purpose of firing unnecessary people, and is likely to enjoy the task of firing. He does not take on roles requiring trust and interdependency. The "company man," a type also portrayed by William H. Whyte, Jr., is essential to large corporations. They believe that they will benefit if the company does; sometimes developing a great deal of love for the company. They tend to lack the risk-taking ability, toughness, and energy of those who reach the very top. They are suspicious of craftsmen because of the latter's desire for perfection and of gamesmen who "use people up." Many company men stick to the rules, resist change, and thus avoid unprincipled manipulation. They sometimes tend to be marketers. Their ethical effect is likely to be positive but not aggressively so. The "gamesman" loves change, competition, new techniques, new methods. He is paradoxical; "cooperative but competitive," fair but contemptuous of weakness, "tough and dominating but not destructive." He is fair but not compassionate. In midlife, he may become unrealistic and manipulative; sometimes quite amoral. Maccoby says the gamesman type may be the most ethical we can get.[19]

Maccoby is nowhere clear about ethical attitudes of his four types, but a few guesses may be made on the basis of some of his remarks. The craftsman is likely to be ethical, but lacks the aggressive qualities that might bring him to the top. The jungle fighter can be quite amoral. The company man is normally moral but can be led to immorality; the gamesman may become amoral. Rosabeth Kanter also believes that corporate work may bring out less ethical qualities in top executives.[20] I am inclined to believe that both Maccoby and Kanter overemphasize the likelihood that top-level administrative work brings out less ethical qualities in top executives. Indeed, almost the opposite—that more trusted people are appointed to top positions—may often be the case. But there are numerous examples of unethical top-level executives.

Pressures of Competitive Business

The argument that pressures of competitive business force managers to be dishonest is frequently heard. Jaspan cites the man he called Waldo who became a crook only because of his small salary (for an important job) and large family obligations. In another case a man was coerced into stealing from a restaurant. Elsewhere Jaspan comments:

> There is a large group of executives, however, who doctor books and manipulate funds but who never personally gain a cent from their wrongdoing. Their fraudulent acts are the result of an impossible profit or work goal set by their superiors or an attempt to cover up their own poor business judgment. Their failing is not so much a lack of ethical candor but courage to say they cannot do the impossible or admit that they had made a mistake.[21]

He follows with an example of the manager of a department store branch who submitted false figures to cover a mistake he had made in recommending an expensive renovation. He stole no money but cost his firm many thousands of dollars in taxes paid on unmade profits.

Some aspects of business provide more pressure for unethical behavior than others. Brooks has pointed out the great demands on the "specialist" in a major stock exchange. Creation of a relatively stable market for a given stock may be very expensive for the specialist. He is under constant temptation to think of his own holdings, rather than of the market for the shares of the company in which he specializes.[22]

Jaspan quotes with approval Donald R. Cressey's conclusion that embezzlers have a "nonshareable financial problem," and gives several examples from his own experience. He cites a sales management survey that asked why prospects or customers resorted to shakedowns. A majority of the panelists believed it to be a result of heavy company pressure for more sales. Cressey's principal conclusion from his studies of over nine hundred embezzlers is that "trust violation takes place when the position of trust is viewed by the trusted person according to culturally provided knowledge about and rationalizations for using the entrusted funds for solving a nonshareable problem".[23] The nonshareable problem is of course usually related to lack of funds. It may, however, be more related to maintaining a standard of living than to actual poverty. Some of the convicted electrical manufacturing executives were receiving very high pay.

Cressey has another interesting comment about the 133 embezzlers he studied. None of them would have considered robbing to obtain the needed funds. Somehow embezzling was less undesirable, an attitude that reflects the need for more detailed ethical education, since the employer suffers just as much from an embezzled $100,000 as from a stolen $100,000.

Cressey makes an effort to tie his theory of the "nonshareable problem" to the theory of association as a source of crime, a theory originally developed by Edwin H. Sutherland. Cressey's efforts to work out a harmony between these theories are not completely successful. However, his explanation of how the embezzler learns the ways in which he can violate his trust leads one to wonder if a similar educational process could not be established in a constructive direction.[24] The rationalization process that Cressey believes all embezzlers go through could be greatly reduced by education about the reasons for fiscal honesty.

There are a number of interpretations of the pressure on the electrical-manufacturing executives who conspired against the antitrust laws. John Fuller notes that in the electrical-manufacturers's case the board chairman Cordiner and president Paxton issued directions for obeying antitrust laws but also put heavy pressure on each division for profits. "In fact, one of the gags going around the company underground was that the only way to succeed as a division manager was to 'brighten the Cordiner where you are.' "[25] The marketing manager of General Electric's switchgear division was said to have been dropped because he religiously enforced the antitrust directive of the company.[26]

Robert W. Austin blames General Electric's organization. The policy of decentralization was a philosophy of management that put heavy pressure on division executives to secure profits. These incentives conflicted with the directive on antitrust-law enforcement. Each man had a clash of loyalty among honesty, family, obligation to company, respect of coworkers, and ambition. Austin grants that a greater personal code of honesty would have helped.[27] Richard Austin Smith also comments on the increased pressure resulting from product division.[28] There is a real danger of competitive pressure transmitted too heavily by corporate superiors.

Influence of Business Associates

Sutherland's theory is that criminals learn their trade by associating with others who already know it. Most people learn their vocations from others. A young man entering business learns from his older associates; if he happens to enter a company or an industry where criminal practices occur he may find himself participating in them.

Examples are numerous. A few years after the episode in which a president of Chrysler Corporation was dropped because he and his wife were principal shareholders of supplier corporations (a clearly illegal conflict of interest), a *Fortune* reporter observed that "in the auto community where auto executives and suppliers live in the same suburbs," they do all social things together and join for business relationships as well.[29]

Another instance is of a former president of an insurance company who was looking for capital gain since his income tax was so heavy. He sat on the board of directors of a great lumber company, whose president obligingly arranged a deal by which the insurance president bought some timber land, which a few years later was sold to the lumber company at a price yielding $400,000 profit. He saw no violation of ethics in this conflict of interest, although it was contrary to the developing ethic in this field.[30]

There are a surprising number of examples in which large parts of a business staff became criminal. Out of loyalty to the company and possible fear of reprisal, many young workers who received no reward cooperated with a high executive in the preparation of elaborate faked business records to cheat lenders to and shareholders of Equity Funding. A few employees began to loot the company when they found the extent to which others were doing so.[31]

The electrical manufacturers' rigged prices (in violation of the Sherman Act) were carried out by a number of executive employees of companies like General Electric and Westinghouse. There appeared to be a group of employees who did not believe in the antitrust laws, in spite of company directives to secure their enforcement. Members of this group persuaded each other that the company did not want to obey the laws.

Norman Jaspan gives an example of an organ factory in which a substantial number of employees stole parts or even whole organs.[32] Another case reported by Jaspan was a routing supervisor of twenty-five truck drivers for a department store, who over the years persuaded twenty men to deliver stolen goods.[33]

Mark Lipman, another consultant to businesses that have problems of employee theft, has a number of judgments similar to those of Jaspan. Like Jaspan he finds employee thieving to be very widespread, and somewhat contagious. In some firms where he has worked, as many as half the employees were stealing, frequently enough so that the firm was facing a major financial difficulty.[34] There seemed to be a kind of guilt by association, leading honest employees to steal heavily in one area. As one delivery helper of a packing plant put it: "Like I said, I had to go along with selling meat because I was there. What was I going to do, say 'no, no, no, don't do it.' I'm here. The guy is going to say 'Take it' ".[35]

Lipman, like Jaspan, found that employees were likely to confess when first confronted with the fact of thieving. He believes that as many as seven out of ten employees steal. He notes that some people steal occasionally and the rest steal quite often. He finds no morality in America today. It is easy to see that no one is obeying the law.

Not all stealing was by lower-level employees. Lipman cites cases in which major division heads, and former owners, now executives, of subsidiaries were stealing.[36] Some of this stealing Lipman ascribed to high income taxes that have encouraged executives to act illegally.[37] Lipman's comments about a pants plant in Texas are worth quoting: "The ones I caught were not hardened criminals; they stole because the company made it easy for them and because everyone else in the plant, and in today's society as a whole, is doing the same damn thing."[38]

Outside of the businesses themselves, there may be antiethical factors in the community. When, for example, a corrupt group like the political machine in Chicago has controlled the politics of an area for decades, it is almost inevitable that some businesses will be tarred with the brush. An interesting example was the group of reputable businessmen who were brought onto the boards of directors of the Chicago racetrack corporations and even consented to "front" for the stocks given to political figures—as a form of bribery.[39]

In another book I have indicated that many political criminals, for example the participants in the Watergate conspiracy and the late Governor Otto Kerner, learned their criminal ways in large part from associates after they had secured responsible political positions.[40] It is also noticeable that political corruption appears in certain areas: it is strong for example in Maryland or West Virginia, but unlikely in Wisconsin or California. Robert E. Lane points out that business violations of law are concentrated in certain cities.[41]

There has been some discussion as to whether Sutherland's differential assoication theory holds for white-collar criminals.[42] Lane supports the theory in his study of government regulation. Marshall Clinard in *The Black Market* believes that the theory does not account adequately for crime but association seems to be at least one factor in developing white-collar criminals; it may be that association is most important in breaking down whatever rudiments of ethical training the potential criminal may have had.

Support for the association theory does not mean support for the theory that competitive business necessarily means crime. John E. Conklin seems to depart from his customary critical objectivity when he reviews several suggestions by sociologists about "learning business crime."[43] Some of the sociologists, such as C. Wright Mills and Sutherland, apparently believed that business crime was a necessary result of the indoctrination of businessmen in the values of competition, individualism, exploitation, and monetary success. The supporting evidence is, however, weak and is partly offset by the evidence of many honestly run businesses in the United States and in other capitalist countries. Conklin concludes that group norms encourage employee theft and price fixing, because there is no business code with strong enforcement sanctions. He ignores the fact that American laws do not permit such codes because of antitrust and due-process-of-law considerations. He also notes that national business associations did not condemn the electrical-manufacturer's antitrust conspiracy; an error of omission but hardly proof of the business origin of bad ethics. Further, Conklin cites Sutherland's conclusion that American businessmen in World Wars I and II viewed profits as more important than patriotism. Some of them probably did, but in my personal experience this was not the general case.

Stealing from Corporations Is OK

Employee thefts were estimated to be as high as $15 billion in 1973; they are probably much higher today. The notion that it is all right to steal from corporations may come from resentment against corporate impersonality or may come from lack of concern about company finances, or from the feeling that it is a custom. Jaspan believes that there is substantial employee discontent or frustration with corporations because they are big or impersonal, and overlook employee needs; hence, the stealing.[44] Sometimes the employee makes his own rules and walks off with company money.

Other analysts have commented about the problem of employees who steal regularly from the companies by whom they are employed. Altheide et al. cite several authors: Dalton found a "gray area" of authorized right of employees to pilfer from the plant, which ranked along with expense-account padding; but Gouldner described a gypsum factory in a semirural area where company tools could be taken home for personal projects, private possessions repaired on company machinery, and reasonable amounts of raw materials taken home, with a resulting group of trusting and trustworthy employees.[45]

Altheide et al. believe that employee theft is a result of a long tradition of workers who expect wages in kind as well as perquisites. The goods taken home or services taken advantage of are not thefts but symbols of the employee's worth. Work-group standards are firmly against efforts to eliminate such takings; workers do not see themselves as criminals.[46] "They will never miss it" is doubtless a frequent reaction. The same authors find that the general American belief in equality results in much employee theft. If lower-ranking employees believe they are not fairly (or perhaps generously) treated, employees will "even it up" with the executives by taking tools, materials, or products.[47] There are variations in these viewpoints. A study by Erwin O. Smigel in the early 1950s found that respondents were more likely to disapprove strongly of stealing from a small corporation than from a large one or from the government. Respondents of lower socioeconomic status were more likely to have their ethical view colored by the size of the organization burglarized.[48] Another way of viewing employee theft suggested by Erwin O. Smigel and H. Lawrence Ross is that the ethics of all higher religion were based on small communities, not on the impersonal corporate structures of today.[49] There are no rules about large corporations to be found in traditional religious statements of ethics. In a survey of plant workers by Donald N.M. Horning, almost 80 percent felt it was wrong to take company property; a slightly larger percentage thought it was wrong to take another worker's property; but a great many small items, such as nuts, bolts, screws, nails, and some tools were viewed as of uncertain ownership. Only one-third of those who had pilfered such objects felt any guilt about it.[50] One-quarter admitted they had given such goods away but only 6 percent admitted they had sold such goods.

Another reason for stealing from corporations may be that the corporations do not seem to care. Jaspan, like Mark Lipman, clearly believes that management has often been quite negligent in overseeing employee honesty. He cites a Price-Waterhouse survey of one hundred cases of white-collar fraud that found that auditors uncovered thirty cases, internal controls found eleven, management found sixteen, and fortuitous events found thirty-six. Management and internal controls should have found more.

Youthful Viewpoints

Thomas Engeman and I have noted in *Amoral America* (Hoover Institution Press, 1975) that a major trouble of American society may be that its youth receive little ethical education. John Brooks in his discussion of the stock-market troubles in the "go go years" (chiefly 1960s) notes that youthful attitudes were a part of the "back office" problems of stock dealers. "This special self-confidence, this belief in having an understanding of the climate of the modern world that their elders could never share was characteristic of the back office people. As well expect them to feel loyalty to the company, or be sincerely pious about small errors in accounts, as ask a modern scientist to devote his life to alchemy.''[51]

Youthful employees were reported to go along enthusiastically with the Equity Funding scandal. One of the vice presidents involved in the conspiracy commented: "We were all just crazy, punk kids, really. Our people were easily led; we were too young to have developed mature, ethical judgments.''[52] Andrew Tobias tells us how cheerily the youthful staff of the National Student Marketing Company contributed to the deception of many shareholders.[53]

In his study *Crime by Computer* Don B. Parker finds that most of the criminals tend to be amateurs and relatively young. The actions seem to be in part because of antagonism to "the organization" and in part because of the impersonality of the computer. There is more collusion in computer crime than in other white-collar crime, and perpetrators are more likely to be persons who work closely with the machines rather than higher executives. The tendency to steal from the organization via the computer sometimes becomes a "Robin Hood" syndrome.[54]

It is well known that the largest number of serious crimes are perpetrated by men under thirty; in recent years such crimes have frequently been committed by junior-high-school boys.

Raymond Baumhart discovered that age made a difference in the answers to his *Harvard Business Review* study of business attitudes. Men under forty were somewhat more likely to use confidential corporate information for private financial gain, to hire personnel from a competitor to acquire information, and to see no ethical dimension in status-symbol advertising. They were less likely to regard padding of expense accounts as unacceptable or to think that providing a call girl for a customer was always unethical.[55]

A survey of managers' attitudes in a major multidivisional corporation in about 1970 on corporate social policy found the lower- and middle-level managers had a sense of futility about corporate social policy. Younger managers showed the lowest sense of personal responsibility and the weakest sense of a need for corporate involvement in social policy.[56]

Reduction of Employee Thefts

Both Mark Lipman and Norman Jaspan are convinced that businesses could cut their losses from employees greatly by installing more adequate controls. The fact that the bill for crime tends to be passed on to consumers or to the Internal Revenue Service makes some businessmen careless; though they will of course be more susceptible to strong competition.[57] Jaspan has a list of sixty-five items to check; they range from requiring bonding of a new employee to checking inventory shrinkage. Unused doors should be kept locked. Everyone should have an identification card. Outstanding keys should be carefully checked.

Both cite too-low wages and salaries as causes of employee theft, although both testify to cases where compensation was not the reason. Gambling and extravagant living standards are also suggested as reasons; not easy ones for employers to eliminate. Jaspan believes that dishonesty of personnel often tests the honesty and capacity of supervisors. The need, then, is to improve the supervisors.

Those in the field of industrial security recommend stricter supervision by the company. Norman Jaspan, describing the experiences of his company, urges selection of strategic control points (shipping, receiving, and exits); development of standards of performance; checking and reporting on performance; and taking corrective and disciplinary action.[58]

It is interesting that in America, where employee thefts total many billions of dollars a year, employers frequently have inadequate controls to prevent such theft. In his book *Mind Your Own Business,* Jaspan states his belief that most persons involved in stealing from the company are not criminal types, and that employee theft is a result of the employer's failure to take adequate protections.[59] I believe the low level of ethical education and low quality of law enforcement in the United States are also important factors.

Kenneth Duber of Duber Industrial Security, Beverly Hills, estimates that employee stealing could be greatly diminished by control methods. He suggests that parking lots should be farther from offices so that stolen objects cannot be put into cars as easily. Entrances and exits should be limited so employees can be observed. Some companies provide clear plastic bags so employees will not have to carry purses. Guards should be hired from outside the company. Employees who are caught should be prosecuted.[60]

Jaspan urges regulations prohibiting gifts from individuals or from corporations doing business with the company, or seeking any loans, services, payments, trips, or gifts. His regulation would also prohibit employees from conflict-of-interest connections with companies that do business with their employers. He also suggests a purchasing policy that discourages the presentation of gifts, tickets, or other favors that may appear to be commercial bribery.[61] He believes that liberal market practices such as variable commissions, cash sales, contests, samples, return privileges, or credits may encourage personnel to collect cash for kickbacks. Many businesses are now trying to eliminate outside gifts to their employees, but are finding that simply sending a letter to suppliers does not accomplish this purpose. In some cases vendors are even asked to sign an agreement that no payments will be made to the purchaser's employees. Sometimes businesses require their own purchasing agents to give financial statements each year. Agreements at the time of employment for such disclosure should also provide for penalties in event of violation of the agreement. State laws are often inadequate protection for companies, and kickbacks are hard to prove in civil suits.

Ethical Education

Jaspan comments that a large amount of white-collar crime is a result of an apparent national indifference to dishonesty, and indifference that also appears in unions, in government, and in nonprofit organizations such as hospitals. The embezzler is described as "everyman," perhaps a well-liked next-door neighbor, a school superintendent, or a fellow clerk in a store. U.S. Fidelity and Guaranty Company surveys, both before and after World War II, found the typical male embezzler was married, age thirty-five, with one or two children, owned his own home in a respectable neighborhood, and had a yearly income in the top 40 percent of the population. The average woman embezzler was a little over age thirty-one, probably married, stealing at a rate equivalent to her annual salary, and with an income in the lower 30 percent of the population. The postwar embezzler was younger, of poorer legal record, lived faster, was more likely to use liquor, gamble or have domestic troubles, and was more likely to abscond.

It is often said that everyone has an understanding of the right and wrong from which criminals (including white-collar ones) happen to stray. In the United States, where many people are never taught ethics, this generalization is questionable. Jaspan writes of a buyer who personally received 5 to 7 percent on all billings: "He explained that since he personally placed his orders directly with manufacturers whom he knew personally, he saw nothing wrong in accepting kickbacks equivalent to what the manufacturers would have to pay their own salesmen. The fact that as a buyer he was obligated to pass on to his own firm any savings he had made on purchases had escaped him."[62] Another case is that of a man who permitted shortages of $1,400,000 in the bank of which he was president because he was literally too good-hearted, and was always willing to help local industry. Jaspan was doubtful whether this man felt any guilt about using or manipulating money that didn't belong to him.[63]

Other writers on business crime have commented on the need for better ethical training of the population. Don B. Parker says in *Crime by Computer,* "Until students are taught that the computer is a sacrosanct, important tool not to be played with in unauthorized fashion, we will continue to have a flow of new graduates coming into our businesses, government, and the institutions prepared to continue their game playing, but where the stakes are real."[64] Robert E. Lane proposes an educational and experimental program involving a government and business interrelationship to build respect for the law.[65] Robert Daley, a writer on crime and law enforcement, writes: "I judge this [crime] as evidence that a new morality exists in America. One which preaches with workers to get away with whatever they think they can get away with, to steal if the joint isn't locked up tight, to terrorize factory owners who suddenly find that after a lifetime in business, they are suddenly about to go under."[66] Daley wants more and better law enforcement; Lipman wants employing companies to have better theft control. But if they are right about American morality, we need more ethical education.

Marshall Clinard believes that the only effective control of white-collar crime rests on the voluntary compliance with societal regulations by most citizens.[67] He discusses the high ethical level of Swiss citizens.[68] This may be attributable to a higher level of ethical education.

Higher Education and the Ethics of Businessmen

Does contemporary higher education encourage businessmen to be honest? Some examples seem to point to a negative answer. There are many white-collar criminals who attended prestigious colleges, graduated with honors, or were respected members of law firms, banks, or stock exchanges.[69] Five of the seven most severely punished electrical-manufacturing executives were graduates of excellent engineering schools.[70] "Today the community is faced with a new kind of thief. He graduated from college and in many cases a very 'good' college. He lives in a lovely home, has a fine family."[71]

On-the-job ethical training might be very valuable. The most difficult problem of corporations, like Gulf Oil, which deliberately set out to improve the ethical level of its executives after 1977, was to find people with the capability to conduct an ethical education in a practical and meaningful way. It would probably be better to select company staff of a known ethical quality than to import academic "ethicians" since the latter would find it difficult to discuss practical business problems.

Teaching of ethics is a difficult task. In our somewhat cynical society, lectures on ethics are likely to be ignored. But careful discussion of why there are antitrust laws and of the scores of millions of dollars lost for example by the electrical manufacturers should indicate to most young executives some reasons for obeying these laws. Similarly analysis of some of the problems of the automobile industry and the heavy costs which came to it from the Occupational Safety and Health Administration (OSHA), the Environmental Protection Agency (EPA) and Consumer Products Safety

Commission might teach young executives reasons for more concern about the safety and health of consumers, of the general public, and of employees.

The amount of white-collar crime could be greatly reduced by more effective government regulation, but the greatest problem is the influence of executives of great ambition but without an ethical code. Boards of directors and top executives need to repeat the reasons for honesty quite frequently. Employees could probably be led by a strong executive into honesty as readily as into dishonesty.

The individual embezzler is another case, however. If Donald Cressey is right in his analysis of over one hundred embezzlers, isolation is a major factor in leading the embezzler to try to solve a personal problem by violating his trust. Perhaps employee counseling on financial matters would help; perhaps better salaries are needed in some cases; perhaps analysis of the ethical problems of the job would be helpful. Cressey cites a number of cases in which embezzlers believed, at least initially, that they were handling money correctly. A frequent rationalization was that the money was "borrowed" from an employing firm. Perhaps better education on the financial responsibilities of the job would have prevented some of these cases.

In several other ways corporations can help create an ethical environment for education of their employees. Codes of business conduct can be helpful, as the discussion in chapter 3 indicates. Special instructions to the internal audit staff to conduct rigorous examinations would probably be more effective than outside audits. Physical control mechanisms can eliminate much employee theft. All these should be viewed primarily as means to the end of training a more honest staff.

What about education for business ethics? When American business schools were started in the early twentieth century, curiously little was said about business ethics. There were statements about excessive governmental control that ran counter to natural law. A majority of top businessmen probably did want honest government, as seen by their support of civil service and municipal reform. But there was little recognition that business might itself be a source of corruption. Millionaires were seen as good because their activities had created economic life.[72] Even today there is not much evidence that business education at the universities has raised the level of business ethics. The prestigious Harvard Business School admits that it has not found the way to ethical education for business.

Religion and Business Ethics

Religious leaders have had some influence on business ethics, usually in the form of social or governmental pressure. The National Council of Churches was a major factor in the reduction of the work day in steel mills from twelve to eight hours in 1922. The churches also heavily backed the civil rights movement.

But it is hard to find evidence of religious support of individual ethical responsibility in business. Certainly some business leaders have been moved to better ethical action by services or sermons or hymns. However, Raymond Baumhart's survey found only one-fifth of the respondents cited "supernatural sanctions" as a major reason for good behavior.[73] A substantial number of white-collar criminals have had substantial religious training or are active church members.

Conclusions

Questionnaire results and white-collar crime statistics indicate that American business suffers from real problems of employee ethics. It is possible that the national costs of our unusually low ethical standards in business equal or exceed the $75 billion governmental deficit of 1980, or three years of our national trade deficit. The low ethics have probably led to many political and public-relations reversals of business, the honest along with the dishonest.

All sorts of reasons have been offered for the relatively low ethics of American business. The various questionnaire results seem to point to inadequate ethical training. There is some evidence that a substantial number of executives are ethical but don't try very hard to stop unethical conduct of others. Executive white-collar thieves seem to be persons who have let themselves get into financial trouble and who then try to steal their way out; or have been forced by corporate financial pressure into law-breaking. Loyalty to the corporation has been used by criminally inclined higher executives to pressure subordinates to participate in crime. In other cases, business associates have encouraged colleagues into unethical action. Some crime comes in part from the belief that it is all right to steal from a large corporation. A greater proportion of young people are involved in white-collar crime. Many businesses fail to take punitive action against employee crime. Some executives may take unethical action because they believe that the welfare of the corporation and its employees justifies illegalities.

There are many suggestions for improving the ethics of businessmen; they vary somewhat with the kind of crime and the administrative status of the perpetrator. Lipman and Jaspan believe that more adequate controls would reduce employee thefts; more honest supervisors are needed. Conklin is probably right in suggesting more publicity and sharper penalties for business crime.

Ethical instruction may help reduce the number of employees who are simply going along with their criminal associates. Parker, Lane, Daley,

Clinard, and Jaspan all make comments that seem to point to better education in the ethics of business responsibility. Institutions of higher education
have to date seemed quite ineffective in teaching business ethics, but are
now displaying a little interest. This chapter has discussed the ethics of
businessmen and businesswomen. The next chapter will discuss the ethical
problems arising from the work of America's major economic
mechanism—the commercial corporation.

Notes

1. Raymond Baumhart, *Ethics in Business,* 1968.
2. Ibid., p. 71.
3. Steven N. Brenner and Earl A. Molander, "Is the Ethics of Business
Changing?," pp. 57-71.
4. George C.S. Benson and Thomas Engeman, *Amoral America;* Benson et al., *Political Corruption in America.*
5. John W. Clark, *Religion and the Moral Standards of American
Businessmen,* p. 98.
6. *Los Angeles Times,* April 19, 1975, quotes Archie B. Carroll,
"Business Ethics and the Management Hierarchy," *National Forum,* Summer 1978, p. 37.
7. *Modern Office Procedures,* May 1981, p. 70, cites the Chamber of
Commerce report.
8. John E. Conklin, *Illegal But Not Criminal,* p. 4.
9. Norman Jaspan, *The Thief in a White Collar,* p. 12.
10. John M. Johnson and Jack D. Douglas, *Crime at the Top,* p. 90.
11. Cited in Gilbert Geis and Robert F. Meier, *White Collar Crime,* p.
41.
12. Norman Jaspan, *Mind Your Own Business,* pp. 6-32.
13. John Brooks, *The Go Go Years,* chap. 11.
14. Chris Welles, *The Last Days of the Club,* p. 64.
15. John J. McCloy, et al., *The Great Gulf Oil Spill,* pp. 226-264.
16. U.S. Senate Committee on Banking Housing and Urban Affairs,
Foreign Corrupt Practices, pp. 98-99.
17. Marshall B. Clinard, *The Black Market,* pp. 236-237; 287 ff.
18. Ibid., pp. 334-343.
19. Michael Maccoby, *The Gamesman,* chapters 2, 3, 4, 5.
20. Rosabeth Moss Kanter, *Men and Women of the Corporation,* pp.
162-163.
21. Jaspan, *The Thief in the White Collar,* p. 127.
22. Brooks, *The Go Go Years,* p. 32.
23. Donald R. Cressey, *Other People's Money,* p. 139.

24. Ibid., p. 153.

25. John Fuller, *The Gentlemen Conspirators,* pp. 124-128.

26. Ibid., pp. 133-134.

27. Robert W. Austin, "Code of Conduct for Executives," pp. 19-27.

28. Richard Austin Smith, *Corporations in Crisis,* pp. 127-130.

29. Seymour Freedgood, "Life in Bloomfield Hills," *Fortune,* July 1961.

30. Walter Goodman, *All Honorable Men,* pp. 64-65.

31. William E. Blundell, "Equity Funding: I Did it for the Jollies," in Moffitt, Donald, *Swindled,* pp. 71-74.

32. Jaspan, *Mind Your Own Business,* p. 45.

33. Jaspan, *The Thief in the White Collar,* pp. 180-181.

34. Mark Lipman, *Stealing,* p. 17.

35. Ibid., p. 26.

36. Ibid., p. 97.

37. Ibid., p. 98.

38. Ibid., p. 145.

39. Hank Messick, *The Politics of Prosecution,* pp. 58-59, 71-72, 81-82.

40. Benson, et al., *Political Corruption in America,* chap. 14.

41. Robert E. Lane, "Why Businessmen Violate the Law," in Geis and Meier, *White Collar Crime,* p. 109.

42. John E. Conklin, *Illegal But Not Criminal,* p. 83.

43. Ibid., p. 78 ff.

44. Jaspan, *Mind Your Own Business,* chap. 5.

45. David Altheide, Peter Adler, Patricia Adler, and Duane Altheide, "The Social Meanings of Employee Theft," in Johnson and Douglas, *Crime at the Top,* p. 90.

46. Ibid., pp. 122-123.

47. Ibid., pp. 102-108.

48. Erwin O. Smigel, "Public Attitudes Toward Stealing," *American Sociological Review,* Vol. 21, No. 3, June 1956.

49. Erwin O. Smigel and H. Lawrence Ross, *Crimes against Bureaucracy,* p. 7.

50. Donald N.M. Horning, "Blue Collar Theft," in Smigel & Ross, *Crimes against Bureaucracy,* pp. 46-64.

51. Brooks, *The Go Go Years,* pp. 199-200.

52. Blundell, "Equity Funding: I Did it for the Jollies," in Johnson and Douglas, *Crime at the Top,* p. 165.

53. Andrew Tobias, *Funny Money Game.* Quoted in John Brooks, *The Autobiography of American Business,* p. 319.

54. Don B. Parker, *Crime by Computer,* chap. 7.

55. Baumhart, *Ethics in Business,* pp. 74-80.

56. John W. Collins and Chris G. Ganotis, "Managerial Attitudes

Toward Corporate Social Responsibility,'' in Sethi, S. Prakash, *The Unstable Ground,* pp. 303-320.

57. Jaspan, *Mind Your Own Business,* pp. 19-20.

58. Jaspan, *The Thief in the White Collar,* pp. 246 ff.

59. Jaspan, *Mind Your Own Business,* p. 205.

60. *Los Angeles Times,* June 28, 1980.

61. Jaspan, *Mind Your Own Business,* pp. 115-137.

62. Jaspan, *Thief in the White Collar,* p. 19.

63. Ibid., p. 81.

64. Parker, *Crime by Computer,* p. 48.

65. Robert E. Lane, ''Why Businessmen Violate the Law,'' pp. 151-165.

66. Daley, in Lipman, *Stealing,* p. xviii.

67. Clinard, *The Black Market,* p. 261.

68. Clinard, *Cities with Little Crime,* chap. 11.

69. Brooks, *The Go Go Years,* pp. 30-31; 35-36.

70. Fuller, *The Gentleman Conspirators,* pp. 92-99.

71. Jaspan, *Mind Your Own Business,* p. 17.

72. Edward Chase Kirkland, *Dream and Thought in American Business,* chapters 4 to 6.

73. Baumhart, *Ethics in Business,* p. 58.

3 The Morality of the Corporation

Corporate organization has been the key to modern industrial life, and has helped boost the living standards of many millions of people. The ability of corporations to keep on going largely eliminates the economic stoppage that comes to proprietary operations when an owner leaves or dies. Also, the pooling of funds in a corporation enables the development of new plants, machinery, or worldwide sales programs, which again a single proprietor or a partnership with full liability would hesitate to undertake. It is hard to conceive of an economic organization other than the corporation that would have given us our national and worldwide telephone service, our ubiquitous automobiles, our speedily delivered consumer products, or our nationwide distribution of worldwide high-fashion clothing. None of these things are all good, but we would protest shrilly if the removal of the corporate form of organization should deprive us of any one of them.

Ethical and Historical Background

The corporation in its modern commercial form was unknown to the Judaic or early Christian world, and there is little in these religious ethics to carry over to the modern corporation except those ethical standards that may be developed from analogical reasoning. Neither have philosophers outlined a code for corporations. It is true that the corporation as a legal person is not allowed to steal, rob, assault, kill, or cheat other persons and corporations with which it may deal. All of these crimes are covered by Mosaic law and other rules of conduct.

So much of American economic life is dependent on the corporation that we think of it in primarily economic terms. But we often overlook the tremendous importance of corporations as a major factor in political and social life, both inside and outside the corporation. While the corporation was developing in the nineteenth century, a variety of ethical questions arose. What were the responsibilities of management and directors to shareholders, especially minority shareholders? Lawrence Friedman correctly comments that in the 1860s and 1870s, "The investing public was unmercifully cheated."[1] What responsibilities did management have to keep directors informed? Was it wrong for managers to own parts or all of corporations that dealt with the corporations they managed? These were not

27

mere theoretical questions. Both New York and Illinois in mid-century were trying to control "watered stock" by requiring that money or property or labor be exchanged for stock. The courts had often to deal with cases in which presidents or boards of directors pillaged the corporation to help themselves. The use of the Constitution to declare legislative acts unconstitutional had the effect of furthering corporate freedom from legal or ethical responsibilities.

Answers to some of these questions could be deduced from the general ethical tradition. But the Mosaic law covered none of them directly; neither did Thomas Aquinas nor Blackstone, the backbone of English law. Ethical rules to cover corporations had to be created in the United States by the clumsy methods of legislative reform or court changes of precedents. Nineteenth-century lawyers were so busy helping to get corporations started that they spent little time devising the necessary controls. Some states entered into a competition as to which had the easiest laws for corporate charters, a competition in which Delaware finally nosed out New Jersey. But it took the rise of the great trusts to bring about the first (weak) federal law governing one aspect of corporations, the Sherman Act of 1890. It took the Great Crash of 1929 to secure the first federal act requiring companies to report to their shareholders, seventy years after England had legislated on this subject.

In 1932, Adolf A. Berle and Gardiner C. Means found unsolved ethical problems in the legal structure of the corporation. In the Van Swearingen railroad-holding structure, the Van Swearingens owned less than 1 percent of the Chesapeake and Ohio Railroad that they controlled through holding companies; other stock owners were eliminated from control. In some cases, the control of major corporations was simply unknown to outsiders. Sometimes the control of the corporation was for sale although some holding companies had already taken undue advantage of their control.[2]

Other ethical problems were bothersome. Sometimes a man was director of two companies that did business with each other; a conflict of interest that could damage one of the concerns. There were no important controls on misuse of insider information but a few courts had recognized the problem. Some mid-nineteenth-century cases, the leading one in New York state, held that directors were responsible to the corporation, not to the shareholders.

The law, according to Berle and Means, has tried to develop three main rules of conduct for management of corporations:

1. A decent amount of attention to business.
2. Fidelity to the interest of the corporation.
3. At least reasonable business prudence.[3]

Friedman expresses the principles of corporate executive obligation as the concept of fiduciary obligation:

> The officers and directors were trustees for the corporation. This meant that officers could not engage in self-dealing; they could not buy from or sell to the company; they were strictly accountable for any profits they made in transactions with the company. This old austere body of doctrine, which courts of chancery had applied to trustees for widows and orphans was also to apply to promoters, officers and directors.''[4]

There were to be many instances in which this high ethical standard was not attained. The Great Crash of 1929 and the subsequent investigations disclosed an unhealthy ethical situation in the banking and security industries; the resulting federal legislation raised standards substantially in both fields, though probably not adequately in the securities industry, as shown in chapter 8. The growth of the federal income tax in the 1930s and 1940s encouraged tax-evasion measures but also provided for more adequate accounting, which raised ethical standards of some business activities. In the 1940s, business in general cooperated with the national war effort and produced the munitions and supplies that defeated the Axis powers; however, some of the price controls and rationing required by the war led to extensive violation of laws by substantial numbers of businessmen.

In the 1950s and 1960s, a surprising number of unhealthy corporate practices continued. Deliberate violation of antitrust laws by high-ranking executives in the electrical manufacturing industry in the 1950s was the most publicized of business misfeasances. The business image was later marred by shifting of accounting practices to show better profits, and massive defrauding of shareholders as in the United States National Bank of San Diego and Equity Funding Corporation cases, and by a good deal of sharp practice in advertising and selling. With the backing of the consumer-protection and environmental movements came laws, intended to be reforms, in Occupational Safety and Health Administration (OSHA) work, Product Liability, and in Truth in Lending; and a revival of the work of the Federal Trade Commission (FTC). This legislation was often marred by overregulation, which has led to congressional revulsion against some regulatory statutes.

Facts on File, a New York commercial-study agency, lists major federal cases against major corporations in the first six years of the 1970s to include at least forty foreign bribes, at least thirteen securities frauds, and twenty-seven other major crimes.[5] These included domestic political corruption, which is sometimes forced on corporations, and antitrust cases, which may hinge on new and technical points. But the other cases involved scores of millions of dollars of misspent money. Two other studies, Edwin H.

Sutherland's *White Collar Crime* (1949) and Marshall B. Clinard et al., *Illegal Corporate Behavior* (1979) calculate a substantial number of crimes by leading corporations. Many of the crimes are perhaps not of great importance or even intentional, but a greater regard for the letter of the law would improve the reputation of American corporations.

Is Corporate Organization Moral?

The view that any large formal organization is antagonistic to morality has been raised by John Ladd. He believes that bureaucratic complexity makes people develop partial sets of skills. No longer functioning as individuals, they are parts of an organization game that has no rules of right or wrong. Administrators in such bureaucracies simply become agents of the whole.[6] Ladd's charges may be true in some cases. As noted, the heads of some corporations have put a somewhat immoral cast on their operations. A critic like John DeLorean gives fairly convincing evidence that General Motors did at times pressure its staff to weigh corporate profit above public safety.[7] However, this is far from saying that all corporations must be unethical. Indeed, if some chief executive officers (CEOs) can make their corporations bad, could not other CEOs make them good?

One writer has concluded that a large part of the task of a corporate chief executive is to maintain moral tone. Chester Barnard, former president of New Jersey Bell Telephone Company, writes in his pioneering *The Functions of the Executive,*

> All these elements of organization in which the moral factor finds its concrete expression, spell the necessity of leadership, the power of individuals to inspire cooperative personal decision by creating faith; faith in common understanding, faith in the probability of success, faith in the ultimate satisfaction of personal motives, faith in the integrity of objective authority, faith in the superiority of common purpose as a personal aim of those who partake in it.[8]

Barnard defined morals as coming from "general, political, religious, and economic environments" and from "biological properties" and "technological practice." Some moral codes are private; in the United States the moral code or codes "derive from or are inculcated by the Christian churches"; but Barnard went on to note that in many respects codes of various religious groups coincide. Every executive possesses personal moral codes but also must conform to codes of the organization (including appropriate laws and charters). In some cases he must create moral codes for the organization, says Barnard. The strength of an organization depends upon the quality of leadership; and that quality derives from the breadth of the morality upon which it rests.

Leadership positions do involve moral leadership. It is hard to think of any important executive job that does not require some exercise of moral leadership. However, Herbert A. Simon, Nobel-prize winner in economics, and many other writers on business management do not discuss the moral factor, indicating that many American academics mistakenly ignore the ethical aspects of business.

Some observers, however, do note a moral factor. Political scientist James MacGregor Burns finds a parallel in political leadership to Barnard's concept of the moral responsibility of the executive. After describing the Franklin D. Roosevelt-Joseph P. Kennedy rivalry, he notes that F.D.R. won because he had a "transcending moral issue in the war." Burns also writes that leadership is a process of morality so long as leaders and followers operate on shared motives, values, and goals. He goes on to point out how effective leadership can broaden the values of followers.[9]

Within the corporate organization there are conflicts that lead to ethical questions, just as surely as do such conflicts in governmental, military, or educational hierarchies. For example, an aerospace-electronics firm learned that a subsidiary company had been sending in fraudulent reports on its finances. The head of the subsidiary was asked to resign but central corporate headquarters wanted to know why the division heads had made the fraudulent reports. Each of the division heads (all but one rather thoughtful man) knew of the wrong reports but believed that their greater loyalty was to the subsidiary president who wanted the fraudulent reports.[10] DeLorean in his fascinating but very personal book on General Motors pictures a corporation in which financially-minded top management overrides the more ethically based judgments of the operating executives who value ethical relations with employees, dealers, and customers more than do the top-level people of sober financial background.[11] Elsewhere corporate pressure on the product division for profit has been described as a reason for dishonesty; Henry Mintzberg confirms this.[12]

Those who have worked in large organizations have most likely encountered conflict-of-loyalty problems. They are similar in kind to the problem of whistle-blowing discussed in chapter 4, but vastly different in degree. Clear-cut organization charts and directives will take care of many of these problems. An ethical top executive will set examples that lead to avoidance of such problems. In addition, however, most thoughtful large organizations have mechanisms that permit information about unsavory local conditions to come to higher levels. Staff channels serve that purpose in many business and governmental organizations; the Inspector General helps accomplish it in the armed forces.

Effect of the Corporation on Individuals

Working for corporations, like working in the armed forces or in a hospital or in a church, may have substantial effect on the character and personality of the individual who works for the corporation for any great length of time, an effect that may lead corporate officials to unethical conclusions about corporate relations to the outside world. It will be shown how certain otherwise moral and legally-minded men came to the conclusion while working for an electrical manufacturing company that the welfare of the company and their own welfare demanded an illegal action, even though the chief executive officer of the company had forbidden the illegal action. Richard Austin Smith concludes that the predominant position of U.S. Steel in the steel industry impressed on its executives a point of view like that of public utilities—that it should raise prices when it needed money and not do so when it didn't need money, regardless of competitive conditions.[13] Gulf Oil for a time seems to have had a few executives who believed in bribing governmental officials to secure what Gulf viewed as favorable official views.

Executives do not today say "the public be damned" as did William Henry Vanderbilt in 1882. But there is still a tendency for some executives to see the world in relation to their companies. David Finn gives several examples.[14] Consolidated Edison of New York City in the 1880s refused to comply with a law requiring elimination of overhead wires, so the mayor sent out crews to cut the wire. Almost eighty years later, *Fortune* wrote that Consolidated Edison was led by old and embattled, proud and thick-skinned men.[15]

Sometimes employees of companies are forced to alter their expressions of opinion for the sake of public image. Finn gives two examples. A junior executive of American Petrofina (Dallas) resigned after the company asked him to screen his public utterances. Bethlehem Steel dismissed a community-relations aide who had joined a local group working to improve race relations in the company.[16] A former B.F. Goodrich employee has written a report on how he and an associate were practically forced to resign by middle-management people because they complained about the company's submission of a false engineering report on an inadequate brake for an Air Force plane.[17] The Merrill division of Richardson-Merrell in 1961-1962 ordered employees to prepare changes in reports to the Food and Drug Administration (FDA) in order to continue marketing a drug, Mer 29, which definitely had harmful effects. Merrill was fined $60,000 and the parent company $20,000 by a federal court.[18] Some corporate employees disagree with their management. But corporations can develop attitudes in a large number of their permanent employees. If the corporation has an even partly antiethical attitude, it can have an adverse effect on the ethical life of some of its staff, as in the case of the electrical manufacturing companies in the 1950s or the bribe-giving multinational companies in the 1970s. A corporate executive officer of Equity Funding Corporation easily persuaded junior staff members who did not profit directly to join his criminal conspiracy; some of the staff even joined in a "party" to forge insurance papers.

Some of this effect comes from an employee's concern to keep his job. Ordinary moral compunctions are overcome by the fear that a superior may discharge you if you refuse to comply with his orders.

Yet a number of big-business bureaucracies continue to develop some dishonesty at or near top levels. Rosabeth Kanter in *Men and Women of the Corporation* suggests that the emphasis on free opportunity toward the top of an administrative hierarchy may keep some "human and humane values" from developing: "Great opportunity—the promise of ever increasing status and power—can breed competitiveness, an instrumental orientation towards relationships, a politically generated focus upward in the organization and an excessive absorption in work that can threaten such outside institutions as the family."[19] Norman Jaspan comments:

> Dishonesty in a company is frequently a barometer of the quality and integrity of supervision. A half-dozen honest supervisors who really do their jobs can keep a hundred employees honest.

> Our firm uncovered more than $100 million of employee dishonesty in the last year. Supervisors were responsible for 62 percent of it. This is not to say that rank-and-file dishonesty is insignificant but the big dollar losses by far are due to middle management and executive personnel.[20]

Another writer wrote about a large corporate scandal:

> Corporations can and do create a moral tone that powerfully influences the thinking, conduct, values, and even the personalities of the people who work for them. This tone is set by the men who run the company, and their corruption can quickly corrupt all else. A startling thing about Equity Funding is how rarely one finds in a cast of characters big enough to make a war movie, a man who said "No, I don't do that. It's wrong."[21]

Does a Corporation Have Rights?

Several commentators have argued that corporations are mere creatures of the state. Even neo-conservative Irving Kristol writes, "Corporations are highly vulnerable to criticism of their governing structure," because they have no basis in political theory.[22] Persons politically further to the left than Kristol have sharp criticisms of corporations. Ralph Nader and his colleagues cite *Hale* v. *Henkel,* U.S. Supreme Court, 1906: "The Corporation is a creature of the state. It is presumed to be incorporated for the benefit of the public. It receives certain privileges and franchises, and holds them subject to the laws of the state and the limitations of its charter."[23]

The theory that the corporation has no private rights is descended from the British practice of licensing trading corporations like the East India Company. In American history corporations secured special charters from state legislatures until the practice of general incorporation statutes was well-established in the mid-nineteenth century. A few commentators have noted that the change to general incorporation has altered the theory of government "creation" of corporations.[24]

Corporations today have assumed the major responsibility for American economic life and can hardly be viewed as whimsical legal creations. They are treated as persons by the law, and are entitled to preservation of their property under due process of law, just as is any citizen. Roger Pilon has developed at length the theory of "Corporations and Rights: On Treating Corporate People Justly." Pilon does not argue against the various charges brought against corporations, but argues that to have a reason for wanting outside control is different from having a warrant or justification to do so. Such a justification should be based on normative grounds. Pilon believes that the corporation is a private association that can arise independently of the state, without violating the rights of anyone. He cites ethicist Alan Gewirth, who maintains that every agent has a right to voluntariness and purposiveness for well-being if these are also the rights of those with whom the agent deals. Pilon sees no reason why a voluntary association like a corporation should not have that same right.[25] Courts do not have a moral right to intercede on a contract for services to aid one or another party. Is Pilon ethically right?

Corporate Citizenship

In view of the importance of business corporations in American life, it is discouraging to have to report a substantial number of major ethical violations by principal officers or directors of major corporations. The recently merged Penn-Central Corporation failed in 1970 with substantial evidence that the board of directors and officers ignored their major function, spending many millions of dollars of railroad money on subsidiaries they controlled and paying out unjustified dividends; these actions sacrificed a major public interest (the continued operation of the railroad) to the immediate financial gain of the insiders. Major automobile manufacturers violated antitrust laws in an effort to delay putting smog-control devices on cars. General Motors sent out over 10,000 school buses with defective brakes and tried to soft-pedal the criticism. Other examples are given in chapter 8 on product liability. The effort to discredit Ralph Nader was discreditable to General Motors.[26] B.F. Goodrich Company was at least embarrassed by an apparent effort to alter the results of some brake testing on a plane destined for the Air Force. Scores of major firms in recent years have violated campaign contribution laws. Major grain companies were convicted of conspiracy to steal grain from the Food for Peace program. A

Lockheed subsidiary was castigated by the court for operating under known illegal and dangerous conditions that resulted in the death of seventeen men. Within Richardson-Merrell Corporation, lab test results were ignored so that a dangerous drug could be put on the market. Officials of Texas Gulf Sulphur were convicted of securing financial benefit before informing investors. Equity Funding followed policies that defrauded shareholders of scores of millions of dollars. Franklin National Bank, on the verge of insolvency, claimed to be establishing itself as a major worldwide financial institution. In 1961, high officials of major electrical manufacturing companies were fined and sent to jail for deliberate violation of antitrust laws. Few, if any, of the guilty executives in all these cases had criminal records in other respects. Many of them had been leaders in their communities. Some of their illegal corporate conduct seems to have resulted from corporate loyalty overriding other loyalties. Administrative or legal action was taken against most of them; one wonders if a program of ethical education of executives could not have forestalled many of these troubles.

With very large corporations exerting great power in the community, a problem arises as to methods of making the corporation become a legal and ethical citizen. It is easy to say that the corporation is a legal person and should assume full responsibility for any illegal action of its staff. However, judges are hesitant to levy major fines on a corporation that is the sole source of income for many families in the community, or the work of which is essential to the welfare of the community. As a result, many corporate fines are too small to be effective. For example, in 1961 the Quaker Oats Company changed the size of grains of certain cereals but neglected to change the weight marked on the packages. Prosecution resulted in a fine of $6,000 but FDA investigators believed that the shortages saved the company some $70,000 in a six-month period.[27]

It is now possible to fine a large corporation $1,000,000 in some federal cases but few judges levy so heavy a fine. The FTC uses its "cease and desist" orders in part because it does not wish to rely on the likelihood of court fines or imprisonment, which require prosecution by the Department of Justice. Corporate executives are rarely sent to prison and those rare occasions are likely to be for very short terms. If corporate executives are given heavy fines, the corporation may find means of reimbursing them. Accordingly, there is a very real problem of adjusting corporate ethics to those of society. The customary danger of punishment that reinforces the sense of rectitude in individuals is frequently not important to corporations.

Christopher Stone has written a book and several articles that suggest means of improving the conscience of corporations.[28] He would begin by increasing the proportion of "outside" directors. Stone would also like to have some public directors backed by staff with specific assignments including assurance of compliance with laws, appearance as liaison in the legislative process, and checking on the effectiveness of internal systems. Such directors would be nominated by a federal corporation commission or the Securities and Exchange Commission (SEC). Special public directors should be assigned to recidivist corporations.[29]

Stone has other recommendations which along with those cited might be contested and would be hotly opposed if proposed as legislation. He may suggest too many controls. But the purpose of his book is a commendable effort to keep the corporate flexibility and drive and imagination, but bring it back into a reasonable ethical outlook. The corporation by itself, largely uncontrolled from outside, has sometimes shown a dangerous tendency to evolve its own ethics, in some cases a strongly antipublic ethic. Stone's notion is to build ethics back into corporate life.

Ralph Nader's group has another proposal for reforming the corporation, largely through federal chartering and civil and criminal sanctions. Penalties are a means of enforcing ethics, but some aspects of the more educational program advocated by Stone are more likely to raise the level of corporate ethics.

The future of corporate boards of directors is not altogether clear. Largely because of the conflict-of-interest problem there has been a nationwide movement toward more "independent" directors, meaning directors not chosen from the executives of the company, nor from the organizations selling legal or financial services or products to the company. Ethically this seems like a highly desirable means of avoiding conflicts of interest and of making corporations more aware of the social, political, and economic repercussions of their actions. In a number of corporations, a small ethics committee, often including outside directors, has been formed.[30] The SEC and the New York Stock Exchange now require that the auditing committee be composed of outside directors. Unfortunately, there is some evidence that independent directors are less likely to be aware of dangers to the business or to contravene mistaken policies of the management.[31] The ethical-director choice thus becomes confused—perhaps an Aristotelian middle way is desirable.

Corporate Political Power

This book will not attempt to probe the difficult problem of whether corporations, or any other economic group, have too much political power; a problem which Edwin M. Epstein and others have analyzed.[32] Instead, it will briefly discuss the ethics of various exercises of corporate political power.

Few people can dispute the desirability of some form of corporate lobbying. Surely the administrators of enterprises that are of basic financial importance to thousands of employees, and of some importance to thousands of shareholders, have a responsibility to let Congress and state legislatures know how proposed legislation may affect the future of jobs and dividends. There may be greater doubt as to the ethics of corporate lobbying for or against general legislation; Massachusetts has attempted to ban such lobbying, but the Supreme Court rejected this ban as an infringement on freedom of speech. Even here, however, it was difficult to say that the corporation had no legitimate interest; the legislation of Massachusetts would have forbidden corporate lobbying against higher personal income taxes, which might well have affected employees of the company.

The spread of governmental activities to include regulation of much of economic life in recent decades has increased the reasons for corporate participation in political life. Legal banning of the use of corporate funds in political elections has made lobbying doubly necessary. Yet to many Americans corporate lobbying still seems reprehensible, and antilobbying laws try to control it. A large part of the reason for this attitude probably is the unethical techniques that a few corporations have used. Since the early 1970s, many corporations put pressure on executives to contribute to political-action funds.[33] Bribing of legislators by corporate funds is odious to many Americans whereas influencing of legislators by union-inspired votes is ignored. The popular distinction here may be correct. Bribing is illegal everywhere; voting by pressure blocks is legal. The only appropriate solution for the corporation is increased intensity of ethical lobbying; with due attention to the ethics of each technique. Like bribing, offering of lucrative jobs to public officials is wrong but portrayal of unemployment as a result of legislation is ethical. The conflict of union and corporate roles in politics also requires ethical consideration, but there is not much chance of developing valid rules. Unions can and do play an active part in elections and in legislation; the party they support has been dominant in American life for a half century. Present federal law prohibits union or corporate contributions to federal elections; however, unions direct much of their ongoing activity to politics. Both unions and corporations may assemble funds through political-action committees of their members or employees. Both approaches present the ethical problem of whether job pressure should force an employee to give to political-action programs that may be opposed to his own political philosophy.

Conflict of Interest

The activities of the modern corporation frequently raise problems of conflict of interest, most of which were not foreseen in the Bible nor Aristotle nor Confucius nor other historical sources of ethics. In those historical sources almost the only relevant conflict recognized and banned was that of the judge or other official who took a bribe. Conflict of interest is an ethical or legal doctrine that forbids a person to make a decision for one side of a controversy when he, his wife, other close relative, or business or professional associate has some economic interest on the other side of the case. Bribery and kickbacks are variants of conflicts of interest but are usually discussed separately. Conflict-of-interest cases in the securities-selling business are discussed in chapter 8.

Since corporations were few and their nature was very different from that of modern corporations, there were few ethical standards for the business corporation as it came into full use in nineteenth-century America. Conflict among managers or employees, or between management and customers, or between top management and lower management, was not adequately foreseen. Yet as America became more and more dominated by legalistic thinking, conflict of interest became more of a problem and more likely to be played up by a press already hostile to business. A group of new ethical rules on conflict of interest in accordance with the Western ethical tradition needed to be developed.

The climax of unethical conflict of interest in corporate management was described by the distinguished brothers, Charles Francis Adams, Jr., and Henry Adams in their famous *Chapters of Erie.*[34] Daniel Drew, long-time treasurer of the Erie Railroad, used its funds and its securities for personal stock-market battles; Jim Fisk and Jay Gould, after driving Drew out, used Erie securities for their personal ends, in a major fight with Cornelius Vanderbilt of the New York Central. All three disclosed almost total lack of concern for other shareholders, driving Erie stock prices up and down for personal financial gain. Unfortunately, leading attorneys, state and federal judges, and legislators seemed ready to cooperate with these totally unethical actions. None of the Western ethical tradition against conflict of interest by officials was taken seriously by these Erie executives, or by the public officials who dealt with them.

Thomas C. Cochran tells of the conflict of interest when nineteenth-century American railroads, seeking to build new lines, created construction companies in which the railroad-board members and top executives had major interests. The construction companies were usually financed by payments in railroad securities, on which the construction company would borrow. Should the construction-company management be frugal to save money for the railroad or should it spend lavishly and demand payment of more shares of railroad-company stock to benefit its investors, who may also be on the board of the railroad company? The possibility of the railroad director cheating the railroad shareholder was great, and apparently this was the case with much railroad construction in the 1850s, 1860s, and perhaps 1870s. However, the railroad-executive letters reviewed by Cochran seemed to indicate that such practices began to be condemned in the 1880s and 1890s. It would be interesting to know how the higher standards entered executive thought processes. In part it may have been because of the difficulty of earning dividends on unduly costly railroad securities. In part the executives may have recognized the basic unfairness of the conflict of interest. In part the fear of legal restrictions may have motivated the executives. Cochran also points out that similar problems arose as to railroad-management interest in corporations supplying steel rails, or in the land and mining companies that railroads developed to secure funds from public-land grants and to secure traffic from economic activities.[35]

Correspondence of railroad executives indicates that some of them were clearly aware of the conflicts of interest. In at least one case, a large shareholder and director succeeded in ousting two other directors from the Chicago, Burlington, and Quincy Railroad because they acted unethically as directors of both the railroad and the construction company.[36] However, no rule forbidding such conflicts of interest was laid down by the companies, and little legislation on the subject was passed by state or federal governments until the 1930s. Saul Engelbourg gives other late-nineteenth-century examples of conflict of interest in railroads and the slow drive toward reducing and eliminating such conflicts.[37] Businessmen themselves seem to have exerted pressure to eliminate some of the worst forms of conflict of interest; but some forms continued into the twentieth century.

For the years from 1900 to World War I, Engelbourg's attention largely shifts to conflict of interest in other enterprises. Charles M. Schwab, first president of U.S. Steel, said, "I believe I am the only man on this Board who has not something to sell to the Steel Corporation." Directors of life-insurance companies participated as brokers in sale of securities to the insurance company. Investment bankers acted as both buyers and sellers. George W. Perkins (executive vice president of New York Insurance Company and partner of J.P. Morgan) even mingled a New York Life Insurance investment with his personal funds. However, morality on these matters was helped by the Clayton Act prohibition of interlocking directorates and by probings like the Armstrong investigation into life insurance.[38]

In the 1920s, Colonel Robert W. Stewart, head of Standard Oil of Indiana, was removed from office after a major proxy fight organized by John D. Rockefeller, Jr. Stewart organized a company that bought over thirty-three million barrels of oil from Mexico Oil Company at $1.50 a barrel, and immediately sold the oil to Prairie Oil and Gas and Sinclair Crude Purchasing at $1.75 a barrel. Sinclair was half-owned by Standard of Indiana. Stewart apparently owned a substantial fraction of the stock of Continental Oil Company, and for several years kept $759,000 of liberty bonds bought with the profits from the deal, depositing at least $33,000 of interest to his own account.[39]

John D. Rockefeller, Jr., as a shareholder in Standard of Indiana, asked Stewart to testify in a congressional probe. When Stewart failed to answer his letter, Rockefeller undertook a proxy battle that ousted Stewart as board chairman. It is interesting to note that the largest number of shareholders, most of whom were employees under a stock-purchasing plan introduced by Stewart, voted for Stewart. It was the larger outside shareholders who were influenced by John D. Rockefeller, Jr.'s drive that Stewart be fired because of his ethical deficiencies. Were ethics confined to the wealthy among the shareholders of Standard Oil of Indiana in 1929? Standard Oil employees had seen great expansion of the company and the employee stock-purchase plan under Colonel Stewart; perhaps they viewed these as more important than the chairman's purchase of stock against the interest of the company or his refusal to give legally requested testimony.

There are more recent examples. In 1927 to 1932 Albert H. Wiggin, head of Chase National Bank, through subsidiary corporations that he owned, made over $10 million speculating in the stock of the Chase bank when it was going downhill financially.[40] A number of years ago a president of Chrysler Corporation admitted that he and his wife had been majority stockholders in two businesses that made much of their annual income by supplying Chrysler. The president was asked to resign and later agreed to reimburse Chrysler for overcharges to the company.

The bankruptcy of the Penn-Central Railroad in June 1970 uncovered another case of conflict of interest. David C. Bevan, financial vice president of the railroad, and some friends, including some employees of the company, organized a personal investment company, Pennphil. This company bought securities of companies in which Penn-Central's later purchase jacked up the prices, then sold the securities at a profit while Penn-Central continued to hold them.[41] Members of the board of directors of Penn-Central were not aware of this venture when it was made.

Numerous cases of conflict of interest arise with no intention of evildoing, as will be discussed in chapter 8 (conflict of interest in security markets). It may be helpful to think of three categories of conflict of interest, each of which calls for different treatment.

First, there are clear-cut cases that should be legally banned under now-fairly-well-accepted ethical standards. These include cases like the profit-making personal corporation established by Stewart of Standard of Indiana. Conflicts like this should be banned, both because they are likely to work against the interests of the corporation, and because the conflict helps build genuine disrespect for business ethics. Ethically speaking, these cases may be the equivalent of stealing from the ordinary shareholder. Another group of cases in the first category involves conflict of interest of corporate employees. Several laws require that a corporate executive, to be indemnified, must have acted in good faith and in a manner reasonably believed to be in the best interests of the corporation.[42] In general, the higher ranking executive bears more legal responsibility than the lower one. A director may not take advantage of his position in a corporation to operate a commercial activity for his own personal profit. Executives may not acquire a business and run it in competition with their employer. Injunctions were granted against executives who planned competing businesses before terminating their employment. American courts have generally tried to forbid a variant form of conflict of interest, the employee who uses company time and knowledge to start a competing company. In a 1936 case, the Massachusetts Supreme Court found conflict of interest and breach of loyalty by three executives who obtained from Lincoln Stores information and money that they used to build a competing store.[43]

In addition to these cases of large conflicts of interest on the part of corporate officers, there is a second class of smaller conflicts that are not easy to ban. Some of those described in chapter 8, including noncompetitive bidding for underwriting, could probably not be eliminated without damage to the raising of funds for American industry. Only large firms like Lehman Brothers or Merrill-Lynch or Goldman-Sachs can sell some corporate issues; these firms are not likely to spend time and money preparing competitive bids for each security sale. So many observers have thought it wise to leave the investment banker with a conflict-of-interest responsibility to his own company, to the corporation issuing the securities, and to the buying public. It appears that in some of this second class of cases, more publicity about the conflict would be desirable. In other cases, such as ownership by an executive of a minor number of shares in a supplier corporation, approval by the board of directors or an appropriate commitee would be desirable.

A third class of cases, even less important, grows out of the nature of modern industrial society, and probably can be controlled only by greater ethical education of the person or persons making the conflict decision. Price setting, wage setting, and work-condition determination may all involve conflicts of interest. Management often accepts a higher wage scale, at a real cost of higher price levels to consumers, because higher wages mean higher executive salaries; any efforts to ban this form of conflict of interest would seriously jeopardize the freedom of our economic system. DeLorean gives two examples of General Motors personnel who used knowledge of company action to make money for themselves.[44]

It may be that the freedom of movement required in a corporate business calls for less rigorous control of conflicts of interest than is needed for a trustee. Trustees are circumscribed by a trust instrument; their duty is to invest, whereas corporate management makes a series of important decisions about choice of products, prices, quality of service, and size of inventories, all of which are subject to an overriding interest in profit.[45]

Corporate Codes

The discussion of the morality of individual businesspersons in chapter 2 indicated that a large majority of business executives and employees are
ethical, insofar as they understand ethical actions. Naturally, out of a large
percentage of would-be ethical persons there come reform movements from
time to time. Some American businessmen are legalistically minded persons
active in reform movements that often try to establish a code for ethical
conduct either in the individual firm or in the industry. Each will be discussed
in turn.

There is no written history of corporate codes, and only a few specific
studies of them. If information from various sources is pieced together,
however, it appears that corporate codes have developed since 1900 in
approximately the following stages:

1. Brief statements of general ideals such as "This company commits
itself to the American free-enterprise system" and just treatment of competitors and consumers.

2. After the electrical manufacturers' cases and jail sentences in the early
1950s, there was a tendency to include some reference to antitrust laws.
Many large concerns issued detailed regulations of how to obey various
parts of antitrust laws, such as no price discrimination and no agreements
with competitors.

3. Today, most of the larger corporations have fairly detailed policy
statements or rules or codes covering a variety of legal and business
problems.[46]

A University of Virginia survey of large and middle-size companies in
1977 lists a number of items of corporate conduct. Large industrial companies seemed to be more likely to have comprehensive codes. Over forty of
the codes were in existence more than ten years, more in insurance and
utilities. About 20 percent of the *Fortune*-500 companies answered the
survey questions.

Most of the answering companies indicated that they have penalties for
the following actions: offering a bribe, concealing knowledge of a bribe,
accepting a bribe, concealing of knowledge of an accepted bribe, accepting
gifts of substantial value, participating in or making decisions that could
result in personal gain, failure to disqualify oneself where a conflict of interest exists, personal conduct injurious to the company's reputation, illegal
political contributions, price fixing, other illegal actions, profiting directly
or indirectly from inside information, falsification of company records, and
unethical conduct.

Commission of any one of five of these acts resulted in dismissal in 83 percent or more of the companies. The five include offering a bribe, accepting a
bribe, price fixing, falsification of company records, and illegal political

contributions. Two-thirds of the companies indicated that one or more managers had been dismissed for such violation in the past two years. A high percentage of companies reminded managers of the standards of conduct, and 71 percent asked them to sign the standards of conduct.

Most common of the ethical problems is that of payoffs (bribes, gifts, or entertainment). This problem occurred especially often in financial and industrial companies. Retailers and utilities listed the gifts and entertainment problem as most frequent; insurance companies listed conflict of interest.

Most of these codes were made by top management, approved by the board of directors or its executive committee, and applied to various levels of management. Only a quarter of the codes applied to all employees, but almost all applied to top management. Chief executive officers participated in most disciplinary actions and were informed of such action in almost all cases. CEOs believed that their managers were almost completely complying with the most important standards.

A survey of officials of somewhat smaller companies who were attending a summer program at the University of Virginia indicated only 45 percent of companies with formal standards of conduct. The smaller companies tended to have lesser penalties in cases of failure to disqualify oneself on account of conflict of interest, illegal political contributions, falsification of company records, and concealing knowledge of an offered bribe. Boards of directors of smaller companies were less likely to participate in drafting the code.

Staff and cooperating professors of the Virginia Center for Study of Ethics had some interesting comments about the results of this questionnaire. The center was gratified that 90 percent of the respondent *Fortune*-500 companies had formalized codes of conduct. Adding the facts that two-thirds of the companies had dismissed one or more managers for violations of standards, and that 100 percent of the chief executive officers believed that their managers were 95 to 100 percent in compliance, the record was a clear indication that large American companies are being guided by a strong sense of ethics. Others are more skeptical; only one-fifth of the *Fortune*-500 corporations had answered the questionnaire, and there is a real possibility that those corporations who used rules least were less likely to respond.

The Virginia Center for Study of Ethics and the cooperating professors were concerned that standards of conduct in most cases referred only to the upper levels of management, leaving most employees with no moral code. They were also concerned that boards of directors and executive committees had little to do with either the writing or application of the standards. One staff member believed the codes were not written in sufficient detail.

A more recent survey of company codes of ethics was made by the Opinion Research Center for the Ethics Resource Center in 1980, without reference to the earlier Heermance survey on industry codes discussed in the next section or that of the Virginia Center for Ethics. Almost three-fourths of the companies on the Opinion Research Center sample reported written codes of ethics; codes were more likely to exist in larger companies. Half the codes were less than four years old and 70 percent were less than ten years old. These percentages are less optimistic than those in the Virginia study.

Ninety-two percent of the companies reported periodical updating. Eighty-three percent believed their employees were familiar with the company's code, although only one-third distributed it to all employees, and only one-fifth distributed it throughout the organization. Sixty percent had only general principles in the codes; only half specified how the code would be enforced. Half used dismissal or possible dismissal as a sanction; 20 percent reported no sanction. Dismissals were more likely in the larger companies, 58 percent of which reported they had dismissed one or more employees for violations. In 68 percent of the companies the code required employees to report unethical activities; 67 percent told the employee how to report. Almost all codes forbid conflict-of-interest activities and forbid giving or taking bribes, kickbacks, or other favors. Only 62 percent forbid abuse of expense accounts or perquisites. Sixty percent believe that it would be beneficial if the code required all public information and advertising to be honest.

Almost all companies with written codes believe the codes are useful. When employees are involved in theft, embezzlement, or fraud, 73 percent require resignation; 65 percent require restitution, but only 44 percent would ask for prosecution. The percentages requiring resignation or restitution seem small.

The end of the questionnaire confirms the impression that a significant number of companies are not sure about some ethical problems such as punishment, nor are they aware of how to attack the problem.

Codes of conduct should be used by companies, and they should be read by all levels of management, and by all employees. A chief concern is that, being legalistic Americans, we may place too much reliance on the codes and not enough on the ethical education that should support their enforcement.

Industry Codes

In addition to corporate codes there are industry codes, which again vary from being broad vague documents to being quite specific.

Edgar L. Heermance made a collection of three hundred codes in 1924.[47] Most of these had been written in the previous four years, as a result of the campaign of Secretary of Commerce Herbert Hoover for better business practices. Some of the codes are a set of ideals like the Rotary Code, helpful "to the imagination of businessmen," but not very easy to enforce.[48] In contrast Heermance gives the specific prohibitions of the code of the National Association of Ice Cream Manufacturers.[49] Unfair trade practices which are cited include: inducing a customer or competitor's employee to introduce foreign substances into a competitor's goods or to otherwise injure its salability or conditions; bribing competitor's employees for any purpose or spying on competitors' plants; trailing competitor's delivery and sales agents; bribing railroad employees for information about competitor's shipments, or the use of any means for the procuring of a competitor's business or trade secrets; inducing competitor's employees to leave in such numbers as to disrupt his organization or embarrass his business; suing a competitor for purpose of intimidation; forcing a competitor out of business if he does not agree to keep out of certain territories; withdrawing advertising if competitor's advertising is not excluded or if certain discriminatory favors are not granted; and withdrawing patronage from a firm supplying materials if the same materials are sold to competitors. Other unfair practices included depriving a competitor of transportation facilities through bribery of railroad employees or otherwise, or the use of any means whereby the movement of a competitor's product is hampered; bidding up prices of raw material to a point where business becomes unprofitable, for the purpose of driving weaker competitors out of business; giving away goods or supplies or samples other than is customary in such quantities as to hamper and embarrass competitors, or in such volume as to have the effect of giving a rebate; or furnishing or offering exceptional and unusual store or advertising equipment to a competitor's customers as inducement to a customer to change.[50]

These unfair practices are relatively new and were not part of American business ethics in 1776. All seem to grow out of keen competition. Several practices, like industrial espionage, continue today, but the existence of the codes indicates that many businessmen wanted better ethics.

In this book of codes, Heermance shows the wide variety of codes resulting from Secretary Hoover's campaign of the early 1920s for such codes. The previously cited Ice Cream Manufacturers' code was one of the best, detailed, with efforts to cover real ethical problems. The Gas Products Association had brief treatment of relations with employees but made a real effort to establish professional-level relationships between competitive firms and in contracts.[51] The garment workers (perhaps prodded by the conduct of their unusual union) had important provisions for relations of the firm with their employees, their suppliers, their fellow manufacturers, and their customers.[52] In contrast, the funeral directors' code skipped over almost all ethical problems.[53] The National Association of Retail Clothiers said almost nothing about ethics.[54] The Iowa Hotel Association talked about "good name" and "professional integrity" but had no real rules.[55] The Straw Hat Manufacturers were in between, covering some real issues, including an entreaty to end the offer of bootleg liquor by salesmen.[56]

Heermance cites several other ethical problems for which rules had not been determined in the 1920s. Most codes had injunctions against "running down" a competitor, from which one can conclude that the practice was frequent. Selling below cost was recognized as a sin; a sin that the Federal Trade Commission might not recognize. "Loss leader" selling was condemned by some codes. So were premiums and trading stamps, which are in frequent use today.[57] Commercial bribery was apparently widespread from the 1880s on. Many codes mentioned by Heermance forbade it, but it is still to be found today.

A good discussion of the legal problems of industry codes is in Ivan Hill's *The Ethical Basis of Economic Freedom*, in which the effectiveness of a number of professional as well as industrial and other codes are discussed by informed writers.[58] Industrywide codes of ethics are likely to run counter to the antitrust laws. A series of court decisions and Federal Trade Commission actions have made it clear that associations can enforce their codes chiefly if the codes are attempting to enforce the law regarding business practices. In the advertising field standards for honesty and disclosure of information regarding products would be valid. As to penalties the authorities would prefer fines to dismissal or expulsion from the association. The FTC would welcome industrial agreements that help to enforce its business-practice rules.[59] The Securities and Exchange Commission has secured some cooperative enforcement from the National Association of Securities Dealers, and from the stock and commodity exchanges.

On the whole, however, industry codes are not nearly as important as the corporate codes already referred to. They are perhaps more useful in fields such as real estate where there are many small operators, for whom a set of corporate rules does not operate.[60] The American Society of Newspaper Editors has a code that is not enforced but which it believes to have the powers of moral suasion.[61] In another field, Abraham Briloff is very critical of the certified public accountants' efforts to determine standards of accounting.[62]

The Direct Selling Association, an organization of firms that operate through door-to-door salesmen, has set standards for membership. Its chief penalty is to ask the federal or state authorities to prosecute a member who violates the law. In the first five years of the code, consumer complaints were handled by the accused company itself. The worst offenders were not covered by the code. The association has suggested to municipalities an ordinance that can be an alternative to licensing procedures.[63] The Public Relations Society of America included 7,500 members in 1975, not a majority of the practitioners. It also has a code and may expel members for violating that code. It reports the same difficulty as did the direct selling group—the problems caused by nonmembers, over which it has no control.[64] The National Association of Broadcasters has established a Code Authority that reviews commercial advertisements and has considerable effect on them. Stanton Helffrich, the director of the authority, is optimistic about the work done by it.

A more recent survey of trade-association codes was made on a sampling basis by Opinion Research Corporation for Ethics Resource Center in 1980. The poll indicates fairly weak codes and enforcement policies, as Ivan Hill and earlier Heermance reports also found. Forty-one percent of the trade associations had codes. Most answering officials believed that codes were beneficial but others pointed to the difficulty of enforcing codes and the fear of conflict with antitrust policies. Half the codes had existed for twenty-five years or more; four-fifths for at least ten years. Sixty-eight percent reported that codes were updated periodically. Sixty-two percent of the codes had enforcement provisions; 82 percent relied on an enforcement committee of members. Sanctions included warnings, censures, reprimands (23 percent), expulsion (56 percent), suspension (29 percent), and fines (10 percent). Only one-fifth of trade-association officials had discussed enforcement with the FTC; only 30 percent of trade associations with enforcement provisions had done so. Almost all preferred self-regulation. One-quarter of the associations had sent key officials to meetings on self-enforcement provisions.

Not all codes of ethics are easily worked out. Associations of engineers for a number of decades have had trouble balancing the requirement of loyalty to the employing corporation with individual professional integrity. If, for example, an engineer believes that a new mechanism is dangerous to public safety but his superior orders him to proceed with construction of the mechanism, does he carry his complaint higher in the corporation, or protest to the press, or resign? A generally accepted ethic on such problems does not yet exist. The Engineering Council for Professional Development says in its code that "Engineers shall hold paramount the safety, health and welfare of the public in the performance of their professional duties."[65] Engineers should inform the "proper authorities" if their professional judgments are overruled. Few corporate codes recognize the right of engineers to do so. Another group of questions are raised by U.S. Antitrust Division attacks on engineering-code provisions that attempt to ameliorate intraprofessional rivalries by ruling against efforts to take jobs away from other engineers.

It can be concluded from this discussion that codes within a business *may* be quite effective; the power lies within the corporation to make them so. Industrywide ethical codes have been established in only a minority of industries. Their enforcement record is poor, largely because government does not delegate authority to the industrial code machinery. Industry and corporate codes should be encouraged but neither is an adequate answer to America's business ethics problem.

Conclusions

The impact of the corporation on American morality has not been as beneficial as its impact on our living standards. There is evidence that corporations can be moral or immoral—largely depending on the executive's choice. Somewhat better standards of corporate managers' responsibility to the corporation have developed, partly through the law and partly through an increasing sense of executive responsibility. Problems of conflict of interest between corporate officials and actions involving other corporations are still far from being solved by laws on executive ethics, but are more nearly solved than they were a century ago. The effect of the corporation on individual employee morals is substantial; whether it is beneficial seems to depend on the attitude of the principal executives. There is now a slow movement toward more recognition of the rights of individual employees within the corporation. The notion that the employee has some responsibility to report illegal or unethical actions of the corporation to the outside world is beginning to spread. Standards of corporate citizenship are slowly rising; a big part of the problem is that government is not as effective in forcing citizenship standards on corporations as on individuals.

Corporate codes and industry codes of conduct have often been tried in this century; the latter tend to be ineffective. All in all, this is a field of ethics in which progress is slow.

Notes

1. Lawrence Friedman, *A History of American Law*, p. 447.

2. Adolf A. Berle and Gardiner C. Means, *The Modern Corporation and Private Property*.

3. Ibid., p. 221.

4. Friedman, *A History of American Law*, p. 450.

5. Facts on File, *Corruption in Business*.

6. John Ladd, "Morality and the Idea of Rationality in Formal Organizations," pp. 488-512.

7. J. Patrick Wright, *On a Clear Day You Can See General Motors*, chap. 4.

8. Chester I. Barnard, *The Functions of the Executive*, pp. 258-284.

9. James MacGregor Burns, *Leadership*, pp. 29-46.

10. John J. Fendrock, "Crisis in Conscience at Quasar," pp. 2-10.

11. J. Patrick Wright, *On a Clear Day*.

12. Henry Mintzberg, "Organization Design, Fashion or Fit," p. 111.

13. Richard Austin Smith, *Corporations in Crisis*, pp. 196-197.

14. David Finn, *The Corporate Oligarch*, pp. 155-190.

15. As quoted from *Fortune*, date not given, in Finn, *The Corporate Oligarch*, p. 168.

16. Finn, *The Corporate Oligarch*, p. 204.

17. Kermit Vandiver, "Why Should My Conscience Bother Me," in Heilbroner, Robert, et al., *In the Name of Profit*, pp. 3-31.

18. Sanford Ungar, "Get Away with What You Can," in Heilbroner, *In the Name of Profit*, pp. 106-127.

19. Rosabeth Moss Kanter, *Men and Women of the Corporation*, pp. 162-163.

20. Norman Jaspan, *Mind Your Own Business*, p. 4.

21. William F. Blundell, "Equity Funding: I Did it for the Jollies," in John M. Johnson and Jack D. Douglas, *Crime at the Top*, p. 156.

22. Irving Kristol in *Wall Street Journal*, May 12, 1978, p. 20.

23. Ralph Nader, et al., *Taming the Giant Corporation*, p. 15.

24. Robert Hessen, "Corporate Legitimacy and Social Responsibility," pp. 18-20.

25. Roger Pilon, "Corporations and Rights: On Treating Corporate People Justly," pp. 1245-1370.

26. Wright, *On a Clear Day*, p. 51.

27. Curt Gentry, *The Vulnerable Americans*, p. 59.

28. Christopher Stone, *Where the Law Ends*, pp. 23-25.

29. Ibid., chaps. 13, 14, 15.

30. Ibid., chaps. 13, 14, 15.

31. Leslie Levy, "Reforming Board Reform," pp. 166-172.

32. Edwin M. Epstein, *The Corporation in American Politics*.

33. Christopher Elias, *The Dollar Barons*, pp. 107-112.

34. Charles F. Adams, Jr. and Henry Adams, *Chapters of Erie*.

35. Thomas C. Cochran, *Railroad Leaders*, pp. 110-121.

36. Ibid., pp. 114-115.

37. Saul Engelbourg, *Power and Morality*, pp. 13-23.

38. Ibid., pp. 98-105.

39. Carl Taeusch, *Policy and Ethics in Business*, pp. 197-221.

40. Frederick Lewis Allen, *Lords of Creation*, p. 334.

41. Joseph R. Daughen and Peter Binzen, *The Wreck of the Penn Central*, pp. 122-149.

42. Leslie W. Jacobs, "Law, Business Ethics and Conflict of Interest," in Tom L. Beauchamp and Norman E. Bowie, *Ethical Theory and Business*, pp. 353-361.

43. *Lincoln Stores* v. *Grant*, 309 Mass 417, 34 NE 2d, 704.

44. Wright, *On a Clear Day*, p. 84.

45. Ralph K. Winter, Jr., "State Law, Shareholder Protection and the Theory of the Corporation, p. 278.

46. Paul M. Hammaker, et al., *Standards of Conduct in Business*.

47. Edgar L. Heermance, *Code of Ethics, A Handbook; The Ethics of Business*, p. 20.

48. Heermance, *The Ethics of Business*, p. 20.

49. Ibid., pp. 36-37.

50. Ibid., pp. 36-37.

51. Heermance, *Codes of Ethics*, pp. 198-204.

52. Ibid., pp. 84-89.

53. Ibid., pp. 516-517.

54. Ibid., p. 90.

55. Ibid., pp. 236-237.

56. Ibid., pp. 231-235.

57. Heermance, *The Ethics of Business*, pp. 35-50.

58. Ivan Hill, ed. *The Ethical Basis of Economic Freedom*.

59. Earl W. Kintner, "Self-Enforcement of Codes of Ethics," in Hill, *Ethical Basis of Economic Freedom*, pp. 387-402.

60. Ibid., pp. 353-363.

61. Ibid., pp. 347-352.

62. Abraham Briloff, "Codes of Conduct," in Richard T. De George and Joseph A. Pichler, *Ethics, Free Enterprise and Public Policy*, pp. 264-287.

63. Neil H. Offen, "Commentary on Code of Ethics of Direct Selling Association," in Hill, *The Ethical Basis of Economic Freedom*, pp. 263-275.

64. Ibid., pp. 283-308.

65. Albert Flores, ed., *Ethical Problems in Engineering*, vol. I, p. 64.

4 Business Relations with Employees

Ethical History

The rights of workmen either as individuals or as groups were not very clear or strong in ancient times, with one exception. The Jews, in the Old Testament, required that workers receive their pay at the end of the day, should not work on the Sabbath, and should not be oppressed. Later Judaic law said a hired man suing for wages was not to be strictly treated, and should have good food while working.

Underlying the specific provisions for individual workers, the Old Testament includes a number of injunctions for good treatment of poor people, which might have included workers. Psalms 9 and 12 are good examples of this injunction.

In the Egypt of the pharaohs, there were frequent references to justice throughout the land but also evidence of exactions from ordinary citizens, and severe punishment for infractions.[1] In Greek law references have been found only to slaves, who were protected against being hit, killed, or jeered at. Roman law was sharp in its repression of workmen striking for higher wages, but had few occasions to meet this problem. It provided for some protection of slaves but, of course, slavery itself seems far from ethical to us today. Thomas Aquinas wrote of a fair wage for a service rendered. English common law recognized menial servants who must work at least a year. Apprentices were bound for a term of years, usually seven; all were entitled to wages, but at minimal levels. Work hours were defined. However, workers were viewed as criminal conspirators when they combined to secure higher wages. Adam Smith was concerned that laborers should be tolerably well fed, clothed, and lodged. Immanuel Kant's argument that every individual should be treated as an end in himself certainly seems to imply freedom for workmen.

It is fair to say that the rights of workmen, either as individuals or collectively, were not well recognized in the Anglo-American legal tradition up to the American Revolution. However, the ethical theory of the Western world was moving toward broader rights for all people, including workers. The doctrine of natural rights that was important in nineteenth-century America clearly had such implications. The Judaic-Christian tradition that every individual had a direct connection with God supported the value of the individual, as did Kant's imperative that every individual should be viewed as an end in himself.

American ethical thought included obligations as well as rights. An ethic that people should work conscientiously was well-developed in literature, sermons, and elsewhere in later nineteenth-century America.

America's relatively new ethical code of recognizing individual values soon encountered major problems. In 1800, common-law principles left few rights for workmen; indeed the principles seemed to view most joint actions of workmen as criminal conspiracies. A few decades later when judicial and legislative action treated workmen somewhat more favorably, employers sometimes called up police and internal security forces against unionists. The unions retaliated with force, and both sides built the background for intense labor-management rivalry, perhaps a sharper rivalry than exists in some other modern industrial democracies. Strike rates also seem to be higher in the United States than in other modern countries.[2] It is curious to have these bitter conflicts in a country where there is great freedom of movement from one social class to another.

"Sweat-shop" conditions, including low wages and poor working conditions, have often been a part of American life and still are to be found in a number of cities.[3] Today these conditions are generally illegal, so the ethical problem is as much one of governmental inaction as of business failure.

At the beginning of the twentieth century, at least two major business approaches toward labor were tried. Some big businesses tried a mixture of "coercion, inducement, and public relations." U.S. Steel introduced a pension plan, an employee stock-purchase plan, and devices to create better working conditions. At the same time, the National Association of Manufacturers had a militant open-shop policy.[4]

In the twentieth century, there has been a growing trend toward treatment of employees in an ethical manner. This includes politeness, regard for them as individuals, and efforts to help them do the work needed by the organization in a way that commands their own self-respect. It is often expressed as a move toward fairness or justice.[5] This trend is far from universal but it is clear. It seems to follow naturally from the growing recognition of individuals in American life. However, neither religious precepts, philosophical generalizations, nor legal enactments provide a clear, ethical background for problems of employee relationships.

Ethics of Compensation

Methods of determining salaries or wages have varied greatly in human history. In many empires and kingdoms, wages were what was necessary to keep workers and their families alive, often on a stingy basis. Slaves were generally rewarded on this basis alone. Nineteenth-century economists wrote of an "iron law" of wages which meant little more than subsistence. This payment of subsistence is more an economic necessity than it is an "ethic."

In America today, there is a wide variety of criteria to determine compensation, mostly more generous than the "iron law"! Companies in some cases pay top executives almost anything the executives ask. Lower-ranking executives are likely to be paid the prevailing rate for persons of their skill and amount of responsibility. Responsibility is the criterion followed also in many governmental administrations. Wages in industries that have been effectively organized by labor unions tend to be at relatively high levels. In other industries, wages may vary from comparable levels to slightly more than subsistence levels. In some companies and most military and governmental units, seniority is a factor in determining wage levels even though at times this practice may run contrary to payment for quality of services rendered. In Japan, wages are to some extent based on security and/or potential ability of the worker.[6] As a result of differences in union pressures, there are many more different jobs with different pay rates in American industry than in Japanese industry.[7]

Economic changes bring in other criteria. During inflationary times, union leaders tend to demand a minimum wage increase equal to the increased cost of living, even though that insistence may result in further inflation and economic damage to independent or nonunion workers. The rise in world trade has made the higher wages of some American industries an economic liability, resulting in heavy unemployment in industries that have international competition. At an earlier time, ironically the higher wages paid by Henry Ford increased the number of potential buyers for cars and other items that were then viewed to be luxuries.

It is difficult to find any accepted ethic in this mixture of compensation schemes. Ethical principles often develop from pressures of various groups, which either become law or generally accepted custom. In the remuneration field, the pressures are many, diverse, and frequently changing. Federal and state governments have adopted minimum-wage laws in an effort to establish a cost-of-living standard, but many competent economists believe that these laws are keeping young people from securing initial jobs and learning how to work. Unions persist in their wage-raising efforts but sometimes drive the employers to financial hardship. Stronger nonunion companies probably tend to follow union wage scales. Most economists and many businessmen would let the marketplace determine compensation, but the competition of a country like Japan makes others question this theory.

An interesting question has been raised as to why a company that furloughed many employees in a time of economic recession could not afford to continue their insurance premiums although it was giving hundreds of thousands of dollars to philanthropy.[8] Was this ethical? Another bothersome problem is the ethic of laying off workers when sales drop or models are changed. Why should the workers bear the economic burden? In some industries, unemployment compensation does.

The whole problem of wage determination almost defies ethical analysis. When one union or one company may determine the wages of hundreds of thousands of people, the free market is not altogether free. At the moment, it seems that wage levels in some industries are a result of large power struggles. Real income of nonorganized employees may suffer as a result of the organization of other workers. On the other hand, complete corporate control of wages may not result in a free market. There are too many sets of wage ethics in America.

National wage ethics also may vary greatly. William Ouchi tells us that in Japan young women workers were upset if pay increases were not based on seniority.[9] In the United States, there is some feeling for seniority; such pay increases are often encouraged by unions on the ground that it prevents administrative discrimination. But many ambitious young Americans would leave a company that relied primarily on seniority for pay increases.

"Blowing the Whistle"

Ralph Nader and his colleagues have written and talked about the problem of "whistle blowing," by which they mean the problem of the employee who publicly criticizes corporate policies because those policies may be dangerous to other parts of the community. For example, one tire-company had research employees who were positive that a brake for an airplane was inadequate, but whose supervisors suppressed their test results, so the employees reported the problem to the FBI.[10] Another example could be that of patrolman Serpico, whose story of general corruption in the New York City police force was disregarded by officials in both the police department and the mayor's office until he told his story to *The New York Times*. He was rewarded with a promotion but was also almost killed as a result of the apparently deliberate negligence of colleagues. Another example is the body-shop inspector who publicized a defect that led to the recall of three million cars. Business frauds at Equity Funding and Investors Overseas Service were partly exposed by employees.

The problem continues. In *Whistle Blowing*, Alan F. Westin published ten cases in which employees complained about antipublic actions or personal discrimination by corporate superiors. Nine of the ten employees were forced out of employment; two received partial damages; one was kept on. The employee criticisms varied greatly. An airline pilot complained to the government about a steering-gear defect that he believed tripped off the auto-pilot and contributed to a crash; the airline suspended and grounded him several times. An in-house counsel told his agricultural-cooperative superiors and later the FBI of illegal payments to political campaigns; the coop fired him and then discredited him, and the coop and the responsible officials were later convicted. A driver for United Parcel Service refused to drive an unsafe truck; he was fired, appealed to the Federal Department of Transportation but received little help, and he also received no help from the Teamsters Union.[11] Westin quite correctly points out that the employees may have been incorrect in their judgments of management's mistakes, or may have chosen the wrong means of protest, or may have been criticizing social policies.

The great difficulties with whistle blowing are that it *seems* disloyal to colleagues and superiors, and may result in discipline or firing or the kind of fellow-employee noncooperation inflicted on patrolman Serpico. The problem has not been studied enough to determine how to balance the requirement of loyalty to a corporation or to management against the ill effect of a corporate or government action on the public. Edward Weisband and Thomas M. Frank have discussed the same problem in political practice, concluding that American public officials are less likely to resign in protest than are British.[12] It may be that American managers and even some workers overemphasize loyalty to the employer.

Sometimes the only right course of action is to resign from a corporation, and to let its competitors or the press or the appropriate governmental agency know the reason for resignation. However, men who have family obligations are naturally hesitant about resignation and loss of salary. Other corporations are likely to view the employee as not cooperative and not hire him. Even more, however, a man may feel a certain hesitancy about public criticism of superiors and colleagues whom he has found to be friendly human beings, and with whom he has worked cooperatively. As a result of these factors, some Americans have almost developed an ethic of not complaining against superiors.

The moral responsibility of an employee to protest some antipublic actions of his employers can hardly be contested. The Golden Rule and Kant's imperative to treat every individual as an end in himself certainly make it desirable to publicize or otherwise prevent the sale of an unhealthy product or unsafe piece of equipment. Almost any student of ethics would agree that if an employer or any member of his staff commits a murder or a robbery, it becomes the duty of the employee to report the offense to the appropriate legal authorities. The problem arises in noncriminal cases in which the employee disagrees as a matter of policy, and believes that he must take his case to the public. Many thoughtful and responsible people who have worked in the public service have come to the conclusion that they must say something to the press, or to Congress, or to some other critic. It is probably good for the public that this happens; some "washing of dirty linen" may be a result, perhaps a result that outweighs any loss of employee morale. The whistle-blowing employee may suffer economically; it is to be hoped that the advantages of a clear conscience would offset the economic disadvantage. A number of recent judicial decisions favor suits of employees who have been discharged because of whistle blowing. Federal civil servants now receive some statutory protection against the economic consequences of whistle blowing.

In private business, the situation is somewhat different. Much whistle blowing is based on concern for the effect of certain policies on the company's economic future. Executives frequently resign because they do not believe in a policy adopted by their employer. Many businessmen understand this and admire such a man for his independence; he frequently receives other job offers.

The more difficult problem is that of a subordinate employee who discovers that his company is selling a below-standard product or otherwise cheating the customer. If his complaints are not acted on, such a man has little choice but resignation, with the hope that he can find a job elsewhere. No person's working life can be satisfactorily accomplished in a dishonest environment.

David Ewing has noted some examples of constructive corporate policy directed against the problems that cause whistle blowing. Thornton Bradshaw, while president of Atlantic Richfield Company (ARCO), in 1978 wrote 50,000 employees asking them to report to the government any examples of use of chemicals that might threaten health or environment. A large division of General Electric Company operates a hotline for employees who have worries about wrongdoing in the corporation; a similar system operates in New England Telephone. Dow Chemical Company publishes employee criticisms and questions in company publications. Delta Air Lines has regular meetings with employees in which worker complaints are heard, after supervisors and foremen have been excused. Pitney Bowes, Inc., has an elected employee council to receive employee complaints. Union procedures sometimes protect employees who make complaints. In some companies elected employee committees administer a due-process procedure to hear and act on employee complaints. However, Ewing estimates that 80 percent of employees have no protection in cases where conscience might force them to "blow the whistle."[13] Westin tells us that General Electric, Control Data Corporation, Singer Company, and McDonald's Corporation have created ombudsmen to receive complaints. However, in none of these companies can there be time to consider every case of employee criticism.

Is there an ethical necessity for the kind of corporate actions discussed here? They are probably not needed in very small business organizations where everyone can go directly to a superior. But in the larger corporation, a good ethical case can be made for a procedure that protects the employee in complaining against corporate action that may threaten public health, safety, or welfare. The principles of *salus populi suprema lex est* and *sic utere tuo*, and injunctions to truth-telling all seem to join in supporting such procedures.

Safeguards of Employee Rights

A.A. Berle describes in *The 20th Century Capitalist Revolution* how in early English and French history people were given the opportunity to demand a hearing from the king if any of their rights were transgressed. The present-day corporation, wrote Berle, has similar problems. A large manufacturer like General Electric is told by a congressional committee that it should not employ communists or communist-sympathizers in security work, for fear of espionage or sabotage. General Electric wishes to do its patriotic duty, but finds itself forced into judging whether employees have communist sympathies, a task for which General Electric has no staff or procedures. Berle suggests that a time may come when large corporations have to be equipped with a procedure for deciding issues of great importance to employees, with notice and hearing and aid by counsel, all of this subject to appeal to federal courts. General Electric perhaps shudders at the amount of personnel time involved in handling such disputes, but Berle wonders if the individual is not entitled to this consideration.[14] Is this right to a hearing a new ethic?

A strong majority of business executives have expressed sympathy with such employees. There are also organizations that have penalized employees for outside activities, threatened no promotion if employees failed to make political contributions, instructed city employees to work on city time as well as outside for reelection of a city mayor, or fired a man because he worked for a league for better black-white relationships. In some of these cases, employees were reinstated; in others they were not.

There are intrusions of corporations or government agencies on employee privacy. For example, employees of a Los Angeles County office in Pomona had their telephone conversations recorded. A senior vice president of American Petrofina in Dallas was told his remarks should be censored by the company when he criticized Dallas leaders for coddling extremists who opposed a requiem mass for President Kennedy.[15] Many companies administer lie-detector tests. However, there is now a tendency toward preserving privacy of personnel records. Many employees wear what they wish to work; but some have been laid off because they violated dress regulations, and managers and arbitrators supported the layoffs.

To settle such problems, Ewing proposes a bill of rights for employees. He would like guarantees, probably through an amendment to the U.S. Constitution, to protect workers so that no organization would discharge, or discriminate against, any employee for criticism of management action. He suggests many other safeguards of outside activity, of privacy of files, and of hearing on complaints.[16]

Ewing overlooks some of the reasons for supervision. There is much to be said for "boss" domination—if the boss is right. The boss is responsible for running a part or all of the company. It is still true that, for good or for ill, many chief executives leave and probably should leave a clear imprint of their desires and ways of doing things on business organizations. If Ralph Cordiner had really dominated General Electric with his antitrust exhortations in 1951, the electrical-manufacturing price conspiracy might not have cost the company millions of dollars. Bradshaw's aforementioned letter to ARCO employees about illegal chemicals seems very sensible.

However, since bosses dominate, education of top executives in human values, including humane personnel procedures, is essential. Boards of directors should consider the qualities of humanity and tolerance as well as of aggressiveness and ambition in selecting chief executives.

Ewing's proposed guarantees ought to become the ethical policy of almost all business firms and government bureaus, particularly with the exceptions from each proposed by Ewing; for example, that the protection against application of penalties to employee critics shall not extend to employees who malign the organization. The underlying notion that managers must recognize the individual freedom of staff members is very good.

However, making these safeguards into constitutional or statutory provisions is a different matter. Courts often make political decisions; their lengthy procedures can cost so much that the expense of the trial is more important to the employee than his loss of autonomy. America needs more ethics, but fewer laws, and the laws here proposed could have a paralyzing effect on some businesses.

Some possible injustices to employees cannot be prevented by Ewing's legalistic code. Employees of the corporation in which the president reserves the succession for a not-very-competent son are handicapped in the fulfillment of their personal ambitions for promotion and possibly as to source of livelihood. Employees of Trans World Airlines (TWA) were seriously handicapped when owner Howard Hughes used a company plane as a personal possession at great cost to the company training program. Employees of RKO similarly suffered from Howard Hughes's ownership-maladministration.[17] Employees and shareholders of C. Arnold Smith's Bank of the United States suffered substantially from his mismanagement of the bank. We need an ethic that prevents such injustices but does not bog down in a morass of legalistic "administrivia."

Company Policy toward Dishonest Employees

One of the reasons for widespread dishonesty among employees in certain businesses is that businesses often do not try to secure prosecution of dishonest employees, especially if the amount stolen is small, or if the employee has been with the company for some time. If the employee has walked off with a few thousand dollars or more, the company is more likely to support a prosecution. If the company does not wish to support prosecution, the law-enforcement authorities normally will not prosecute; without evidence from company sources, conviction would be impossible.

The policy of not asking prosecution of employees who commit lesser offenses is based on various considerations: it saves the time of the firm's security force, which under America's disorganized court procedures may have to attend several court sessions before it is finally asked to testify; unions will often oppose criminal action if the offense is light; fellow employees also may resent a big company coming down hard on a small offender; the firm's chances of being prosecuted for false arrest are lessened if no prosecution of employees is undertaken; judges are very likely to give light or no penalties to white-collar employees; it may be felt that the fact that the employee is discharged and compelled to make restitution is in itself adequate penalty; the employer may be more concerned with securing restitution than with any possible advantage to public morality resulting from prosecution; or the employer may wish to avoid undesirable public relations attitudes, such as condemnation of the firm because it hires dishonest workers.

Is this permissive attitude toward clear-cut crimes by white-collar workers a denigration of ethical standards? It is certainly the more popular attitude. One study found that respondents viewed food adulteration as more comparable to serious traffic violations than to burglary.[18] Most retail organizations are quite aware of the desirability of remaining popular with employees and customers. As noted, in some firms a custom of allowing minor thefts has developed. Employees may take home minor tools or clothing items. It is difficult to keep this attitude from broadening into more serious theft. The problem for companies that follow this policy is whether they are encouraging dishonesty. Even if the company discharges the dishonest employee (which is usually the case, although a few long-time employees may be excepted), other employees will be aware that dishonest employees are not prosecuted.

A careful study of this problem cites the experience of the U.S. Post Office, which turned over all employee violators for prosecution. Department of Justice officials found in most cases that prosecution was warranted. As a result, the rate of apprehended dishonest postal workers was one-quarter the rate of apprehended workers in nonprosecuting department stores. Of course, there may be other factors such as the tenure and retirement provisions of post-office employment that made dishonesty more undesirable.[19]

Court sentences of department-store offenders have been quite light; most frequently a small fine or a light suspended sentence. There is a circle of reactions here. Judges are easy on white-collar offenders, so employers don't ask prosecution of white-collar offenders, so offenses increase in number, and judges become easier.

A few firms have found losses from employee thefts so high that they take a firmer stand and request prosecution much more frequently. These firms are usually ones selling expensive portable products.

An overall ethical answer for such a confused situation is not easy to find. Perhaps a specialized commercial-offense court with power to order restitution or fines quickly would have better results. Quicker punishment may be more important than severe punishment.

Ethics of Union Relationships:
One Bad Turn Deserves Another

Business dealings with unions have included some of the worst of American business ethics, on both the union and management sides. The nineteenth-century reaction of many American businesses against unions was wrong, both ethically and legally. Pinkerton's, Inc. and other quasi-police agencies were used by employers until statutes forbade it; force was freely applied by strike-breakers; numbers of businesses showed a desire to keep unions out completely, operating on what might be called the nineteenth-century ethic of the complete control of supervisors over all workers. Local governments were generally friendly to businesses, who were the largest taxpayers, and added their relatively weak local police strength to the men hired by businesses. It should be added that not all American businesses used violence against unions; there were some offers of friendly relationship in spite of the general coolness, but in many cases unions have responded with violence.

The advent of the New Deal in the 1930s turned the tables rather completely. Federal laws made it difficult, if not impossible, for many businesses to oppose unions. Unions have become "quasi-state institutions." "[T]he legal spider's web that surrounds labor relations in the United States maintains incumbent union officials in power over the workers, and it insulates the power and status of those officials against possible rejection by the workers over whom they rule."[20]

Federal laws heavily handicap employer opposition to unions; U.S. Department of Labor attitudes have made it very difficult for workmen to oppose the positions of their union leaders.[21] Federal laws permit appeals to the Department of Labor, but that very union-minded agency offers little help to workers who complain about union practices. The unethical anti-union position of nineteenth-century businesses has swung to the present position, just as unethical, of government-supported unions, some of which are more unethical than the businesses were.

The relative invulnerability of unions to democratic control has brought many undesirable agents into the unions. It is generally thought that organized crime has many connections with the Teamster's Union. It is not so generally known that organized crime has been operating in several other national unions, and racketeers in several more. As early as 1934, racketeers were employed "in a program of intimidation and violence" in the dress industry.[22] In the 1970s, hired thugs were brought into meetings of the respected International Ladies Garment Workers Union to intimidate members.[23] The longshoremen's unions have had fairly steady organized crime ties.[24] A later section of this chapter on organized crime gives other examples.

Statistical summaries are hard to find, but it seems clear that organized crime and individual racketeering have penetrated organized labor more effectively than they have other portions of American society, except perhaps the corrupt political machines of cities of the Northeast. This is not because union members are more prone to crime; in fact, they are probably less so than some other classes of society. A more credible possibility is that union leaders have often had close ties of acquaintanceship, religion, or politics with local-machine politicians who have had close ties with organized crime. More important, however, are the legal and administrative difficulties that keep union members from reforming their unions.

Two comparative studies indicate that the internal operations of American unions are indeed less honest than those of Australia or England. Seymour Martin Lipset advances the interesting theory that this is because there is less class spirit in American unions.[25] American union leaders think more of establishing themselves financially than of advancing the status of labor if this theory is correct.

Two ethical comments should be made. The first is an obvious but often overlooked ethical lesson: if you treat someone else unethically, a time may come when he treats you unethically. The difficulties that some businesses have today with unions are in part a result of businesses' earlier unethical treatment of unions. The other comment is related: all honest elements in society have a stake in honest, effective law enforcement. Unions would not have been so badly treated in their formative years if local government had been more impartial and had enforced laws against violence; unions would not be pushing honest businesses around so much today if federal, state, and local government were able to enforce the law more vigorously.

Few businesses have a combination of participative management and profit-sharing or other employee-satisfaction programs that does not leave a "hard core" of dissatisfied workers.[26] This dissatisfaction of bottom-level workers results in unions that at least purport to give employees an opportunity to express their own ideas. As unions gain strength, they frequently fall into a kind of competitive relationship with the employing firm. Management often resents the existence of unions. John DeLorean tells us that in the last dozen years, at least one ranking General Motors executive advocated closing a large plant to show the union it had no authority.[27] These relationships raise a variety of ethical problems.

Nonunion Firms

If a majority of employees has not voted for unions, it is not legally or ethically wrong for companies to establish a variety of plans for employee participation in management that may blunt the edge of demand for unions. Xerox, IBM, and Hewlett-Packard are examples of firms that secure worker participation in management with few problems from outside unions. Efforts of employees to express their own wishes in the management of a concern are reasonable and ethical; the employer owes to employees substantial recognition of this desire for self-satisfaction on the job. But there is no ethical precept that states that an outside union must furnish this employee representation. In bargaining in which unions are recognized, attitudes imply ethical demands. Each side should be truthful with the other; whether each side should always tell the *whole* truth is not an easy question to answer, but the answer is probably yes. A firm that needs a layoff on economic grounds and tries to put the blame for this layoff on the union is clearly unethical. As the National Labor Relations Board has said, the employer should make a "forthright candid effort" to reach a settlement.

Benjamin M. Selekman, a former teacher at Harvard Business School, has tried to describe management attitudes. He found management cynical about labor attitudes. He believed that in 1946 and 1947 capitalists worked with communists in order to secure lower wages. He sharply criticized the attitude of General Electric's vice president Lemuel R. Boulware that, as Selekman described it, management should take a position on union matters and hold firmly to it, thus giving labor representatives no chance to learn of political, economic, and social matters through negotiation.[28] "Boulwareism" has not prevailed as Selekman feared in the late 1960s. However, it is probably still true that a majority of managers would be glad not to deal with unions, or would rather deal with a weak union.

Selekman, who is more understanding of unions than of management, also cited the frequent failure of local union branches to follow principles to which the central union has agreed. Selekman's judgment overlooks the ties of some unions to gangsters and to corrupt political machines. Union tendencies toward inflationary wage demands have been noted. Some of these troubles may be a result of management's failure to welcome and help build strong unions, but the employers' reluctance to deal with corrupt unions is also understandable.

The attitudes of neither manager nor employee are modified much by the Western injunction to love your neighbor as yourself. The industrial battles of the late nineteenth and early twentieth centuries live on in the ideologies of both sides. Modern methods of supervision have taken some but not all of the sting out of class rivalry.

Union Attitudes toward Supervision

A major ethical problem in some negotiations between business and unions is that certain demands that seem reasonable to union negotiators may endanger great loss, in some cases even bankruptcy, for the firm. Richard C. Smyth and M.J. Murphy give a few examples.[29] War production at one aeronautical plant was seriously disrupted because the labor agreement specified that any disciplinary action required mutual agreement of the shop committee of the union and a representative of management. The shop committee did not agree in most discipline cases, so chaos resulted. The management could have been circumscribed in its disciplinary action and still have functioned effectively but mutual consent was disastrous, and employers would have good ethical grounds to oppose it. Unions may also push for joint management-union committees, which can be very useful in an advisory way but again could paralyze management if given veto power.

"Featherbedding" rules are demanded by some unions, but frequently not by the large industrial unions. These rules seek to perpetuate obsolescent methods of doing work in order to keep jobs. Sometimes they bankrupt the companies that agree to them. Other companies agree and lose out in competition to firms that are not handicapped by such rules. Smyth and Murphy give examples that are still true today of featherbedding rules by railroad, musicians', longshoremen's, stage hands', and some building-trades unions. It is certainly not unethical for employers to oppose make-work rules of the sort that have damaged economic operations and, hence, employment in some of these fields. Nor is it unethical to oppose such rules when they impose severe burdens on the national economy.

In *Men Who Manage* Melville Dalton gives some sidelights on operation of southern California local unions in industrial plants with regard to national contracts secured by an unnamed union.[30] Both union and management would have preferred local work-practice agreements; perhaps this is a sign that the national union's agreement was running counter to the development of local participative management. One union grievance committeeman said, "Top union and management are always bothering the local plant. We can work out our own arrangements if they'll leave us alone."[31] Both militant and lukewarm union members kept pressuring the shop steward or a member of management or both for items of personal satisfaction such as extra pay, or a better work position, or a desirable time of work. Neither union nor management resented these efforts. In at least two of the plants, first-level foremen often yielded to pressures from the union with something of a feeling of revenge on higher managers. Unofficial favor bartering between a union member with grievances and management often reached up to the division level. Lower-level management often liked unions because union-supported wage increases became a basis for higher management salaries.

The unions in these plants did not represent all members on a fair and equal plane. The union local did, however, provide a partial check on arbitrary management action. Union and management accepted each other easily. Neither was concerned about inflation. The situation was not likely to produce adequate regard for ethics.

Seniority

The union quest for recognition of seniority in transactions regarding employees has interesting ethical aspects. With or without unions, many employers would agree that if all workers were equal in ability, and a layoff of half the force was required, they would feel an obligation to keep the half who had been with them longest. Unions, however, argue for seniority in most aspects of personnel policy because they do not trust management, and fear that management would lay off the most union-supportive employees; or because seniority rules have become popular with employees. There is little ethical difficulty in yielding to such feelings until the problem of promotion arises. In that regard, the company which follows the union desire and promotes on the basis of seniority (not ability) may be endangering its own future and hence that of its employees, clearly an unethical action. It is interesting that the emphasis on seniority is not as strong in other countries as in America.

Must Employees Accept Union Attitudes?

There may be union members who support the principle of unionization, but do not wish to have to follow the union's political or social leadership. Paul Sultan suggests that this problem of values cannot be solved until unions become much more open to discussion and varying ideas than they are today.[32] In the meantime, the employer may find himself forced to yield to a closed-shop contract that constricts the freedom of his employees.

Peter Drucker believes it possible that the shift from manual to mental work may destroy the usefulness of the unions to which we have become adjusted. If so, the change may be good, for unions have perhaps been a bad ethical influence as often as a good one in American life. But if the old-style unions do go out, employers would be wise to make sure that there are adequate means for the worker to participate in the decisions of the organization. The desire of man to be heard about his work will not disappear, and the ethic of recognition of individual wishes is an increasing part of the Western tradition.

Closed Shop

Another difficult ethical question is raised by the closed shop. Unions maintain that without a closed shop, they are forced to maintain collective action against non-dues-paying "free riders," to the union an unethical result. Employers, and at least some employees, maintain that it is unfair to force a worker to support a union with whose political and economic goals he may disagree. If we do value rights of individuals in America, the ethical case seems to be against the closed shop.

Unions and Organized Crime

Organized crime (popularly but incorrectly called the Mafia) is strongest in the Northeast, but is to be found in most other sections of the country. It has strong political ties in New York, Chicago, and northern New Jersey, among other places, and sporadic ties elsewhere. It is probably spreading. Most strong firms try to avoid contracts with organized crime; in some parts of industry, however, "the mob" is unavoidable and legitimate business has to deal with them.

It is not completely appropriate to discuss organized crime in a chapter on business relations with employees. Most businesses that are drawn into connections with organized crime are caught because of connections with unions of their employees. However, others are brought into such relationships by force or monopoly; they cannot do business in an area without paying organized crime directly or indirectly.

Organized crime is descended from but is not part of the Sicilian Mafia. It uses Mafia techniques such as strict discipline, the punishment of death for what is considered disloyalty to chieftains, and personal movement in and out of respectable circles. In the United States organized crime ususally started with operation of brothels or gambling houses, and later became involved in drugs, thus leading many writers to say that it existed only because of America's severe laws on such "victimless" crimes. Today, however, organized crime operates in many fields of business.

Jonathan Kwitny gives several examples of the business operations of organized crime. Meat of various kinds (including tainted meat), mozzarella cheese, trucking, the waterfront, banks, stockbrokerages, clothing, and liquor are among the businesses that have extensive gangster ownership.[33] In many cases organized crime functions through some part of the Teamsters' Union, the Amalgamated Meat Cutters and Butcher Workmen, or other transportation, food, or construction unions. One of Kwitny's examples will be described here to illustrate the ethical problems of businesses.

The Iowa Beef Packing Company gave bribes, probably totaling millions, to Moe Steinman, a racketeer who with assistance from three organized crime families and adequate payments to key individuals controlled the Amalgamated Meat Cutters. Through union control, and again with organized crime backing, Steinman had become a meat wholesaler to a dozen supermarket chains in the New York-New Jersey-Connecticut area. The bribes were given to pay off union executives, supermarket executives, organized crime leaders, union executives, and Steinman himself. Thus the meat industry in a large urban area was controlled by one man for the benefit of himself and his conspirators, in violation of numerous state and federal laws. Ultimately, the huge bill for these bribes was paid by shoppers at the supermarkets.

Steinman's arrogant authority could not go undetected for long. Eventually the federal government, working at times with the New York County prosecutor's office, prosecuted Steinman, the president of Iowa Beef, and a number of recipients of bribe money. Organized-crime suspects are usually well defended, and this case was no exception. Steinman was convicted but received a light sentence; the president of Iowa Beef was convicted but received no penalty at all. The Internal Revenue Service secured a number of convictions for unpaid taxes but again the penalties were light.

Kwitny finds similar crimes in other industries where organized crime is actively functioning in unions. On the waterfront, shipping companies still have to pay organized crime to get their goods moved. In the trucking business many companies of good nationwide standing contract with organized-crime-related firms. The Teamsters' leaders have been very effective in pocketing their share of these funds.

There is evidence that American unions have a high proportion of ethical trouble. The largest and most potent of unions, the Teamsters, has an unenviable record of frequent racketeering, that is, securing funds from industry as a condition of operations. Investment of union pension funds, especially the large Central States Pension Fund, has been under constant surveillance by the U.S. Department of Labor, and there has been constant public criticism for the investment of such funds in Las Vegas gambling houses and elsewhere. International Longshoremen's Union officials on the Atlantic and Gulf waterfronts have often been arrested and tried for racketeering payoffs, kickbacks, embezzlement, and extortion.[34]

The federal and state governments find it difficult to stop the flow of this organized-crime lawlessness. What ethical questions does it raise for business? One of the most significant is whether an ethical firm should enter into business relationships with an organized-crime-controlled or related firm. The excuse for doing so was stated by the judge who sentenced the president of Iowa Beef: "There are very few people in American business who would have acted differently in these circumstances. In a certain sense this court will always consider you a victim of the extortionate practices of union officials and supermarket executives in New York."[35]

The judge was right and wrong. It was Steinman and organized crime that did the extorting. However, Iowa Beef Packing, which had already out-sold all other meat companies, could have refrained from entering the New York market until the control of organized crime was broken. Several supermarket chains refrained from buying Iowa Beef products because of the overcharge. If laws create ethical standards at all, the president of the company was wrong and should not have been treated so generously. Nor should Steinman have been sentenced so lightly; he was a real criminal.

A more borderline case arises with a score of nationally known firms (one known for its purported honesty) that have saved on trucking rates by using a firm with known organized crime connections, a firm that had con-tracts with its drivers below standard Teamsters' rates, and was probably paying bribes to union executives (in the case of the Teamsters' Union, possibly to organized crime) in order to operate on this substandard basis.[36] People who deplore Teamster's Union actions generally may think it good to pay a lower rate for hauling than standard Teamsters' wage rates would permit. But is it good to do business with a clearly unethical operation?

Several American business firms have become careless about organized crime connections. A nationwide brokerage house hired the nephew of an organized crime leader a week after his uncle was featured in a *Life* article for his murder trial and armed bank robberies. The firm was surprised when the FBI caught up with the nephew and uncovered a multi million-dollar securities-fraud scheme.[37] A butchers' union head with syndicate backing used a campaign of arson to try to force A&P stores to sell a mediocre deter-gent.[38] A distinguished nationwide firm buys a major food product from gangster-controlled facilities.[39] Syndicate figures control at least twenty firms in New York's garment center.[40]

The major ethical responsibility of business against organized crime is one of good citizenship, to back honest legislators and judges and prosecutors until organized crime can be suppressed in the area. When a union has become a center of nonethical activity, an employer is hardly to be blamed for working to keep his business from being organized by one of these. Some businesses should be critized for entering into agreements with crime-controlled unions, thus subjecting their employees to gangster rule.

Strikes

American labor has been damaged by an unusual number of strikes. From 1956 to 1965, American workers lost 477 days in industrial disputes per thousand workers in nonagricultural work, compared to 289 days in Belgium, 334 in Canada, 226 in Denmark, 191 in France, 174 in Great Britain, 32 in West Germany, 26 in the Netherlands, 6.6 in Sweden, and 3.9 in Switzerland. Only Italy with 901 days was higher in the reporting group.[41] Between 1961 and 1971 inclusive, there were 40,055 work stoppages in the United States, costing 306.7 million man-days, lost income of $6.7 billion, and lost income tax of $1.2 billion.[42] In the early 1970s, the rate of strikes continued to be high.[43]

The purpose of strikes is to secure higher wages, certain fringe benefits, better working conditions, and power for the union. Although economists differ on their effectiveness, it is clear that the results have sometimes been significant.[44] During inflationary times, the effort of the union is usually to secure wage increases beyond the inflationary guidelines set by the government. The union often succeeds, at least partly because the government administration is often politically allied to the union.

Strikes often produce a substantial amount of violence.[45] Usually the first objective is to keep nonstriking workers from going to work, an effort that is illegal everywhere but is often not stopped by local law-enforcement authorities who have political ties to unions. Nonstrikers may have their cars upset or have rocks thrown through their car windows, or be physically damaged, usually without penalty to the union lawbreaker. Companies may legally discharge strikers who violate the law in this way, but often agree not to do so. Unions will almost invariably oppose efforts to discipline employees involved in strike violence; but union discipline may be applied to employees who refuse to participate in strike efforts. In unions with criminal connections, strikes may result in shootings and physical beatings, aimed at nonstrikers. Thus the effort to establish unions as an ethical check on employers has become a source of nonethical activity.

Union efforts to stop wildcat strikes vary, but some unions do their best to end such strikes. The Electrical Workers' Union is reported to endorse them. There are scores of ways in which illegal work stoppages can be started. Sometimes political factions within unions lead to such strikes.

The amount of strike violence in the United States is clearly not inevitable. Switzerland, a highly industrialized country, has almost no strikes. Efforts have been made in America to establish systems of arbitration and detailed grievance procedures, or contracts including no-strike pledges, but strikes go on. The U.S. Steel Company has had an agreement for arbitration for several years, but has doubts if it should be continued. Strikes must be viewed as an unproductive weakness of American business. Attitudes of both employers and unions toward any strike or strike possibility may vary so greatly that it is almost impossible to find a general ethical standard. It can, however, be suggested that the introduction of illegal force by either side is unethical; whether it be the armed strike-breaking of the early twentieth century or the physical attacks on cars or people by strikers or strike pickets today. If local government did a better job of maintaining law and order, the strike process would be more nearly ethical.

An interesting ethical question is whether the government should pay a substantial part of strikers' pay, as it does under the unemployment-compensation laws of some states. This policy, coupled with supplementary unemployment benefits, shifts most of the financial burden from strikers to the union or its members, and may mean that the only real limit on wage increases becomes the solvency of the company; inflation becomes an unethical final result. On the other hand, pitting a union with small strike funds and no unemployment compensation for workers against a powerful corporation may also be inequitable.

Some new intermediate principle needs to be discovered and propounded. An English student of American strikes concludes that conflict has been institutionalized, and that both labor and management view each long strike as a battle for bargaining structure and for job control. Workers in America are not campaigning for socialism. Governmental agencies do not try hard to stop most strikes.[46]

Whatever the reason, it is clear that both unions and management should sit down together and find a less disruptive means of settling their problems. Continued fights, even though sure to end, are rarely the ethical means of settling a contest. There are ethical arguments for employers to oppose the potential corruptness of unions; equally there are ethical arguments for workers to oppose arbitrary job supervision. Both of these ethical reasons, however, could be resolved into an ethical code.

Responsibility for Health and Safety of Employees

It is difficult to avoid the conclusion from the principle of *sic utere tuo* that every business has an ethical obligation to be concerned that the life and health of employees is not affected adversely by any work done to create or sell the business's product. There is of course a partial exception for especially hazardous occupations like those of test pilots or deep-sea divers, whose hazardous work is additionally reimbursed and who receive special insurance. Military service is another exception, in which the U.S. government tries to recognize hazards with insurance and combat pay. Test pilots, linemen, cowboys, firefighters, and police all know there is some danger in their callings, which should normally be recognized by higher rates of pay, and greater insurance coverage.

Perhaps a large majority of American businessmen are deeply concerned with the health and safety of their employees. In well-conducted businesses, the problems are more technical than ethical. What are the best ways of avoiding accidents or explosions in a coal mine? How can an electrical lineman be safeguarded from falling or from contact with live wires? Such technical problems are ones this book will not attempt to discuss. But there is a real ethical problem if a corporation fights against a particular safety law or regulation, claiming that enforcement of this regulation would be so expensive that it would put the firm out of business. One study recounts generations of resistance against mining-safety regulations by the mining industry. Methane gas in a concentration of 5 percent or more will ignite or explode, so the legal limit in a mine was 1 percent. Coal dust in the air lowers the limits of explosion. For decades scores of men were killed each year because of mine owners' unwillingness to install equipment adequate to control methane gas and coal dust. Eight hundred and fifty miners were killed in mine accidents between 1941 and 1952, almost half the accidents because of obsolete machinery. State mining laws were feebly enforced. Federal laws were not effective until a Nixon-administration bill of 1969 became law. The United Mine Workers moved slowly on legislation, perhaps because it wanted to keep royalties flowing into a retirement fund that it administered.[47]

The real ethical question is that of the mining industry's constant (until 1969) resistance to passage of adequate safety laws by Congress or state legislatures. The main argument against better regulation was that the industry could not afford the substantial cost required by safety machinery and devices. Background data on unemployed miners and on many unprofitable mines were used to bolster the cost argument before many legislative committees. It was argued that the high costs that shut down mines deprived miners of jobs and users of coal for heating homes and operating businesses. One can imagine circumstances in which this argument is valid and the loss of human life is justifiable. However, the argument was not universally valid in the industry, and industry leaders were ethically indictable for their decades of resistance to adequate safety regulations.

Another episode may help outline the ethical problems in company reaction to worker environment. This is given in some detail, not as a horrible example but because it tells us how corporate resistance has continued. The chemical firm Rohm and Haas explored and remedied the hazards of production of bischloromethyl ether (BCME) and chloromethyl (CME), but not until cancer created by the chemical had killed scores of workers, mostly in the Bridesburg plant (near Philadelphia). Dow Chemical Company in 1951 published the results of tests that indicated dangers from work with CME by persons who have sensitivities, asthma, or lung disorders. Rohm and Haas was aware of this statement, but found no hint of carcinogenicity in its plant. In 1962, the company became aware of a lung-cancer problem in Building 6, where CME was produced; but it took six years to shift the process to the much safer closed-kettle operation, in which the chemical was kept inside of containers and tubs. A list of 102 chemicals including BCME was sent to Sloan-Kettering Institute for Cancer Research to check on their carcinogenic potential, but Sloan-Kettering, primarily a cancer-therapy institution, did not find any. Although workers continued to die, the cause remained unknown to company management. By 1975, at least 27 workers had died of respiratory cancer from exposure to the chemicals.[48]

In 1964, Rohm and Haas refused to contract a study by a New York University (NYU) group, because the group demanded the right to publish results. In 1967, a more cooperative lab still found cancer in mice caused by BCME. Subsequent studies by Dr. Norton Nelson of NYU did find that BCME was highly carcinogenic to mice, a fact reported to Rohm and Haas in 1971. BCME production was then shut down until new procedures could be established.

At an industry meeting called by the government in July 1971, there was considerable argument against the NYU conclusions; Rohm and Haas was more open-minded than some other chemical companies. Under an OSHA act of 1970 companies were required to report deaths of workers. Rohm and Haas failed to do so at first. Later the company refused to give exposure data to scientists who were publishing on the problem. Dr. Ellington H. Beavers of the Rohm and Haas staff, still maintaining that there was no evidence that bis-CME was a human carcinogen, was put on an OSHA advisory committee, using the opportunity to oppose successfully a "zero-exposure" standard for BCME. In October 1972, Rohm and Haas made an argument to the National Institute of Occupational Safety and Health against stringent government controls of BCME although the company knew that a study of another plant in Redwood City, California, had produced clear evidence of high cancer risk among men who worked with BCME. In 1973 similar results were reported from a West German plant and from a Japanese plant. Yet Dr. Beavers continued to maintain in OSHA committee meetings that BCME was only an animal carcinogen, not a human one. OSHA inspection of the Bridesburg plant yielded no information; in January 1974 OSHA issued rules that failed to set standards for carcinogen exposure. It required the closed-kettle system, and a regulated area, which Rohm and Haas already had. Lack of adequate inspecting force was part of OSHA's explanation for its failure to delve into the deaths at Rohm and Haas.

The company's policy over the years is difficult to appraise. At the time when production of BCME began, almost no one was aware of its carcinogenic properties. Rohm and Haas did not press for information. It turned to a less-well-equipped research laboratory for information; it withheld data from the government and the press. Its representatives tended to talk down the danger both to press representatives and to OSHA's Standards Advisory Committee on carcinogens. Curiously, while Rohm and Haas disregarded the carcinogenic situation of its workers, the Haas (later William Penn) Foundation was distributing small funds for cancer research and large funds to hospitals.[49]

What ethical judgment does one pass on the long-delayed remedial action and the resistance to information by Fritz Otto Haas and other executives of the company? No one accuses them of wanting the death of the workmen. The real charge against them is that they took important and well-paid responsibilities in Rohm and Haas without vigorously recognizing their own responsibility to keep their business from harming others. The general lack of information about the effect of new chemicals was an excuse; the failure of local authorities and of OSHA to investigate adequately was a second; the inability of the chief executive officer to assume all the responsibility for every company action was a third. At an industry gathering in 1971, representatives of various companies seemed to join Rohm and Haas in an almost belligerent resistance to the human implications of the very strong evidence that BCME was consistently fatal to mice.[50]

It is this resistance of some industrialists to unpleasant information from outside that seems to call for a broader ethical outlook. Despite their excellent educations, these executives did not seem to feel a responsibility to take aggressive steps for the health and safety of their workers. Perhaps the loss of individual responsibility in a large corporation had dulled their senses of ethical responsibility; perhaps they had not had that sense in the first place; perhaps what ethical education they had received was all on the negative injunction side, and they did not recognize the harm that could be done by failure to initiate action for better treatment of fellow humans.

Conclusions

Relations of business firms with employees are diverse, constantly changing, and hardly follow a single ethical rule, unless perhaps it is that every employer needs to be constantly attentive to the ethics of his relationship to his employees.

Labor-management relations in America have often had a violent aspect that has done no good to anyone. Each side is convinced that the other side is at fault; a situation that leaves only one ethical response—that is, to find another way to handle the disputes. The efforts of politicians to find compromises have been weakened by the efforts of both labor and management to secure maximum political support.

The problem of wage and salary determination has found no ethic and has been one of the most "squeaky wheels" in the economic mechanism. Elliot Jaques's effort to find an equity of compensation may be the closest to an ethical answer. Complaints of employees against company policies that are illegal or dangerous to public health and safety need to be treated fairly and effectively within the business organization as well as outside of it. The trend toward governmental protection of "whistle blowing" seems tendentious and clumsy, but may be unavoidable. The rights of employees to be free citizens, however, deserve special company safeguards.

Ethics of business relations with unions are very complex. There are ethical reasons for wishing to avoid labor organization of plants by some unions—unions include more than their share of corrupt or criminal leaders. But if a firm has unions, it should treat them fairly; if it does not have unions, it should provide appropriate worker representation. Businesses should act more firmly than they have to resist trade with organized crime, which some unions force on them. Unions have a role in politics as do employers. Management and unions should try to be fair and friendly with each other. Strikes and the violence connected with them do the country no good; efforts should be made to substitute a peaceful negotiation process. Business has too often been too slow in thinking and planning ahead for the health and safety of its employees. The ethical requirement for full concern is indisputable. The problem of the ethics of supervision will be discussed in chapter 5.

Notes

1. Alan Gardiner, *Egypt of the Pharaohs*, pp. 115, 244.
2. Everett M. Kassalow, *Trade Unions and Industrial Relations*, p. 157.
3. Jane Addams, *Twenty Years at Hull House*, chap. 10.
4. Roger H. Wiebe, *Businessmen and Reform*, p. 165.
5. Wayne A.E. Leys, *Ethics for Policy Decisions*, p. 282.
6. Robert E. Cole, *Work, Mobility and Participation*, p. 4.
7. Ibid., pp. 106-111.
8. Robert Ackerman and Raymond Bauer, *Corporate Social Responsiveness*, p. 25.
9. William Ouchi, *Theory Z*, p. 48.
10. Robert Heilbroner, et al., *In the Name of Profit*, pp. 3-31.
11. Alan F. Westin, *Whistle Blowing*, pp. 17-106.
12. Edward Weisband and Thomas M. Frank, *Resignation in Protest*, p. 163.
13. David Ewing, "Constitutionalizing the Corporation," in Thornton Bradshaw and David Vogel, *Corporations and Their Critics*, pp. 253-268.

14. Adolf A. Berle, *The 20th Century Capitalist Revolution*, pp. 61-115.

15. David Finn, *The Corporate Oligarch*, p. 204.

16. David Ewing, *Freedom inside the Organization*, pp. 144-151.

17. Richard Austin Smith, *Corporations in Crisis*, pp. 41-66.

18. Donald J. Newman, "Public Attitudes toward a Form of White Collar Crime," p. 228-232.

19. Gerald D. Robin, "The Corporate and Judicial Disposition of Employee Thieves," in Erwin O. Smigel and H. Lawrence Ross, *Crimes against Bureaucracy*, pp. 119-142.

20. Burton H. Hall, ed., *Autocracy and Insurgency in Organized Labor*, p. 257.

21. Ibid., pp. 267-283.

22. John Hutchinson, *The Imperfect Union*, p. 90.

23. Hall, *Autocracy and Insurgency*, pp. 292-293.

24. Hutchinson, *The Imperfect Union*, chap. 8.

25. Seymour Martin Lipset, *The First New Nation*, p. 230.

26. Milton Derber et al., *Plant Union-Management Relations: From Practice to Theory*, pp. 101-103. Also Sidney Peck, *The Rank and File Leader*, p. 144.

27. J. Patrick Wright, *On a Clear Day*, p. 206.

28. Benjamin Selekman, "Cynicism and Managerial Morality," pp. 55-65. See also Benjamin and Sylvia Selekman, *Power and Morality in a Business Society*.

29. Richard C. Smyth and M.J. Murphy, *Bargaining with Organized Labor*, pp. 132-159.

30. Melville Dalton, *Men Who Manage*, chap. 5.

31. Ibid., p. 111.

32. Paul Sultan, *The Disenchanted Unionist*, pp. 242-245.

33. Jonathan Kwitny, *Vicious Circles*.

34. *Wall Street Journal*, June 9, 1978.

35. Kwitny, *Vicious Circles*, pp. 357-358.

36. Ibid., p. 178.

37. Ibid., p. 212.

38. Ibid., p. 275.

39. Ibid., p. 104.

40. Ibid., p. 23.

41. Kassalow, *Trade Unions*, p. 157.

42. Walter E. Baer, *Strikes*, p. 7.

43. P.K. Edwards, *Strikes in the United States*, pp. 12-17.

44. Baer, *Strikes*, pp. 17-19.

45. Ibid., chaps. 6-8.

46. Edwards, *Strikes in the United States*, chap. 8.

47. Ben A. Franklin, "Death and Injury in the Mines," reprinted in Harry M. Trebing, *The Corporation in the American Economy*, pp. 146-163.

48. Willard S. Randall and Stephan D. Solomon, *Building 6*.

49. Ibid., p. 116.

50. Ibid., pp. 132-176.

5 Does Supervision Require Subordination?

Slow Evolution of Western Ethics

In the Western tradition, ethics usually include regard for other people, for their rights, for their needs, and for their feelings. "Love thy neighbor as thyself" should certainly apply to employees in a common enterprise. In ancient history, the Jewish effort to aid poor Jews by giving them a chance to start work in their own trade may have been a beginning of the Western tradition of valuing the individual. Even slaves in Greece and Rome ran businesses for their masters with some benefits for themselves and with some legal protection. Medieval guild systems had a clear-cut role for apprentices and for journeymen, although the masters ran the operations. Maimonides recognized the ethical importance of the psychology of such relationships when he expressly recommended that employment or other favors to a fellow Jew should be given with kindness, consideration, and regard for the individual worth of the recipient.

These very general aspirations have been negated at many times in Western history. Reference has been made to the common law's repressive acts against workmen and their associations. Continued Negro slavery was America's worst mistake. In Sweden farmers were allowed to administer corporal punishment to their workers as late as 1920. In early nineteenth-century America, courts permitted employers to cheat farm workers out of their annual salaries. However, in the last half of the century, American laws became more favorable to workmen, although some corporate actions almost brutally disregarded the interests of laborers.

As a result of a shortage of labor, of laws, of union pressures, and of humanitarian drives like those of the Social Gospel movement, American attitudes toward workers have become much friendlier in the twentieth century. However, the growth of large administrative organizations operating under strict hierarchical supervision has brought about a series of new problems. In 1919, Woodrow Wilson told Congress that the labor problem would be solved only by a genuine democratization of industry that would enable all workers to participate in some organic way in every decision that affected their welfare, or the part they were to play in industry.[1] The Western aspiration or ethic of recognizing individual values was asserting itself more strongly. It is, however, still true that American industrial output is costlier, mistakes more frequent, and strike rates higher than in Japan, where supervisory techniques are more cooperative.

Mechanisms for Better Supervision

Administrative organizational pressure may lead some executives to commit acts almost directly opposing the Judaic-Christian-Western philosophic tradition. If a high-ranking executive decides that his staff should work half the night or all of the weekend in order to get a job done, he makes that decision. In most civilian organizations, overtime pay must be granted; but in the military forces there is no such pay and the executive decision for overtime work is generally approved as an example of hard-driving effectiveness. Few employees would oppose the extra work for fear of discharge or transfer or disciplinary action. Yet it could be quite unethical to hold a staff at great personal cost for speedy action which is not urgently needed.

A number of counter-hierarchical devices have been developed as means of preventing unnecessary authoritarianism at the middle-management level. Appeals against unfair disciplinary action or removals are frequently established in the personnel machinery of many governmental and business administrations. Some major firms allow an "open door" to the chief executive officer or personnel officer for employees who believe they have been unjustly treated. Layoffs are eased by unemployment compensation, largely but not entirely as a result of laws. Many firms who close plants or departments try to find other jobs for their workers. All of these devices are in part results of a greater ethical regard for the value of the individual. Most of them work with only partial success; a supervisor who wants to goad a subordinate can usually find means to do so.

There are also a number of mechanisms for moving ideas upward in the administrative hierarchy which also may be used to prevent the nonethical use of hierarchical power. More than one "little Caesar" who exerts despotic control over a field office has been upset because visiting staff men from a higher headquarters have, sometimes inadvertently, secured information about his arrogant actions. Procedures for complaints to a personnel office or for termination interviews may serve the same purpose. The Army uses an inspector general who, among other duties, posts himself at an appointed time and place in or near enlisted men's barracks to hear complaints of enlisted men without interference from their commanding officers. It is clear that all of the above mechanisms are useful only if a higher official investigates the complaints and takes action designed to secure a more ethical relationship. Often ethical relationships may be restored only after transfer or discharge of the overbearing superior.

Other administrative devices have been tried to secure a sense of employee participation in work. In several European countries, most notably in Germany, there are union representatives on the boards of directors of companies. In America, the president of the United Auto Workers is a member of the Chrysler Corporation's board of directors. This experiment in "codetermination" to date does not indicate that it has solved the problems of supervision. Union representatives on boards of directors are far removed from workers on the assembly line; there are few signs that union democracy carries its message that far. Codetermination is succeeding politically in western Europe and may do so elsewhere, but how much does it do for the worker when it operates counter to the consumer's interest.[2] Campbell Balfour thinks that American unions still want management to manage.[3]

Another proposal to secure workers' interests in the job is profit sharing, a device that has been fairly widely used in American industry. Although in many cases it may work out well, profit sharing does not solve the problems of supervision. In years where the business does not do well, some employees will be unhappy.

Psychological-Ethical Techniques of Supervision

It is surprising how many ongoing industrial conflicts and wildcat strikes are related to methods of supervision. Some discipline has to be preserved in a workplace where things of value are made or used. But a few other lines of action would be helpful. If supervisors were more uniformly courteous, (and courtesy is simply a form of ethical respect for other human beings), disputes would arise less often. Spurred on by Japan's industrial success, some American firms are establishing an ethic that workers are entitled to be informed of the purpose of what they are doing and how it fits into the company plan, and are asked to plan how to do it.

An excellent book on *Grievance Handling* by Walter E. Baer gives 101 guides for supervisors. Many of the points are legal and technical. But at least a dozen deal with matters which a supervisor of good ethical character should decide on the basis of some ethical education. These guidelines suggest that the company must be consistent in its policies, it must give the union a fair opportunity for presenting its case, and the company must prove its point in discipline and discharge cases. It should treat union representatives and employees as people, it should help its employees understand economic realities, and it should encourage their loyalty to the corporation. The qualities of leadership Baer prescribes are: "Be faithful to principle," "Inspire others," "Criticize constructively," "Admit your own mistakes," "Reprove tactfully," and "Cultivate moral fiber."[4] Baer supports some of his points with decisions made by arbitrators. But it is interesting to note that a substantial number are ethical decisions.

One problem needs special attention. Many workers seem apathetic. Union stewards find it hard to respect such people, so supervisors perhaps should not be blamed for not doing so.[5] Yet our entire American system of thought requires respect for the individual, whether worker, steward, or supervisor. Perhaps that respect requires educating the employee out of apathy.

Supervisors encounter many problem cases that are not dependent on money, or at least not on money alone. Frequently, there is a clash between an individual's interests and the particular job to which he/she is assigned. If a would-be salesman is appraised by something like Paul and Sarah Edwards's PSE Preference Survey, he may find that he ranks low in "affiliating" and high in "controlling," and a shift to accounting or a related occupation should be suggested if possible. A woman who ranks high in "conserving" doesn't belong in a "challenging" job. Someone with high research capacity does not belong in sales. Making these observations is only the beginning; the difficulty is to find the more appropriate job and to transfer the employee.

Supervisors are increasingly becoming aware that certain employees may perform poorly in times of stress. There are many questionable mental-stress claims that appear in court, but there is evidence that job stress may produce a variety of job ailments.[6] The Edwardses list heart trouble, spastic colon, ulcers, diverticulitis, and many other diseases as job-related.[7]

A new variety of difficulty in supervision is presented by harassment and related charges. Sexual harassment is now frequently charged, often with good cause; yet it could be easily exaggerated. Methods of supervision such as asking questions about an employee's family or chronic teasing have been grounds for successful court actions. There is considerable feeling against employer use of lie detectors, but employers who face many millions of dollars of losses from embezzlement or employee theft are using lie detectors more often.[8]

Ethics are not going to form easily in these confusing fields. Will employees shift jobs because of psychological-test results? Can harassment charges stand up against the long-standing custom of mildly flirtatious greetings between men and women? Can or should supervisors understand all the motivations of each man or woman on their staffs? It will take time to produce new ethics in these areas.

Participation in Work Planning

An important part of worker participation in management is a developing ethic that workers should have something to do with planning their own work. Farm laborers, artisans, machinists, teachers, salesmen, and many other vocational groups have long been allowed this freedom. Should not workers in factories or elsewhere have the same privilege? Is it not part of a man's individual right to determine the way in which he moves his body in a long work day? Should not he and his colleagues be given an opportunity to organize the details of the work they are doing, provided cost and quality of the product are not unduly affected?

Sydney Harman wonders if the adversary relationship of management and workers would not largely disappear if workers had more to say about how their own jobs are to be done. It would take years in some cases to build up mutual trust, but there is evidence to indicate it can be done. Stephen H. Fuller, a General Motors vice president, reports from a study of four GM plants:

> What we learned is that there is a close relationship between an organiza-tion's performance and how employees feel about the organization—how they feel about the work climate, the quality of management, and employee-management relationships. The project showed us that we could improve performance and human satisfaction by creating conditions in which peo-ple can become more involved, work together, and experience personal growth. . . .[9]

Quality of Working Life

For many decades it has been recognized that employers have some respon-sibility for the quality of working life. It is true that if companies are to sur-vive economically, factories and workshops must sometimes be utilitarian and somewhat drab, but it seems to be increasingly agreed that employers have a responsibility to make work surroundings as cheery as possible. This probably is an ethical responsibility. If we should love our neighbors as ourselves, as both the Old and New Testaments tell us, and if neighbors in-clude employees, a not-unreasonable assumption, employers need to fur-nish attractive working conditions. However, a qualification on the ethical principle is that of how much it costs.

Partly voluntarily, partly though pressure from the government, some corporations have succeeded in sharply reducing plant noise. This ac-complishment can improve the work environment of many workers; a clear ethical accomplishment.[10] The Occupational, Safety, and Health Ad-ministration (OSHA) has issued regulations lowering the decibel level of noises to which workers are subjected all day from 90 decibels to 84, and perhaps to 80 decibels. To secure results like these, General Motors has covered ceilings and walls of plants with sound-absorbing materials. Cur-tains of noise-absorbing fiberglass surround particularly noisy departments. Elsewhere, other methods are used. Again, the ethical responsibility is somewhat limited by the extra cost.

There are other changes that General Motors and other leading com-panies are making to improve the quality of working life (QWL). In those plants that are unionized (a minority of American workers—perhaps 20 percent—belong to unions), the companies are increasingly working with the unions on QWL. It is a matter of survival for both, and unions should be consulted on changes in QWL.[11] Similar efforts to improve QWL are being conducted in nonunion companies like IBM, Xerox, and Hewlett-Packard. An interesting feature of QWL efforts is the creation of larger work modules, so that the monotony of assembly-line work is reduced. Instead of spending all day screwing in a bolt on a part of the car chassis, the worker becomes part of a unit which assembles a section of a car with methods the unit has joined in creating.

As the recognition of worker interest in the job increases, it becomes reasonable to give the workers more education in what their jobs are about. Japanese recognition of the importance of worker education is far ahead of American viewpoints on that matter. A minority of American managers, however, are recognizing the importance of worker participation in determining job procedures.

How much beyond group participation in work procedures can worker choice go? There are reports of cases in which worker participation in selection of supervisors has helped to increase worker productivity.[12] University faculties usually participate in choice of department heads and deans, with fair success. One study, however, cautions that while it might increase productivity if workers selected their own fellow workers and participated in selection of their supervisors, it could cause great confusion for the personnel department if workers selected coworkers from outside the organization. The enforcement of federal affirmative-action policies by fellow workers could become very difficult.

Michael Maccoby discusses some further expansion of worker participation. In one union-management project, there was a feeling on the part of the workers that the work should be redesigned so that all could share in the clerical work. "They don't believe it is right to have some people do clerical work while other people do higher level work."[13] This theory of equity in work is unlikely to be accepted. If a hard-driving executive in business or government must take time to do his share of the typing, the affairs of the firm are going to be badly handled, and a less "equitable" system will have to be installed—such an ethic of equitable work is unworkable.

Japanese Management Methods

In recent years Americans have become aware of sharp industrial competition from other nations. The success of the Japanese in manufacturing products that were long known as American specialties more cheaply and with higher quality has been especially noticeable. One reason for this success is that although Americans have long thought of themselves as the leaders in democratic business methods, the Japanese are leading in the participative management methods that are an industrial counterpart of political democracy. Some of the lower costs of Japanese products are a result of lower wage levels. It is possible that centuries of feudal leadership have made Japanese workmen more acquiescent; if so, a few more decades of industrial life may make them more disputatious. However, a careful review of various studies does not show that Japanese now like to work more than do Americans.[14] It is possible that the Japanese have discovered a method of worker-management relationship that is more truly ethical and hence likely to continue to give them a competitive edge.

It is clearly not possible to reproduce all Japanese methods of business management in the United States. The following distinctive features of Japanese management are found in large concerns employing perhaps 40 percent of Japanese workers.

"Lifetime employment," followed by large companies and government bureaus, covers perhaps a half of the work force. Young people are hired upon graduation from school or college with expectations of staying with the company until age fifty-five unless they commit a major criminal offense. After age fifty-five all except a few top managers retire, receiving five or six years' salary but no pension. Retired persons may be sent to a small satellite company where they may secure part-time employment for a decade. "Lifetime employment" has interested American observers, but has not been seriously promoted as an addition to the American work ethic except that some high-technology firms mention its desirability.[15]

Japanese workers are paid bonuses, typically twice a year, each bonus adding up to five or six months' work. This method of pay gives workers an incentive to feel a part of the firm. Workers tend to save a large part of an unexpectedly large bonus; Japanese policy encourages savings. Each firm has a large number of temporary employees, typically women. Their working hours are very flexible to accommodate those who have children to care for, but they are immediately laid off in slack periods. Satellite firms will sharply contract or go out of business in slack times; the major firms contract out to them only those services most likely to fluctuate.

A Japanese employee's service is evaluated very differently from an American's. For ten years he receives exactly the same pay increases as those of the other young men who entered company service with him. This procedure is very slow for aspiring young men but it presumably promotes an attitude of cooperation with other employees, and enables a careful long-term evaluation.[16]

Workers function within a number of small groups. These groups have a tremendous impression upon their psychological outlook. Typically, young employees will work in a variety of different jobs, resulting in a nonspecialized capability when, after ten years, the worker gains his first major promotion. The result of this broad training is a high degree of coordination within the organization. Matsushita rotates 5 percent of employees (managers and workers) from one division to another each year.[17] The Japanese firm does not like to specify immediate objectives, but prefers to inculcate a philosophy of values in its employees so the employees can set their own objectives. The values are chiefly of relationships with other employees and of policies of the firm.[18] Decision making is likely to be of a cooperative nature in Japanese business. As many as sixty or eighty people may be consulted on a particular decision, and a real effort is made to arrive at a consensus. This results in slow decision making; but the Japanese claim that they implement the decision more quickly because the employees all understand it. The decision has been based on their sense of common values, which in Matsushita's case includes national service, fairness, cooperation, courtesy and humility, adjustment, and gratitude. The Japanese also have an indirect method of conversation that softens the harshness of administrative intercourse. Senior-junior relationships tend to become partnerships.[19]

American businesses have begun to pay attention to Japanese methods of supervision. The automobile industry is experimenting widely with such methods. According to a recent *Business Week* article, three major steel companies have started participative management teams.[20] There is some union opposition; teams are established only where there is union agreement.

Can the United States make a major shift to a participative management ethic? In other words, can America establish an ethic by which workers in a company are polite and friendly to one another and anxious that each worker has something to say about the process of his work, and are working in cooperation with the company for a better product? Such an ethic seems to fit with the Judaic-Christian tradition of respecting each individual's judgments about himself and his work; it seems also to fit with our democratic heritage. If it could be established, much of the bitterness of American industry might be mollified.

But there are powerful arguments against such an ethic. Some union leaders do not want it for fear that their own reason for existence would disappear. Employers in industries in which unions have been dishonest or belligerent will have grave doubts about extending the authority of individual workers, even if it is only to discuss and determine their own immediate jobs. Much of our industrial engineering and supervision has had a long basis of authoritariansim. There is doubt if brilliant young executives would stay with an employing firm that tried to establish the slow promotion processes of Japanese firms.

Americans have long been used to calling each other bad names. Our politicians fire verbal brickbats at one another as a means of attracting attention to themselves. Our sports enthusiasts are often savage in their verbal criticism of opposing teams. Our farewell occasions for departing employees tend to become "roasts." Will this attitude of controversy change to an ethic of cooperation because of the pressures of Japanese and western-European competition? A thorough answer to these questions requires an ability to foresee major philosophical and sociological trends. Perhaps the Western version of individualism will handicap the development of cooperative administrative relations. Union rules and judicial consideration of cases of unfair supervision may be so thoroughly engrained in the American work ethic that they cannot be extracted.

Peter Drucker, one of America's most perceptive writers on management, has suggested that the fundamental concepts of Confucian ethics might help America develop an ethic of supervision. It is true that Confucian ethics outline personal responsibilities for the superior as well as for the subordinate in the supervisory relationship, an important part of what American industry needs to strive for.[21] Drucker's idea deserves investigation.

American Industrial-Psychological Theories
of Supervision

Curiously, while Japan has been employing more ethical means of supervision, several American industrial psychologists have been trying to persuade industry to move in similar directions. Douglas McGregor's Theory Y is based on the assumption that it is natural for people to work; that they will exercise self-control and self-direction if they are committed to their objectives and will be rewarded by satisfaction of ego and self-actualization needs; that the average human learns to seek responsibility; and that the capacities for imagination, ingenuity, and creativity are widely distributed in the population.[22]

Like most social scientists, McGregor does not specifically mention ethics, but an observed code of ethics is implied in his advice to management as to how employees should be treated in a Theory-Y organization. The organization is likely to suffer if it promotes or transfers individuals without regard for personal needs and goals. And it seems that ethics, except perhaps in military organizations, requires consulting with employees about change of jobs.

McGregor gives an example of a supervisor who corrected his subordinate's work through careful and polite efforts to arrive at a joint agreement on the nature of the man's job. McGregor criticizes formal appraisals of an employee's record, on the ground that such appraisals may cause trouble, do not secure integrated thought about the subordinate's task, and can easily though unintentionally be rude. In the administration of promotions and placement, the individual's interest needs to be considered. McGregor discusses with enthusiastic support the "Scanlon plan" which includes an effort to see that every member of an organization contributes his brains and ingenuity as well as effectiveness to improving the effectiveness of the organization. Discussing the managerial climate necessary for better supervisorial relations, McGregor first lists "Confidence in a Fair Break." This is to be secured through ethical actions, such as management's admitting errors and rectifying them. James G. March and Herbert A. Simon in a cautious review of research come to similar conclusions:

> We have already argued that an individual is more likely to identify with an organization in which he has considerable interaction than one in which interaction is limited, that he is more likely to identify with an organization that he perceives as accepting him than one he perceives as rejecting him, that he is more likely to identify with an organization that permits him to satisfy personal goals than with one that frustrates the satisfaction of personal goals. Now we are arguing that an individual is more likely to identify with an organization that he perceives as high in prestige than one he perceives as low.[23]

Rensis Likert says leaderships consists of:

1. *Support*—behavior that serves the function of increasing or maintaining the individual member's sense of personal worth and importance in the context of group activity.
2. *Interaction facilitation*—behavior that serves the function of creating or maintaining a network of interpersonal interrelationships among group members.
3. *Goal emphasis*—behavior that serves the function of creating, changing, clarifying, or gaining member acceptance of group goals.
4. *Work facilitation*—behavior that serves to provide effective work methods, facilities, and technology for the accomplishment of group goals.[24]

Likert also notes how top corporate officers fail to give information to subordinates, surely unethical treatment of people who are supposed to tell their superior about anything important to the company. Neither Likert nor McGregor nor March and Simon mention ethics or its subsidiary, politeness. Baer, the management man, interestingly does emphasize politeness. Yet all five advocate a form of supervision that is largely one of simple ethical conduct toward fellow employees and especially toward subordinates. Education of all employees in ethics, largely an education in decent regard for fellow human beings, would be a big step toward participative management. The Western ethical tradition prescribes that people deserve to be told what they are to do and what is to be done, and asked how they think it should be done. These distinguished industrial psychologists are rephrasing ethical precepts that were developed centuries ago. Perhaps a good course in interpersonal ethics for business supervisors would accomplish much of what these scholars are promoting.

Conclusions

Is the notion that man has a right to be informed and consulted about his work likely to become an ethical principle? The course of American development in the nineteenth and twentieth centuries seems to be a move toward a greater ethical regard for the common man; through better wages, shorter hours, and better working conditions, and recently with some emphasis on teaching each worker more about his work and giving him some control over it. The clumsiness of bureaucratic administrative machinery of the kind described by Michel Crozier in *The Bureaucratic Phenomenon* often increases the pressure toward worker control.[25]

Ethical trends in a matter as complex as this are difficult to discern. The predominance of political power favors greater action by the union; the logic of the work situation, as Leon Trotsky once pointed out, favors participative management. Either answer will be an addition to our economic ethic, but one that will not really become incorporated until it has lived through years or decades of experience.

Participative management will prevail in a number of what Drucker calls "knowledge industries," simply because it is a natural means of functioning there. The unions may prevail through political control, but they will have to raise their ethical standards substantially if their participation is to become meaningful. Congress would hesitate to inflict on the public a regime of brutal exploitation of consumers through criminal union operations like those described by Jonathan Kwitny.[26] It is, however, also true that workers in industries that in the past have treated workers arbitrarily will not change their prounion, antiemployer attitudes for a long time, at least until employers accept the workers as an integral part of the human machinery of their businesses.

Notes

1. Daniel T. Rodgers, *The Work Ethic in Industrial America*, p. 59.
2. Alfred L. Thimm, *The False Promise of Codetermination*, p. 265.

3. Campbell Balfour, ed., *Participation in Industry,* p. 2.

4. Walter E. Baer, *Grievance Handling.*

5. *Sidney Peck, The Rank and File Leaders,* pp. 143 ff.

6. *Wall Street Journal,* September 17, 1980; *Los Angeles Times,* June 18, 1980, part I, p. 24.

7. Edwards, Paul and Sarah, *PSE Preference Survey,* privately printed, Los Angeles, 1981.

8. *Forbes Magazine,* January 15, 1941.

9. W. Michael Hoffman and Thomas J. Wyly, *The Work Ethic in Business,* pp. 69, 215-219.

10. Fred Luthans and Richard M. Hodgetts, eds., *Social Issues in Business,* p. 284.

11. Hoffman-Wyly, *The Work Ethic in Business,* p. 260 ff.

12. Edward E. Lawler, III, "Reward Systems," in J. Richard Hackman and J. Lloyd Suttle, eds., *Improving Life at Work.*

13. *Michael Maccoby, "Discussion," in Hoffman and Wyly, The Work Ethic in Business,* p. 60.

14. Robert E. Cole, *Work, Mobility and Participation,* chap. 8.

15. Ibid.

16. William Ouchi, *Theory Z,* p. 26.

17. Richard Tanner Pascale and Anthony G. Athos, *The Art of Japanese Management,* p. 53.

18. Ibid., pp. 50-53.

19. Ibid., pp. 51, 95-102, 134-139.

20. *Business Week,* June 19, 1981, p. 132.

21. Peter Drucker, "What is Business Ethics," *The Public Interest,* Spring 1981.

22. Douglas McGregor, *The Human Side of Enterprise,* pp. 47-48.

23. James G. March and Herbert A. Simon, *Organizations,* pp. 74-75

24. Rensis Likert, *The Human Organization,* pp. 72-74.

25. Michel Crozier, *The Bureaucratic Phenomenon.*

26. Jonathan Kwitny, *Vicious Circles.*

6 The Social Responsibilities of Business

Ethical Background of Corporate Social Responsibility

Parts of the Western ethical tradition deal with social responsibilities. The Western tradition has not been exact in outlining the social responsibilities of employers to employees or other individuals, but it has not ignored the problem. The Mosaic code expressly ordered Jews to leave the gleanings in wheat fields or vineyards for the poor. Workers were to be paid at the end of every day. There were careful instructions on how not to force collection of debts, and debts were to be forgiven every seven years. In Maimonides' writings, there were instructions on *how* to give so that the psyche of the recipient would not be damaged. Aristotle's Nichomachean ethics gave instruction on appropriate amounts of giving. At times in Egypt giving to the poor was important, as was also the case in Babylon. Charitable giving was clearly recognized in Roman law and in English common law.

Christianity also greatly emphasized the responsibility of charity in some areas. The Judaic-Christian doctrine of "love thy neighbor as thyself" has at times led to a strong conception of charitable giving, especially within organizations. The "Merchant of Prato" near fourteenth-century Florence found that his responsibilities included giving to a variety of people in straitened circumstances.[1] Protestantism was supposed to emphasize salvation by faith rather than by works, but as any twentieth-century American knows, many Protestant denominations have encouraged generosity among their members. The United States, the country that separates church and state, interestingly encourages such generosity in its tax laws—much more than do most other countries. Individuals may be exempt from income taxes for gifts of up to 50 percent of their adjusted gross income. Since 1935 corporations have been able to give up to 5 percent of their annual income. The amount was changed to 10 percent in August 1981.

Along with these obligations to charity, the Judaic-Christian-Anglo-American religious and legal traditions have consistently recognized the employer's social responsibility for running his business in a way that does not damage others. Under Old Testament strictures, if a man knew that his ox gored others, he was responsible for keeping the ox under control. In the Code of Hammurabi and in Roman law the same principle is followed in several cases. English common law developed the principle that a man must not use his own property in a way that damages others (*sic utere tuo ut alienum non laedas*). In the flexible common law judges have ignored or overridden this principle at times but in modern times there has been a strong legislative movement to make it more important.

In the early twentieth century, some associations of businessmen worked for social goals such as better housing, urban beautification, and industrial health-and-welfare programs. The National Association of Manufacturers (NAM) supported a pure-food-and-drugs act.[2] However, in the 1909 to 1914 period the NAM opposed all "reform" legislation except workmen's compensation.[3] It seems that America entered the twentieth century uncertain about the ethics of corporate social responsibility.

The ethical obligation for the health and safety of employees discussed in chapter 4 has in the past not been stated clearly, in part because the working conditions that caused ill health or endangered an employee were not clearly known, nor were remedial measures. However, looking out for the safety of employees and customers can be inferred from the Golden Rule, from the prohibitions against killing people in all ethical codes, and from the special values placed on individual life in the Judaic-Christian tradition, the philosophy of Kant, and elsewhere. Again, the common-law maxim *sic utere tuo ut alienum non laedas* applies.

In modern America there has been a steadily growing demand for corporate social responsibility and a growing tendency for corporations to meet the demand; however, the practices of corporations are diverse. It is clear that the social responsibilities of business can be carried to excess. A Harris poll in 1973 found that the following percentages of Americans expected businesses to: wipe out poverty (83 percent), rebuild cities (85 percent), eliminate racial discrimination (84 percent), control air and water pollution (92 percent), and decrease accidents on highways (72 percent).[4]

This list illustrates some of the problems that arise out of the modern concepts of businesses' ethical responsibilities. Business leaders have no legal authorization to do all of the tasks mentioned; indeed, a voluntary effort on their part to do so might result in antitrust prosecutions, in suits by irate shareholders, in resentment from the poor, or in bankruptcy. But businesses do have legal and ethical responsibilities to control pollution or to prevent racial discrimination, and they share a vague but general ethical responsibility to try to reduce unemployment.

Does a Corporation Have the Charitable Responsibilities of an Individual?

American law is clear that a corporation has the rights and privileges of an individual. A corporation is treated as a person in statutes and court actions.[5]

Obviously, a corporation cannot be imprisoned or executed, but it can be fined, in some federal statutes today up to a million dollars.

It follows that the responsibilities attached to an individual, that is, those of a business (not a family) nature, also attach to a corporation. Milton Friedman has taken the opposite point of view, that the corporation's sole responsibility is to make a profit, operating within its legal boundaries.[6] There is something to be said for Friedman's position. A wealthy corporate director feels more free to give away his own assets than does a corporate board that has a responsibility to its shareholders and to its employees. Corporations frequently are operated on the assumption of continuous performance, taking on pension and other obligations to employees that may extend for decades. Corporations may not have the right to give away earning power. The fact that existing federal and state income taxes usually take over one-half of a corporation's net income seems to imply that the government itself has taken over most of the corporation's social tasks.

On the other hand, there are circumstances in which a corporation *must* assume charitable responsibilities. A corporate executive once told how his corporation supported a drive for building a local hospital. The corporation operated a cement plant in the area, which lacked wealthy donors. Many of its employees were poor. The corporation was among the very few persons or firms in the area who could assume any important charitable responsibility for building a hospital. No public hospital was within reasonable driving distance, nor would one be built in that area. Even Professor Friedman might grant that the cement company had to contribute to the construction of that hospital if it wished to retain the loyalty of its employees, the cooperation of the community, and to satisfy the ethical sense of its executives.

Many similar examples can be raised. If a flood or other catastrophe comes to a financially straitened city, corporations in the area should aid in reconstruction efforts as any other person would. If an organized crime group starts to take over an area, the resident corporations should contribute to a responsible group that is fighting organized crime. Corporate gifts to community funds are necessary in most communities. Even if a corporation has a deficit year, a token gift is often expected. Gifts to major hospitals, to colleges and universities, and to community events are often viewed as almost obligatory.

Most business leaders have not accepted Friedman's point of view for ethical reasons of the sort just cited. Nevertheless, many businessmen believe there must be real limitations on corporate giving. The 5 percent of net corporate income authorized by Congress in 1935 for deduction from net income as donations has not yet been given by any substantial number of corporations, and indeed seems unlikely to be given. Gifts to date are about 1 percent of corporate income. Many businessmen who give generously of their own incomes will be cautious about giving from the profits of a corporation owned by many shareholders. No one has maintained that there is an ethical responsibility to give gifts beyond the reasonable financial and legal capacity of the corporation.

A thoughtful business executive, president T.F. Bradshaw of RCA, comments that Friedman overlooks the fact that businessmen "exist in a real world where people's needs go far beyond their economic needs," and that the rules are changing so "we may yet reach that state in which a businessman is judged by the social goals he accomplishes, as well as the profits he makes." Bradshaw suggests that businessmen should stick to their own competencies, but within those fields they should fight for constructive change.[7] The real problem for many corporations is to choose the social purposes to which they give. There is not much question about giving to social-welfare activities related to the company's employees. There is little question about gifts vital to community social organizations such as those patronized by the community chest. But as the corporation considers educational and other cultural agencies of the community, the problem of choice becomes difficult. Some solve this by giving small amounts to all area colleges and universities, or to all the private ones, since corporate tax payment supports the public institutions. Other corporations give to all local cultural agencies or to one of few the executives value highly. It is difficult to find an ethic emerging in this process; it is more nearly a charitable marketplace in which the corporate attitude seems to be "convince us of your needs and we will give it to you."

Affirmative Action

"Affirmative action" is a new ethic, yet one that is now written into U.S. statutes and is becoming imbedded in company policies. The principle behind affirmative action is that a firm which employs any substantial number of persons has a responsibility to offer employment and opportunity for promotion to qualified persons in proportion to the representation of ethnic groups in the area where possible employees are living. Government also uses a similar policy toward employment by sex.

This principle was not recognized in early legal-ethical traditions. It is derived from a practical problem in America, that minority groups demand economic recognition and that they often have been victims of discriminatory employment policies. Its underlying principle comes from features of the Judaic-Christian tradition that underlies the recognition of individual rights—from the doctrines that each person is the same in the eyes of God, and from natural-rights philosophy and Kantian emphasis on the value of each individual. Affirmative action may also be essential to maintaining social peace and individual opportunity in a country with as many different ethnic groups as in the United States. Although compliance with affirmative-action programs has been expensive and time-consuming for many businesses, industry opposition to affirmative action has been much less than opposition to other regulatory laws, partly because many businesses like a wider market for labor and partly for ethical reasons.

But it is difficult to find complete support for governmental affirmative-action programs in the Western ethical tradition. Philosophers like Thomas Hobbes, John Locke, and Jean Jacques Rousseau were more concerned with the individual's relation to society than with an ethnic group's relationship to employment. Aristotle wrote of commutative and distributive justice. Commutative (or compensatory) justice is a corrective transaction to offset injury.[8] Distributive justice is an equitable distribution of goods and services in society. Both these kinds of justice could be said to be found in affirmative-action programs, but the precedent is not precise.

One precedent for affirmative action was the order of Alexander the Great to his soldiers to marry Persian women. Another was the long-delayed decision of the Norman kings to accept Anglo-Saxons as equal to Normans in England. Another was the British treaty with France that guaranteed that French-Canadians could retain French education and language. All of these recognized that harmonious survival could not be attained in a society which discriminated against one group; but none of these acts corresponded exactly to affirmative action.

Although this principle of affirmative action is firmly set in federal laws and regulations, and apparently is accepted by many corporations, there is still substantial opposition to this new ethic. One philosopher finds it hard to accept the theory that ethnic groups have rights (partly because ethnic groups are hard to define) but can support affirmative action as a step against discrimination.[9] Affirmative action has involved detailed government regulation of the personnel policies of many companies, and, as pointed out in chapter 12, regulation frequently becomes obstructive to the workings of a free-market economy. Employers have had to pay some very large penalties for discrimination. Racial quotas were used in nineteenth-century European countries to keep Jews out of positions for which they were well qualified. Regulations trying to secure ethnic mixtures in public schools have met intense opposition at times.

There are several possible approaches to the problem of racial employment discrimination. Simplest and ostensibly fairest is nondiscrimination; hiring and promoting every person on the basis of qualifications regardless of race or sex. Yet at the present time, this method would almost certainly leave many minority-group members and many women completely out of employment in many firms. They would not know when the jobs were available or how to procure them. They would probably have to be hired by personnel staff of a different ethnic background or sex. The ethical goal of nondiscrimination would probably not be accomplished. A second possibility for affirmative action is to expand the pool of applicants by advertising or other methods, but to hire strictly on the basis of qualification. Adequate minority representation, the ethical goal, would still come more slowly. A third method is to systematically favor women or minority groups in hiring or promotion. This is what happened in *United Steel Workers V. Weber* [443 U.S. 193, 200 (1979)] in which the Supreme Court upheld the right of a company to favor minority employees for promotion. If company officials hold to this policy, discrimination against minorities will lessen, but some qualified people will be discriminated against. Is this an ethical result, or does it run contrary to the ethic of awarding the more important jobs to the best qualified? Fourth, fixed quotas may be used; that is, so many blacks, so many women, and so on, shall be hired. Again, some people will be unjustly treated: those who are better qualified but not members of a quota group will suffer. The last two methods are the most effective but the least fair. It seems improbable that a new ethic will follow either of these directions in individualist America, although they may be of temporary value.

Daniel Seligman raises the question of whether affirmative-action programs should require hiring less-able or less-well-trained minority employees for lower-level jobs as long as their qualifications are equal to those of the lowest-trained person on the job. Some government lawyers view this as necessary only in special cases in which a minority group has been discriminated against sharply in the past. Others view it as generally desirable. There is some evidence that hiring requirements for some positions have been overly high, so that room can indeed be found for less-qualified minority or female employees in lower positions.[10] Of course, if a firm hires less-qualified people for bottom-level jobs, then it may be committing itself to giving these new people a chance for greater opportunity for extra training which would qualify them for eventual promotion.

Should these responsibilities for nondiscriminatory employment be placed on business firms when through taxes businesses already help pay for public-school systems that should give minority members chances to qualify? Businesses have little chance to raise this question. Administrative interpretation of civil-rights acts requires businesses to secure minority-group employees at various ranks. So the ethical responsibility of businesses becomes the legal one of hiring female and minority employees and, second, the ethical one of working to help these employees adjust to the discipline of industrial life.

A number of companies have worked hard on affirmative-action programs. American Oil Company found that it could easily triple the size of a minority purchasing program by integrating affirmative action into normal corporate operations.[11] The placement of blacks on boards of major corporations is a sign that they will be more widely placed in corporate employment. Recent publications have shown that there is still a long way to go to achieve proportional distribution of minorities but progress has been made.[12]

There are important arguments against affirmative action as a business ethic. Thomas Sowell speaks of affirmative action as a "transitional policy."[13] He wonders, reasonably, if a transitional policy can be a constitutional one; if not, can it become an ethic? He believes that ethnic-cultural factors, not discrimination, underly most of the differences in income and education among ethnic groups in the United States. Second-generation West Indians in the United States, although black, have incomes higher than the national average or than the Anglo-Saxon average; discrimination against those blacks would be hard to prove. Sowell also cites evidence that single women who work continuously do financially as well as or better than single men. He believes that the Supreme Court majority in the Weber case affirmed quotas "in the spirit" of the Civil Rights Act of 1964, when the legislative history of the act clearly denied the intent to require preferential quotas.

Such doubts about the legal usefulness and indeed legal justifiability of affirmative-action policies can indeed raise the question of whether these policies will become part of a continued national ethic. It is, however, hoped that an ethic will be established against voluntary discrimination by employers, an ethic that may have been aided by the Civil Rights Act, as a number of newer business ethics have been aided by statutory action.

Psychological Adjustment

In *Men and Women of the Corporation*, Rosabeth Moss Kanter appraises the psychological problems involved in the entrance of women into higher ranks of corporate work.[14] Some of these problems involve fairly clear ethical decisions. The ethics of corporate life, as of any other aspect of life, require treatment of each individual with the respect due him or her as a person and the respect due to his or her office. Women entering executive positions frequently find themselves oppressed by nuances of male executive thought. How would the women react to frequent male profanities? Some men tested this for little reason other than slightly malicious curiosity.

Kanter found frequent evidence that women executives were viewed as too "bossy." She counters that this is because women have been powerless and their powerlessness produces this characteristic. In the corporation she was studying, women were to be only in first-line executive positions, with little chance of moving higher. Hence the powerless-boss syndrome; something like "the corporal complex" in the military. If Kanter is right, the ethical responsibilities of the male executive become clear. The first responsibility is to respect the reason for the bossiness. The woman's immediate superior should advise her to use other less-"bossy" methods. Second and much harder is to try to ensure equality in advancement for capable women.

As American industry hires and promotes more of our "largest minority," women, more than obedience to affirmative action is required of executives and staff colleagues. Women in executive positions are too often made aware that they are token employees by a "male front" that does not include them in discussion groups or talks down to them. A somewhat earlier study of shop stewards showed a deep resentment of working women, except perhaps widows and single women.[15] As women slowly made their way into Milwaukee plants their reception by fellow workers must have been less than cordial. Many unionists blamed women workers for juvenile delinquency, a belief unsupported by most statistical evidence.

James E. Post gives an interesting account of Polaroid Corporation's adjustment to the women's-rights-in-industry movement. Polaroid, which had been quite rapid to recognize the concerns of minority groups, was slow to recognize the ethical problems of treatment of women employees. Post suggests that management gave first priority to minority programs. It is possible that Polaroid management felt the economic problems of minority groups more acutely than those of female employees. Polaroid finally did respond to pressure from women employees and from the Office of Federal Contract Compliance, and wrote an affirmative-action plan for women.[16] American businesses are slowly developing a new and badly needed code of ethics in this field. Many men have been aware that women's capabilities were not adequately employed, but few have realized that they themselves were partly responsible, through discouraging remarks to female staff, through the closed-mindedness of a dominant male group, through careless remarks about imaginary undesirable qualities of women. A new ethic of conversation is needed and is slowly developing.

Hiring of ethnic minorities also presents ethical requirements beyond an affirmative-action policy. Blacks in particular meet suspicion and hostility, less from supervisors and managers than from fellow workers. In four industrial plants studied in Chicago; Lynchburg, Virginia; Buffalo; and Memphis there were sometimes no differences reported as to black and white workers' attitudes. But in Chicago there was a real difference in attitudes of young and disadvantaged black hourly workers. A majority of both blacks and whites got along with and respected their foremen but a larger proportion of blacks, especially in Chicago, did not. Promotion was a difficult problem in all plants; although some blacks had been promoted, between one-third and one-half believed that they did not have fair opportunities for promotion.[17]

It was generally found that foremen believed that blacks work at least as well as other workers on the average, but problems of black absenteeism and tardiness did occur, especially in the North.[18] White workers generally were open toward black fellow workers, but blacks and whites immediately separated in the cafeteria, on breaks, and after work. Theodore V. Purcell and Gerald F. Cavanaugh advocate a vigorous "systems" approach to get more blacks into higher positions. They recommend extra efforts to inform the foremen of cultural differences and reward them for outstanding work in recognizing minority efforts. In the plants they studied they found some executives who worked hard to help put black people into businesses. However, they add a warning that management cannot be expected to shoulder the whole burden of bringing minority groups into American economic life.

What has been described here is an effort to develop more fully the American ethic of equality of opportunity for all. There is little question that blacks have been excluded from many economic opportunities in the past and deserve better breaks. The sharpest ethical problem arises if and when harder-working or better-educated or more-senior employees of the majority group are deprived of economic opportunity because they are not minority-group members. It is still not clear what form the new ethic of equality of opportunity will take. Highly competitive universities or law firms or businesses will probably not award top posts to minority members who do not meet the exacting standards for such positions. Because of the complexity of modern problems, it is increasingly clear that able people are needed in such top competitive posts. At the same time, real efforts will be made to help minority groups get employed, if necessary at the cost of lower-economic-level whites. The greater impact on these whites may seem undesirable, but an ethically better answer is hard to discover. These new arrangements for minority groups require great psychological concern by management.

Nondiscrimination is an ethic that needs to be developed carefully. Affirmative-action policies can be abused as a means of securing promotion. This kind of action weakens competitive forces for professional or administrative advancement, forces necessary if our society is to move ahead with development of qualified leaders.

There are other moves needed to apply the Western ethical tradition of equality of individuals to both men and women. Capable women should be encouraged to expand their job tasks and responsibilities. Many secretaries are quite capable of doing administrative assistant work; a fact which is only sometimes acknowledged. The natural desire of most human beings to progress can be met in this way.

Treatment of the Environment

Throughout history there have been remarks about the effect of human activities on the environment. Business activities have been discussed most in recent years because business controls such a large part of our contact with the natural environment. Increasing use of chemical products in industry and agriculture has affected the environment in ways that were often unforeseen by users or manufacturers.

There were few laws on environmental matters other than sewage disposal until the publication of Rachel Carson's *The Silent Spring* in 1962, followed by other books and periodicals of environmental concern, and the activation of environmental societies. Now there are federal acts to secure water quality, solid-waste disposal, national air-quality standards, and resource recovery. Most of this legislation is a reasonable reaction to difficulties caused by an increasingly technological society. Business should not be ethically blamed for the difficulties except in some instances in which it has refused to inquire into or recognize the danger to the environment.

Most of the corrective legislation is clearly here to stay. A new ethic is being created, and most responsible businesses can be expected to respect it, though the cost may be great. It is probably true that businesses could have avoided some of the excesses of environmental regulatory legislation, had they been more aware of and alert to the dangers to the environment.

The religious and legal ethical heritage clearly sets an absolute standard of not damaging other property through misuse of one's own (*sic utere tuo*). Modern writers are more likely to think in terms of a more flexible utilitarian code: How much does it cost to prevent pollution? and How much does pollution cost? There sometimes is merit to this method of consideration, but it cannot set absolute legal or ethical standards.[19]

Since most people recognize the need for not damaging the environment, the sharpest ethical questions are raised in connection with cost. Recently Standard Oil of Ohio (Sohio) was forced to withdraw its proposal for a pipeline to bring Alaskan petroleum from Long Beach, California, to the west. The pipeline would have saved long, expensive shipments of Alaskan oil through the Panama Canal to Gulf ports. But Sohio would have been required, among many things, to pay $85 million for a new "scrubbing" device at a Southern California Edison plant to offset the pollution that might be caused at Long Beach harbor by oil transmission. Government imposed costs killed the project. Somewhat similar questions must be faced all over the country. Should a corporation shut down a plant that requires many millions of dollars of environmental-control machinery, but at great economic cost to the town in which the plant is located?

In an effort to reduce air pollution, Congress in 1970 required automobile companies to reduce new-car emission of hydrocarbons into the atmosphere. Most of these requirements have been met by the car companies, but at the costs of more efficient use of fuel, of difficulty in starting the cars, and greater expense in production. The auto companies opposed these requirements and asked for delays in putting them into effect. Were they unethical in doing so? The whole area of emissions control is new, and ethical responsibilities are not clearcut.[20] Clearly the companies were unethical in conspiring to keep new devices for control of noxious emissions off the market.[21]

Some corporations tend to delay ethically desirable actions through prolonged legal delays. Several years after it had become clear that the taconite mining operation and the associated dumping of used ore into Lake Superior was both illegal and unhealthy, Reserve Mining Corporation continued to fight legal action with delay as its main goal. Clearly Reserve had a legal right to conduct its court appeals and other delaying actions, and the executives liked the company's profit status better before Reserve was required to meet expensive antipollution requirements. But the officials and the public who became concerned with the problem probably concluded that Reserve Mining's management was wrongfully ignoring the health of the people living in its area of operation. That type of unconcern about the health of others is clearly counter to the *sic utere tuo* tradition, and is hardly likely to help the ethical reputation of American business.[22] Donald Mac-Donald suggests in relation to U.S. automobile companies,

> It is quite probable that if automakers had faced reality and suggested an equally arbitrary goal of, say, 70 percent purity, credibility would have been established and the lawmakers would have acceded to a reasonable timetable for achievement of the goal. But no. Detroit pursued the indefensible protests with fresh vigor by appointing vice presidents to carry on the war against Washington.[23]

It is, however, only fair to add that in the 1970s the auto industry put a great deal of effort into reduction of automotive air pollution, undoubtedly pushed by laws but with a genuine desire to secure results. Similarly, Bristol-Myers Company and Nestle "stonewalled" on the policy of selling infant food in developing countries. Real health problems resulted from such selling.[24]

On the other hand is the example of the Aetna Insurance Company and no-fault auto insurance. As a result of its own losses and public pressure for reform of insurance, Aetna broke from the rest of the industry and favored no-fault insurance.[25]

Most of America's large corporations respond to criticism of their environment-affecting actions, but they often respond so slowly that the public continues to view them as selfish and unethical. The Du Pont and Gillette companies were both slow to recognize the danger of fluorocarbons to the earth's ozone layer, finally requiring governmental action. In both cases there was an initial problem of uncertainty as to the scientific evidence of danger, and a larger problem of millions of dollars invested in fluorocarbon production. But when the scientific facts were clear, neither responded with the speed which an ethical regard for the welfare of their fellows would have required.[26]

In other cases, industry has simply opposed what many people would view as changes toward a more ethical environment. Brewers, bottlers, bottle makers, can makers, and others spent a million dollars to oppose an initiative bottling bill in Massachusetts in 1976 which would have required a deposit on containers, except for milk and fresh-fruit-juice containers and biologically degradable containers. Other states had reported substantial drops in littering as a result of such legislation.[27] Were the business firms who opposed this measure (chiefly on the grounds of the nuisance of paying for, storing, and transporting the bottles and cans for reprocessing) really conscious of their ethical responsibility to their fellow Americans? Is this opposition one of the reasons why politicians continue to pass legislation that *is* unfair to business?

It is to be hoped that many corporations have by now changed their views about environmental factors. General Electric Company, for example, had decided a decade ago to consider environmental effect carefully in all its strategic decisions.[28] In doing this, questions were raised as to the service of a "social needs" market, the effect of the product and manufacturing facilities on pollution, the effect of public acceptance of the company as a major social asset, the political viability of the project, and its employment attractiveness.

In some of the larger environmental problems, the ethical responsibilities of companies are shifting from the legalistic damage liability envisioned in *sic utere tuo* to a utilitarian process of balancing or "trading off" social goods and social evils in particular corporate activities. An example already cited is Sohio, which wished to pipe Alaskan petroleum from Los Angeles to the midwestern area. Since it would be introducing some uncontrollable pollution, it was required to pay $85 million for a pollution-control apparatus on a Southern California Edison power-generating plant. This requirement plus other difficulties finally forced the oil company to abandon the pipeline project, at real cost to many users of petroleum.

The trade-off theory of ethical responsibility seems fair and is particularly attractive to people with economics or engineering backgrounds. It probably is more flexible than the *sic utere tuo* principle. But the latter rule remains more ethically justifiable, and the fairest one to apply in most situations.

Business Policy and Social Standards

There are some cases in which the interests of a business seem to run directly contrary to those of the national community, though the business does not violate any clear-cut ethical precept. Some of these are cases, not directly related to health or safety, in which most Americans do not want governmental dictation. What, then, is the ethical responsibility?

Most noted of these cases is that of the use of violence on television. Of all modern countries, the United States certainly has the highest number, and probably the highest proportion, of television shows that emphasize violence. Since television came into most American homes (about 1955), America's rate of crimes of violence has risen sharply. There are currently four to twenty times as many murders per 100,000 people as in any other modern democracy. One important national study commission, with substantial representation from people who have worked in the industry, reported that television was a major cause of violent action in at least some youth. A Rand Company analysis of many other studies concludes that television does have an effect of making some youngsters more violent.[29]

But the television industry does not accept this evidence. It points out that much entertainment is based on violence, including many of Shakespeare's plays. The social experiments in the effect of television violence on youth are not absolutely convincing; one, for example, is a study of a class of school children, half of whom have seen a violent film and are more likely to press a button which gives a shock to someone than the half who have not seen the film. This is not overwhelming evidence; the coincidence of the rise of television and of violent crime is more important evidence, suggesting at least an experiment in crime reduction through nonviolent television.

Are the television executives morally wrong to continue to display violence to American youth with an already-high crime record? This author thinks so, but it is a difficult judgment. Few people believe that a small amount of violence has much impact; where and how do we know what is too much violence? There is nothing in Mosaic law or Thomas Aquinas's writings, or the common law that forbids showing scenes of violence. Must we make our judgment of a new possible cause of crime and legislate against it on a trial-and-error basis? Americans dislike the idea of censorship, therefore few are likely to legislate against television violence. The television industry's support of violence may last for decades; perhaps violence will eventually come close enough to the lives of television executives or their descendants so that they themselves will decide that they have been ethically wrong. In the summer of 1981, a group of right-wing religious fundamentalists planned a television boycott, but they have dropped it, at least temporarily. Television programs in the fall of 1981 were reported to have less violence.

Some advertisers, perhaps fearful of boycotts from unhappy customers, have agreed not to support violent films. Is this a case in which a new ethic—"thou shalt not lead thy children or thy neighbor's children into crime"—is slowly forming as a result of commercial connections?

There are somewhat similar cases in which a new, more egalitarian America is creating a new ethic contrary to established business practice. One case is *redlining*—the practice of banning or making very difficult conditions for mortgages on homes in poor, badly maintained residential areas that lack adequate public facilities such as transportation, shopping, or cultural agencies. A Federal Home Mortgage Disclosure Act of 1975 requiring federal banks and savings-and-loan associations to report on areas in which they made mortgage loans was opposed by the bankers. Is redlining poorer districts unethical or is it merely prudent business? Most likely the latter; but bankers are wrong if they oppose loan pools or other means of solving the problems of such areas.[30]

A similar problem has been raised about insuring properties in core-city areas like those where riots occurred in 1960. Legislation was passed in 1968 to established state pools for loans in such areas, with the federal government serving a reinsurance role. One-half of the states generally have supported this program with legislation. Insurance companies also backed this plan.[31] Are loan pools and federal support undue interferences with a free economy? Time will tell whether the United States has established a new ethic requiring insurance for all properties.

Welfare and Social Betterment Activities

There is another group of activities for which an employing firm deserves ethical credit, but which are not so universally applicable as to be ethical obligations. A thoughtful employer who wishes to keep his employees happy may do some of them, but there is no legal or strong ethical requirement to do so.

Some firms build up "credits in heaven" with welfare activities for employees. If an employee is unjustly arrested, the personnel department may help him find a lawyer or appear in court for him, or give him some financial help when he is ill. Some firms prefer to keep employees happy with this service. As a result of union pressures, many businesses now pay large sums for employee-pension schemes and health insurance, as well as the legally compelled amounts for workmen's compensation and unemployment compensation. Usually, the original compulsion in such cases was union pressure. It is doubtful if an ethic has been established by this process. Frequently there is failure to realize that such a requirement may add greatly to consumer costs or may endanger the company's future. A number of smaller companies dropped pension plans when a federal Employee Retirement Income Security Act (ERISA) made them more expensive. However, with or without legal obligation or union pressure, prosperous firms will continue to make financial arrangements for retired employees.

In the later 1960s, a large number of corporations undertook some social-betterment projects perhaps in reaction to riots and to ensure social peace. In 1967 Smith, Kline, and French Company organized a self-help street-cleaning project in a part of Philadelphia. Inland Steel Corporation found jobs for three thousand unemployed persons in five weeks. Xerox Corporation paid future employees while they attended classes which fitted them for further employment. Lockheed Corporation in Georgia hired six-hundred hard-core unemployed blacks. Hallmark undertook a $115-million project to help urban renewal in downtown Kansas City, Missouri. Many other well-known corporations undertook urban-renewal projects or training of the unemployed.[32] DeLorean gives an example of Pontiac Division's real efforts to employ blacks in Pontiac, Michigan.[33]

David Finn comments that these projects were subject to the criticism that companies were "dabbling." Efforts were too small to solve the problems of securing employment for the hard-core unemployed. Finn's criticism is valid, but such projects should continue. Private businesses, with their alert staffs, may be more likely to stumble on answers to social problems than is a ponderous government bureaucracy. The ethical justification may be the experimental value of dabbling. Private corporations, legally confined to competitive actions, half their profits taken by taxation, should not be expected to solve huge problems like unemployment. But it is possible that these corporations can help the government find the way to solutions to which all businesses might contribute. In Sweden the Rehn plan called for cooperation of government and business to retain employees whose occupational skills had become obsolete.

In 1971, 239 companies (48 percent) of the *Fortune*-500 companies disclosed some social-management activity. In 1972 the number of such disclosures increased to 290 or 58 percent. The largest number of actions was 214 (environmental controls), minority employment was second (88 mentions), then responsibility to personnel (64), community activities (75), and product improvement (58).[34]

Review of the various voluntary possibilities of corporate social reform indicates that the real problem is one of choice. Very few corporations could undertake the whole gamut of welfare activities plus profit sharing and miscellaneous activities on the 5 percent of net income for such projects allowed by the law. If a corporation dipped into nonexempt profit, it would probably face shareholder suits. So the real problem is to select the few things that can be done from the voluntary list on the basis of needs and of what the company can do best. The compulsory projects discussed in later chapters must come before these voluntary ones. Few of the above are *ethical obligations* in the full sense of that term.

The late Neil Jacoby made an excellent suggestion that may help businesses decide which welfare activity they should support. He urges companies to establish "social sensors" through surveys and other methods of finding public values and attitudes toward the company's products and its methods of work. Within the company, feedback processes should evaluate and act on the information secured from the social sensors. Two-way communications with social groups in the community should be established. Social accounts and social audits should be made.[35] If these or similar methods of appraising company relationships are followed, there will be a more informed approach to the ethical needs of corporate social responsibility.

Conclusions

American corporations are only beginning to understand their social responsibilities, which flow from a long Western tradition of philanthropy and general social responsibility. Most corporations have rejected Friedman's argument against philanthropy. Most have accepted the doctrine of affirmative action forced on them by the government; business leaders have usually recognized the desirability of a broader labor market. There are, however, real doubts whether affirmative action in the form of ethnic quotas for all positions can become an ethic. Many psychological problems of affirmative-action administration require special attention.

After undue delay, corporations are beginning to be more attentive to the effect of their actions on the environment. Though some government-forced programs have been unduly expensive, we can expect an ethic of attention to the environment to form.

Welfare and social-betterment programs of corporations vary from expensive pension programs that may endanger the company's financial health to small grants that have been perjoratively characterized as dabbling. An ethic has yet to be formed in this field.

If American corporations expect to keep their present freedom of action, they need to keep reviewing the adequacy of their social-responsibility programs. There may even be years in which that adequacy is of paramount importance. Social responsibility is a *sine qua non* of our modern complex society.

Notes

1. Iris Origo, *The Merchant of Prato*.
2. Roger H. Wiebe, *Businessmen and Reform*, pp. 19, 49.
3. Ibid., p. 219.
4. Louis Harris, *The Anguish of Change*, pp. 162-163, cited in Fred Luthans and Richard M. Hodgetts, *Social Issues in Business*, p. 477.

5. *Santa Clara County* v. *Southern Pacific Railroad* (118 U.S. 396). Also *San Mateo County* v. *Southern Pacific Railroad* (116 U.S. 396).

6. Milton Friedman, *Capitalism and Freedom*, pp. 133-136.

7. T.F. Bradshaw, "Corporate Social Reform: An Executive Viewpoint," in S. Prakash Sethi, ed., *The Unstable Ground*, pp. 24-31.

8. Aristotle, *Nichomachean Ethics*, pp. 111-145.

9. William T. Blackstone, "Is Preferential Treatment for Racial Minorities and Women Just or Unjust?" in Richard T. De George and Joseph A. Pichler, *Ethics, Free Enterprise and Public Policy*, pp. 99-115.

10. Daniel Seligman, "How Equal Opportunity Turned Into Employment Quotas," cited in Luthans and Hodgetts, *Social Issues in Business*, pp. 218-230.

11. Philip T. Drotning, "Organizing the Company for Social Action," in Sethi, *The Unstable Ground*, p. 264.

12. Moskowitz, "Affirmative Action and the Urban Crisis," in Thornton Bradshaw and David Vogel, *Corporations and Their Critics*, pp. 93-101.

13. Thomas Sowell, "Weber and Bakke, Presuppositions of Affirmative Action," *Wayne Law Review* 26, p. 1309.

14. Rosabeth Moss Kanter, *Men and Women of the Corporation*.

15. Sidney Peck, *The Rank and File Leader*, pp. 180-223.

16. James E. Post, *Corporate Behavior and Social Change*, pp. 30-38.

17. Theodore V. Purcell and Gerald F. Cavanaugh, *Blacks in the Industrial World*, passim.

18. Ibid., p. 295.

19. Barry Shore, "A Framework for Procurement Decisions Dominated by Environmental Constraints," p. 46-53.

20. Ernest S. Starkman, "Imposed Constraints on the Auto Industry," in Sethi, *The Unstable Ground*, pp. 328-344.

21. Kenneth Hahn, *Record of Correspondence . . . .*

22. Post, *Corporate Behavior and Social Change*, pp. 168-184.

23. Donald MacDonald, *Detroit 1985*, p. 60.

24. Post, *Corporate Behavior and Social Change*, pp. 257-269.

25. Ibid., pp. 219-232.

26. Ibid., pp. 87-105.

27. Ibid., pp. 150-166.

28. Ian H. Wilson, "Reforming the Strategic Planning Process," in Sethi, *The Unstable Ground*, pp. 245-255.

29. George Comstock et al., *Television and Human Behavior*, pp. 13, 211-261.

30. Post, *Corporate Behavior and Social Change*, p. 131.

31. Ibid., p. 149.

32. David Finn, *The Corporate Oligarch*, pp. 236-237.

33. J. Patrick Wright, *On a Clear Day*, p. 273.

34. Dennis R. Beresford, "How Companies Are Reporting Social Performance," *Management Accounting* (August 1974), pp. 41-43.

35. Neil Jacoby, "The Corporation as Social Activist," in Sethi, *The Unstable Ground*, pp. 224-244.

7 Business and Consumers

Ethical Traditions

This chapter deals with the business frauds that are likely to be directed against individual consumers, especially lower-income consumers. In other chapters security sales, advertising, product liability, and other problems that involve groups of consumers are discussed.

The ethical standards of the Western world relevant to this chapter include several principles. Of some importance for this subject is the responsibility to "love thy neighbor as thyself." This counsel of perfection probably boils down to a more practicable maxim like "Your neighbor, a customer, is one of us. Help him, don't cheat him. We will all get along better." "Thou shalt not steal" is also a rule covering business-consumer relations. Most good businessmen follow these rules. A harder rule to follow is that against deceiving the other party in a sale. This appears in Roman and Mosaic law. Thomas Aquinas wrote "It is altogether sinful to have recourse for deceit in order to sell a thing for more than its just price, because this is to deceive one's neighbor so as to injure him."[1] This rule was perhaps intended for closer-knit nomadic or agricultural societies but it is also important in modern society, especially since America in mid-twentieth century has succeeded in largely eliminating the spurious *caveat emptor* doctrine, discussed more fully in chapter 12.

In modern American business, the injunction to not deceive in commercial transactions has been awkwardly expanded into institutional mechanisms to prevent either party to a transaction from being cheated. In order to maintain good customer relations, some sellers will permit buyers to cheat them. For example, some department stores operate on the principle that the customer is always right. In general, the law provides adequate means for sellers to protect themselves against buyers, but inadequate means for buyers to protect themselves against sellers. Consumers are not as well organized as are merchants or manufacturers. However, recent consumerism movements have attempted to broaden the ban on commercial deception, to forbid not only fraud and intentional misrepresentation but also coercive and high-pressure tactics of marketers such as bait-and-switch advertising, chain-refund selling, free gimmicks, and fear-sell. They also mention "the right to be informed, which concerns questions about unfounded claims, exaggerations and misrepresentations of product attributes and also questions of partial or incomplete information or disclosure."[2]

Many lawyers and businessmen would not agree that these expansions of the rule for truth in commercial dealings have become an ethic. Obviously, most advertisers do not follow them. But the consumerists, a substantial number of political leaders, and much of the general public would agree.

The principle of *Salus populi* also seems to have importance for business's relations with consumers. The seller, especially the manufacturer, knows much more about the product than the consumer; he becomes a trustee for the part of public health or safety affected by his product.

Historical Sketch

Little has been written about consumers prior to the Civil War. Most Americans lived on farms where they made many of their own necessities or engaged in barter or similar transactions for them. There was little in the way of specific legal protection, except in the form of control of ferry and similar charges (a merchantilist holdover), but there was also not much opportunity for cheating.

After the Civil War, because of the general lowering of American business and political ethics, consumers were in many cases very badly treated. The development of canned goods and the generally greater exchange of goods permitted a good deal of exploitation of consumers by careless manufacturers. No federal protection was secured until Dr. Harvey Wiley tried to secure some supervision of food products in the 1890s. The reform movement, plus Upton Sinclair's scathing criticism of meat-packers in *The Jungle,* resulted in a meat-inspection law and a pure-food-and-drug act, both in 1906. But state and local agencies were poorly equipped to protect consumers. This is still the case.

Business attitudes of the time were not helpful. Cornelius Vanderbilt made his "public be damned" remark in the 1880s; the remark was misconstrued, but the effect was bad. A little earlier, Henry O. Havemeyer, president of the American Sugar Refining Company, said, "Let the buyer beware; that covers the whole business. You cannot wet nurse people from the time they are born until the time they die. They have got to wade in and get stuck, and that is the way men are educated and cultivated."[3] This was obviously an unrealistic attitude since many consumers had almost no means of knowing what was in various products. There was a consumer outburst. Pure-food-and-drug and meat legislation encountered difficulties from business criticisms, but the protection of consumers had become important in the 1890-1914 period of reform.

What was the situation in 1900? Advertisements were frequently deceptive. However, reputable retailers like Wanamaker's tried to sell only reputable products. *Good Housekeeping* tried to advertise only worthwhile goods. Responsible manufacturers tried to sell only healthy products. But the lack of adequate technical knowledge and of regular inspection meant that consumers were frequently misled. Probably few of them knew how badly off they were; publication of *The Jungle* in 1906 is said to have startled people so much that meat consumption fell sharply for a year or so.

A new outburst of consumer consciousness came with the publication of *Your Money's Worth* by Stuart Chase and F.J. Schlink in 1927. This volume lists patent medicines, quack medicines, adulterated and misrepresented products, inadequate production standards, very large price markups, and overadvertised brands. American ethics in dealing with consumers had advanced since 1900 but there was still dissatisfaction.

The Great Depression swelled the new wave of consumer consciousness. Another outburst in the late 1960s added to the legislation designed to protect consumers. The following sections review some of the problems raised by that outburst, many of which still exist.

Consumer Health Problems

One charge against business ethics is that some business executives have taken a corporately selfish view of the attacks on some business activities which threaten health. The slowness of the automobile industry to act on air-pollution control is a policy decision few ethical considerations could support. In the 1950s, people with lung problems were dying of air pollution in southern California because the automobile executives would consider only changes that made their cars more salable. Ralph Nader cites a conversation between Kenneth Hahn, Los Angeles County Supervisor, and a senior official of one of the automobile companies, in which the latter refused to consider an air-pollution device if it would not sell more cars.[4] Air-pollution-control devices were installed only after federal and California laws compelled such action. In 1955 the four major automobile companies and the Motor Vehicle Manufacturers Association agreed not to go ahead with the production of air-pollution-control devices until all were agreed. The agreement delayed production of such devices. In view of the clear evidence of the dangerous impact of smog on persons with lung trouble, this action was irresponsible. The agreement was finally ended by a consent decree in 1969.[5]

A book of *New Republic* articles that appeared in 1969 summarizes some of the main complaints of some more articulate consumer advocates; much of the book is devoted to products that may damage health.[6]

Ralph Nader was concerned about infants being exposed to nitrate residues from overuse of nitrate fertilizers, an exposure which, wrote

Nader, the food industry did not want to know about. He also feared the use of antibiotics for artificial growth and health in poultry and red-meat animals. Fat content in meat was being pushed by the meat industry as a means of reducing cost. Sausage samples, including most brand names, included some varieties of filth. Nonfederally inspected plants were allowing diseased meats to go on the market. The fish industry was fighting off efforts to regulate its inadequately inspected products. Water pollution was damaging shellfish and fish, with little or no effort by the industry to develop techniques for detection of such pollution. Cyclamates were worrying the Food and Drug Administration (FDA). Questionable additives were added to food to give flavor, color, or texture.[7]

Nader did not present a large amount of evidence supporting these charges. A decade later some of Nader's points have been confirmed and some at least partially refuted. The scope of this book does not permit a lengthy reconsideration of the validity of the charges. But if Nader was correct that the food industry was "dragging its heels" on development of inspection techniques, either public or private, its ethics were questionable. For at least four-thousand years, most of the Western world has respected the principle that one's property should not be used to damage others and that the seller should inform the buyer of potential difficulties in the object of sale. There is surely a defect in the ethics of the entrepreneur who continues to sell foods known to be dangerous or diseased, without warning to his customers. This type of unethical practice was probably stimulated by the unhappy reign of the policy of *caveat emptor* in nineteenth-century American courts.

The recent lax inspection of meat in Pennsylvania is reminiscent of Upton Sinclair's *The Jungle* and of the controversy over federal inspection of meat in the 1950s and early 1960s.[8] It is difficult to approve of companies like meat-packers which resist governmental regulation, after decades of experience has made it clear that they or some of their competitors will produce unhealthy meat products unless they are strictly inspected.

In 1972 the Federal Trade Commission charged the makers of *Anacin, Bufferin, Excedrin,* and *Bayer Aspirin* with misrepresentation in advertising. Resulting cease-and-desist orders required 25 percent of their advertising budgets for two years be spent on corrective advertising. Makers of and advertisers for *Geritol* were sued by the Justice Department in 1978 for false claims as to the effectiveness of *Geritol* in overcoming tiredness.

An interesting problem with drug costs is raised by David Sanford. Drug companies insist on marketing brand-name products, which are heavily advertised and much more expensive than the same material sold as generic drugs.[9] The drug companies are doing nothing illegal. But are they following the Western ethical tradition in their representations to their customers; is it in accord with *salus populi suprema lex* to jack up the price for brand-name drugs? No ethic has been determined.

Between 1964 and 1968, under new legislation the Food and Drug Administration filed thirty-three actions against twenty-six drug manufacturers including some of the largest.[10] Most of the actions were for false or deceptive advertising promotions. If the drug companies made misstatements, they were clearly violating an ethical principle going back to the book of Leviticus in the *Bible,* which states that a seller should be honest with a buyer.

Sanford Ungar has written an account of Mer/129, a drug manufactured by Richardson-Merrell in the late 1950s and early 1960s for cholesterol control. One Food and Drug Administration specialist feared the drug, but somehow it secured FDA approval in 1960. Reports of unfortunate side-effects began coming in quickly. Instructions as to how to combat these reports were issued to salesmen. A competitor reported to Richardson-Merrell that test animals went blind on Mer/129, but Merrell disputed this result. Finally, under heavy FDA pressure Merrell agreed to a warning letter in December 1961, but followed it with a sales letter. By April 1962, the FDA had learned that Merrell had given altered reports on drug results to the FDA. In 1964, a federal judge fined the company and its parent firm a total of $80,000, a small fraction of its $180 million sales. However, civil damage suits cost the company more.[11]

A General Accounting Office (GAO) report in April 1972 attacked deteriorating conditions, especially of sanitation, in the food-processing industry. The Food and Drug Administration answered on May 17 that it needed 300 more inspectors than the then-current 210 for the inspection of 60,000 plants. Lax inspection of meat in Pennsylvania led the United States to start inspection of plants in that state in July 1972. Mercury-tainted swordfish were recalled in 1970, and similarly tainted eels in 1971.

In the 1970s, a wide variety of other hazardous projects were banned, publicized, or criticized by the FDA, the Environmental Protection Agency (EPA), the Department of Health, Education, and Welfare (HEW), the National Commission on Product Safety, or the Federal Trade Commission (FTC).[12] Most remedies for the common cold were found to be ineffective by a National Academy of Science-National Research Council report released by the FDA on July 7, 1972, three years after it was submitted to FDA.

Attacks by individual businessmen on meat regulation frequently offered free enterprise as the reason they should continue to be allowed to sell diseased meat. This position is wrongly thought out. Free enterprise was not guaranteed in the original U.S. Constitution, but it has become a part of the American business ideology since the Civil War. It has never been defined by any thoughtful thinker or writer as including the right to sell unhealthy products.

It should be added that government, often with the real cooperation of many businesses, has succeeded in eliminating many of the hazards to consumer health. The ethical responsibilities to love one's neighbor as oneself and to not deceive the customer are becoming more clearly recognized in American society, although the situation is still far from perfect.

Consumer Fraud

Consumer fraud is even more important than street crime in its toll on the poor, and in the resentment it causes against American institutions. This kind of white-collar crime probably costs American customers several billion dollars a year. It has been cited as one reason for the Watts and Detroit riots.[13]

Most large, well-established businesses are anxious to keep their customers, so they maintain a reasonably high standard of quality goods and are generous to consumers on complaints. However, there is a commercial underworld that lives on exploitation of poor and ignorant persons. The amounts stolen by this underworld are small, but the impact on the lower-income customer may be great because of his financial insecurity. The impact on the general reputation of business is also very damaging. Most respectable businesses would condemn these practices if they learned the facts.

Federal Trade Commission files show many complaints about deceptive methods of selling freezers, vacuum cleaners, sewing machines, correspondence courses, fire alarms, aluminum siding, and encyclopedias. For example, a deceptive salesman advertises a very low price, then sells a defective product for a very large price. Another ruse is a phony contest in which everyone wins a prize, enabling the customer to be oversold with an elaborate contract for overpriced merchandise. A third ruse is use of a survey or contest.[14]

More affluent customers sometimes have problems with overselling. Sharp selling practices, for example, are much more likely to occur with car salesmen, whom the customer may never see again, than with grocery clerks, who want to see the customer back the next week.

The automobile business has its troubles with consumers.[15] A "takeover" house was closed down by the district attorney of Los Angeles County in Torrance in 1978. A series of salespeople misled customers with the objective of increasing the final sales price. Some of the techniques included using pictures of vehicles that depicted options not included in the advertised price; charging or attempting to charge customers for services performed prior to delivery without fully disclosing the fact; representing that specific equipment was included in the purchase price, but without the equipment installed and operative at that price; failing to give advertised discounts or rebates; failing to pay off unpaid balances on a vehicle taken in trade, after the dealership has agreed to do so as an inducement to close the deal; and misrepresenting the authority, directly or by implication, of a salesperson or other representative of the dealership to negotiate the final terms of a transaction with a customer. (In other words, the whopping discount or trade-in you have been offered by the salesperson will be reneged on at the last moment by the closer.) Quality dealers do not use such practices. However, Donald MacDonald comments that more than a few dealers who abhor such practices are forced into them to protect their franchises. He also comments that he has not heard of cases in which the factory closes the takeover dealer, only of cases in which law-enforcement agencies do so. In addition to cheating customers, dealers sometimes cheat the factory and vice versa.

Legal Difficulties of Consumer Debt

Studies have clearly shown a good deal of difficulty for buyers on installment-sales or similar credit plans who have difficulty in making payments or who are incensed by what they view as bad treatment if they fail to make payments.

Frequently the consumer finds that he must make payments on sales contracts regardless of the justice of his complaint against the seller, because the seller may have sold the contract to a finance company or bank. Under the holder-in-due-course legal doctrine followed in most states, no action could be brought against the financial agency. The sales firm sells its merchandise with false promises, trades the signed contract to a finance company, leaves town, or has too few assets to be sued. The customer finds himself saddled with a recently purchased car, refrigerator, or other item in poor condition, with no chance to sue for damages yet bound to pay principal and interest to the financial institution. He then becomes a debtor.

If the debtor is unable or fails to make payments, he may be subject to several penalties. The merchandise may be repossessed through legal action. It will then be sold, often at a price far below the price the customer originally agreed to pay. Since this forced legal sale price is inadequate to repay the debt, the financial institution (holder in due course) continues to put on considerable pressure to secure payment. In most states it may secure by legal process the garnishment of a portion of the debtor's wages. This garnishment may also result in unemployment, since many employers do not wish to go through the extra work of paying some of the wage to the financial institution, and may become distrustful of the employee. Another method of securing payment from defaulting debtors is the filing of liens on their personal or real property. In one extreme case, a woman lost her house because she had cosigned a $150 note for her daughter and had then been unable to pay it off. In most of these matters, many buyers do not understand the legalistic wording of contracts. They may be unable to afford legal aid. The machinery of the law appears to them to be very one-sided. It is important for buyers to recognize the obligations entailed before they sign documents. It is clearly not ethical to design the contract and sales talk so that there is deception, and legal redress is impossible.

Consumer Complaints

A very large part of American dissatisfaction with business grows out of consumer complaints about poorly manufactured products, or failure of producers or dealers to meet their legal or ethical obligations to consumers.

An analysis was made of several hundred letters by complaining consumers sent to Ralph Nader between November 1969 and December 1971. Since Ralph Nader had no legal authority to rectify consumer complaints but was only a widely known sponsor of consumer rights, many of these letters were copies of letters sent to company officials, political figures, media personalities, or organizations. Women wrote more of such letters than men; their complaints were primarily in the areas of food, medical care, or appliances. Complaints about appliances were more likely to be typed; all complaints were more likely to come from cities.

Half the appliance-complaint letters dealt with defective merchandise. Most writers expected some defective products but were surprised at how quickly defects showed up, and at the unwillingness of dealers to exchange defective merchandise for better products. Replacement parts were all most dealers would furnish. Frequently appliances expected to last a decade or more broke down after six or seven years, after expiration of the warranty. Warranties were found to be too short. Warranties often left purchasers responsible for repair labor charges. On small items, the warranty was good only for repair at the factory. There were often design defects. Seventy percent complained about service, including slow shipment, improper connection, little or no repair service, excuses for not giving service, high repair charges, and monopolistic high prices for repair parts.

Food complaints dealt largely with the quality of foods purchased: vitamin deficiencies, presence of pesticides, mercury contamination, presence of insects and rat droppings, et cetera. Twenty percent of complaints worried about additives such as DES, water injected into meat, mislabelled products, or alien objects found in packaged or canned goods. Advertising of products was often viewed as false. One theme that runs through many of the letters to Nader is an exasperation with the failure of some companies to respond quickly and generously to such complaints.[16]

Business Self-Regulation

The suggestion has been made that businesses could avoid detailed government regulation by handling such complaints through their own trade associations. A number of consumer-action panels were established during the Nixon and Ford administrations. Among others these included a Major Appliance Consumer Panel established by manufacturers of home appliances and gas appliances and by the National Retail Merchants Association; Automobile Consumer Action programs created by the National Association of Automobile Dealers and the Automotive Trade Association managers; the Furniture Industry Consumer Action Panel; the Carpet and Rug Industry Consumer Action Panel; the Office of the Impartial Chairman of the Moving and Storage Industry of New York City, established by six movers' trade associations and a Teamsters' local; and the Home Owners' Warranty Program adopted by the National Association of Home Builders. Each of these panels was established for business reasons, to avoid government regulation and to reduce competition by lower-quality operators. The apparent selfishness of these reasons need not be a cause of concern; higher ethical standards often grow out of similar circumstances.

But the troubles of each panel have been substantial. David I. Greenberg and Thomas H. Stanton comment that some of the panels have refused to review cases until an agreed statement of fact has been reached. Panel procedures assume consumer satisfaction with explanations unless there is positive evidence to the contrary. Panels do not systematically inform consumers that if they are dissatisfied with the manaufacturer's response, they can continue the case with the panel. Panels fail to monitor business promises to resolve disputes, and tend to treat complaints arbitrarily. Panels also take great care to safeguard the privacy of the firms against which there are complaints. The obvious conclusion is that the rules and procedures of these panels are weighted against the consumer.[17]

It does indeed seem possible that efforts of industry at self-regulation may take the side of the businesses that are supporting the self-regulatory effort. A careful study of a Better Business Bureau in California confirms this impression. Some Better Business Bureaus date back to the reform era of the early 1900s when they were an offshoot of an almost evangelical truth-in-advertising movement. They are supported largely but not entirely by retail businesses and some manufacturers. There were perhaps 130 such bureaus in 1970 and there are far more today, as part of a movement for self-regulation to avoid government regulation. The bureaus are financed by voluntary contributions, not always given on a generous scale. One Better Business Bureau studied (probably in San Francisco or Oakland) receives numbers of complaints about consumer goods or services. After asking the business to adjust the problem, a task the Bureau does well, it puts some pressure on both parties to settle if the matter is not amicably determined. Its role is more that of liaison than of arbitrator or mediator. The Bureau also tries to encourage arbitration panels and sponsors some opportunities for consumer education. The only actual penalty it inflicts on any business is to indicate in a letter to inquiring customers that the Bureau has received some complaints about the business. This is not an imposing penalty, although it might damage a few businesses.[18]

There are several reasons why industry self-regulation is unsatisfactory to consumer analysts. Self-regulation combats a level of business ethics that for a century has been too low. Our antitrust laws place severe limitations on the punishment of offenders by exclusion from trade, a problem discussed in chapter 3. Perhaps the American sense of individualism is a further limitation.

However, there are many cases in which individual businesses go a long way to meet the customers' demands. A study of large department stores indicate that they will often give a complete refund for damage to an article that has been used and repaired many times.[19] All of us have dealings with grocery or hardware stores that are scrupulously honest. If the Western ethical tradition is developing in many such areas of business, it should be encouraged as an alternative to cumbersome governmental regulations. Few want to be part of a society in which every commercial move must be made in accordance with statutes and regulations. Perhaps a supervised exemption from antitrust laws would permit some businesses to form effective self-control groups, and thus establish a better business ethic.

State and Local Regulation

A number of state and local governments have attempted to protect consumers from deliberate fraud. All states have laws against fraudulent sales though some laws are rudimentary. The majority of state laws against consumer fraud are not well enforced for lack of prosecutorial staff and for other reasons. Many local governments also seem unable to cope effectively with fraud against consumers. In Illinois in the 1970s, the state attorney general's Division of Consumer Fraud and Protection seemed to give up hope of driving fraudulent merchants out of business and to be content with recovering the money of the deceived customers where possible.[20] The common-law background of most states was sensitive to the property rights of merchants—a sensitivity that the Depression and the selection of liberal judges overturned only slowly. The tendency of the courts to treat white-collar offenders lightly perhaps came because such offenders did not seem like ordinary criminals. The growth of consumer credit facilitated fraudulent enterprises, especially since the laws of most states permitted financing companies to escape responsibility for any defects in products.

In an account of his experience as Consumer Counsel of New York City (April 1970-June 1971) and an earlier experience working for the National Association for the Advancement of Colored People (NAACP), Philip G. Schrag describes several episodes in which poor people were criminally deceived but in which appropriate governmental help was very difficult to find because of the dilatory, ineffective New York legal system.[21]

The first case was of a New York resident who earned about $5,000 a year (in 1966). Super Fine Furniture, a large Harlem store, sold him and his wife a "budget saving plan." All foods but milk and fresh vegetables would be sent him; he would pay $30.22 per month for three years for a freezer, (he was not aware of the three-year period of payment) and $74.83 per month for the food. The food proved to be inadequate. The customer was told that he could cancel the food contract but that he must pay for the freezer for three years, at the then-very-high price of $1,087. The store had promptly sold the contract to a credit company; under New York law the buyer could secure relief from paying the store on the grounds of fraud, but not from the finance company, which could garnishee his wages. Efforts to secure punitive damages dragged on in the courts until, after four years, the case was settled by the bankruptcy of Super Fine.

A woman was talked into signing a contract to pay $525 for a vacuum cleaner and use of a shoppers' service, with the promise that the contract would be torn up if she phoned in her change of mind the next morning. She phoned to cancel the next morning and was told it could not be cancelled because her contract had by then been assigned to a finance company. The shoppers' service seemed useless to her and the vacuum payments became burdensome. Court action was brought by the city's Department of Consumer Affairs; in the hearings it became clear that the so-called finance company was the original company. But the New York City Corporation Counsel's office was very dilatory; the court finally refused to grant an injunction, and the only gain for the complainant was a promise that the company would behave itself.

Kramer's Appliance Repair Company was frequently complained against. It would take in television sets for repair, charge very high prices, do work without orders, not complete repair jobs, and otherwise cheat its customers. After lengthy legal proceedings the cheated customers won judgments against Kramer by default but were unable to secure any money, partly because of lack of cooperation from city marshals. The Department of Consumer Affairs sued Kramer, but the court decided that Kramer's admission of false advertising did not prompt judicial action (shades of *caveat emptor*).

Standard Magazine Service sold five-year subscriptions to six major magazines for payment of a small "publisher's service charge which is only sixty-four cents a week," actually the full cost of the magazine subscriptions. The service was a franchise agent of a nationally-known corporation. When threatened with unfavorable publicity of a mass restitution suit, the national company agreed to a consent judgment, and later stopped all sales by Standard Magazine Service. But it was difficult to get the New York courts to agree to the consent decree. The court clerk who finally recommended approval to the judge initially viewed this kind of cheating as only "puffery," following the *caveat emptor* doctrine, which the clerk probably did not know was legally almost obsolete.

Foolproof Protection Inc. sold to residents of high-crime slums a crime-protection system for $769.28 that did nothing the salesman promised. It did not even ring in police or fire stations. It was sold at more than ten times the cost to the company. The president of Foolproof, a man with a previous record of harsh sales tactics, had nevertheless secured a license as a home-improvement contractor. Salesmen were trained to say that customers in default were not sued; in actuality they were vigorously prosecuted. The Department of Consumer Affairs decided to inform customers of their right to cancel because they had never been given cards required by the law. The department worked out a consent agreement with the corporation but had real difficulty with Mayor Lindsey's office and with the judge. Foolproof would not follow its agreement. Foolproof fought the consent decision but eventually lost in court. Schrag notes that the company had help from major companies as well as from city hall.[22] Another company gave one-day training sessions to sixty sales girls who sold an "information service" on child guidance. The goods and services sold cost $38; the customers paid $264.33.

In almost all the cases cited by Schrag, the chief complaint is against the slowness of government or the unwillingness of government to act. Major business had responsibility only in one case.

A study of *Consumers in Trouble* by David Caplovitz reviews legal action against debtors in Chicago, Detroit, New York, and Philadelphia in 1967. These default debtors whose names were taken from court docket books, included an overrepresentation of blacks and Puerto Ricans. Their incomes were low, but not a great deal below the mean income of nonfarm family heads. The purchased items that produced the debt were automobiles (26 percent); furniture (20 percent); household appliances (13 percent); entertainment appliances (11 percent); clothing and soft goods (16 percent); jewelry, watches, and wigs (10 percent); and miscellaneous. Loans were from banks, small loan companies, and credit unions, the latter being by far the great majority. Direct sellers (door to door) did 30 percent of the selling, automobile dealers (used cars) and low-income retailers did 25 percent each, and general retailers only about 18 percent.[23]

More than a third of the debtors indicated that they had been deceived either at the time of sale, or when the wrong merchandise was delivered.

Direct sellers (47 percent) and automobile dealers (42 percent) were more likely to have been represented as deceptive. Less than half of those who dealt with direct sellers and automobile dealers were told the true cost of their purchase at the time of the sale. Eighteen percent claimed they never received a copy of the contract of sale, the worst offenders being the same two groups, direct sellers and auto dealers. As might be anticipated, the debtor's income was negatively related to deception in the sale. Also, education was an antidote to deception only among those better-off debtors who dealt with automobile dealers.[24] The college-educated are almost as likely to be deceived as the less educated, when direct sellers or low-income retailers are doing the deceiving.

Caplovitz has an interesting description of reasons for the defaults.[25] This discussion will be limited to those which bear on specific problems of business-consumer ethics. Reasons like overextension of funds, loss of job, or loss of health raise only the general ethical problem of whether salesmen may ethically persuade indigent or near-indigent purchasers into costly installment sales contracts.

More than a third of the debtors gave reasons for default for which the creditor was at least partly responsible. Frequently, there were violations of express warranties: the car required repairs but the seller refused to do anything about it, so the debtor declined to pay until he was legally forced to do so; the used car would not run or the wrong vehicle was delivered; or all merchandise was not delivered. Forty-five percent of the debtors who were told a price at the time of sale claimed to be misled about the actual cost, sometimes substantially. Life-insurance, health-insurance, and property-insurance charges, about which the buyer had not been informed, were added. Salesmen made false promises. For example, a freezer was promised if the customer contracted for a food-purchase plan, when actually the freezer had to be bought at a high price. Another promise was that the customer could pay for his vacuum cleaner through commissions earned by finding other customers. Some debtors claimed they were tricked into buying contracts. In the home-repair field, fraudulent firms promised but failed to deliver. Banks and governmental agencies did little to protect the consumer.

A few comments on these findings may help appraise their importance for the general ethics of business-consumer relationships. First, the results are fourteen years old; change in laws regarding consumers and in public opinion regarding such sales may have improved the situation. Second, the information was secured from debtors who may not have been the most trustworthy informants. Third, there is a Direct Selling Association that is attempting to improve the standards of its members.[26] Fourth, the types of goods sold, such as cars and furniture, are those which do not involve speedy new purchases, and hence are likely to be oversold, in contrast to groceries and other commodities that are purchased frequently.

A home-renewal project of similar character occurred in the Washington, D.C. area in the years 1963 to 1967. Nathan H. Cohen along with some relatives and a convicted forger, put together the Monarch Construction Corporation to merchandise an aluminum townhouse front to be applied to the exterior of old row houses. A large sales staff, a "boiler room" of telephone solicitors, and a booklet advertised and sold the projects. Sales, mostly to poor blacks, were handled with complete disregard for the homeowner's interest. Buyers were asked to sign blank contracts, and they later received new contracts with vastly increased costs. Provisions of original contracts were often disregarded by Monarch workers. Mortgaged properties were speedily sold under District of Columbia laws which gave little protection to homeowners. The homeowners who had signed Monarch contracts usually had no place to move.

Although Monarch's sales to one-thousand Washington families were often cruelly fraudulent, the victimized homeowners usually were pressed for payments by respectable savings and loan companies that had bought the notes from Monarch and by the Federal Housing Administration which had a policy of helping enforce loans made by insured lenders. As in other cases, Citizens Building and Loan (a holder in due course) did not investigate the ethics of Monarch Corporation, but did press hard to secure payment of the loans it bought from Monarch, not hesitating to foreclose on victims of the fraud. Two other banks ceased business with Monarch after they discovered what was going on.

The first real trouble for Monarch Corporation and Nathan Cohen came in 1964 when a suit was filed against them, a trustee broker, and a trust company that had bought a Monarch note. In January 1965 Monarch responded to some bad publicity with a costly advertising program for its townhouse fronts; a program endorsed by prominent senators of both parties. The advertisements, however, backfired and led to investigations by several government agencies. The investigations clearly showed Monarch's poor work and the heavy debts forced on purchasers. Congressman John Dowdy was bribed to try to stop the investigations—a bribe that later led to his prosecution. Finally in 1969, three years after Monarch Corporation died, a federal prosecution of Cohen and Associates on mail-fraud charges was begun. Cohen secured some immunity by testifying against Congressman Dowdy. Cohen and his associates agreed to make some retribution, but received no jail sentences; a small penalty for inflicting $6 million damage on over one-thousand indigent or near-indigent families. Congressman Dowdy was sentenced to eighteen months in prison and was fined $25,000 for perjury.[27]

A recent California example shows how the Trane Company, a successful nationwide business, let its subsidiary, Trane Home Comfort Center (said to be the largest home-improvement company in California), become involved in fraudulent sales to consumers. A major savings and loan association bought the contracts and through a legal technicality avoided responsibility to the consumer. Trane and the savings and loan association both promised to mend their ways when the California Attorney General's Office, the California Contractor's State License Board, and the Los Angeles County Department of Consumer Affairs carried on a five-year investigation and won a million dollars from the company to pay legal and past and present investigatory costs.

Trane Home Comfort Center was charged with selling air conditioning equipment to lower-income people who were unlikely to be able to meet payments and thus might lose their homes; claiming that the purchaser could make medical-tax deductions for the purchase price of the equipment; stating that their equipment would result in savings in utility cases; stating that homeowners would be subject to health and safety rules if they did not replace existing equipment; distributing a flyer that asserted their equipment would help relieve arthritis, asthma, high blood pressure, heart strain, would lead to longer children's naps, help pianos stay in tune, help preserve sets in women's hair, and other claims; lying to a blind woman that her house would not be taken away from her; and using "undue influence" on a couple with mental disabilities.

San Diego Federal Savings and Loan Association bought Trane contracts regularly until November 11, 1980, two days after the *Los Angeles Times* reported that hundreds of low-income Californians had lost their homes or been threatened with loss of homes because of signing contracts with Trane Home Comfort Center. Trane did not admit guilt but did agree to pay civil penalties, to not use the lien foreclosure provision in its contents against low-income persons who had bought their equipment in the last four years, to try to persuade others not to use those provisions, and to place a large-type warning on future contracts. There was no provision for repaying defrauded customers, but suits could be brought.[28]

Two comments seem necessary. It is surprising that such a large company should have continued such methods of sales to, and harsh treatment of, low-income homeowners in an era of consumer consciousness. The California legislature could also be criticized for passing an act with several consumer-protection clauses but which left a loophole for direct loans from lender to consumer. Trane Home Comfort Center Corporation and San Diego Federal worked out a procedure that used this loophole as a means of avoiding the consumer-protection act.

It must be admitted that state and local regulation has been ineffective in Illinois, New York City, Chicago, Detroit, Philadelphia, the District of Columbia, and until recently, California. Most of the fraud was not by major businesses, although Trane Company and some savings and loans were large. State and local governments were less effective chiefly because of poor statutes, slow court operation, and inadequate prosecutor staff. The indictment of big business here is that it has not urged on state legislatures the enactment of laws and provision for law-enforcement machinery adequate to punish the fraudulent-sales companies. The general position of chambers of commerce and other business associations against most regulatory measures needs to be reexamined.

Improvement of Laws of Consumer Relations

Philip Schrag has written about the heavy costs to ghetto customers of suing a merchant for fraudulent action. He suggests laws to provide that consumers who win court cases could collect costs from merchants, and that the same action that can be raised against merchants for fraudulent sale could also be raised against companies that buy debt certificates coming from a fraudulent sale, a change of the law in most states.[29] This raises an interesting ethical question. The poorer consumer needs help; costs of going to court are too high for ghetto customers. But how far is it good public policy to help law firms that may begin to argue cases for the fees?

Legislation to protect consumers against quasi-fraudulent actions like those just described is frequently attacked as undue pampering of the consumer. This argument has some validity. If a person is willing to pay $400 for an item known to be worth $200, perhaps he should suffer the consequences of his own stupidity, a price he must pay if he expects to be a free agent in a modern world. But if the law is drafted in a way the consumer does not understand, to make him responsible for paying $400 for an object that is worth $200, then the seller who takes advantage of that law is violating the Western tradition of truth telling.

Consumer fraud is frequently hard to investigate because it looks like a normal, commercial transaction. Many examples of it can inundate state and local law-enforcement agencies. It is necessary for prosecutors to prove that the defendant intended to do a prohibited act, a real problem when the fraudulent corporation has few or no records of its own operations. A corporate hierarchy may obscure defenders. Astute defense lawyers may use a process of delay. Real punishments are difficult to secure.

Donald P. Rothschild and Bruce C. Throne believe that some new methods of legal operation will solve some of these problems. They cite an effort in the District of Columbia that brings together national and local officials. Restitution schemes have had some good effect but are often hard to organize. These authors also note a critical gap in defense against criminal exploitation of the poor. There are no efforts by civic leaders, churches, schools, the press, or government to condemn these crimes against the poor.[30] New York State passed a law in 1977 that makes it easier to establish felony fraud in smaller cases.[31]

Small-claims courts have been used in some areas to help consumers who cannot afford regular court action. In some jurisdictions, small-claims courts work out well; in others they share the slowness and expense of larger judicial processes. Laura Nader and Christopher Shugart suggest that small-claims courts may help the development of "in-house mechanisms and intermediaries." They also suggest a consumer-fraud bureau and class-action suits.

Federal Action

Several government agencies, the Federal Trade Commission, (FTC), the Justice Department, and a few courts moved against a surprising variety of business firms for deceptive practices or antitrust violations which were damaging to consumers in the late 1960s or early 1970s.[32] A few examples of significant ethical nature will be given.

False tests on television were banned by a Supreme Court ruling of April 5, 1972. Dupont de Nemours and Company agreed with the FTC to inform consumers when damage might result from use of its antifreeze. In 1975 Allied Van Lines was fined $20,000 and some of its operations suspended for fifteen days because of consumer complaints of faulty estimates, failing to report underestimates, and failure to deliver on schedule. The action was by the Interstate Commerce Commission. A consent agreement with Chrysler Corporation in 1980 provided for repaying to persons whose cars or trucks had been repossessed any profit from the sale of the repossessed vehicle. There are parallel agreements with Ford and General Motors. The FTC announced an interpretation of nationwide rules to provide consumers with information about home insulation before purchase. The rules involved procedures for determining the insulative quality of the product being sought. The FTC also gave final approval to a consent agreement with Ford Motor Company on methods of informing Ford customers about repair information and possible postwarranty compensation for defects of which Ford was aware.

These samples of Federal Trade Commission activities on behalf of consumers leads to several observations. Most of the activities are those which individual consumers of average or less-than-average means could not undertake to litigate on their own. Almost all seem to be directed largely toward the age-old Western ethic of telling the truth in business transactions; the development of more honest techniques of salesmanship which is a commendable ethical goal if not carried to excesses of detailed regulation. Most of the activities dealt with larger companies or industry groups, not with the small "fly-by-night" concerns of the type encountered by Schrag in New York City.

There is sharp criticism of the Federal Trade Commission. One commentator satirizes this policy of consumer protection: "General stupidity is not the only attribute of the beneficiary of FTC policy. He also has a short attention span; he does not read all that is to be read, but snatches general impressions. He signs things he has not read, has marginal eyesight, and is frightened by dunning letters when he has not paid bills. Most of all, though, he is thoroughly avaricious."[33] When one considers the age and lack of education of some of the persons the FTC is trying to help, this satirical attack may be unwarranted. However, the best answer may be to find another way to help protect the interests of the aged poor. Other critics note the many sins against which the Federal Trade Commission has not taken action.

Congress has tried at other times to help the consumer, sometimes not very successfully. Legislation for a consumer department has been defeated. The Truth in Lending Act has sometimes resulted in added credit charges. The Employee Retirement Income Security Act had the result that a good many companies dropped their pension plans. The Magnuson-Moss Warranty Act had some vague language which is said to have stopped some warranties. The Product Safety Commission has met with many criticisms.[34]

Some of the above setbacks may be reduced in time. But ethics might have been better than laws in helping the consumer on these points.

Conclusions

This chapter has reviewed the ethical principles that are generally accepted and may be applicable to business-consumer relations. It has listed a number of cases in which certain businesses have shown insufficient regard for the health of consumers but has concluded that these problems are slowly being remedied by government and businesses. It has discussed some of the defrauding of consumers, especially poorer ones; an evil for which most legitimate business is not responsible but which it could help to remedy through support of necessary actions on the parts of state, local, and federal governments. A series of efforts to eliminate unfairness to consumers through industry panels and Better Business Bureaus have been only moderately successful. The ethical traditions listed in the beginning of this chapter have not been followed in many business dealings with consumers.

Poor ethical conduct between business and consumers is very damaging, especially to poorer consumers, and to the average American's general regard for business. Firms that have done their best to secure honest and thoughtful contacts between their staffs and consumers may be among the first to suffer when an irate pubic or legislative body passes antibusiness legislation. The successful future of a free-enterprise system is in part dependent on control of the type of consumer fraud discussed in this chapter.

What is the responsibility of business executives in these matters? Most fraudulent or partly fraudulent sales are made by irresponsible, often highly mobile people. Reputable businessmen cannot be blamed for such sales. However, it is questionable if banks or other financial institutions should buy the contracts of semifraudulent sales without at least looking into the quality of the product sold and the capacity of the purchaser to buy the product on credit. The method of collection employed is completely contrary to the high standards set by the Old Testament, and the business that financially supports this unethical conduct surely deserves some blame.

The other indictment of reputable business in this field is against its frequent delaying of or complete opposition to appropriate governmental action. Legal considerations, principally connected with antitrust laws, make it impossible for business to establish systems of self-regulation like some of those which exist in Europe. But the wise businessperson should encourage establishment of laws and governmental machinery needed to keep the kind of schemers whose activities have been described in this chapter out of business.

A major responsibility for forward movement of American business ethics in the consumer area lies with government, especially state and local governments. State attorney-generals' offices need more prosecuting staff for consumer concerns, and the county attorneys need to take more action. Many state laws need strengthening. Consumer groups and business groups can help secure governmental action; some of both do now. The ultimate force for establishing an ethic for honest treatment of consumers is governmental.

Notes

1. Thomas Aquinas, *Summa Theologiae,* pp. 318, 277.

2. Jagdish N. Sheth and Nicholas J. Mammana, "Recent Failures in Consumer Protection," in Fred Luthans and Richard M. Hodgetts, *Social Issues in Business,* p. 434.

3. James Bishop, Jr., and Henry W. Hubbard, *Let the Seller Beware,* p. 25.

4. Ralph Nader, *Unsafe at Any Speed,* pp. 153-154.

5. Mark J. Green, et al., *The Closed Enterprise System,* pp. 256 ff.

6. David Sanford, et al., *Hot War on the Consumer.*

7. Ibid., pp. 3-9.

8. Harrison Wellford, *Sowing the Wind.*

9. Sanford, et al., *Hot War on the Consumer,* pp. 81-90.

10. Ibid., pp. 91-94.

11. Sanford Ungar, "Get Away With What You Can," in Heilbroner, *In the Name of Profit,* pp. 100-127.

12. Lester A. Sobel, ed., *Consumer Protection.*

13. Donald P. Rothschild and Bruce C. Throne, "Criminal Consumer Fraud: A Victim-Oriented Analysis," p. 675 ff.

14. Bishop and Hubbard, *Let the Seller Beware,* pp. 153-154.

15. Donald MacDonald, *Detroit 1985,* p. 172 ff.

16. Eric Freedman, "Dear Mr. Nader, A Study of Consumer Complaint Letters," in Nader, *No Access to Law,* pp. 113-170.

17. Greenberg and Stanton, "Business Groups, Consumer Problems: The Contradiction of Trade Association Complaint Handling", in Laura Nader, ed., *No Access to Law,* pp. 193-231.

18. Marian Eaton, "The Better Business Bureau," in Nader, *No Access to Law,* pp. 233-281.

19. Angela Karikas and Rena Rosenwater, "Department Store Complaint Management," in Nader, *No Access to Law,* pp. 283-316.

20. Eric H. Steele, "Fraud, Dispute and the Consumer: Responding to Consumer Complaints," pp. 1107-1186.

21. Philip G. Schrag, *Counsel for the Deceived.*

22. Ibid., p. 15.

23. David Caplovitz, *Consumers in Trouble,* p. 44.

24. Ibid., p. 44.

25. Ibid., chapters 4-9.

26. Ivan Hill, ed., *The Ethical Basis of Economic Freedom,* pp. 263-282.

27. Jean Carper, *Not With a Gun.*

28. *Los Angeles Times,* November 9, 1980, p. 1 ff; and December 12, 1980, pp. 1, 3, 20.

29. Philip Schrag, "Ghetto Merchants: A Study in Deception," in Sanford, et al., *Hot War on the Consumer,* pp. 33-36.

30. Rothschild and Throne, "Criminal Consumer Fraud: A Victim Oriented Analysis," p. 661 ff.

31. Robert I. Clarey, "The Prosecution of Consumer Fraud, New York's New Approach, pp. 197-201.

32. Sobel, *Consumer Protection,* pp. 113-137.

33. Cited in Simon Rottenberg, ed., *Occupational Licensing and Regulation,* p. 113.

34. Congressional Quarterly Inc., Editorial Research Reports, *Consumer Protection Gains and Setbacks,* pp. 4-8.

8 Investment in Land or Securities

As a nation that developed the larger part of a continent and as one of the leading nations in the Industrial Revolution, the United States has constantly faced the problem of the sale of speculative ventures that cost far more than the financial strength of the originator of the venture. There were not many specific rules of ethics to cover the problems of such investment.

Ethics and History of Land Sales

One ethic that can be cited in relation to land sales is the responsibility of the seller not to deceive the buyer. The right to hold property seems to imply the right to a clear title. Much of English common law was concerned with the right to land. However, in colonial times, the King and sometimes royal governors or other leaders of the colonies used grants of land for political patronage or colonial development. Shortly after the American Revolution came a number of land-development booms that often involved prominent political leaders. The Yazoo land frauds, covering land in present-day Alabama and Mississippi, were perpetrated by giving stock to all members of the Georgia legislature in 1789.

In the first part of the nineteenth century, the United States recovered from the collapse of various schemes of wholesale land-grabbing that occurred in the post-Revolutionary period.[1] However, the Louisiana Purchase in 1803 brought millions of new acres. "Squatter's rights" and "Spanish grants" were claimed. Land speculation occurred in Texas in the 1820s while it was part of Mexico. In the 1830s, public land offices did a "land-office business" and much speculation developed. Senator Daniel Webster had a significant part in such speculation. There was intense land speculation in California in the 1850s and again in the 1880s. The collapse of the Florida land boom of the 1920s contributed to the Great Depression. In more recent decades American suburbanization has introduced many land-sale problems.[2]

In spite of all the difficulties that attended America's continuous land growth and speculation, the U.S. government, through the Homestead Act of 1863 and earlier policy, may have succeeded in distributing land more freely and equitably than has been the case in most other countries. Public lands were widely distributed; most losses from speculation were offset by later increases in land value. However, land sales have introduced important ethical problems.

127

Land speculation in itself may be perfectly ethical, and we can assume that many Americans from George Washington on who indulged in land speculation were ethical. The recurring cycles of boom and bust, however, may lead to doubts about the ethics of overselling, which spurred on the cruelty of the cycle for those buyers who were caught in the boom and bust period, a damage only partly mitigated by the possibility that if the buyer was able to hold on to his land long enough he could probably recover his money or even make a profit. Many buyers could not hold on so long.

It is difficult to find the point at which the selling of speculative land becomes unethical. If we go back to the biblical standard set in Leviticus, chapter 25, the seller should be fair with the buyer. If the seller describes the economic possibilities of the land, should he also indicate problems such as hostile Indians, danger of drought, danger of storms, or unhealthy aspects of the terrain? The general distrust of land speculators at times in American history is probably in large part a reaction to overselling of land. It may also be related to a rash of fraudulent practices such as forging of land titles, lying, and swindling.[3]

Another constant ethical problem in land business in the United States has been the foreclosure of mortgages. In times of prosperity, land values were bid up high with the aid of mortgage borrowing; in times of adversity money was often not available for mortgage payments. From the operations of the Second Bank of the United States in the first quarter of the nineteenth century to the Florida land bust and Midwestern agricultural slump a century later, this phenomenon occurred and recurred. Should banks or other mortgagees foreclose on landholders who had probably paid too high a price because they were the innocent victims of a land-speculation fever? Mortgagees arrived at different answers to this problem. State legislatures often altered laws to make it harder to foreclose on mortgages, an action that may have been unethical to the moneylender but seemed to be justified by the necessity of the borrower.

Real-Estate Investment Trusts

In the 1960s and 1970s, a major development in land handling was the Real Estate Investment Trust (REIT). The REIT, established by well-known banks, investment houses, brokerage firms, and others, seemed in the late 1960s to be a major new type of investment, but they crashed sharply in the mid-1970s. The story as told by Roy Schotland is one of a new institution, brought down by conflict of interest, a poor enabling law, and lack of regulation.[4] Schotland begins the REIT story with the 1960 law in which Congress thought it was giving small and medium-size investors a chance to take part in professionally run real-estate developments, and so to promote construction of residential units. REITs were given a corporate tax exemption like that given to mutual funds if they invested at least 75 percent of their assets in real estate and paid out 90 percent of their income annually. These two provisions, intended to insure the purpose of the statute, operated to weaken the REITs when interest rates rose and when some real-estate values dropped in 1974. REIT difficulties were greatly exacerbated by the almost universally used adviser system which most REIT sponsors said was required by the 1960 act. Most REITs secured financial direction from advisers, who were usually sponsors of the REIT. Mutual funds and closed-end investment companies were usually managed by advisers, but their advisers were subject to detailed regulation by the Securities and Exchange Commission (SEC). The Investment Company Act of 1940 barred leveraging by borrowing, regulated use of public money in the investment fund, and required that advisory fees be reasonably organized and established. No such regulatory apparatus was authorized for REITs or their advisers, and the troubles that had been experienced in investment funds in the 1930s reappeared in REITs. When bargaining is as unequal as that between REIT shareholders and their "advisers," it requires some rules to make the process more ethical.

Most REIT advisory fees were scaled to percentages of the total assets of the REIT, thus encouraging financial advisers to borrow more at the risk of the shareholders, not of themselves. When prime-interest rates rose to 12 percent in 1974, REITs, which largely had short-term commercial loans, found themselves under staggering debt burdens. Sponsor-selected advisers had frequently allocated to the REITs the poorer properties on which the sponsor was not willing to lend. REITs also suffered from management conflicts. The REIT board had no real power, since external management by the financial firm that started the REIT also serviced it. REIT trustees were independent of advisers but they had little authority. REIT managements had interest in raising fees. Overcharges were estimated at $100 million.

Many REIT trustees prohibited their officers or employees from dealing with the trust, but made lesser limitations on the advisory firm, which actually made the decisions. Self-dealings of REITs with advisory firms were common. The only formal regulation of REITs came from the states, where it was generally not well done. The midwestern Securities Commissioners Association produced a policy statement but it was formally enacted only in eight states and was often disregarded.

REITs were established slowly at first, but made many large public offerings from 1969 to 1974. They rode through the 1966 and 1969 stock-market drops rather well. But they bottomed out in 1974, a recession year that was especially difficult for real estate. In 1973, REIT share prices declined 41 percent, whereas stocks declined by only 16 percent. Dividends, of course, dropped precipitately in 1974. In 1974 REIT stocks dropped 73 percent while the stock market went down 30 percent. Since 1974 REIT prices have recovered somewhat; in early 1978 they were 29 percent above the 1973 value.

Of greatest ethical interest in the REIT debacle are the built-in conflicts of interest in the adviser structure. Most high-ranking corporate executives have some shares or options to buy shares in their companies; executives have some personal interest in their corporations, whereas most REIT adviser staff held only a few shares in the REIT. REIT shareholders were informed only of the total cost of advisory services, not of top individual salaries, as are corporation shareholders. A majority of REIT trustees were "independent," but were in fact chosen by the sponsoring firm, which also chose the advisory service. The fees of REIT advisers were also full of potential conflicts of interest. The total of nonadvisory as well as advisory payments made REIT advising one of the best-paid businesses of the country. Eventual REIT board revolts, class-action suits, pressure from lenders, anxiety for the reputation of the sponsoring firm, and perhaps some ethical considerations have resulted in changes in the advisory system.

Bank and insurance-company sponsors often imposed a right of first refusal on their REITs. The sponsor could have the loan first if it wished it. Some sponsors were more generous, participating in 10 percent or 20 percent of REIT loans. There were substantial examples of self-dealing among REITs and their trustees, or among REITs and their advisers. These connections were usually disclosed. When trouble came some of the sponsors, especially the banks, went through real difficulty to assume REIT loans in order to maintain their own reputations.

Will competition straighten out the REITs? Schotland, following the mutual-company analogy, believes that some regulations would help the industry. He grants that the SEC has been less than dynamic in pursuing the few powers it had over REITS or in asking for new powers, but believes that the public interest and the interest of the REITs would be served by regulations like those for mutual funds. It is a judgment in line with American ethical trends that REITs should not have been established with the conflicts of interest that existed between them, the advisory services, and the sponsors. At the very least, they deserved the autonomy of judgment that an ethical outlook increasingly demands for corporate sponsors and managers. Not all conflicts of interest are bad, but the REIT advisory-system conflicts were almost designed to encourage mishandling.

The REITs have had an unhappy history, although some of them are returning to health in the 1980s because of inflation. As of early 1978, nine were bankrupt and fourteen of the fifty largest had negative net worth.

History of Security Sales

Slightly later than but parallel to the growth of the land business, another major source of ethical problems developed, the sale of securities in business enterprises. In this field, Americans could not use English law as a precedent, but had to solve new problems. As the nineteenth century progressed, a variety of manufacturing concerns, railroads, and later banks and insurance corporations were formed. The states for a time moved slowly on granting corporate charters but by the time of the Civil War were granting them freely. Today it is probable that over 90 percent of most business is conducted through corporate organizations, almost all of which are chartered by state laws, frequently Delaware or New Jersey laws. All such corporations have issued shares of stock; needless to say, shareholders are anxious to see their shares rise in value.

The large number of financial panics in American history have frequently had bad economic results, but all were not necessarily a result of ethical lapses. The lack of laws or government or industry regulations to prevent market "corners," the lack of a stable monetary supply, the absence of a central bank, the weakness of banks and trust companies, and the lack of regular auditing and supervision of financial enterprise were all causes of American financial unrest. Though unethical actions may have contributed to many of these difficulties, the sins were more of omission than of commission, and were often a result of the lack of appropriate governmental action to ensure stable and honest financial operations.

Almost all financial losses were expensive to shareholders, and sometimes to bondholders and employees. Personal losses like those of professional speculators Daniel Drew and William C. Durant could be attributed to the risks of the game. Speculation is perhaps necessary for fast buildup of a free-enterprise economy. Some men will win; some will lose. The issues are not necessarily ethical. However, a major ethical problem that goes back to the thousands-of-years-old tradition of fair representation of facts to buyers is whether the financial reports of speculating corporations to their shareholders are fair and adequate. In the nineteenth-century United States, which accepted most business ethics without much question, the speculator was singled out for criticism. The customary view was that investors helped the common good by helping business. Speculators made profits but helped no one. Andrew Carnegie advised would-be gamblers to avoid speculation and go to gambling houses where "they cheat fair."[5]

Even if accounting practices are fair, what right does a corporate head have to risk the funds of bondholders and shareholders, the jobs of employees, and the economic welfare of host communities in speculative ventures? There are a variety of answers to this question depending on circumstances. Most enterprises are started as at least partial gambles, and this is not necessarily unethical. If, however, a new executive or new board of directors takes an established, steady business and quickly puts it into a highly speculative situation, an ethical question is raised. Neither shareholders nor employees anticipated such a venture, and both may be economically damaged. Board action and a report to shareholders seem minimal protection for present or prospective shareholders.

Courts of law have slowly built some legal ethical principles pertaining to speculative operations. The judges know that risk-taking may be essential to economic progress, and that holders or buyers of securities may be entitled to "expectation damages" if a seller delays unduly on delivery. Similar decisions have been made regarding dealings in commodities. The newer view of contracts as strictly legal documents that courts should enforce literally has encouraged transactions that might prove to be of speculative values.[6]

The "prudent investor" rule adopted by the Massachusetts court in 1830 permitted the investment of trust properties in banks or stocks subject to the degree of care, diligence, and skill a prudent man would use in handling his own property. It slowly became a general rule, establishing a new ethic.[7]

It was and is still true that an executive or director who speculates too heavily with the property of the company owned by his shareholders may face court action for fraud and negligence.[8] But there are not clear legal or ethical rules to determine what is undue speculation.

Marketing of Securities

There are very ethical uses of markets for securities as well as for commodities. Well-organized markets may help avoid disorderly conditions in which the price of a security or commodity may fluctuate wildly as investors receive alarming or favorable news. Markets usually develop aids in securing information that decrease uncertainty about basic values of an asset. In an impersonalized market, trade practices are standardized, so it is easier to determine the risk of default, and it is easier to enforce contracts. Speculative holding of inventories may reduce swings in commodity prices. Market liquidity contributes to competition and reduces the possibility of monopolies and price manipulation. Techniques of market organization such as low margin requirements and clearing houses promote market liquidity.[9]

It should also be noted that markets generate their own ethics. The broker who has knowingly unloaded low quality securities on his customers, will faithfully complete a disastrous purchase or sale made on the floor of the exchange evidenced only by holding one finger in the air. The reason for the difference in ethical attitudes is simple. The stock exchange would bar a broker who reneged, whereas the usual customer has no such authority.

Methods of selling securities in the United States have varied from the completely unethical to the highly ethical. In the last half of the nineteenth century, fake-stock exploitations were so frequent as to be the subject of many articles and books.[10] Large-scale sales of fraudulent stock continued into the twentieth century. In the 1920s in New York and Chicago over 100 *bucket shops* cheated customers out of many millions of dollars. Customers paid from 10 percent to 33 percent more to buy low-grade stocks. Orders to buy were issued by the *bucketeer*, but sell orders of the same amount were usually issued too. The customer's account was closed out if the stock dropped below the margin requirements, a drop in which the bucketeer sometimes aided. If too many stock values rose, the bucketeer might leave town. Sometimes the bucketeer sold valueless stock. Sometimes he built up the value of nearly worthless stock. Prosecution in New York in the 1920s was not likely to be successful if bucketeers made appropriate payments to Arnold Rothstein, who was a major link between organized crime and city government.[11] Similar bucket shops existed all over the country. Most large brokers opposed the bucket shops, but a few helped them to complete securities transactions.

Bucket shops have been largely closed down, sometimes by SEC action, sometimes by state "blue sky" commissions, or by local prosecutors. "Boiler-room" sales tactics are still used and fraudulent stocks are still sold by individuals, but the blatant overadvertising that occurred in the first third of the twentieth century has been reduced.

Watered Stock and Unethical Stock Transfers

There are many ways in which stock transfers have been used to secure funds unethically. Chapter 3 referred to the use of railroad stock to finance new construction, providing unethical gains for railroad executives. Similar abuses have happened in other fields of industry. A leading San Francisco banker was found drowned in San Francisco Bay after his directors discovered that he had overissued the stock of his bank by several million dollars and used the money for himself.[12] In 1901, U.S. Steel Corporation was launched with $508 million in common stock, $510 million in preferred stock and $304 million in bonds. Henry Clews refers to these stocks as "heavily watered."[13] The investment-bankers' syndicate headed by J.P. Morgan put up only $25 million of its own money and received a 200-percent dividend. In three years time, the stock was worth only 8-7/8 in contrast to a 1901 offering of 24 to 25.[14]

The ethical problem here is more easily described than solved. The House of Morgan doubtless justified its large fees and the liberal treatment of the companies included in the merger on a market basis—"If we can sell it, the price of the stock is justified." But there may have been partners in the Morgan firm who wondered if this overcapitalization was really ethical. Persons who bought stock on Morgan representations lost heavily. The House of Morgan violated the three-thousand-year-old Biblical injunction, "if thou sell to thy neighbor or buy of thy neighbor's hand, ye shall not wrong one another."[15] Morgan was not the only one creating ethical problems. E.H. Harriman in 1906 ordered very generous dividends on Union

Pacific and Southern Pacific railroad stocks and increased his personal fortune by $10 million through the rise in stock values resulting from these
dividends.[16]

Samuel Insull paid $7.54 a share for common stock of Insull Utility In-
vestments in January 1929 which in August was selling out of the corporation at 149-¼ a share. Thus the public was paying ten or fifteen times the
price at which Insull had bought.[17] Cornelius Vanderbilt, after securing control of the New York Central Railroad, drove the price of the stock up and
down as he wished, and as it helped his pocketbook, according to Clews.[18]
Such use of a company's management role to force security prices up and
down for personal benefit is unethical and is today illegal. Such actions certainly seem to be in violation of the philosophy of commercial honesty outlined in Leviticus 19:35, "ye shall do no unrighteousness in judgment, in
measures of length, of weight, or of quantity." Stock transactions like the
ones just described would be found by an observant SEC today, and the
defrauding executive would probably be punished. The Pujo Committee, a
1913 House of Representatives subcommittee on concentration of money
and credit, found a great concentration of financial control and recommended government supervision of investment bankers.

Although the Pujo Committee's recommendations were not passed
directly, they did influence other legislation like the Federal Reserve Act of
1914, and forced the investment bankers to rethink their positions. In January 1914, J.P. Morgan, Jr. announced that he and his partners would resign from the boards of directors of twenty-seven corporations.[19] The fear
of legislation thus helped to bring about an ethic against one kind of conflict of interest in security issues. At the same time, state "blue sky" laws
were being passed, largely to compel disclosures of financing conditions and
to further regulate security issues. Better-business bureaus, which were business supported, worked to secure passage of these acts. The acts were poorly
enforced by the states.

Holding Companies and Investment Trusts

The pyramiding of holding companies or the establishment of certain kinds
of investment trusts by corporations can be as ethically dangerous as the
direct mishandling of securities. Any such subsidiary lessens the ethical
responsibility of the parent company. The holding company, a company that
exists primarily to hold parts or all of the stocks of other companies, flour-
ished in the 1920s. There were ninety-two pure holding companies listed and
active in the New York State Exchange in 1929; fifteen had existed in 1910.[20]

Holding companies were used for a variety of purposes. Some may have
had the genuine economic purpose of bringing together related companies

to offer joint services, or pool electric power. Many of those which developed in the 1920s were simply a means of maintaining control over many corporations with a minimum of investment. Some were compounds of various purposes.

James C. Bonbright and Gardiner C. Means in 1932 listed four major charges against the unregulated holding company: it encouraged "unwieldy and uneconomic" forms of consolidation; it facilitated stock watering, capital inflation, and similar forms of misfinancing that injure consumers and impose losses on small investors; it made for secrecy of corporate accounts and made it easier to manipulate constituent companies in the interest of controlling management; and its service charges enabled holding companies to financially drain the operating companies.[21] To judge the validity of these charges (all except the first dealing with unethical deception of stock buyers), the activities of one holding-company will be reviewed. The Insull structure of utilities that collapsed in 1932 is widely known. Samuel Insull, who owned several small utilities, formed the Middle West Utilities Company in 1912 to help raise more capital. Insull so organized the company that outside buyers paid for it, but he kept 50,000 shares, which gave him control. One of his companies furnished management services to local companies and collected almost 100-percent profit. Insull's companies sold securities to each other at high prices. Local utilities were bought at three times their value.[22] The holding-company structure was almost incomprehensible. Insull's brokers also bought and sold shares of his companies in an effort to stimulate the market.

It is probably true that Insull built up his complex structure of holding companies in part because of the general economic euphoria of the 1920s—the belief that a new economic era had dawned. But it is hard to believe that Insull was not also aware of the fact that these complex levels of companies defeated effective government regulation of utilities, confused customers, and vastly increased the shares that went to Insull and his associates. On balance, the ethical motivation was faulty. The Great Crash of 1929 proved that the financing was also faulty.

As a result of cases similar to Insull's the Public Utility Holding Company Act of 1935 was designed to eliminate the use of the holding companies as tools for speculation in the utilities field.[23]

The investment trust as developed in the 1920s was a financial variant of the holding company. There was sometimes elaborate pyramiding, as in the Goldman-Sachs organization of several companies that private purchasers probably did not understand. Shares were also sold to the public at a price well above that paid by the organizers of the trust. Handsome fees were charged for "organizing" these companies, some of which had no genuine economic function. Benjamin Graham and David Dodd tell us that the early investment trusts abandoned research and analysis, "finding prominent companies with a rising trend of earnings and then buying their shares regardless of price."[24]

"Corners" and "Bears"

From the 1830s to the Great Depression there were a number of successful attempts to *corner* stocks on the New York Stock Exchange. As the price of a stock was driven up, prudent but unwary men would sell the stock short. When there were more short sales than stock to be bought, the managers of the corner could set their own price; though at times the stock exchange would establish a high but not exorbitant price. The breakdown of a cornering effort could also cause huge losses to the *bulls* trying to engineer the corner.

Bear pressure was sometimes used to force down the value of a stock. A bear can pound away at the value of a stock by selling blocks of stock at a price lower than the public is willing to pay. This selling process frightens out timid holders. When the price is low enough, the operator buys large quantities of the stock at a lower level, then pushes the price back up to a more normal market level at which he can sell at a substantial profit.

A somewhat similar operation can bring the public to drive a stock price upward. The manipulator may buy a few shares to drive the price upward, let the price drop a little, and then buy again. The process is repeated until public support comes. When a high enough price is obtained, the manipulator may sell all his holdings.[25]

Mid-nineteenth century battles between stock-market bears and bulls were sometimes large and destructive; fights more for prestige than for constructive efforts to build up the economy.[26] Innocent people may have been ruined by the rise and fall of stocks in the hands of some amoral operators. Both of these types of pressure are now illegal, although the Securities and Exchange Commission does not find or prosecute all cases. Such artificial actions serve little useful free-market purpose, but are tricks designed to enrich a few people; they violate ethical injunctions for truth and fairness in business transactions. It is interesting that the stock-exchange machinery for such actions developed long before they were forbidden. "Cornering" stocks may have seemed like a fair game to some of the participants, reflecting the lower ethical levels of the later nineteenth century.

Legislative Control of Investment Banking

The Pecora Committee, a 1932 subcommittee of the U.S. Senate Banking and Currency Committee, recommended better disclosure requirements and regulation of investment houses. The committee hearings were not impartial in nature but they did uncover evidence of investment-banker practices that several brokers granted were much in need of reform.[27]

New Deal legislation in 1933, 1934, and 1935 established the Securities and Exchange Commission, reduced holding companies and investment trusts, and made it possible to require larger margins. The stock-market crash and the Depression taught Americans some ethical lessons, at least temporarily. But major and minor programs to cheat investors continued to appear, such as the McKesson-Robbins drug-company case in the 1930s, the forced reorganization of the American Stock Exchange in the early 1960s, the Investors Overseas Service scandals late in the 1960s, the Equity Funding scandal in the early 1970s, and the bankruptcy of brokerage firms in the 1970s.

How did the investment bankers react to the New Deal legislation? In the 1930s, the president of the Investment Bankers Association (IBA) announced opposition to several features of the Securities Act, especially the provision for civil liability of security issuers and underwriting houses. It also opposed enactment of the provision of the Banking Act of 1933 that required separation of security affiliates from commercial banks. However, under the National Recovery Act in 1934, the IBA tried to make the investment banking code one of the best. Reformers and conservatives alike probably now admit that the governmental actions of the early 1930s plus the shock of the stock-market crash have helped raise the ethical quality of investment banking in the United States.

"Boiler Rooms"

In the 1950s there were several exposés of Wall Street "boiler rooms," offices from which high-pressure salesmen sold worthless or near worthless securities by telephone.[28] In 1956, unscrupulous boiler-room salesmen cheated many thousands of people out of an estimated $150 million.[29] Estimates were that $350 million of nearly valueless stock was sold from 1950 to 1956. Some five hundred high-pressure boiler-room salesmen were operating in New York, some of them ex-prisoners. Rewards were high; one sales manager drew $150,000 in commissions from a single boiler room and one salesman pocketed $75,000 for six months' work.

In 1958, an organized-crime-supported boiler room under the name of Lincoln Securities secured stock of an almost worthless Canadian mining company and sold $500,000 of it with various misleading statements. In this case the government secured fast action and in 1960 the boiler-room leader was sentenced to three and one-half years in prison with the promise of additional sentences.

Hillel Black quite rightly points out that this type of crime occurred in part because it was a time of speculation, with resultant substantial increases in the price of cheaper stocks, which made small investors anxious to get into the market. He also points out that organized crime had a good deal of money to invest in new businesses. Boiler rooms required such money.[30] The involvement of organized crime usually changed the boiler rooms from partly legitimate to completely crooked operations. A considerable number of illegitimate securities came from foreign sources; often Canadian or American issues originated from "Swiss type" trusts.

Troubles on the Stock Exchange

In 1951 the Congress asked the SEC to make a full study of Wall Street. The illegal manipulations discovered were substantial. One well-educated swindler fled to Brazil to escape the SEC. Two other men had illegally sold over 1 million shares of nine corporations with a total value of over $10 million. The president of the American Stock Exchange Edward T. McCormick, a well-educated man who had worked his way up on the SEC staff, was forced to resign because he had let Alexander Guterma pay $5,000 in gambling debts for him at a time when Guterma was seeking a listing for his Shawana Development Corporation. The SEC report, which was highly critical of the American Stock Exchange, pointed out that McCormick had been a salesman, not an administrator of the exchange. Specialists on the exchange were both buying on their own and creating a market—a clear conflict of interest. The SEC reported a clear lack of adequate rules of conduct on the American Stock Exchange.

Black concludes that the stock-exchange pirates of the 1960s were not nearly as bad as the manipulators of the "lawless years" of the 1950s.[31] If so, American business ethics in security sales are improving. This is probably true but there should be concern about the slowness of the improvement process.

In the late 1960s many brokerage firms found themselves badly behind in their "back-office" work, so that several firms were forced into bankruptcy or forced mergers with other concerns that needed support funds from the stock exchange before they took on the obligations of the disappearing firms. Stock-exchange firms borrowed on securities owned by customers, most of which were classified in the records of the firms by security issue, not by customer ownership. In 1969, ten key firms had pledged "in error" a total of $87 million in customers' fully-paid securities.[32] Much more than most industries, the securities industry was financed by its customers' cash and securities.[33] The failure or near failure of several brokerage houses thus threatened disaster to many investors. Yet In 1970 the president of the New York Stock Exchange publicly said that the exchange's Special Trust Fund was not near depletion, and that the exchange information on member firms' condition was adequate. Within two or three months the exchange's Special Trust Fund was more than committed. Poor records of the securities businesses resulted in extensive thefts of securities in 1967 and 1968. Even some New York Stock Exchange members supported "shell" corporations during this period while the exchange president maintained that excessive speculation did not exist. Although the exchange had legal responsibility to enforce antifraud and antimanipulative legal provisions on its members for off-exchange action, it never did so.

The New York Stock Exchange in the early 1960s was operating under a fair degree of home rule with general approval of the Securities and Exchange Commission. The exchange recognized its responsibility by making considerable efforts to aid solvent brokers to merge with insolvent ones so that customers's cash and security accounts might be safeguarded. Certain individual members performed a public service in keeping the crisis from becoming a national controversy.[34] However, several small firms failed, without any effort by the exchange to have the customers' accounts taken over by solvent firms. The stock-exchange sins were of omission rather than commission. The exchange knew that a number of brokers had too much business to handle, but its management failed to take action to protect the shareholders of these corporations.

Christopher Elias believes that the large amount of money received by Wall Street firms in the late 1960s was spent on private pursuits, not on building stronger firms. He notes that in 1968, the year of the back-office breakdown, an exchange survey found 14 Wall Street firms planned to train 2,250 new salesmen. It was a year of many speculative new issues; in view of the inability of the firms to handle the securities they had, these expenditures for more sales are ethically questionable.[35]

Wall Street research, according to Elias, is mostly a sales tool. Corporate executives hire financial public-relations firms that give rosy reports on a firm, which reports stimulate buying of corporate stock, and create higher stock prices for the executive who has options to buy at existing or lower prices. This kind of "research" is hardly ethical, even violating the rule in Leviticus that the seller should be honest with the buyer.

Elias cites a good many instances in which salesmen violate the rights of their customers. One is the practice of *churning* or buying and selling the customers' stocks in order to secure more commissions. Others have used customers' accounts for their own purposes. The stock exchange will discipline in such cases but sometimes rather too easily. "Tales of loose ethics and downright dishonesty are endless, as official records of the Stock Exchange and the SEC show. It is practically a daily occurrence for each to release reports of brokers' suspensions, fines, and firings."[36] Readers of the *Wall Street Journal* in 1981 found a continuing series of similar offenses.

The record of the New York Stock Exchange is especially disappointing because of the efforts for over forty years of both government and some businesses to secue self-regulation in the securities industry.[37] Is there not some fault in the ethical education of the leaders who have so often been unable to fulfill the responsibilities of their very significant businesses. The unwillingness of the exchange to regulate its members has damaged the general standing of business in the community.

After disastrous losses in the 1910s, the 1930s, and the early 1970s, American securities have still greatly enhanced in value, financed important productive companies, and enriched millions of shareholders. The ethics of Wall Street have certainly improved. What, then, is the real concern about the losses from the trusts, the holding companies, the bull-and-bear playing, the corners, or the land exploitation? The most important disadvantage of these actions is the lack of public confidence in a system of free American business that they have caused.

Conflicts of Interest in the Securities Business

Problems with security sales are not yet ended. In a recent Twentieth Century Fund report, a lengthy study of commercial-bank trust departments, many conflicts of interest were found to still exist in security marketing, some of which would be very difficult to eliminate. Only a few of the more important conflicts will be summarized here (see also the section on conflict of interest in chapter 3).

If banks sponsor investment companies, there is a danger that the banks may be weakened in order to support failing investment funds; banks may also dump bank-underwritten securities into controlled portfolios at the cost of the investment funds. If a bank sponsors a corporate-trust business, it may have to press for bankruptcy in the interest of the trust while it wishes to keep the company alive to salvage credits in the interest of the bank's commercial side.

Bank trusts have owned sizable proportions of securities in small, closely held companies. May a bank use its power as a lender to acquire such companies? Should it dispose of the assets of such companies if a customer relationship is damaged as a result? Available evidence seems to indicate that banks tend to view such holdings as investments rather than control. The bank may refrain from control other than of mergers, which banks view as investor business. There is some evidence of interlocking directorates but this is not adequate evidence of a desire for control. Some banks have limits of buying not more than 10 percent of the stock of a company.

A desire for customer accommodation may lead a bank to buy securities from a customer corporation for the bank's trust account. The potential for abuse is not great if the bank secures adequate valuations or competitive bids. However, pressures on the bank to stay in the good graces of the company management may be severe. Sometimes too much of a pension fund is invested in the stock of a single company. Mergers frequently lead to pressure on banks to support either side with its trust shares. The problem of selling trust-owned securities of customer corporations has been troublesome, but the increased autonomy of trust departments is reducing it.

Before the failure of the Penn-Central Transportation Corporation in 1970, three major banks, Chase Manhattan, Morgan Guaranty Trust, and Continental Illinois, sold over a million shares of Penn-Central stock. Some have criticized this action as a use of inside information; others have wondered that such sophisticated banks stayed so long in ownership of the mismanaged Penn-Central. In either case there was a potential conflict of interest.

A number of court cases have turned on the erection of a *wall* which keeps information from flowing between the trust departments and the commercial operations of banks. The purpose of the "wall" is to keep information secured in making loans from being available to trust departments in determining how to handle stocks; it would be unfair and illegal if banks used their commercial-loan knowledge to buy or sell stocks ahead of other purchasers or sellers. It is not legally clear, however, that this responsibility to keep an information barrier (under SEC Rule 10b-5) saves the bank from liability for not using information to sell trust stocks on time. The use of such walls continues to create many questions. The barrier is obviously penetrated in some cases; not all banks have made such restriction of knowledge part of their rules.

It has been proposed that most of these possibilities of conflict of interest in commercial-bank trust departments could be reduced by attempting to prevent further combinations of major trust banks, by enlargement of competition, by limits on some forms of conflict, by preservation of class-action possibilities for smaller customers, and by increased public disclosure.[38] A recommendation of strong ethical education of bank employees who administer fiduciary relationships could be added to or substituted for these proposals.

Private pension funds, the overwhelming majority of which are sponsored and funded by corporations for the benefit of their employees, probably have assets well over $200 billion.[39] The fundamental conflict of interest in these funds is between the board of the corporation which handles the funds and the pension-plan participants. The Federal Employee Retirement Income Security Act of 1974 (ERISA) is the first federal legislation to address this problem. The United Mine Workers' welfare and retirement fund was flagrantly misused. In 1971 trustees (union- and company-appointed but with union psychological leadership) deposited 44 percent of fund assets, $75 million, in a union-owned bank with *no* interest paid, clearly an unethical action.

The most obvious conflict of interest has been the investment of part of the assets of a pension trust in stocks or other assets of a company. In the case of the conglomerate Genesco, stock dropped from 60 in 1965 to 6 in 1974, with great loss to pension funds. Pension funds had been used to drive up the price of stock in order to buy additions to the conglomerate through exchange of stock, a process that today would be illegal.

The new pension law (ERISA) has required open disclosure of pension-fund transactions, which will limit much of the inside trading with corporations. Interlocking directorates present the bank with more of a dilemma than a conflict. Reciprocity of deposits is now said to be a thing of the past.

Investment banks, through their intermediate position between the stock-issuing company and buyers of the new stock issue, are automatically put into a conflict-of-interest position.[40] Theirs is a risky venture, and they usually charge highly for it. If, however, the underwriting function and the retail brokerage were separated, they would have to form joint syndicates to sell securities. Fortunately, the entry of Merrill-Lynch into the investment banking field has made it more competitive. The questions of what is due diligence on the part of the underwriter, what is a good prospectus, how the stock issue should be priced, what is the underwriter's compensation (3 to 13 percent of revenue from the stock offering), and how to handle a hot issue all include possible conflicts of interest. Nicholas Wolfson concludes that more disclosure of investment bankers' operations is the most useful reform. He also suggests ethical education.

There are further suggestions for decreasing the danger of this conflict of interest. For example, Wolfson suggests that every prospectus of a new security issue should include a section on the conflicts of interest of the underwriter. Similarly, the underwriter's decision on price of the new security tempts him to buy cheap and sell dear, but his responsibilities to the company and the buyers are great. The SEC has ordered that the price be estimated the day before SEC approval, and that the prospectus include a "bona fide estimate of the maximum offering price."[41] Neither provision will completely eliminate the underwriter's conflict of interest.

Broker-dealers also suffer from a basic conflict between their desire to serve their customers fully and their support of the price of the stock that belongs to them.[42] Goldman-Sachs in 1970 was still pushing Penn-Central stock to its customers while it was getting rid of its own. Brokerage houses often make a good deal of interest on customers' balances. Very occasionally brokerage houses promote stock of questionable value to customers. Sometimes investment brokers have promoted commercial paper (notes of indebtedness) that was questionable. Bank-customer relations may affect the purchase or sale of the customer company's securities by the bank trust department. "Going private" may involve unfair treatment of minority shareholders whose stock values shrink. The ability of stock specialists to outbid and underoffer the customer has been questioned. Block-trading positioners also may get into situations in which their customers are mishandled. Margin accounts may be abused against the customer. Mutual funds sometimes benefit their investment advisers and underwriters through reciprocal brokerage.

Conflicts of interest like those described in *Abuse on Wall Street* are not easy to eliminate, and probably can never be entirely eliminated. The investment bankers' setting of prices for new issues is a conflict that cannot be eliminated if new capital is to be secured. But efforts should be made, and are made, by the SEC and the courts to eliminate the most obvious conflicts such as reciprocity between deposits and commissions or use of loan-department information to help trust-department operations. Further-progress will come slowly from court suits and SEC actions. More rapid progress would come from a general program of educating the financial community in its own ethics. Such a program could lead to the development of new ethical standards for most of the problems discussed in this section.

Is Disclosure of Corporate Finance an Ethical Necessity?

The fundamental ethical purpose of SEC regulations on disclosure is to give information of a corporation's financial condition so that possible stock purchasers, stockholders, lenders, suppliers, and other purchasers have equal opportunities to know what they are dealing with. It would clearly be a violation of the ethical tradition of truth telling if corporate executives were allowed to give false impressions to shareholders, whose money was being used, or to banks, whose money the executives want to use, or to suppliers, to whom the executives may soon owe money. The whole theory of corporate disclosure is to present the financial facts. However, this theory is often questioned and there is much dispute about what constitutes adequate disclosure.

William H. Beaver writes that the competition of financial analysts results in security prices that reflect a broad set of information. Recent trends toward diversification may reduce investor demand for information about specific firms. Should the SEC impose disclosure requirements on companies to accommodate investors who have chosen not to diversify? It is clear that few individual investors use complete SEC reports on corporations; only analysts and institutions go to that trouble. The statutory concept that disclosure should be limited to "material" information is not very clear; SEC rules and the courts interpret it to mean information needed by the average prudent investor. If it should be decided to give the individual investor a larger amount of information, the move would be counter to the current trend toward recognizing the professional. Beaver concludes that the amount of disclosure should be an economic issue: Will rules for details of disclosure damage the investor more than they help him?[43] Lauren K. Newton believes that more than economic analysis is needed; the accountant determining the amount of disclosure must also consider the possible costs of liability for failing to make disclosure of what may prove to be a material item.[44] Does legal liability help make an ethic? It probably does.

Arguments against statutory disclosure requirements are raised by George J. Benston in an interesting comparison of disclosure requirements in the United Kingdom and the United States. Not surprisingly, the United Kingdom places more emphasis on the responsibility of the stock exchange and of the accounting profession (which started in Great Britain where there is greater emphasis on quasi-public actions by professional or business groups). The United States places more emphasis on government regulation, partly because Americans view ethical problems more in legalistic terms, and partly because our antitrust laws limit business self-regulation. The greater emphasis on ethical education in the United Kingdom may also encourage the use of quasi-public agencies.

Benston reviews several recent theoretical analyses and cost-benefit analyses of a number of benefits that presumably come from governmental regulation of securities. These include the obligation of government to enforce contracts, a concept of fairness in dealings among people, protection of nonshareholders who are affected by companies, improved efficiency of resource allocation, improved administration of government, and the public's and employees' "right to know." In each case, according to Benston, the analyses show that these benefits are not a necessary result of disclosure of financial information of companies. He places special emphasis on studies of stock-market responses, which do not seem to be affected by changes in accounting methods, or by reported accounting data, or by manipulation of securities pools. Share prices seem to change independently of published corporate information. The information on financial statements is generally known before the statements are available to the public. There is evidence in the United Kingdom as well as in the United States that adequate financial statements would generally be available without government requirement.

Benston's analysis concludes that SEC requirements have not decreased the amount of private placement of securities. He finds rankings almost perfectly correlated—the greater the bias imposed by the SEC, the higher the percentage of privately placed debt. He does not believe that having detailed financial statements is useful to employees. He does grant that if required disclosure of financial information and auditing of statements reduces the incidence of scandal, "the benefit from avoiding circumstances in which punitive or special interest legislation can be passed may exceed the cost (of disclosure and auditing) to private corporations."[45] There is an ethic that the requirements of disclosure may help fulfill, that is, confidence of the public in the most important of American institutions, our commercial corporations.

If Benston is correct, the Western ethical tradition that stipulates that the seller should not deceive the buyer is not expandable into the position that the corporation should tell its shareholders in its financial reports about everything of importance that has happened to it during the period under review. His evidence of the heavy cost of existing SEC requirements is impressive; in fact, the SEC has partly recognized this fact by reducing the disclosure requirements for smaller companies. Yet some want fuller disclosure. This is apparently another area in which a generally accepted ethic has not yet evolved. So long as America remains a competitive society, there is not likely to be an ethic that all technical research results must be revealed in each quarterly report. But a quarterly report that does not mention a sharp drop in sales during the quarter would be ethically very questionable.

In the last decade there has also been discussion of extension of the SEC power over disclosure to force corporations to release information about matters that do not have great effect on corporations' financial positions, but are or may be of substantial public-policy importance. Does the ethical requirement of frankness in business dealings make such nonfinancial disclosure a matter of ethical importance? The SEC did require disclosure of all bribes of public officials, in the United States and abroad, a disclosure that resulted in legislation forbidding most of such bribes. This legislation is discussed in chapter 14. The SEC has been asked by environmental groups to force disclosure of corporate acts affecting the environment, but has avoided the acceptance of that responsibility.

Is it ethically desirable that the SEC or the courts or the Congress force corporations to disclose possible criminal actions? As Russell B. Stevenson, Jr., comments, "One does not have to be irredeemably cynical to recognize the virtual impossibility of operating any large American corporation within the enormously complex, confusing, and occasionally contradictory body of legal rules to which its activities are subject, without continually being at least in technical violation of a few of them, however conscientious the management may be in its efforts to comply with the law."[46] Stevenson suggests that disclosure should be compelled only when the crime is important enough to subject the corporation and corporate officers to substantial public censure.

Insider Information

The Securities Exchange Act of 1934 forbids sales of shares by owners, directors, or officers of a corporation within six months of purchase.

SEC Rule 10b-5 forbids any act that defrauds or deceives any person in connection with the purchase or sale of any security. Suit may be brought in federal court by a shareholder who believes that fraudulent action was perpetrated against him by officials or directors. In the 1964 Cady-Roberts case, the sale of shares by a director, just before a dividend cut and a telephone call to his firm that made more sales just after the cut, was held by the Securities and Exchange Commission to be a violation of Section 10b of the SEC act of 1934 and of SEC Rule 10a-5.[47] In the Texas-Gulf Sulphur case in the late 1960s, district and appeals courts supported the Securities and Exchange Commission in ordering restitution of profits made from insider trading while there was a slight delay in announcing the discovery of important bodies of ore.

Henry G. Manne has attacked the SEC position on insider trading. He cites original defenses of the rule against insider trading, most of which view such trading as unfair use of corporate information to the advantage of the insider, and to the disadvantage of the ordinary shareholder who lacks such information. None of these defenses satisfy Manne, who points out that there were no such legal rules prior to 1909. He grants that a "special facts" rule allows action if there is some danger of fraud against shareholders by corporate management.[48]

Manne's arguments against the insider-trading rule include his conclusion that shareholders will receive the benefit of good news in their shares regardless of such trading. Almost no insiders could receive full value from insider information; possession of all shares of stock would be necessary. If free use of all information is permitted, inside information cannot be accurately distributed to a wide variety of shareholders. The speculator who has purchased a stock because he gambled on good news is the outside trader who may lose from insider trading. Manne also believes that the role of entrepreneur in a large corporation should be recognized and rewarded by gains on the basis of insider information. This is a reward for being what economist Frank Knight called the organizer of uncertainties. Manne also notes that a number of outsiders have inside information: corporate raiders, executives of major suppliers, or buyers may know of information that will affect stock prices. It is difficult to see how their trading could be forbidden.

Manne's position has been countered by Roy A. Schotland's strong defense of the ban on insider trading.[49] Schotland points out that in the Securities Exchange Act, Congress called for fairness in no less than six sections, several of them relevant to this problem. The Manne thesis fails to consider that restraint on insider trading helps "the quality of our society and our human relationships." Earlier court decisions and several decades under the federal securities laws have built up animosity toward insider trading. But more important is the public's confidence in the stock market.

If a large number of persons are to "invest in America" by buying common stocks, the market must "not only be fair, but also appear to be fair." Contrary to Manne's view, empirical studies suggest that insider trading does not have the effect of causing stock prices to reflect values more accurately; insider trading is rarely large enough to have such an effect. Schotland denies Manne's argument that long-term investors are not hurt by insider trading because price of the stock is not important for them. Price is important to any stock investor. Insider trading should be unlawful because the opportunity for it may be a means for delaying disclosure, disclosure which has been the goal of both SEC regulations and self-regulatory bodies. Legal insider trading is likely to increase the temptation for stock manipulation. Long-term shareholders are especially likely to feel aggrieved if they sell shares while executives are withholding information to facilitate insider trading. The corporation's welfare may be affected adversely by insiders who make faulty judgments to aid their trading profits.

Short-term investors, or speculators, may gain from the increased attention to a stock caused by insider trading, but are their interests as important as those of the long-term investor? Insider trading on bad news simply means that the manager is rewarded for his failures. The entrepreneural act which Manne wants to reward is very hard to isolate. Confidential information may be leaked to nonentrepreneurs. There are better ways of rewarding entrepreneurship.

The arguments pro and con partly cancel themselves out but the balance appears to be clearly against insider trading. Corporate executives and directors should, like Caesar's wife, be above suspicion. A new ethic against insider trading is developing, at least among directors or officers or large shareholders. This ethic flows from the Western tradition that the seller should not deceive the buyer. In insider trading, the trader simply delays passing out information to his presumed ally, the shareholders, but the delay can amount to deception. The effort to eliminate insider trading is slowly gaining acceptance as an extension of this Western ethical tradition, although the problem of enforcement remains real.

Conclusions

Sales of land and securities are ethically troublesome areas. The superior knowledge of the vendor makes it easy for him to defraud the buyer. The latter, however, is often looking forward to a chance to oversell in his turn and make a capital gain. Government regulations are needed to eliminate the fraudulent aspects of the sales, but governments have difficulty in regulating because they do not know how to eliminate fraud without handicapping the free market.

Land sales have often been very speculative and buyers have lost large sums of money. Luckily, inflation and the growth of the country have reduced some of these losses. The ethics of land sales still leave much to be desired; in most states regulation of such sales has not been very effective. The REITs were unfortunately organized in a manner that increased conflict of interest on the part of sponsor-advisers, with unhappy results for most shareholders.

The sale of securities, especially in New York City, has been aided by organization of principal dealers, who have among themselves maintained a fair level of honesty. They have, however, often yielded to times of excessive economic euphoria, at times almost criminally neglected the keeping of their own records, and fairly consistently fought against governmental regulation. They have not been able to keep major speculators from damaging other persons in the market. Their record on conflict of interest has often been bad, using their advisory sales role to unload undesirable stocks. As a result, the brokers have not added to public confidence in their industry.

The role of speculators, that is, professional operators, has often had real ethical problems. Driving stock prices up and down involve deception and fraud; the concern for victims of such price variation has often been negligible.

Investment bankers are fewer, stronger, and more concerned about their reputations. However, they too have succumbed to economic euphoria. Their profit on some stock issues has been too large, but this is the kind of marketing transaction that is not easily regulated. Their effort to keep certain customers tied to them is less ethical. There is real ethical objection to financial blocs led by investment bankers, similar to the objections to the concentrated power of trusts.

Commercial banks have a large number of responsibilities for securities, which inevitably create conflicts of interest. There are a half-dozen types of cases in which banks have conflicts of interest; they talk of information "walls" between the loan and investment departments but there is skepticism about them. Some of these conflicts will continue, though there is a slow trend toward an ethic opposed to conflict of interest.

Corporate disclosure of financial information to shareholders (and of course to others) does not yet have a settled ethic. Regulations compelling disclosure are advanced by some scholars, opposed by others. Someday a compromise ethic should develop: the corporation will tell shareholders promptly of all major events, but not of trade secrets. Limitation of action on insider information is similarly subject to scholarly dispute. It is difficult to predict what kind of ethic will emerge.

Notes

1. Aaron M. Sakolski, *The Great American Land Bubble*, p. 191.

2. Thornton Bradshaw and David Vogel, *Corporations and Their Critics*, pp. 171 ff.

3. Sakolski, *The Great American Land Bubble*, pp. 182-183, 195, 228-229, 235, 260-261, 341.

4. Roy A. Schotland, "Real Estate Investment Trusts," in Twentieth Century Fund, *Abuse on Wall Street,* pp. 158-223.

5. Irvin G. Wylie, *The Self-Made Man*, p. 77.

6. Morton J. Horwitz, *The Transformation of American Law*, pp. 175-185.

7. Lawrence M. Friedman, *A History of American Law*, pp. 368-369.

8. Ibid., p. 452.

9. Joseph M. Burns, *A Treatise on Markets*, pp. 5-29.

10. H.J. Kenner, *The Fight for Truth in Advertising*, p. 13.

11. Nat Ferber, *I Found Out*, pp. 201-202.

12. Henry Clews, *Fifty Years on Wall Street*, p. 469.

13. Ibid., pp. 761-762.

14. Dana L. Thomas, *The Plungers and the Peacocks*, p. 68.

15. *The Bible*, Book of Leviticus 25:14.

16. Clews, *Fifty Years on Wall Street*, pp. 780-787.

17. Frederick Lewis Allen, *The Lords of Creation*, p. 283.

18. Clews, *Fifty Years on Wall Street*, p. 350.

19. Vincent P. Carosso, *Investment Banking in America*, p. 178.

20. Adolf A. Berle and Gardener C. Means, *The Modern Corporation and Private Property*, p. 205.

21. James C. Bonbright and Gardener C. Means, *The Holding Company*, pp. 153-154.

22. Allen, *The Lords of Creation*, pp. 266-303.

23. Thomas, *The Plungers and the Peacocks*, p. 241.

24. Benjamin Graham and David Dodd, *Security Analysis*, p. 356.

25. Thomas, *The Plungers and the Peacocks*, pp. 59-60.

26. Clews, *Fifty Years on Wall Street*, pp. 425-436.

27. Carosso, *Investment Banking in America*, pp. 153, 349.

28. Hillel Black, *The Watchdogs of Wall Street*.

29. Ibid., p. 54.

30. Ibid., pp. 74-75.

31. Ibid., p. 232.

32. Hurd, Baruch, *Wall Street: A Security Risk*, p. 37.

33. Elias, *Fleecing the Lambs*, pp. 208-209.

34. Baruch, *Wall Street*, p. 309.

35. Christopher Elias, *Fleecing the Lambs*.

36. Ibid., p. 111.

37. Baruch, *Wall Street*, pp. 298-322.

38. Edward S. Herman, "Commercial Bank Trust Department," in Twentieth Century Fund, *Abuse on Wall Street*, pp. 23-157.

39. John Brooks, "Corporate Pension Fund Asset Management," in Twentieth Century Fund, *Abuse on Wall Street*, pp. 224-266.

40. Nicholas Wolfson, "Investment Banking," in Twentieth Century Fund, *Abuse on Wall Street*, pp. 365-432.

41. Ibid., p. 381.

42. Martin Mayer, "Broker Dealer Firms," in Twentieth Century Fund, *Abuse on Wall Street*, pp. 433-497.

43. William H. Beaver, "Current Trends in Corporate Disclosure," pp. 44-52.

44. Lauren K. Newton, *Journal of Accountancy* (August 1978), pp. 45-47.

45. George J. Benston, *Corporate Financial Disclosure in the U.K. and the U.S.A.*, p. 150.

46. Russell B. Stevenson, Jr., "The S.E.C. and the New Disclosures," *Cornell Law Review* 62:82. Copyright © 1976 by Cornell University. All rights reserved. Reprinted with permission.

47. *Commerce Clearing House Federal Securities Law Reporter*, 1961, p. 76803.

48. Henry G. Manne, *Insider Trading and the Stock Market*.

49. Roy A. Schotland, "Unsafe at Any Price," pp. 1425-1478.

**Is There an
Antitrust Ethic?**

This chapter will discuss the historic background of antitrust laws, their general acceptance by the U.S. government, and the continuing doubt as to their value. Despite its common-law origins, laws requiring business competition were not really a major feature of English or American law until the Sherman Act of 1890. Here, more than in other chapters, the question is asked whether a country can create a new ethical obligation more or less by itself in a complicated field of human endeavor.

Judaic and Roman Law

The general ethical tradition of the Western world gives only a partial basis for the theory that government should try to maintain business competition through antitrust activity. There is a biblical statement against monopoly in the book of Isaiah: "Woe unto them that join house to house that lay field to field 'til there be no room and ye be made to dwell in the midst of the land."[1] Roman law included a provision against monopoly apparently directed at both merchants and professional people. Monopolies were strictly forbidden:

> Moreover, if anyone should venture to practice monopoly, he shall be deprived of all his property, and sentenced to perpetual exile. Again, we decree that those who are at the head of other professions, and hereafter venture to fix the prices of their merchandise, or bind themselves by any illegal contracts of any kind, shall be punished by a fine of forty pounds of gold, and that your tribunal shall be condemned to pay a fine of fifty pounds of gold if it should happen that, either through venality, dissimulation, or some other vice, the provisions of our most salutary constitution with reference to prohibited monopolies and forbidden agreements of corporate bodies should not be executed.[2]

However, neither Judaic nor Roman law was written against monopolies of the contemporary American type.

Anglo-American Legislation against Monopoly

There was a general tendency of the English common law to encourage business competition because of its emphasis on individual liberty and economic independence. Grants of privilege to guilds worked in a more communal or group direction. Also, royal monopolies, granted since the fourteenth century to foreigners to bring in new ideas or new products, became a means of aiding court favorites under the Tudors. Objection to these government monopolies led to the Anti-Monopoly Act of 1624. The common law was then readying for change to a more competitive economy.

As the principle of contract replaced the guild structure, a clear trend toward control of monopoly came into British life in the sixteenth and seventeenth centuries, when *forestalling* (controlling the bulk of commodities going into a market), *engrossing* (controlling wholesale purchases), and *regrating* (buying and selling in the same market) were forbidden by common law.[3] In 1772, the restrictions on market price control were repealed but some judges continued to condemn price control until an act of 1844 prohibited such suits. The enlargement of markets had reduced the danger of cornering local markets.[4] However, the common-law objections to all three practices did carry over to the United States, and were part of the philosophy behind the Sherman Antitrust Act of 1890. This common-law and statutory effort at control of monopolies should be classified more as an aspiration than an ethic, but it did represent a general aspiration.

There was also a common-law doctrine of refusing to enforce contracts in restraint of trade. Originally the ban may have grown out of a fear that men who agreed not to practice their trades could become public charges, but the ban also seemed to be supported as an antimonopoly measure. The ban began to be relaxed in the seventeenth century and was gone in England by the end of the nineteenth century. Although it was much narrower than the restraint-of-trade concept in the Sherman Act, it furnished some precedent for the Sherman Act.[5] And though this concept is important in modern times in America, it is now unimportant in English law.

In American common law, rules against forestalling and engrossing were not as important, but doctrines against restraint of trade did develop. There were sharp differences among states but a substantial majority of the arrangements involving restraint on business competition prior to the passage of the Sherman Act were held legally valid if market control was not too great.

In the last half of the nineteenth century, American businessmen began to form "pools" in railroads, petroleum, and other industries including coal, grain, candles, salt, meat, powder, and whiskey. The pools were aimed at regulation of production, market sales, profits, or patents of the participants. There had been simple agreements immediately after the Civil War, leading to more formal trusts by the mid-1880s. In the trust, as established first by the Standard Oil Company, each corporation received trust shares in return for its stock and properties. The trust had power to admit new corporations, as well as to buy and sell stocks of other corporations. Trusts were also formed in the oil, cotton oil, linseed oil, sugar, cordage, and lead industries. A few of the trusts were opposed by state legal action.

Formation of some of the trusts was accompanied by questionable ethical practices. The trusts were born in one of the ethically low periods of American business, and some trusts lowered the level further. These difficulties led to the federal Sherman Antitrust Law of 1890. The trusts were clearly contrary to American legal theories of economic freedom. However, there was no unanimity of opinion on how to handle the problem. The economists, a small group who were not consulted by the Congress, were not in agreement. There was more agreement among the muckrakers—journalists who attacked monopolies increasingly in the 1880s and 1890s. The brunt of their attack seemed to be that monopoly was costly to labor, farmers, and small businessmen. In the Social Gospel movement, which was especially strong among Protestant clergy at the time of passage of the Sherman Act in 1890, there was again a variety of opinion about monopolies. Newspapers and magazines followed the controversy fairly closely; the bulk of magazine writers opposed monopoly.

Underlying the support of the Sherman Act was distrust of price raising by the trusts and a typically American reaction against placing vast economic power in the hands of a few trust officials. A National Anti-Monopoly League was established by prosperous businessmen in New York in 1881, and in the early 1900s the National Association of Manufacturers lobbied for more effective antitrust action.[6] Executives of smaller businesses were also concerned about the growth of large concerns and trusts.[7] Many Americans probably agreed that the concentration of economic power in a few hands, like the concentration of political power in a few hands, was contrary to American moral principles that emphasized the worth of each individual. The particular sins of some trusts probably added to the moral and political fervor of antimonopolists.[8]

Louis Galambos's study of the public image of big business covers the 1880s and 1890s, in which antitrust law was conceived and enacted. His study is based largely on expressions of opinion in certain magazines catering to occupational groups: professional engineers, Congregational clergymen, farmers, and skilled laborers. The four sample groups were deeply concerned about the growth of trusts in the 1880s. However, improving economic conditions made both farmers and workers feel better about the economy by the 1890s. Similarly the clergymen had a placid view of the trust problem by the early 1890s. The professional engineer was generally inclined to sympathize with the corporations. If Galambos's interpretation of group attitudes is correct, the Sherman Act of 1890 was not a result of profound social discontent.[9] From 1875 to 1912, progressives in both parties discussed antitrust policy, and some legislative, administrative, and judicial steps were taken to improve execution of the policy, but again there was no sign of great popular discontent over the issue.[10]

After the economic depression of 1921 and, of course, during the Great Depression of the 1930s, Galambos again found clergymen, farmers, and workers critical of big business. But as World War II brought higher wages and higher farm prices, it once more became clear that Americans were learning to live with big businesses and indeed found the products of those businesses useful.

If almost a century of federal antitrust law has not yet made an ethical evil out of anticompetitive acts, it may be in part a result of the process that Galambos has described, the adaptation of Americans to big businesses as economically useful.

The primary purpose of the Sherman Act was the advancement of consumer welfare, according to Hans B. Thorelli, a point supported by Robert H. Bork of Yale Law School.[11] However, Thorelli adds a second purpose, the protection of small businesses, which Bork concludes is *not* one of the purposes of the act. Suzanne Weaver agrees with Thorelli's position.[12] It can be concluded, after review of Thorelli's analysis of congressional debates over the Sherman Act, that Congress did have in mind the protection of smaller businesses, although its ultimate aim was the protection of the consumer.

In view of the history of ethical principles suggested earlier and the Anglo-American legal history of opposition to monopoly, it is not surprising that the rapid development of trusts in the last quarter of the nineteenth century resulted in serious protests. Many Americans had been worried earlier about concentrations of financial power such as that of the Second National Bank, but their concern became far greater as the trusts appeared to be taking over the country's economic life. The Sherman Antritrust Act of 1890 passed very readily. Debates in the House and Senate indicated few opponents of the legislation. Only one vote was cast against final passage. Most senators believed that they were simply making the common-law restrictions on monopolies in restraint of trade into a part of federal law affecting interstate commerce. Little was said about the vastly different problems of enforcement of antitrust laws in a modern economy, nor did senators mention the fact that common-law restrictions against monopoly had largely disappeared in Great Britain.

The United States is one of the few modern democracies that has made antitrust legislation a fundamental policy of government toward business. Some legislation favoring competition has been passed in modern times by several nations. Canada has legislation somewhat similar to that of the United States. West Germany has a federal cartel office, active since 1973, but not as powerful as U.S. authorities.[13] France has a Technical Commission of Alliances and of Dominant Positions. The greatest extension of antitrust activities outside the United States has come from the European Economic Community (EEC) over the multinational corporations (MNCs) that do much of the business in the EEC. There is no uniform pattern of administration in each member country but MNCs have had sharp reduction in prices ordered by individual nations. The EEC itself has antitrust laws pointed primarily at concentration and restrictive practices—more sharply defined goals than those of the U.S. legislation. Big MNCs have been forced to follow orders by the European Economic Community's commission, whose decisions are not reversible by national sovereignties.[14] England has a cartel commission which, however, has not opposed some near-monopolistic mergers.

There are still some sharp critics of antitrust measures. Some believe that antitrust laws create only "economic crimes," deserving only mild punishments. Some argue that antitrust offenses are not traditional criminal offenses, that they are difficult to define, that corporate liability for crime is hard to define, and that antitrust forces owe more to political forces than they do to economic theory or ideology.[15]

There is much evidence to oppose these contentions. Numerous writers have advocated criminal action against trusts. The framers of the Sherman Act believed they were following a common-law doctrine. Congressional action for over a century has generally favored strengthening the antitrust laws, although there are important exceptions.

It is probably true that careful analysis of English and American court decisions would show changes of viewpoint and major uncertainty in antitrust policy. These uncertainties, plus the great ability of lawyers to argue cases for corporate clients and the inability of judges to deal with economic problems, often did produce confusion in antitrust-law administration. But there seemed to be enough initial agreement to present a national consensus, perhaps enough to justify an ethical obligation. Law alone, however, does not create ethical obligations, or creates them very slowly.

Early Antitrust Administrative and Legal Problems

The history of federal antitrust-law administration confirms the impression that the United States had a partly moral and partly economic purpose in passing the Sherman Act, but did not know what would happen under it. Presidents Benjamin Harrison (in office 1889-1893), Grover Cleveland (1893-1897), and William McKinley (1897-1901) did not push or did not ask their attorney generals to push antitrust cases vigorously. President Theodore Roosevelt (in office 1901-1905), however, talked about more vigorous antitrust policies. The courts initially seemed unfriendly to the antitrust act but in time began to see that it was a genuine part of national policy. In the first fifteen years of the twentieth century antitrust problems became of national interest, and the Sherman Antitrust Act was supplemented by the Clayton Antitrust Act and the Federal Trade Commission

Act of 1914. Since that time, antitrust policy has not been in question except for the brief period under the National Recovery Administration codes in the first two years of the New Deal. When the NRA was declared unconstitutional in 1934, President Franklin Roosevelt made no effort to revive its code authorities, which were quite contrary to antitrust principles.

Later Antitrust Legislation

The history of antitrust legislation has been summarized by Mark J. Green et al.[16] The Rule of Reason introduced by the Supreme Court in the 1911 Standard Oil and American Tobacco cases severely stunted the growth of antitrust policies. However, the Clayton Act of 1914 prohibited stock acquisition to lessen competition, certain interlocking directorates, and some price discrimination. Many economists now view the effort of the Clayton Act to ban price discrimination as an unhappy measure. The next important antitrust legislation included two New Deal acts, the Robinson-Patman Act (1936) which forbade price discrimination in "uncertain" language, and the Miller-Tydings Act (1937) which legalized manufacturer-dealer price arrangements. Both acts were really departures from the antitrust philosophy. In 1950 the Celler-Kefauver Act prohibited corporations from acquiring the assets of other corporations when the effect would be to lessen competition or to create a monopoly. The Miller-Tydings Act was repealed in 1975.

However, Congress has also weakened antitrust legislation by exempting farmer and labor organizations in the Clayton Act (1914), by permitting businessmen to act together in foreign trade (Webb-Pomerene Act of 1916), by allowing common-carrier agreements approved by the Maritime Commission (Shipping Act, 1916), and by exempting agricultural cooperatives in various acts. Insurance companies have been exempted if regulated by state laws. The Reed-Bulwinkle Act of 1948 permits "rate bureaus" of carriers to set common tariffs although a carrier can take independnet action. Bank mergers prior to June 17, 1963 have been forgiven. Mergers of failing newspapers are allowed by an act of 1970.

Although antitrust laws were adopted with much business support and accepted as a matter of national policy, they have not been accepted by businessmen as well as have other national laws regarding business. The antitrust laws have been fought regularly in the Congress and in the courts. Some businessmen realize the basic importance of the laws to the continuance of free enterprise in the United States, but many do not. The antitrust ethic is only partially established.

The Electrical Manufacturers' Case

In 1961 the nation was shocked by news that high-level executives of several nationally important electrical-manufacturing concerns had deliberately violated antitrust laws and rigged prices. According to one estimate, customers were overcharged about 12 percent.[17] Reviewing the rationalizations for the illegal actions of these highly placed executives gives some insight into the ethics of corporate executives.

General Electric (GE) had inaugurated a program of decentralization under which division managers were allowed to determine prices. The company's chief executive officer, who believed in free competition, had several times issued a circular requiring obedience to the antitrust laws. But in certain heavy-machinery divisions, the circular had not been taken seriously, or the oral remarks of one or two top executives had been interpreted as signs that GE did not really care about enforcing the antitrust laws. So prices had been agreed upon with competitors (in some fields there were only three manufacturing companies in the United States) in an effort to keep prices and hence profits high. When various employees told what was going on, the Department of Justice investigated. The final result included almost $2 million of fines on the companies, thirty-day jail sentences for seven defendants, and suspended jail sentences for twenty-three others. In addition, suits for triple damages under the Sherman Act cost the companies sums in the neighborhood of $500 million.[18] The General Electric executives concerned were almost all removed by the company; some other companies demoted or rebuked executives.

For the purpose of this discussion of the acceptance of antitrust laws as an ethical principle, it is interesting to note that sixty years after the passage of the Sherman Act, thirty-two electrical-manufacturing executives implicated themselves before a grand jury. Some believed they were following company policy. The collusionists themselves believed nine out of ten GE executives shared their point of view.[19] These executives were predominantly college graduates, had no other criminal records, and had been philanthropic leaders in their communities. They had apparently received little instruction in the purpose of antitrust laws, or in their basic role in maintenance of free enterprise.

Clarence Burke, who walked into an already long-established price conspiracy in circuit breakers, learned about it from executive vice president, Apparatus Group, Henry V. Erben. Burke recalls Erben saying that he had talked to (president) Cordiner about this policy, that Cordiner was not pleased with the idea of getting together with competitors, but that he, Erben, had said he would do it in a way that would not get the company into trouble. He further explained:

> Erben's theory had been live and let live, contact the competitors. He gave us that theory at every opportunity and we took it down to other levels and had no trouble getting the most innocent persons to get along. Mr. Erben thought it was all right, and if they didn't want to do it, they knew we would replace them. Not replace them for that reason of course. We would have said the man isn't broad enough for this job, he hasn't grown into it yet.[20]

An interesting example of the reaction of an "organization man" to ethical problems was furnished by W.S. Ginn, a vice president of General Electric, a graduate of Georgia Institute of Technology and for fifteen years a GE employee. He had been asked by his superior to meet with competitors to discuss prices and allocation of government jobs. Ginn did not let his plant manager or the president of the company know of his actions. Ginn signed the antitrust directive several times on orders from Erben. Even when president Cordiner told him to obey antitrust laws, vice president Erben told him to keep dealing with competitors. Ginn thought he was following a GE "philosophy" that violation of antriturst laws was necessary. After Erben's death and Ginn's promotion to vice president he realized that his "air-cover" was gone and told his sales managers to obey antitrust laws, but they disregarded him. He recognized his action was morally wrong, but he believed in administered prices.

Ginn made a confession that was also a charge against the company's ethical-education program: "I think certainly on matters of ethics, business ethics, and I think this is true not only of antitrust laws, the conflict of interest, expense accounts, and all of this, there has got to be a better job sold on the moral principles involved."[21]

A more complicated case is that of Mark Cresap, president of Westinghouse Corporation. Cresap's appearance before the Kefauver committee in 1961 has been cited as the result of a corporate failure to respond to the legal or moral requirements of the antitrust laws. From 1940 to 1960 Westinghouse had been involved in fourteen antitrust cases. Later it had nineteen more cases brought against it. Cresap told the Kefauver committee counsel that the company was starting a new course for young men on morals and ethics in business. He was determined that more violations would not occur; they were fruitless, immoral, and wrong. Yet a year later, Westinghouse was again indicted for antitrust violations. Incidentally, Westinghouse did not remove its convicted employees, as did General Electric.[22] However, it did order a general training of key executives in economics.[23]

It is difficult to speculate about Cresap, but a few remarks are in order. As he himself noted, this kind of electrical equipment accounted for only 5 percent of Westinghouse products, and he may have been unable to keep track of the operations of the whole company. No evidence was adduced that he knew of the violations in advance, but the Kefauver committee wondered if he had not failed to be suspicious enough. Certainly the steps he took to avoid repetition of monopolistic actions seemed inadequate. Did the high pay, hard work, or prestige of being president of Westinghouse weaken the ethical strength of the very hard-working and effective executive? Or did he fail all along to understand why American political leaders almost universally have seen antitrust legislation as essential, and hence an ethical obligation in American society?

Another possible explanation of the conduct of Cresap is that it is a twentieth-century commercial version of *raison d'état,* that a king or his high-ranking representatives could lie, cheat, or otherwise be unethical for reasons of state or for the advancement of the state. Perhaps Cresap believed that the welfare of many thousands of Westinghouse shareholders and employees justified his lack of frankness before the Kefauver committee.

Richard Austin Smith has another explanation for the behavior of the GE defendants: "In the instance of General Electric, the crisis came about because top management made the mistake of piling on the pressure for profits without keeping itself adequately informed of how the recipients of that pressure, the department and divisional managers down the line, were reacting to it."[24]

The antitrust laws, which seem to be very generally accepted as a matter of public policy, have apparently not moved into the active mental workings of a substantial number of business executives. Is this perhaps a proof that no ethical precept is valuable until people have been educated on the reasons for the precept?

Antitrust Problems Continue

Mark J. Green and his coauthors point to evidence that some businessmen did not accept the antitrust ethic. Raymond Baumhart's questionnaire to businessmen found that half of the respondents regarded antitrust policies as antibusiness.[25] On the other hand, a large number of firms have intrafirm programs explaining the reasons for legality on antitrust matters.

Attacks on antitrust laws by individual businessmen have frequently referred to free enterprise as the reason for continuing to be allowed to fix prices. Free enterprise was not guaranteed in the U.S. Constitution, but it has become a part of the American ideology (not always action) since the first half of the nineteenth century. It has never been defined to include the right to create monopolies. And of course, antitrust laws were designed to support free enterprise, not as something for free enterprise to oppose.

Reviewing prosecutions of antitrust violations, Green and his coauthors found that almost half the major violations were by trade associations. One of the largest, the Plumbing Fixtures Manufacturing Association, in the early 1960s secured substantial increases in prices of its products. Its conspiracy was discovered almost by accident by the Internal Revenue Service. Another trade association, a quinine cartel, secured full support from the U.S. State Department for a scheme that resulted in vast profits to the businesses involved and very high prices to consumers.

Some figures indicate that commission of antitrust crimes may be profitable for corporations even after payment of triple damages. Green and his colleagues suggest remedies of higher fines, advertisement of conviction, forfeiture of corporate divisions that have been consistent violators, and more antitrust-enforcement machinery. Would these controls create an ethic?[26]

Antitrust-law administration has remained a problem. The Federal Energy Administration on March 19, 1975 secured indictments against six oil refiners for conspiracy to fix wholesale gasoline prices in the western states. Eight chemical companies, including E.I. Du Pont de Nemours and Co., were allowed by federal district courts on December 15, 1974 to plead not guilty on charges of conspiring to fix dye prices. Three well-known clothing stores—Saks Fifth Avenue, Bergdorf-Goodman, and Genesco, Inc.—were fined the maximum amount by a federal court for fixing the prices of women's clothing (February 27, 1975). In the late 1960s and early 1970s several government agencies (the Federal Trade Commission, the Justice Department, and a few courts), moved against a surprising variety of business firms for deceptive practices or antitrust violations that were damaging to consumers.

In spite of the political and judicial difficulties antitrust legislation has met, there have been a good many judgments in favor of the government. Between 1900 and 1956, the prosecution won dissolution, divorcement, or divestiture in sixteen of the twenty major industries studied by Simon N. Whitney.[27] Whitney remarks that in three cases in which the dominant firm (U.S. Steel Corporation, American Can Company, and International Harvester Company) was not broken up after prosecution, it subsequently did a substantially smaller percentage of industry sales.

State governments have antitrust laws but do not use them much. An exception was an action brought by California's attorney general, together with several county attorneys, against practices of real-estate boards that required members to meet strict, unnecessary requirements to gain access to multiple-listing services.

Antitrust Laws and Politics

Although antitrust laws have been generally accepted by leaders of both parties since 1890, there has been a great deal of weakness in enforcing them. Congress has the largest responsibility, but high officers of national administrations have shared the blame for this lack of enforcement.

Sometimes antitrust laws have been misused by the government for political purposes. In 1948, suits were brought against farm-implement companies and meat packers, presumably to attract farm votes. In the early 1960s, President Truman is said to have ordered a suit against the *Kansas City Star,* which had opposed his administration. The Kennedy administration in 1962 ordered a grand-jury antitrust investigation of the steel industry in an effort to pressure that industry into accepting administration price policies. Some of these administrative actions may have been ethically justifiable, but the fairness of using the powers of a statute to secure ends not envisioned in that statute must be questioned. The formation of an antitrust ethic is not aided by this kind of statutory misuse.[28]

What Green and his colleagues call "defensive politicking" is frequent. Senator Pat McCarren (D., Nevada) was said to have asked the antitrust division head to stop 1952 grand-jury probes into RCA and most major oil firms. In 1956 Senator Wallace Bennett (R., Utah) and Secretary of Agriculture Ezra Taft Benson pressured Attorney General Herbert Brownell to drop a projected suit against an agreement between the *Deseret News* (owned by the Mormon Church) and the *Salt Lake City Tribune*. Representative Morris Udall (D., Arizona) persuaded Attorney General Nicholas Katzenbach to bring suit against a Republican-oriented chain that was taking over a Democratic Arizona newspaper.

A merger of two rice-milling companies in Louisiana in 1964 went undisturbed in part because of the intervention of Senator Allen Ellender (D., Louisiana), although the merged firms clearly exceeded permissible percentages of market control. Attorney General Katzenbach is said to have confessed, "Why not get a political benefit from what you are going to do anyway?"—thus raising interesting ethical problems.

Business firms soon learned to use the argument (which may or may not have been valid) that plants might be closed, with resulting unemployment, if a merger was not approved. Senator Abraham Ribicoff (D., Connecticut) used this argument at least twice with the Department of Justice to prevent prosecution of mergers. Senator Pastore (D., Rhode Island) used it to undo a court decision against Kaiser Aluminum Company's securing a plant in Bristol, Rhode Island. There have, however, been cases in which the Anti-Trust Division staff has resisted political pressure to drop antitrust suits.[29] Representative Emmanuel Celler (D., New York), chairman of the House antitrust subcommittee, was said to have used his power not so much for his district as for his law firm.

In the Nixon administration a suit against International Telephone and Telegraph Corporation for absorbing Canteen Corporation (a leading vending-machine producer) was comprised when the White House staff and the Attorney General participated in negotiations. Similar action was taken on a merger of Warner-Lambert Company with Parke-Davis and Company; again, political considerations seemed to be very important. Green and his colleagues review the record and conclude that the two political parties have had equally bad records on enforcement of antitrust laws.[30] This may surprise Democrats, who view Republicans as a big-business party, but apparently big business has had influence on Democrats, too. The Republicans, as more fervent supporters of free enterprise, may have felt more commitment to antitrust legislation, even though they have more big-business ties. Neither party has cared to challenge the ethic of antitrust, but neither has given it real support.

A comment should be made about the unfortunate political interferences with antitrust laws. Much of the difficulty lies in the general American practice of permitting the chief prosecutor, in this case the attorney general, to have complete authority as to whether action should be taken. Such final authority should be vested in a judge or a civil servant, (as in Canada), or in someone less susceptible to immediate political pressure, someone with clear ethical obligations. The United States has committed itself through nine decades to an antitrust policy; it is clearly unethical for one official to give up that policy because it is politically inconvenient to enforce. There could be sympathy for a president who needs a senator's support for an important bill and hence considers placating the senator by permitting a merger in the senator's state; but this practice should not be called ethical.

It may be that antitrust laws are basically incompatible with the kind of government regulation of industry to which our national government has been tending; witness the wide variety of special-group pressures. Perhaps Congress was wrong in placing antitrust work in an office as subject to political pressure as that of the attorney general. Perhaps we should have followed the German practice of having associations of industry and of consumers bringing civil actions against firms that violate fair-trade practices. The antitrust division is said to be primarily reactive to outside complaints; perhaps we should help the outsider do the prosecuting. The damaged party may sue for triple damages under the present law.

Several conservative academics have written forceful pleas for judicial adoption of a more economic definition of the purpose of antitrust laws. Robert Bork of Yale Law School believes antitrust legislation should be interpreted only to protect consumer welfare—not to control the structure of business.[31] Richard A. Posner of the University of Chicago also believes that the protection of small businesses is not the purpose of antitrust legislation; the emphasis should be on control of collusive price fixing.[32] Yale Brozen has written eloquently against what he believes are mistaken efforts of antitrust officials to prosecute companies for expanding trade.[33]

Brozen, Bork, and Posner (all somewhat conservative) agree on many issues, and all of them would narrow and simplify the field of antitrust law to the protection of competition for the benefit of consumers. These changes might develop a more supportable antitrust ethic largely because the process of enforcement would be more comprehensible.

Many economists believe that present antitrust laws are confusing and misleading. An important consideration is that antitrust law covers only the

American market, but much of American competition is now worldwide. The United States cannot use tariffs and quotas to withdraw from the world market; it needs to sell much to it and buy much from it. Instead of worrying about General Motors and Ford monopolizing the American automobile market, we need to worry whether General Motors and Ford can compete successfully against Datsun, Toyota, Volkswagen, and Renault.

Against these views is the hard-line position of Senator Edward M. Kennedy in favor of strengthening present antitrust laws.[34] A number of economists and lawyers deplore the ineffectiveness of present enforcement of antitrust laws.[35]

Viewpoints of critics and proponents of antitrust legislation are so far apart, and there is so much to be said on each side, that a balanced commission of inquiry might serve a useful purpose in helping to restore an antitrust ethic. To secure general adoption, an ethical principle needs to be clear enough to be understandable and at least partly enforceable. Antitrust philosophy has not yet attained this degree of clarity.

Will there be an antitrust ethic in the future? The difficulty of securing firm decisions from a government that is separated into three different powers makes it likely that differences of opinion on antitrust actions will continue for decades to come. Businesses that find antitrust legislation an obstacle will continue to assail it and secure some political support for their efforts; devotees of an American tradition of economic freedom, including freedom of opportunity to enter business, will continue to support antitrust legislation. World competition of very large companies will sometimes eliminate the possibility of domestic competition; if there are to be only a half-dozen world automobile companies, perhaps an American car manufacturer can survive. Whether the conglomerate movement will be economically successful and become a back-door means of eliminating competition in some industries remains to be seen. Fortunately, the United States appears to be developing an ethic that favors the market for many decisions. This renewed interest in the market may keep the antitrust ethic alive.

A Critical Look at Conglomerate Mergers

As a result of the wording of the Sherman Act and of various court decisions, antitrust laws have been consistently applied only to various legal concepts of restraint of trade. A formal effort through agreement or purchase of another business to control a substantial percentage of a particular industry, a control that might raise prices or eliminate competitors, is likely to have been disapproved by antitrust action. However, the growth of a specific business from within has not been disapproved. The antitrust laws also have not been applied to mergers of companies whose activities are not related to each other, no matter how much economic power such a merger of unrelated business might produce.

In the early 1960s especially, this feature of the antitrust laws permitted the formation of a substantial number of so-called conglomerates. In 1966 about 60 percent of the fifteen-hundred mergers reported by the Federal Trade Commission crossed industry lines.[36] In 1968, twenty-six of the nation's five-hundred largest corporations were merged out of existence. Forty-five hundred mergers were affected during that year.[37] The rise of conglomerates was a striking feature of the 1960s. Conglomerates had substantial setbacks in the stock market's drop in the late 1960s and early 1970s, but they were still in business and mergers continued at a rapid rate with governmental approval in 1981.

The Case for Conglomerate Mergers

The case for conglomerates is forcefully made by George J. Benston.[38] Mergers are often an investment for the acquiring company, an investment preferable to paying out more dividends which would be taxed at higher rates as a result of inflation. Often merger is preferable to investing more funds in an industry that already has underutilized capacity. It may also be better for the corporation than starting a totally new business with the incumbent problems of finding and training personnel, developing plant space, and working out distribution systems.

Smaller nonpublic companies are often glad to be merged to avoid an inheritance tax that might cause dissolution of the company, freedom to start a new business or for leisurely retirement, or to secure new capital through the stock issues of a larger company. Mergers may bring about important economies. Some economies may come from joint production, some from integrated facilities that reduce transportation costs and supply uncertainties, some from more efficient distribution such as joint warehousing and shipping, some from savings in research and development, and some from wider possibilities of use of management and other talent, from lower cost of financing because of economies of scale, and from lower administrative costs. Mergers usually result in diversified cash flow, which is easier to handle, they permit acquisition or sale of unusual talent, and they permit displacement of poor managers. Aside from these advantages to management, Benston finds advantages to consumers, workers, communities, and society from mergers.

Benston believes that conglomerate mergers are likely to *increase* competition, largely through reinvigoration of the acquired companies. Employees are benefited by provision of greater opportunities for promotion, training, and location. Statistical studies indicate that conglomerate mergers do not increase the concentration of economic power. The growth of economic and political power as a result of such mergers is not alarming.

The Case against Conglomerates

However, conglomerates have been developed for somewhat less worthy reasons. Men who have wanted to build financial empires under their own control have discovered that they can attain control of a corporation that had a low price-earnings ratio, a diversified ownership, and substantial quantities of cash or assets readily transferable into cash. Since many such corporations are controlled through relatively small percentages of stock ownership, it has sometimes been possible to gobble them up rapidly. If the merged company continues to be operative on a reasonable basis, there is not much financial objection here. If, however, the empire-builder takes the cash and near-cash assets of the company and uses them to buy other companies, there may indeed be several ethical questions. Is it right to deplete assets? Will the merged companies continue to develop economically? Mergers are frequently accompanied by increases in the market values of stock of both companies, but the use of assets in the case just described may not result in increased economic productivity in the long run, and may endanger the economic position of employees or shareholders.

Some mergers are ethically questionable in an accounting sense. If the purchasing company uses the "pooling" method of merging the new company and operates as one company, it may carry the assets of the newly acquired company at a book value far below the amount paid for that newly acquired company. Since the new company had a good price-earnings ratio, it is possible to show an increased income for the conglomerate, an income that unfortunately does not have a solid economic basis. An analysis made in 1968 by Marvin May, president of Tubular Structures Corporation of Los Angeles, concluded that rate of growth in reported earnings per share is not an appropriate benchmark of growth for valuing mergers or acquisitions.[39]

In some cases the shareholder may be damaged by the apparent profitability of a conglomerate that takes on several mergers, but since the conglomerate is not required to publish operating results by divisions, the shareholder is being deceived and eventually will have to pay for the deception. As noted earlier, many conglomerates showed a sharp loss of earnings in the 1970s.

The uncontrolled process of merging companies to produce conglomerates may of course also raise ethical questions of treatment of long-time employees: are they to be dropped at the whim of the conglomerate management? The merger movement of the early 1960s may also have introduced an understandable and perhaps unethical fear-provoking force into the economic community. Studies seem to indicate that much of the existing management after a merger does not remain with a merged company. Management that while independent was doing a good stable economic job finds itself suddenly subject to the new policies of the conglomerate administrators. However, these objections have not produced legislation against conglomerates aside from Senator Kennedy's suggestion.

Colleagues of Ralph Nader put together in 1972 a number of objections to conglomerates.[40] Granting that conglomerates can help competition, the Nader associates find that conglomerates are anticompetitive in several ways. There is a potential loss of competition when a conglomerate buys a firm in an industry into which it might have gone. Reciprocal buying and selling arrangements between firms could presumably be greater with conglomerates. Purchases of a leading firm by a conglomerate may strengthen that firm against competition, by giving it conglomerate backing and advertising. "Soft competition" among conglomerate units may replace real competition. These fears are probably unfounded, but the drop of conglomerate stocks in their own crash of 1973-1974 perhaps does indicate some real weaknesses.

The formation of conglomerates is not always an ethically desirable process. Chris Welles gives a fascinating account of the takeover of the asset-rich United Fruit Company by the relatively smaller AMK conglomerate. Unlike the old-fashioned proxy fight, the conglomerate takeover was based largely on securing the support of institutional investors in the stock of the desired corporation. The attitude of institutional investors tended to turn on the opportunity for quick financial gain on the shares already held. In the case of United Fruit, a brokerage house that had sold much of the United Fruit stock to its customers decided to promote the takeover so its customers would not be disappointed in their United Fruit stock holdings. Goldman-Sachs, a distinguished investment-banking house, aided the brokerage house. Support of other institutional investors was gained. A group of banks agreed to loan $35 million to AMK for the takeover. The management of United Fruit finally decided they could not avoid the takeover and agreed to go along. AMK and its competitor for takeover of United Fruit, Zapola Norness Inc., worked out package offers for United Fruit stock, involving a 60-percent premium over current market values. AMK finally secured United Fruit for $540 million worth of AMK securities. Once the deal was completed, most of the institutions that had profited by selling their United Fruit shares for AMK "casually dumped their new shares." The four firms running AMK's side of the takeover fight secured at least $5 million in fees and commissions. The institutional portfolio managers gained a short-term profit. But AMK stock (no longer United Fruit) soon went down in value.[41] The whole takeover game apparently was of value to all participants except the continuing shareholders.

The role of banks in financing conglomerate mergers is open to some question. By financing stock purchases, by exerting pressure on holders of stock, and in other ways, a big bank can help to "put over" its client. The bank can then gain substantially by requiring the newly merged subsidiaries to shift their banking business to it or to other banks designated by it. For example, Chase Manhattan Corporation supported Gulf and Western Industries, Inc. in acquisition of New Jersey Zinc, and received the stock-transfer business of Gulf and Western and numerous subsidiaries, compensated balances on loans, and received advance information on proposed mergers (to aid stock profits).[42] Is this kind of transaction the business of prudent, helpful bank loaning, or is it simply gaining profit from financial power politics?

On another occasion, Chase Manhattan sold reputable stocks from its own accounts and trusts to help Resorts International try to take over Pan American World Airways.[43]

In other instances, banks have avoided using their power to investigate questionable conglomerate practices. For example, the banks represented in the Penn Central board of directors did little to control its nonrailroading financial misadventures. This nonattention is somewhat reminiscent of banking attitudes in the late 1920s.

After mergers come other problems. One executive who believed that merger had resulted in his demotion promptly formed a group that embezzled $2 million from their company, now a subsidiary. When company headquarters move after a merger, company lawyers and accountants are changed. Payroll increases may drop from 15 percent to almost nothing. Earnings of subsidiaries are diverted. Few conglomerates are perceptive enough to know how to use the executives of the old company.

Norman Jaspan, whose firm has had decades of experience in locating employee crime, believes that mergers foster disloyalty as a result of insecurity and unfulfilled expectations.[44] He cites the case of a conglomerate that bought a large Canadian construction firm. The construction firm's reports looked good to conglomerate headquarters for a few months, but soon heavy losses were reported. Managers had milked the company for all they could get, and then disappeared. In another case accounts were fixed so that a construction company looked like a good buy. But its long-time manager (not owner) was securing money through under-the-table arrangements with contractors and dummy suppliers, and through black-market sales. In another case, an executive of twenty-five years' experience was downgraded to line supervisor when a conglomerate took over his company. The executive set up his own business using the company's dies, equipment, and personnel. In yet another case, the engineers of the conglomerate and the engineers of the subsidiary were literally spying on each other.[45]

Conclusions

It is, and perhaps long will be, debatable as to how much of American policy on competitive business relations is ethical and how much is a groping for the most effective economic policy. American national thought has generally assumed that concentration of power over a phase of economic life is unethical. Common-law precedents, the Sherman Act of 1890, the Federal Trade Commission, the Clayton Act of 1914, and subsequent legislation for the most part confirm this policy and should by now have acquired an ethical value that goes beyond a simple fear of being illegal. Yet individual businessmen and groups of individuals have made continuing sporadic efforts to evade these laws, and to establish complete economic power; the majority were men who had not otherwise stolen or committed assault or violated major ethical precepts.

Whatever the purposes of antitrust laws, and whether the courts are foolish in trying to use such laws to protect both consumer and competitor, the United States has not succeeded in establishing antitrust laws as a basic ethical value. The relative agreement of the politicians on the fundamental principle has not carried over to courts, lawyers, or business leaders.

What does this mean? Must it take a millennium instead of a century to establish a new ethical principle in business? Or is the antitrust principle unenforceable, or so economically undesirable that it cannot be enforced? Or have hostile groups destroyed the antitrust ethic? Or is the American government, handicapped by a fragmented law-enforcement system, simply unable to enforce the law? Would a sales campaign in favor of the antitrust laws have been a better approach than prosecution?

The rise of conglomerates makes these questions more difficult. Is the antitrust ethic sidestepped by the free formation of conglomerates? Will the conglomerates continue to move toward concentration of economic power that could result in monopoly? Are conglomerates permissible in an economy that is presumably based on an antitrust ethic?

Perhaps several of these reasons apply; perhaps there are other reasons not mentioned here. The conclusions to be certainly drawn are that relatively new ethical principles are hard to establish, and that the enforcement authority of the U.S. government is weak when important economic pressures are applied.

What of the future? Is it possible that the antitrust ethic will still become a workable principle. Many American business leaders seem to have accepted it. It helps to keep a vital, changing economy. But there must be much hard thinking and teaching, and learning from experience before antitrust ethical principles become accepted.

Notes

1. *The Bible*, Book of Isaiah, 5:8.

2. S.P. Scott, ed., *The Code of Justinian*, p. 121.

3. William Blackstone, *Commentaries on the Laws of England*, pp. 154-160.

4. Hans B. Thorelli, *The Federal Antitrust Policy*, pp. 12-17.

5. Ibid., pp. 17-20, 27-35.

6. Roger H. Wiebe, *Businessmen and Reform*, pp. 13-14.

7. Thorelli, *The Federal Antitrust Policy*, pp. 1-9.

8. Ibid., pp. 9-163.

9. Louis Galambos, *The Public Image of Big Business in America 1880-1940*, pp. 47-78.

10. James W. Hurst, *Law and the Conditions of Freedom*, p. 93.

11. Robert H. Bork, *The Antitrust Paradox*, pp. 15-71; Thorelli, *The Federal Antitrust Policy*, p. 227.

12. Thorelli, *The Federal Antitrust Policy*, p. 227; Suzanne Weaver, "Anti-Trust Division of the Department of Justice," in James Q. Wilson, ed., *The Politics of Regulation*, pp. 129-131.

13. *Wall Street Journal*, August 21, 1979, p. 38.

14. Gladwin and Walter, *Multinationals Under Fire*, pp. 349-358.

15. Cited in Harry V. Ball and Lawrence M. Friedman, "The Use of Criminal Sanctions in the Enforcement of Economic Legislation," pp. 201-202.

16. Mark J. Green, *The Closed Enterprise System*, chap. 2.

17. Ibid., p. 174.

18. Ibid., p. 174.

19. Richard Austin Smith, *Corporations in Crisis*, p. 120.

20. Ibid., pp. 124-125.

21. John Herling, *The Great Price Conspiracy*, p. 253.

22. Ibid., pp. 139-143.

23. Smith, *Corporations in Crisis*, pp. 165-166.

24. Ibid., p. 113.

25. Green, *The Closed Enterprise System*, p. 150.

26. Ibid., pp. 145-177.

27. Simon N. Whitney, *Antitrust Policies*, pp. 386-387.

28. Green, *The Closed Enterprise System*, chapters 2 and 3.

29. Ibid.

30. Ibid., p. 114.

31. Bork, *The Antitrust Paradox*.

32. Richard A. Posner, *Antitrust Law*.

33. *National Review*, November 24, 1978.

34. *Fortune*, August 14, 1978, p. 195 ff.

35. Robert A. Wilson, "Barriers to Trust Busting: 'Efficiency' Myths and Timid Trustbusters," pp. 19-39.

36. Fortune Editors, *The Conglomerate Commotion*, pp. 8-15.

37. John Brooks, *The Go Go Years*, p. 154.

38. George J. Benston, *Conglomerate Mergers*, chap. 2.

39. Fortune Editors, *The Conglomerate Commotion*, p. 99.

40. Green, *The Closed Enterprise System*, pp. 26-29.

41. Chris Welles, *The Last Days of the Club*, pp. 335-345.

42. Christopher Elias, *The Dollar Barons*, pp. 246-251.

43. Ibid., p. 95.

44. Norman Jaspan, *Mind Your Own Business*, p. 205.

45. Ibid., pp. 41-59.

10 The Ethics of Government Regulation

Ethical and Historical Background

Efforts of governments to regulate business prices, means of business operation, or services rendered have existed with sporadic continuity since Western culture began. Some Egyptian pharoahs enslaved skilled and unskilled workers for months or years in order to build their elaborate tombs. The economy of ancient Greece relied on the enterprise of individuals, but government officials often determined prices as well as amounts sold. The Roman government used *annonia*, (public associations) to move the foodstuffs required to feed Rome and other cities and the Roman legions; in fact, the later Roman empire had a very regulated economy.

In medieval Europe, every institution was part of a system of economic control. Churches controlled large bodies of land, often a third or more of a total province, and ordered the economic as well as the spiritual lives of tenants. Prices of goods sold at local markets were often determined by ecclesiastical courts, which also penalized merchants for selling bad or overpriced merchandise. Agricultural operations on manors were controlled by local nobles. Medieval guilds were instruments of control of wages of journeymen and apprentices, of quality of products, of methods of manufacture, and of parties to which sales could be made. Governments sometimes controlled guilds, sometimes used guilds as their own instruments of control, and sometimes were made up of guilds. Most guild control was intensively local and hence often ineffective since goods came from other areas. Underlying both market and guild control was the vague philosophical-theological concept of a just price.

Governments were themselves inconsistent in their economic outlooks. English kings granted monopolies over sale of specific products to particular friends. Prices and wages were set by statute after the Black Death in the fourteenth century, but the statute was no more effective than was Prohibition in the United States.

During the later Middle Ages and early Renaissance, international commerce had developed a large degree of freedom and its own "law merchant." In the time of the Renaissance (fourteenth to sixteenth centuries) and Reformation (sixteenth century), national governments became stronger than their feudal subdivisions and tried to set national economic policy, usually called mercantilism. Government officials knew little about how their economic controls worked, so Adam Smith's advocacy of less-controlled economies in *The Wealth of Nations* (1776) was welcome to many merchants, and was followed especially in the United States in the nineteenth century.

The Americans who began the Republic had two kinds of ethical precedents. They had revolted against British mercantile control, but still had some forms of local mercantilism. Adam Smith's *laissez-faire* doctrine (that government should not control the economy) was not generally accepted until the second quarter of the nineteenth century, and even then it operated side by side with state-owned banks, canals, turnpikes, ferries, and railroads. Government power to license many businesses was recognized and exercised by the end of the nineteenth century.[1] J. Willard Hurst says of the whole nineteenth century, "There was a mass of contemporary commercial regulation which was throughout accepted as normal and lawful."[2]

So in the eighteenth and nineteenth centuries Americans could believe either that it was right for government to regulate business, or that it was not right to do so.[3] The failure to have a developed ethic for or against government regulation does not mean that the founding Americans were lawless. They had been reared in European, especially British, monarchies and courts to have a fairly good sense of obedience to the law, somewhat handicapped by the fact that the law itself was often far from clear or reasonable.

The nineteenth-century American government was often handicapped by its inability to enforce its regulations. For example, an act of Congress in 1838 to make the life of passengers and employees safer on steamboats in the navigable waters of the United States was weakly administered by the U.S. Office of Patents. The law failed badly.[4] An act in 1852 that established a steamboat-inspection service was somewhat more successful.

Detailed Regulations of the Twentieth Century

Today, governmental regulation of business is a real problem in the United States. Why are relations between government regulators and regulated businesses so much sharper in the United States than in European countries? Why is government regulation so much more extensive in the United States? One American businessman asked, "Why is it that I and my American colleagues are being constantly taken to court—made to stand trial—for activities that our counterparts in Britain and other parts of Europe are knighted, given peerages or comparable honors?"

Alfred D. Chandler Jr. discusses this question in an unpublished, undated talk on "Government versus Business: An American Phenomenon." Chandler ascribes the phenomenon to several facts. Governmental bureaucracies developed more slowly in the United States than in Europe, so quite different governmental cultures appeared in each. In the United States, antitrust and rate-regulation laws (which do not exist on the same scale in Europe) appeared because some shippers and merchants pressed for such acts to protect themselves against the great railroads and trusts of the 1880s and 1890s. Hostility toward big business, which was intense in the early 1900s, returned with the Depression in the 1930s, and with the conservation and pollution problems in the 1970s. John Rae has suggested that government regulation came to the United States very suddenly at the end of the nineteenth century; hence its detail may have been a result of an overreaction to long-ignored problems.

According to Chandler, in Europe there was much less cause for hostility between government and business. On the Continent the railroads were built and run by existing public hierarchies. The railroads there fit into a network of existing waterways and roads. Wholesalers were not put out of business by new industrial grants. European dependence on foreign trade necessitated close working between government and business. Cartels at home helped expansion abroad.

At least one other explanation could be added to Chandler's. The United States has more lawyers and much more legalistic thinking than Europe. Lawyers tend to work and think in an adversarial environment. In a lawyer-dominated country like the United States, a formal regulatory system can be filled with conflict. Attorneys for regulated companies try to advance their clients' interests to the maximum point; attorneys for the regulatory bodies often ask too much. At times, a regulatory commission assumes a paternalistic attitude, at other times a regulatory agency pushes for literal enforcement of extremely expensive statutory mandates. In both cases, lawyers tend to argue with statistics the court will accept. Few people attempt to figure out the ethically best result of the regulatory process.

Robert B. Reich, a lawyer and economist with the Federal Trade Commission from 1976 to 1981, and now a professor at the John F. Kennedy School of Government at Harvard, has written an article that makes a similar point. He believes that regulatory officials and corporate officials could negotiate directly with each other on many matters, and save a good deal of time and written regulation. The difficulty on both sides lies with the business-government intermediaries—the lawyers, trade-association officials, public-relations offices, and lobbyists whose skills are for the most part strategic, not substantive. They apply political pressure, manipulate administrative procedures, and inform "their side" of the arguments of the "other side." Such officials, whose purpose is to develop confrontations, are not likely to start negotiations or develop a cooperative ethic of regulation.[5] It may be that Americans are too litigious a people to conduct the regulatory process by the simpler means of negotiation that Reich suggests. In a way, the open public confrontation seems more ethical even if it wastes time and money.

Americans have shied away from governmental ownership of businesses, for the good reason that their government does not seem well adapted to running business operations. Instead, they have turned to government regulation when the market mechanism does not seem to work well. However, regulation sets up a bureaucratic government office to control bureaucratic corporations, which may lead to friction. The following sections will describe the extent of some of the government regulation of business now existing in the United States and look for an underlying ethic.

Regulation for Health and Safety of Employees and the Public

Action for the health and safety of persons connected with a business has long been part of the Judaic-Christian ethical tradition. Examples are found in the Pentateuch, in Roman law, and in the *sic utere tuo ut alienum non laedas* provision of common law; clear evidences of personal responsibility for the health and safety of people affected by property. In America today the corporation is considered the legal equivalent of a person. "Love thy neighbor as thyself" is also a precept that requires at least respect for the safety of employees, who at work can be considered "neighbors." *Salus populi suprema lex est* is another relevant principle.

Perhaps because of its ethical certainty, much regulation in the health-safety category is readily accepted by most businesses. Few concerns object to regulations in the interest of health or safety of many people. Contractors usually do not try to weaken building codes. Railroads and trucking companies cooperate with safety regulations. The Airlines Traffic Association on May 29, 1979 responded with alacrity to the temporary grounding of DC-10s to check on metal fatigue in the attachment of motors to the planes, after a disastrous crash that killed 272 people. The public could feel sure that every DC-10 received this check, since no airline would wish to endure the obloquy against a company that failed to check.

However, some safety and health regulations have not been so favorably received. In this century about 100,000 Americans have been killed in coal mines, and from 1930 to 1969 over 1.5 million serious mine injuries were recorded.[6] Coal mining is an industry of great dangers, but there are reasons to believe that in many states mine-safety regulation has not been adequate and that some mining companies have opposed stricter regulations. Mines owned by steel companies have better safety records than independently owned mines. It is difficult to avoid the conclusion that mine owners and their political representatives (who have fought against regulation in several states) simply did not place a high enough value on the lives and safety of individual workers, in violation of the American ethical traditions.

It should perhaps be added that this lack of concern for miners' safety may not be an ethical failing of mine owners alone. Americans seem to have little concern for the large number of their fellow citizens killed or injured in highway accidents, as many as 50,000, equal to the number of soldiers lost in seven years of the Vietnam War. Automobile manufacturers have been very slow to emphasize safety features on cars.[7] However, the ethical responsibility for traffic deaths is not so easily placed on particular individuals as is the responsibility for deaths in mines.

As pointed out in chapter 3, the chemical industry fought long and hard to resist the Toxic Substances Control Act of 1977, even though members of the industry were well aware of the deaths and injuries of employees in the Rohm and Haas plant from manufacture of chloromethyl acetates, or the neurological injuries caused by kepone, or the asbestosis in factories in Texas and New Jersey.[8] The industry's objection in 1971 was initially to the requirement of premarket notice and testing before a product could be issued, an objection based largely on the experience of slow premarket testing of drugs by the federal government. Later, the industry lobbied against any strong regulatory measures.[9] In 1974 and 1975 it began producing evidence of the substantial costs of compliance, about which it was only partially correct. The chemical industry's objections did contain some validity. But members of the industry were slow to recognize their ethical obligations to their employees. In the long run the bill for federal control became law. The ethically deplorable slowness of the industry to show concern for this aspect of employee safety added one more count to the criticisms of business ethics made by many Americans.

The automobile industry was slow to do anything about its large proportion of the responsiblity for smog.[10] While local industry was spending $55 million of capital costs and $5 million of operating costs to reduce smog, the auto industry was spending only $1 million a year on smog research. David Finn comments on how the auto industry continued to emphasize the capacity of new cars for speed even after the National Traffic and Motor Vehicle Safety Act of 1966. The chemical industry's reaction to Rachel Carson's *Silent Spring* seemed to Finn to be neither considerate nor cooperative.[11]

It is hard to imagine how some industrial leaders could so long ignore the ethical responsibility for their actions. Most likely they committed primarily sins of omission; the executives simply refused to study the consequences of their actions, and remained in deliberate ignorance. It is possible that the corporate attitudes discussed in chapter 3 helped suppress inquiries on the part of staff. The expense of such measures as smog control or mine-safety devices was also a major factor; if competitors did not follow the safety measures, a complying company might be priced out of the market.

Today many corporations are doing much better in regard to health and safety measures. OSHA and the EPA are forcing very expensive programs on them. It is probably the case that if companies had been less negative toward regulation against accidents such as the death of employees in mines or by chloromethyl, regulation would have been more gradual and less expensive. An ethic has been established at considerable expense as a result of conflict, with some bad results for both businesses and employees.

Regulation of Industry Rates and Services

The type of government regulation of business with which Americans have longest been familiar is the control of rates and services in a particular industry that has been "affected with a public interest," to use a legal phrase. The Interstate Commerce Commission (ICC) has had some power over railroads since 1887; more recently, other methods of transportation like buses and trucks have been regulated. The Federal Power Commission has had authority over hydroelectric power sites on navigable streams since 1920, later was given authority over interstate shipments of gas, and in 1935 over interstate transmission of electric power. The Federal Communications Commission (FCC) has regulatory power over radio and television. Meat shipped in interstate commerce has been regulated by the Department of Agriculture since 1907; recently the department has been given some power over intrastate shipments. Food and drugs have been regulated for health purposes since 1906. The Civil Aeronautics Board (CAB) has had broad powers over the service routes and rates of airlines. The Army Corps of Engineers has had charge of inland waterways. The Federal Reserve Commission and the Office of Controller of the Currency oversee federal banks. Most of these agencies regulate rates and safety.

The states have regulatory authority in intrastate operations. State regulation is, however, much more likely to be exercised over energy and transportation than in other fields. In general, states have been much less aggressive regulators than has the federal government.

It should be said that the industries concerned have often supported regulation, sometimes in order to keep a monopolistic or oligopolistic position. In state and federal governments, the quality of regulation has been lowered by the ineffectiveness of many of the men appointed to regulatory commissions. All too often presidents and governors have thought more about the appeasement of political factions or geographical areas than about the quality of work likely to be done by a commissioner. Several presidents have shown an interest in reforming regulatory agencies but few have followed through to accomplishment.[12] President Carter's support of deregulation of airlines and other means of transportation is the first major exception, and the Reagan administration is now pushing deregulation very forcefully. Although a few great public servants have been members of regulatory commissions or served on their staffs, the average has been disappointing. This mediocrity of government representatives has often led to lack of respect by businessmen and poorer performance by the committees.

A part of the ethical problem in the regulated industries is the tendency for the regulatory commission to be viewed as a "godfather" of an industry, to be expected to make decisions intended to help the industry rather than the public. Industry has often initiated a regulatory statute (to help preserve its monopolistic position) and then carefully cultivated the regulators. Commission members are often visited by executives of businesses under regulation.[13] Maritime-agency employees work very closely with the National Maritime Council, made up of shipping companies and unions.[14] Commission members who oppose the regulated industry are not likely to receive senate confirmation or reappointment. One airline president publicly suggested an airlines committee to nominate new members of the Civil Aeronautics Board.[15] Cooperative commission members and senior staff members are often appointed to good positions in the industry they had regulated when terms expire, or when it seems convenient to move on. Commission members are invited to address the industry and enjoy recreation or entertainment at industry expense. Some commissioners or agency heads avoid these allurements; a very few are appointed as industry gadflies and will be offered no "soft-soaping" by industry. Congress has legislated against industry assignment of former officials to matters that were part of that person's official responsibility until two years after he has left the government. But in general, the regulated industry has been successful in taking on ex-regulators. The fact that presidents and governors frequently use commission appointments for patronage purposes means that some commission members need jobs after leaving the government, a fact that adds to the likelihood of securing regulators who wish to be part of the industries they regulate.

Ross Eckert's studies of the careers of regulatory commissioners show that large proportions of retiring commissioners (their terms are usually seven years) either go to work in the regulated industry or in a law firm that deals with problems of the regulated industry. Most commissioners are lawyers. Between 13 percent (CAB) and 25 percent (ICC) had some relationship with the industry before service on commissions. After commission service, 43 percent (ICC) and 59 percent (FCC) had affiliations with the industry they had regulated. About two-thirds of each commission had industrial affiliations before or after commission service. Half of the precommission jobs in the regulated industries were held in the public sector; that is, in commission staff, congressional committee or staff, or related federal or state staffs. Postcommission service was from three to six times more common in the private sector.

The possible ethical implications of Eckert's studies are numerous, but none lead to clear-cut recommendations. It looks as if service on a one-industry regulatory body was filled with conflicts of interest. Would not the industry be more likely to find positions for persons whose decisions had been friendly? On the other hand, is it not perfectly reasonable that a man retiring from a seven-year term should work in the industry about which he has learned much from his commission service? Perhaps the fault is that of Congress in establishing a seven-year term for commission members rather than a lifetime term like that of judges.

There is evidence that industry regulators have not always taken the side of the regulated industry. Utility rates are raised in times of inflation, but only over public protest, which often causes delays or rate reductions by the regulatory bodies. In 1979-1980 the Civil Aeronautics Board fought for reduction of regulation against the wishes of the airlines. The governmental agencies regulating all businesses are much less likely to side with the regulated businesses than are the single-industry regulatory agencies.[17]

The results of "family-type" regulation of individual industries have rarely been outstanding and are often less than mediocre. The Interstate Commerce Commission has frequently been charged with giving the railroads, bus companies, and trucking companies what they want, with bad results for the public, and not very good ones for industries themselves.[18] The deregulation of railroads and trucking is now progressing. The Federal Communications Commission has been erratic in its watch over what some people think is the greatest modern danger to American values—the television industry. Although banks have grown greatly in recent years, few people assert that the Federal Reserve has succeeded in establishing a sound financial system. The Federal Power Commission has shown little foresight into the immense problems it faces.

Most outside observers would probably agree that the regulation of individual industries has not been very successful. Such observers might differ as to the causes of this. An economist is likely to say that most of these industries need not be monopolistic, or as in the case of television, oligopolistic, but that the market could better handle their problems. Public administration experts might point to the hopelessness of trying to get expert objective judgment from commission members who see their only career future in the industry they are regulating. Lawyers might point out that court supervision is a reason for many delays and much inconsistency in regulation.

How much ethical responsibility do business executives have for the frustrations of this variety of governmental regulation? Obviously the blame on business, if any, is only partial. Congress selected the unworkable commission form of regulation, and jurists are responsible for the all-too-frequent habit of court intervention in regulation. Presidents under heavy pressure from Congress are responsible for politically motivated appointments.

But could not a more ethically-minded business community have helped the regulatory commissions secure a more respected position and do a better job, to the long-run advantage of both public and industry? There have been a few cases in which an industry has backed the reappointment of a strong commissioner such as Joseph Eastman of the Interstate Commerce Commission. But the industry attitude has primarily been one of "who knows him?" to the mediocre political choice of the president or a governor. Much of the ethical fault in the processes just described belongs to the government, which has adopted strong laws but put inadequate people in charge of their enforcement.

Regulations Affecting All Businesses

One of the earliest forms of overall federal regulation of businesses was the Sherman Antitrust Act of 1890, which was followed by several subsequent acts, chief of which was the Federal Trade Commission Act of 1914, establishing the FTC. The Pure Food and Drugs Act was passed in 1906 and strengthened by later legislation.

The next large group of federal regulations covering all businesses came with the consumer, environmental, and labor movements in the 1960s and 1970s. Legislation included the Labeling Act of 1960, the Truth in Packaging Act of 1966, the Truth in Lending Act of 1968, the Occupational Safety and Health Administration (OSHA) in 1970, the Environmental Protection Act of 1970, the Consumer Product Safety Commission Act of 1972, the Clean Air Act of 1970, the Equal Employment Opportunity Commission, the Federal Employee Retirement Income Security Act of 1974, and the Noxious Products Act of 1976.

Two of these acts, the Consumer Products Safety Act and Equal Employment Opportunity Act, are administered by new commissions; most of the others are administered by agencies of an already-established federal department. Instead of a commission with close ties to industry, as described in the last section, administrative agencies set up by these acts usually have had a certain amount of anti-industry missionary zeal. Many of the administrators are civil servants, have lasting jobs, and often believe that rigorous enforcement of the law is the policy most advantageous to their personal careers. Other executives have been appointed from the pressure groups supporting the legislation. It is these all-business regulatory agencies whose policies raise much sharper business criticism than the policies of the single-industry commissions.

The ethical problem involved in these agencies was frequently that the government required too much rather than too little of industries: not too much clean environment or too much safety but too many billions of dollars in industry expenditures. Reasonable people would agree that a healthy, clean environment for work as well as for community life is desirable; but should such regulations be enforced at the cost of bankrupt industries? One economist suggests that the costs of regulation were passed on to consumers but the quality of life was not improved. The evidence suggests that national equipment standards provided no significant improvements through the mid-1970s.[19]

Business reactions to these regulatory programs have been indignant. Some concerns received deservedly rough treatment because they had ignored the health or safety of employees, the public, or their customers. As indicated in chapters 7 and 8, there are some genuine cases of business ethical opacity that perhaps should be balanced by governmental action. Nevertheless, businesses that have honestly tried to produce a safe, healthy product in a safe, healthy way find that the costs imposed by federal administrative rules have sometimes been staggering. Murray L. Weidenbaum estimates that in 1979 business and industry spent $102.7 billion for compliance with federal regulations, ranging from extra paperwork to major technological changes. A number of small foundries have been forced to quit, and some of our larger businesses, for example the steel and auto industries, are having real financial difficulty; the expense of regulation is a major factor in these troubles.[20] The losses of the auto industry in 1980, a real financial threat to the health of the American economy, are relatively close to the annual costs imposed on the industry by the EPA, OSHA, and miles-per-gallon regulations enforced by the Department of Transportation, about $4 billion. Some automakers and some observers believe that federal agencies have taken over control of the auto industry.[21]

Yet some of these costs are necessary. Clearly the death of scores of workmen should not be allowed to continue in a society that values every individual. Air and water pollution must be eliminated as rapidly as is financially possible. There is obviously an ethical need to improve the quality of working life.

Government regulatory officials have recently recognized more utilitarian goals by increasing the use of cost-benefit analyses, which make an effort to estimate the costs of regulation to government and to business and the resulting saving in terms of human life, health, wealth. Unfortunately, cost-benefit analyses suffer from the problem of utilitarianism, that there is no firm standard to protect a person or company from unjust treatment. Unions and proregulation groups have opposed such analyses, stating that human lives should not be considered in mathematical formulas. However, the analyses can be helpful in reducing the inflationary effect of regulatory processes.[22] Such studies may also be a useful check on regulation, as Murray Weidenbaum has pointed out.[23] Dollars are already traded for lives when a higher speedlimit for cars is permitted. He states that government regulation should be carried to the point at which the added benefits equal the added costs, but no further. The federal government now requires inflation-impact or economic-impact statements of major new regulations. More effort is needed to bring regulatory costs under control. Labor unions and public-interest groups have opposed efforts to require cost-benefit analyses of regulatory controls. Their belief is that human life, safety, or health are absolute values that should be preserved regardless of cost. But is this argument valid when these absolute values threaten to eliminate important American industries, without which many workers would lose their jobs and livelihoods? In cases like this, should not the ethical judgment be more utilitarian than Kantian? An ethic has not yet been established.

Other difficulties arise from excessive regulation. Several large companies find that growing percentages of their research-and-development work are spent on compliance with federal regulations. Innovation in pharmaceutical products is shifting to foreign countries in part because of the detailed U.S. governmental regulation. The Federal Employee Retirement Income Security Act has resulted in abandonment of many small-company retirement plans.

The Occupational Safety and Health Administration (OSHA) is an example of a regulatory agency that has sharply exacerbated government relations with business and business relations with labor. Curiously, OSHA was started under Republican president Nixon as a concession to labor. Its purposes of occupational safety and health are commendable. But the decision to staff it with federal inspectors cast aside the chance to use state and local inspectors, who tend to be well-informed and fairly tough. Staffing by Department of Labor inspectors brought in a not-very-well-qualified group, whose tendency from their labor-union background was antimanagement. There were only four hundred inspectors for five million worksites. The power to levy small penalties without court action made these inspectors appear to be arbitrary, as some undoubtedly were. The lack of available regulations led OSHA to effect many volumes of privately prepared regulations that had sometimes been prepared for quite different purposes. The agency itself set up poor inspection priorities; over half of the inspection visits were to small firms, which had less than one-fifth of the accidents.[24] Fortunately, changes in administrative policy have reduced some of these difficulties. Business specialists suggest more emphasis on helping companies develop their own safety programs.[25]

The result of OSHA regulation to date has been tense feelings between labor and management, large additional costs to companies, and criticism of many managers, without substantial savings of lives or reduction of accidents.[26] Also, the example of OSHA has led some state and local regulatory bodies into a parallel type of excessively bureaucratic rule-enforcement.

A more cooperative (or ethical) type of regulation is needed. Michael Levin suggests a revision of enforcement priorities to maximize accident prevention, creating incentives for change such as disclosure to shareholders of accident rates above the industry average, deduction only of average workers'-compensation premiums as a business expense establishment of a broader constituency, and reduction of the adversarial nature of enforcement through the development of plantwide safety committees.[27]

Is There An Ethical Reponsibility to Obey Excessive Regulations?

In all types of regulation, some rules are viewed as unnecessary or highly controversial. Recent academic discussion favors elimination or reduction of many of these regulations. Each regulation raises the ethical problem of its necessity. Many governmental regulations seem to be petty, inconvenient, or expensive. Many of the original OSHA rules seemed to those regulated to be of a controversial nature. For example, a hand railing which under local building codes was three feet high would have to be three -and-one-half-feet high to satisfy some OSHA inspectors. Federal drug-approval rules worked well in the thalidomide case but have kept Americans from using new drugs the English and Canadians find useful. Interstate Commerce Commission (ICC) regulations for decades forced truckers to empty back-hauls, and ICC gateway restrictions forced trucks to use unnecessarily long routes.[28] Banks were ordered to make only good loans, but not to "redline" areas of bad loans.[29] The use of a newly designed, more efficient railroad car to haul grain was delayed five years from by ICC regulations.[30] Until recently it was much cheaper to fly from Los Angeles to San Francisco than a similar distance across state lines because the Civil Aeronautics Board determined interstate but not intrastate rates. Regulation by the Federal Communications Commisssion (FCC) enabled Mr. and Mrs. Lyndon B. Johnson to build a fortune in the television industry while they were actively engaged in politics that helped the FCC. The Federal Trade Commission, which does many things in keeping with the Western ethical tradition, has also engaged in picayune regulations like setting the price of frozen fruit pies in Salt Lake City.[31] The state of Wisconsin in 1965 had laws making it a crime to furnish oleomargarine to inmates of publicly supported hospitals, or to sell baking powder without a list of the ingredients printed in type not smaller than eight-point bold-faced Gothic capital letters.[32]

The tremendous cost of environmental- and worker-protection measures aimed at zero pollution or zero work danger adds greatly to inflation; alternatives such as use of protective equipment on workers, or a system of taxing industry heavily for pollution, or the setting of antipollution goals rather then following detailed regulations, might achieve equally good results at a cost of billions of dollars less. If the United States loses its auto industry, expensive regulation will be a significant reason.

Attitudes of businesses toward excessive regulations vary greatly. Some accept regulation cheerfully as a necessary nuisance that is wise to obey in order to avoid the danger of illegal operations. Others try to evade such rules whenever possible. Frequently, ignorance of the rules or failure to understand them is used as an excuse for failure to obey them. Big business tends to obey regulations more than do smaller businesses.[33]

What is the ethical obligation of a business confronting a useless or too-detailed regulation? It seems clear that the regulation should be obeyed, with the possible exception of obsolete or forgotten laws. Regulations must be obeyed because responsible business executives, like all responsible individuals, wish to have laws enforced; otherwise there would be chaos. The business should also do its best to persuade legislative and administrative agencies and the public that the useless or undesirable regulation should be repealed. Perhaps ''sunset'' legislation, which calls for periodic review of the necessity of laws, may aid in this process.

The General Problem of Enforcement of Regulations

Several observers have noted hostile business attitudes toward governmental regulations which are intended to create a better, more acceptable business environment. Insofar as legal responsibilities produce ethical responsibilities, some businessmen become unethical because of their resentment of the application of governmental regulations. Robert E. Lane points out that certain features of government are annoying to businessmen, and arouse resentment in government-business relations. These features include the confusion caused by the many sources of decision in government, the conflict of governmental policy resulting from alternate pressures in Congress (for example, the Sherman Act, which enforces competition, and the Miller-Tydings Act, which works against it), and the ensuing lack of certainty and consistency in government policies.

Since Congress is the ultimate architect of federal administration and federal policy, the average government official can do little to change these factors. Businessmen must learn to accept these difficult working conditions, but it is easy to understand why some of them become impatient and follow unethical policies.[34] Lane ventures an opinion that Edwin H. Sutherland's theory of differential association (that association with persons favoring violation of law makes one tend to be a violator) also applies to businessmen. He cites a geographical example, that in some shoe-manufacturing communities none of the shoe firms violated the law whereas in other communities almost half the firms violated it. He also notes that big-city businesses seemed less likely to violate the law than did small-city firms.[35] These results seem to him to confirm the theory of differential association, which perhaps should be extended to include a theory of differential ethical standards.

Through a survey of the contents of the magazine published by the Connecticut Manufacturers' Association, Lane concluded that the principal objection of businessmen to government regulation was that the restrictive effect of the legislation was detrimental to public good. Further, there were frequent comments on defective administration of the government regulatory agencies. Over a period of time the critical references on each piece of regulatory legislation began to decline.[36]

There is much truth in these comments. The differential-association theory may indeed fit businesspeople better than it does other groups in society. In America, where little ethical instruction has been given by parents, teachers, or in company policy, it seems very likely that businesspeople will secure their ethics from the actions and statements of the people around them. Resentment of limitation of a businessperson's authority to run his or her own business is also very natural, even if the government and the public believe that the limitation is called for. As executives discover that their businesses continue to operate successfully in spite of forced union recognition or a government decision against a proposed merger, the business executives become more accustomed to the new laws.

Most of these reasons for business reactions against government are somewhat negative; these attitudes might have been overcome by a strong education on the desirability of regulations. Lane also mentions a general business belief in free competition, which, of course, would tend to make many government regulation seem antibusiness.

The very nature of governmental regulation makes its ethical problems more complex. The regulator is supposed to push aggressively for the public interest. The regulated business executive is supposed to push aggressively for the interests of his business, whether monopolistic, oligopolistic, or competitive. Statutes often fail to define the standard of regulated conduct clearly, as a result of conflicting interests in the legislature, and the problem of decision is transferred to the administrative agency. Under these circumstances the decision of the regulatory agency cannot be considered a Kantian universal law. It is more like a utilitarian rule, the greatest good for the greatest number. It is objective, but it often pays little attention to the added costs of doing business under regulation.

Are there ways in which government officials could work more effectively with regulated businessmen? Lane suggests polling businessmen to find their expectations from government, their values, their mores. If regulators understood the "established symbols and customs" of businessmen, they could better explain how the regulations would help maintain free enterprise.[38] The desirability of stressing those points of regulations that strengthen a common ethical code should be added.

Weidenbaum has some helpful suggestions to government officials to help make a more ethical and workable regulatory process. Most of them are points on which both conservative and liberal economists would agree.[39]

1. *"The individual should have maximum opportunity for personal choice."* This grows in reaction against the type of regulation which would keep a heart drug from an older man because it might be toxic. In an individualist society, should he not have a choice?

2. *"Whenever possible, the government should provide information rather than coercive commands."* Would results not be more economical and ethical if manufacturers were told how to improve their products rather than ordered to change the process of manufacture?

3. *"Whenever possible, the government should provide incentives rather than directives."* As the experience of other countries has shown, companies can often find cheaper ways of eliminating pollution if they are given an opportunity to select from alternatives.

4. *"Good public policy should avoid the simplistic notion that all short-comings originate in business."* The government and the public make mistakes, too.

5. *"Government should set an example and not put itself above the law."* There are still many examples of governmental pollution, for instance.

6. *"The vast power of government should not be aimed at trivia."* Did the loss of the one-hundred-sixteenth variety of snaildarter (since discovered elsewhere) justify holding up a $120-million dam?

7. *"Government should learn that its decisions often can produce long-term and unexpected consequences."* Should, for example the National Labor Relations Board deny freedom of speech to employers?

These suggestions come, as do most ethical principles, out of unfortunate experiences. Perhaps the underlying ethical principle from which most of them are developed is that of allowing other individuals and companies the freedom to learn and perform their own tasks in their own ways, provided they meet their public responsibilities. This is the lesson participative management is slowly teaching American business; a lesson some Oriental civilizations may have learned ahead of us. Should not government learn that same lesson and try to teach ethics to businessmen rather than coercing them with regulations? The long-run results may be better.

A more important reform is one neither business nor government can make. If our intellectual leaders would decide to advocate a return to teaching of ethical concepts by parents, teachers, clergymen, and political and business leaders, both government and business would soon become more moderate and thoughtful in their debate on regulation.

Conclusions

The ethical problems raised for business by government regulation are those in which ethical obligation (sometimes supported by opposition to competition, sometimes by genuine public need) is pitted sometimes confusingly against corporate self-interference or against dilatory or stubborn bureaucracy. Few general ethical principles have appeared, but some possibilities can be presented.

Businesses should, and most now do, recognize that the health and safety of the public is the supreme law. Failure to do so results in unduly restrictive legislation, and in a much lower political standing of business. There are many regulations of questionable importance that must be obeyed for legal reasons, but which should be repealed or changed. The sharp reduction of regulation of single industries in 1981 indicates that a regulatory ethic has not been clearly established. Events of the next few years may develop an ethic; if not, corporations should follow the policy of obeying the law.

Regulations affecting all industries have aroused much resentment, chiefly because of the heavy, sometimes crippling, costs imposed on certain industries. Nevertheless, it is probable that long-stated underlying ethical principles such as the injunction to respect the life and health of employees and the public will continue to be respected, if not immediately put into effect.

Both business and government would do well to rethink the ethics and methods of their approaches to problems of regulation. Business has erred in fighting all governmental regulation and too often has ignored the long-standing ethical principals that underly most regulations. Government has erred in its failure to consider the costs of regulation, and in using a strictly legalistic rather than an educational approach.

Notes

1. Ernst Freund, *Administrative Powers Over Persons and Property.*
2. J. Willard Hurst, *Law and the Conditions of Freedom in the Nineteenth Century*, pp. 50-51.
3. Louis Hartz, *The Liberal Tradition in America*, pp. 53-54, 99-100.
4. Louis C. Hunter, *Steamboats on the Western Rivers*, pp. 532-535.
5. Robert B. Reich, "Regulation by Confrontation or Negotiation," pp. 82-93.
6. Robert Coles and Harry Huge, "Black Lung: Mining as a Way of Death," in David Sanford et al., *Hot War on the Consumer*, p. 189.
7. Ralph Nader, *Unsafe at any Speed*, chap. 5.
8. Willard S. Randall and Stephan D. Solomon, *Building 6*, p. 212, 256.

9. Ibid., p. 234.

10. Nader, *Unsafe at any Speed*, chap. 4.

11. David Finn, *The Corporate Oligarch*, p. 179.

12. Kohlmeier, *The Regulators*, Ch. 20, pp. 265-286.

13. *The New York Times*, December 8, 1973, pp. 53-55.

14. *Los Angeles Times*, July 21, 1978.

15. Louis M. Kohlmeier, Jr., *The Regulators*, p. 48.

16. Ross Eckert, "The Life Cycle of Regulatory Commissions," *The Journal of Law & Economics* 24:1 (April 1981).

17. James Q. Wilson, ed., *The Politics of Regulation*.

18. Robert Fellmeth, *The Interstate Commerce Commission*.

19. Paul W. McAvoy, "Overview of Regulatory Effects and Reform Prospects," in Timothy B. Clark, et al., *Reforming Regulation*, pp. 9-20.

20. Murray L. Weidenbaum, "The Future of Business Regulation," *Amacom* (1980).

21. *Los Angeles Times*, June 17, 1979, part 6.

22. James C. Miller III, and Bruce Yandle, eds. *Benefit and Cost Analyses of Social Regulations*.

23. Murray L. Weidenbaum, *The Future of Business Regulation*, pp. 55-56.

24. Michael Levin, "Politics and Polarity," *Regulation* (Nov.-Dec. 1979), pp. 33-39.

25. *Wall Street Journal*, December 26, 1980, p. 8.

26. Steven Kelman, "Occupational Safety and Health Administration," in Wilson, *The Politics of Regulation*, p. 263.

27. Levin, "Politics and Polarity," p. 33.

28. Mark J. Green, *The Monopoly Makers*, pp. 144-145.

29. George J. Benston, *The Anti-Redlining Rules*, Univ. of Miami, Law and Economics Center, 1978.

30. Louis M. Kohlmeier, *The Regulators*, pp. 121-128.

31. Ibid., p. 256.

32. Harry V. Ball and Lawrence M. Freidman, "The Use of Criminal Sanctions in the Enforcement of Economic Legislation: A Sociological View," pp. 197-223.

33. Robert E. Lane, *The Regulation of Businessmen*, p. 101.

34. Ibid., p. 102.

35. Ibid., pp. 100-107.

36. Ibid., pp. 45-51.

37. Ibid., pp. 87-88.

38. Ibid., p. 120.

39. Weidenbaum, *The Future of Business Regulations*, pp. 131-138.

11 The Ethics of Accounting

The ethic of telling the truth in commercial transactions has had a long existence. It was submerged in nineteenth-century America but is now revived. The establishment of systems of weights and measures and of keeping accounts are corollaries of the truth-telling principle. Accounting has become especially significant in an era of corporate activity in which managers are responsible for the property of thousands of other people. Careful accounts must be kept if the truth is to be told to shareholders, fellow employees, creditors, debtors, suppliers, and customers. Certified public accountants (CPAs) attest that the figures prepared by a company in its reports present fairly its financial condition to the shareholders and the public. It has taken many decades to develop a system of accounting more or less adequate to the ethical responsibility of account-keeping.

History of Accounting

Accounting is a very old profession. In ancient Babylonia there were men who made most of their living by keeping track of other peoples' affairs. In the Roman Empire debt records were regulated by systematic practices under legal requirements.[1] In the Italian Renaissance careful recording led to the invention of double-entry bookkeeping, which was used to some extent in Genoa, Florence, and Venice as early as the fourteenth century. The double-entry system was not the great activator of capitalism as Werner Sombard has suggested, but it certainly facilitated the art of accounting.[2]

Basil Yamey has written or coauthored a number of articles on the purpose of double-entry bookkeeping. Although he disputes Sombart's view, he deals with ethical material. Of both the single-and double-entry methods it was said,

> . . . the object of bookkeeping is peace and rest of mind, such as is looked for in another world.

> . . . we can wrong others, and even ourselves, without doing any wilful injustice, and that is, by giving our Memory too much Trust and neglecting to write down every Transaction of our Affairs, or setting them down in so disorderly and confused a Manner, that every Person's Right is not truly distinguished but they are charged too much or too little.[3]

Yamey comments that fifteenth-century (and earlier) Italian account books usually began with a pious inscription invoking the name of God. There were numerous references at the beginning of ledgers to the name of God and to good fortune. Similar religious account-book openings were found in England, but lessened in number earlier in England than in Italy.

It is doubtful if much ethical significance can be drawn from the expression of devoutness of fourteenth- to eighteenth-century Italian bookkeepers. Perhaps account books were blessed as were all other major commercial objects—the fishing fleet, the departing galleon. However, the recognition that individual property rights were supported by adequate accounting records indicates the role of accounting in supporting ethical standards.

Double-entry bookkeeping did not become universal even in Italy for several centuries, but it did spread to other countries like Holland and Germany. British merchants picked it up and it was often employed in seventeenth-century England. In both England and Scotland, public auditing occurred with governmental action for tax collection, forfeited estates, and similar items. Public auditing of private business did not become a main part of accounting practice until the 1880s or 1890s. In 1855 in Scotland and 1880 in England, the government-chartered associations of accountants raised professional standards. The Scotch Institutes of Accountants began examinations in 1855 or 1856. Scotland led in accounting because the Scotch used independent accountants for settlement of estates, not official masters of chancery as in England.[4]

An impetus for accounting in England came from the Joint Stock Companies Act of 1856. A schedule of forms of articles for associations included a provision for auditors. A similar table was included in the Companies Act of 1862. An act of 1879 made auditing compulsory for all banking companies registered as Limited after the passage of the act.[5] Chartered accountants were frequently used in British business at that time. The maintenance of accounting standards was the responsibility of the Association of Chartered Accountants rather than of the government.

Examination of a book of speeches, statements, and discussions of English accountants' views of their responsibilities in the last two decades of the nineteenth century shows how the ethical strength of public accounting was built up; the profession helped create its own standards. Sometimes this standard-building was in reaction to the claim that only solicitors were important names on a prospectus of stock. Sometimes it was serious inquiry as to what procedure would be of greatest value to the shareholders. Sometimes it was fear of lawsuit. The fact that the ethical responsibility of the accountant was to the public as well as to his clients seemed to be accepted by all accountants.[6] The ethical bases of this enlightened attitude of British accountants were rarely stated, but they may have grown out of the general ethical background of educated Englishmen of the time.

The training of expert accountants spread from England to the United States, and associations of public accountants were established in America a few decades after those in England. The American Association of Public Accountants was established in New York in 1887, and a bill for licensing such accountants was passed by the New York legislature in 1896.[7] The audit requirement came much more slowly in the United States than in England. It was not firmly established in federal law until the Securities and Exchange Commission Act of 1934, seventy-two years later than establishment in England, and then only applying to larger companies. A large part of the delay was a result of the American federal system that left most of the responsibility for the integrity of companies to the states until the New Deal changes of the 1930s. The states generally limited themselves to passage of "blue sky" laws around 1910 against sale of fraudulent securities. These laws were weakly enforced and were not of great importance to the American accounting profession. It is probably fair to say that late-nineteenth-century and early-twentieth-century Britain was much more concerned about accounting standards than was the United States during the same period. James T. Anyon, an English accountant working in the United States, expressed this opinion in New York in 1886.[8]

The delay in development of accounting practices in the nineteenth-century United States may have been one of the causes of the financial chicanery preceding the 1929 stock-market crash, the continued use of "bucket shops" into the 1960s, and the questionable aspects of the con-glomerate boom of the 1960s. Perhaps the securities problems and the slow development of accounting were both results of poor American business ethics in the late nineteenth and early twentieth centuries.

Business financial reporting improved in the years from 1900 to 1914.[9] Even so, some corporations provided little or no information to shareholders or even to directors; profit-and-loss statements were often nonexistent. However, regulated industries were supposed to publish financial reports. The Hepburn Act of 1906 required reports from railroads, and Interstate Commerce Commission regulations forced better practices of depreciation and replacement accounting. Price, Waterhouse and Company, a firm that was a transplant from Britain where accounting standards were more advanced, set standards for all its clients, thus leading Federal Steel, a part of U.S. Steel, to issue a complete report which U.S. Steel later followed. Price-Waterhouse required consolidated accounts of both holding-company and subsidiary-company accounts.[10] Standard Oil in this period instituted an important internal audit system. New York's Armstrong Investigation of insurance (1905-1906) showed evils resulting from inadequate accounting. The internal moves of business and outside pressures both seemed to push toward better accounting standards.

Collection of the federal income tax in 1914 increased employment of public accountants, but initially only to prepare tax figures.[11] Other accounting services sometimes became necessary, a process speeded by the war-revenue bills of 1917. State legislation requiring work by certified public accountants moves slowly, partly because of opposition from accountants who were not certified and partly because of some negative state-court decisions. The American Institute of Accountants was established in 1916 in an effort to overcome the differences among state requirements for CPAs. By 1924 all states and territories had enacted CPA legislation.[12] All states now use a uniform CPA examination, although requirements vary from state to state.

In 1933 the New York Stock Exchange adopted the requirement that companies wishing to list their stocks must have an audit report by an independent CPA; a majority of companies already did this. The Chicago Stock Exchange soon followed, and the Securities Act of 1933 required a CPA report of registration statements for securities sold on interstate markets. Thus the calamity of the crash and Depression resulted in a long-delayed but much needed reform.

Accountants were alarmed by a provision in the 1933 Securities Act making them liable for damage suits, but were relieved when the Securities and Exchange Commission Act of 1934 reduced the period in which suit might be brought from ten to three years. In the 1970s, accounting firms were the object of many suits and had to pay multimillion-dollar claims for false or inadequate statements.

Along with the better organization and growth of the accounting profession, another factor developed—the Securities and Exchange Commission (SEC), which had statutory power over accounting but made an effort to leave that task to the profession. In 1938 the SEC was informed that McKesson and Robbins executives had taken $3 million from the concern and then covered the theft with fraudulent inventories and warehouse data which the auditor, Price-Waterhouse, had not discovered through use of then-normal auditing procedures. The SEC scolded Price-Waterhouse, which refunded its half-million-dollar audit fees. In the 1960s, one CPA firm and one partner were briefly suspended from practice because of inadequate investigation of a business firm.[13] A writer on financial matters suggests that the accounting profession's great mistake came in the 1920s when accountants devised misleading ways of writing up book values of companies in order to raise stock-market prices.[14]

College education as a standard for CPAs began to be adopted in the 1930s and 1940s. Unfortunately, college education does not necessarily bring higher ethical standards.[15] In 1936 two national accounting societies were merged into one American Institute of Accountants. This became the American Institute of Certified Public Accountants (AICPA) in 1957. The Institute adopted expanded rules of professional conduct in 1958.

American Accounting Standards

Accounting still seems to command greater respect in England in one regard than in the United States. John Brooks comments:

> In the late sixties, thirteen members of the House of Lords were professionally qualified accountants, as were nine members of the House of Commons, including the Chancellor of the Exchequer himself; on this side of the Atlantic, not a single accountant was to be found among the 535 members of Congress.[16]

Of course, membership in Congress is not necessarily as much a sign of distinction in American life as is membership in Parliament in England. The British usually include a chartered public accountant on government investigatory commissions; the Americans rarely include a certified public accountant. Brooks believes that American accountants are more likely to yield to their clients' wishes than are British accountants.[17] George J. Benston notes that

> U.S. accountants are subject to much greater restrictions than are their counterparts. U.S. accountants are penalized for not following the letter of the law and regulations which are presumed to protect the public. In the U.K. much more reliance is placed on accountants' professional judgment and integrity, and their desire to protect their reputations. Perhaps for this reason U.K. accountants appear to enjoy more prestige than do their U.S. counterparts.[18]

Benston is very skeptical of the value of government supervision of corporate financial matters. He believes that commercial pressure on accounting firms would provide adequate control, and that criticisms of this approach are exaggerated.

In recent decades the public-accounting profession has prospered greatly in the United States. Statutes and regulations now require professional audits of all firms listed on stock exchanges and those with over one-hundred shareholders. The SEC, which has legal power to prescribe accounting methods, has until recently left the authority over accounting rules to a body established by the American Institute of Certified Public Accountants (AICPA). Many substantial philanthropic and educational institutions have annual audits by CPA firms. Some, but not enough, governmental units do also. The income of the accounting profession in America today is several billion dollars a year. Resident partners of the "Big Eight" auditing firms in large cities may have incomes as high as a quarter-million dollars a year.

All of this emphasis on auditing and accounting has certainly helped to raise the ethical standards of American business. However, the requirement of an audit does not bring an ethical Utopia. Amost all auditing firms are selected and paid by the management of the business being audited (although in recent years the accounting firms usually report to a committee of independent board members). The AICPA codes have tried to ban formal connections between auditors and their clients. Auditors may not serve on the boards of, borrow money from, or conduct joint business with clients.[19] Yet there is still some pressure on auditors to be sympathetic to their employers. A number of accounting firms sell management services to the business firms they audit. Funds received for these services, often more than for auditing, are thought by some accountants to push in the direction of less effective auditing, although many accountants deny this.

The basic economic function of public accounting is to preserve the integrity of capital markets by fairly presenting the financial condition of a company to holders or buyers of the company's bonds or stocks, or to its creditors or debtors. A firm of certified public accountants which deliberately misreported financial figures would lose its reputation and some accountants would probably lose their licenses. However, mistakes do occur. At least two surveys of audit reports to banks for credit purchases show that inadequate audit procedures had been followed.[20] There can be little question that in recent decades CPA firms have sometimes rendered reports that have been deceptive to present or prospective shareholders.

A dissenting group of CPAs has been the academics, some of whom bemoaned the failure of the profession to set firmer technical accounting principles. Accountants in practice reacted against the academics and kept them in minority roles on the boards dealing with accounting principles, thus emphasizing the importance of flexibility in business, but sometimes overlooking the opportunity to keep fiscal reports clear and accurate for shareholders.[21] Reports of the Accounting Principles Board, and of the Financial Accounting Standards Board after 1972, were weak in that they did not clearly require disclosure of financial conditions. The SEC has had an increasing number of staff members who are unhappy about the results. For years the SEC threatened action.[22] In recent years the SEC has more clearly indicated its intention of laying down principles if the accountants fail to do so, and on some occasions the SEC has intervened.

Further proof that the academic critics were at least partly right comes from a symposium sponsored by the AICPA, the Financial Analysts Federation, the Financial Executives Institute, and Robert Morris Associates.[23] The conference was held in late 1971 after the artificial stock values of the conglomerate boom had begun to crash. A majority of the reported talks clearly indicated dissatisfaction with the vagueness of accounting principles.

Certified public accountants have attempted, with endorsement and prodding from the SEC, to establish bodies that would set up firmer accounting principles. First, the American Institute of Accountants established a Committee on Accounting Principles that published some bulletins between 1938 and 1959. Then the Accounting Principles Board (APB) was established to undertake the task from 1959 to 1972. Finally the Financial Accounting Standards Board (FASB) was established in 1973. None of these have been completely successful, but they have made some progress in defining accounting principles. In general, the active accounting professionals preferred to use alternative methods of handling accounting problems.[24]

Robert Chatov believes that the SEC gave up its powers over accounting methods because of heavy political pressure from accountants and related financial groups. The series of organizations established by the public accountants all tended to avoid making more specific accounting principles because big-business employers of CPAs wanted leeway to change accounting methods when business or general accounting pressure made changes seem desirable. Although this is not proof of Chatov's point, it is important to know that a U.S. Senate subcommittee staff in 1977 also reported that the FASB and its predecessor the APB yielded to business viewpoints on accounting for foreign-currency fluctuations in charging for research expenditures, and other accounting problems. However, the big accounting firms had some good answers to the subcommittee-staff criticisms.[25]

Changes or uncertainties in accounting methods may act against the disclosure of corporate financial conditions. They were, says Chatov, one of the reasons for overdevelopment of conglomerates in the 1960s, and the conglomerate crash of 1971-1972. According to Chatov, the SEC should sponsor the development of accounting codes, and enforcement of the codes should come from private or SEC actions in special federal courts. Chatov's suggestion is somewhat like the method used to enforce the law of business operations in West Germany.[26]

Since Chatov wrote his book, the SEC has on a few occasions set up its own regulations on accounting matters, sometimes overriding the FASB, and not always in the interests of better accounting. There have also been efforts of CPAs and others to strengthen the FASB.[27] However, there is no general tendency in the SEC to regulate all accounting, and the Reagan administration's deregulation program will probably move in the opposite direction.

Only some of Chatov's thesis is acceptable. Chatov is properly aware of the tendency of some one-industry regulatory agencies to assume the attitudes of the industry, and the SEC has often, though not always, done this. But Chatov thinks primarily in terms of greater SEC control, not recognizing that business ethics are often developed on the job. Joint SEC and accounting-profession efforts might be more likely to prevail than Chatov's program of codes and courts. The already existing investor actions for damages from CPA firms may help secure a more thorough CPA attitude.

When Accounting Has Not Worked

Here are some examples of the failure of accounting to prevent the loss of several billions of dollars of shareholders' money. Three of the country's large public-accounting firms were involved in the first example; the fault was not all theirs, but a more aggressive attitude toward the public good on their part might have stopped much of the deception and fraud. These are only sample cases; others could be cited.

In 1960, Investors Overseas Service (IOS) was formed in Panama by Bernard Cornfeld and Associates. Its purpose was to sell securities in a mutual fund, at first in the Dreyfus Fund, and later in securities of IOS, which owned the Interstate Investment Trust (IIT), the Fund of Funds (FOF), and other funds. IOS was exempt from Securities and Exchange Commission control, as it operated overseas, had headquarters in Geneva, and presumably did not sell securities in the United States. IOS did, however, strive for some aspects of financial respectability. Arthur Andersen and Company were auditors for IOS from 1960 on, Price-Waterhouse helped prepare the prospectus for the Fund of Funds, and Lybrand, Ross Brothers, and Montgomery (now Coopers and Lybrand) audited the FOF and Robert Vesco after his takeover of FOF in 1970.

The Fund of Funds, registered in Ontario, Canada in 1960, increased spectacularly after 1962.[28] By 1970 the combination of funds under IOS issued new stock for $110 million. Arthur Andersen and Company, auditors for IOS and ITT since 1960, "took no specific responsibility for the accuracy of the prospectus at this point, but they did not report any omissions or distortions."[29] The prospectus also obscured the fact that IOS sales were operating at a loss and that a subsidiary, Commonwealth United Corporation, was "illiquid" and was forced to borrow $4.5 million from its subsidiary, Investment Properties International.

In 1969, the Fund of Funds secured an $11 million participation in King Resources Company rights to drill for petroleum in an Arctic area of Canada. A sale from King Resources to a closely related company, Consolidated Oil and Gas, of a small part of King Resources' interest, and another small sale to John Mecom and Lake Share Associates established, according to IOS, a great increase in the value of its Arctic holdings. IOS sold back to King Resources a roughly equivalent share of its rights. The Fund of Funds report in the summer of 1970 glossed over the questionable nature of the transactions on which an increase of value of FOF's holdings from $11 million to $156 million was based. Arthur Andersen and Company declared themselves not competent to judge the values, but did not object to a very questionable increase in valuation.

Also during 1969 and 1970, IOS paid out large sums for various schemes enabling senior staff members to charge off income tax due from their recently sold stock earnings. Eight of the early IOS employees became millionaires through these processes. IOS also bought a large number of its own shares, presumably to keep the price up. Finally, by May 1970 it became clear that IOS was not earning profits but was in great financial difficulty. Values of shares dropped tremendously and Cornfeld was fired. The loss to IOS shareholders was very great.[30]

In 1971 what was left of the IOS group came under the control of Robert L. Vesco and his allies. This group siphoned $224 million of former IOS assets into close-ended units outside the United States controllable by Vesco. A partner of Lybrand, Ross Brothers, and Montgomery (now Coopers and Lybrand) audited the accounts of Vesco's company, International Controls, while this step was taken. SEC action against this siphoning of assets originally named the accounting firm as codefendant but later dropped it.[31] Vesco still lives outside the United States to avoid prosecution.[32] In 1980, Coopers and Lybrand paid $150,000 to International Controls as part of a settlement of a shareholder action on the Vesco deal.[33] A New York law firm and a large bank also had large liabilities in 1980 for the Vesco deals.[34]

There were relatively few illegal actions in the history of IOS, but many shareholders lost hundreds of millions of dollars because of the highly unethical actions of Cornfeld, his collaborators, and Vesco. Two nationally known independent certified public-accounting firms furnished inadequate protection to the investors. The auditors did not commit fraud, but they deserve criticism for failure to discover the fraud.

Equity Funding Company of America (EFCA) is another example of a company that took millions of dollars away from its shareholders with almost no warning from its independent accountants. EFCA sold a combination of mutual-fund shares and life insurance. Beginning at least in 1964 and continuing until discovery of the frauds in 1974, the EFCA reported inflated commissions on sales. In 1968 the conspirators began borrowing funds without showing the liability in the accounts, by not recording the source of the funds or by involving funds in bogus transactions through subsidiaries. In 1969 income was inflated by $17. 2 million by a sham sale of supposedly valuable future commissions to a foreign corporation controlled by the conspirators.[35] Foreign subsidiaries were used to record other fraudulent income. As these and other frauds failed to produce the desired income, a subsidiary, Equity Funding Life Insurance Company (EFLIC), in 1970 began to record wholly fictitious insurance policies and then to reinsure those policies with other companies to secure funds. The frauds were discovered in 1973 after $143 million in fictitious income had been reported. Thousands of investors found their Equity Funding stock, for which they had paid substantial prices and about the value of which they had been constantly misinformed, to be practically worthless.

During all these years of fraud the small CPA firm Wolfson-Weiner, discovered nothing. When the auditors requested additional information they were stalled off, finally referred to the president of the company, and after a conference with him closed the audit. There is evidence to indicate that some staff of the auditing firm, later merged into Seidman and Seidman, were not unaware of what was going on, and probably helped to conceal the fraud. A trustee reported the EFCA's accounts and records were "in relative disarray" over the entire life of the fraud. The takeover by Seidman and Seidman did not result in adequate auditing. The large national accounting firm, Haskins and Sells, (now Deloitte, Haskins, and Sells) audited the subsidiary, Equity Funding Life Insurance Company; the same trustee suggested that the auditors failed to review internal controls.[36] The three accounting firms jointly agreed to pay $39 million to share and debenture owners.

The question raised by these spectacular failures is again to be raised about a series of smaller failures or great drops in stock values. Why were the CPAs not more careful, more anxious to see that a full report went to shareholders? Some accountants view these errors as technical rather than ethical but some technical errors are important enough to become ethical errors.

Even George J. Benston, who in general opposes government regulations, commented:

> . . . there is reason to believe (though there is no supportive evidence) that auditors may not be willing or able to report possible conflicts of interest or misrepresentation which obscures unfavorable operations by the management which employs them. Therefore government required disclosure that is directed towards preventing or reducing the incidence of management violating its fiduciary responsibilities to shareholders appears justified and beneficial.[37]

Others have noted that in addition to the small accounting firm Wolfson-Weiner, other more influential groups had approved Equity Funding for its New York Stock Exchange rating. Both the American Stock Exchange and later the New York Stock Exchange had approved Equity Funding. A leading underwriting firm had sold Equity's funds and had a senior partner on its board of directors. Its tax returns were examined by the Internal Revenue Service. Seidman and Seidman had signed its 1972 prospectus and Haskins and Sells had audited the subsidiary, Equity Funding Life Insurance Company. The insurance regulators of some of the largest states, including New York, California, and Illinois had examined it. An actuarial firm certified its reserves. A consortium of large banks, including Citibank and Wells Fargo gave Equity Funding credit of over $100 million, just nine months before its assets were discovered to be largely fraudulent. Five experienced insurance companies reinsured $1.2 billion of largely fraudulent life-insurance policies. It is true that one insurance company, Ranger National Life, prodded by Anderson, Clayton, asked Peat, Marwick, and Mitchell (PMM) to check out the insurance policies in 1970 and PMM almost found the fraud. But that check was put off by Equity Funding, so the existence of false policies was not discovered.

What can be understood from this failure of regulators to regulate and of other financial companies to discover fraud? The chief point may be that too much is taken for granted in American accounting and financial circles. Robert Loeffler, court-appointed trustee for Equity Funding and lawyer, blamed the Equity Funding situation primarily on the independent auditors. J. Seidler, Frederick Andrews, and Marc J. Epstein, all accountants or closely related to accounting, believe the blame could be more generally spread. Some fraction of the blame should be placed on the general failure of Americans to teach active ethics to accountants as well as to others. Men who are responsible for other people's affairs need "a disposition to find out and respect the relevant facts and a disposition to think clearly."[38]

In any event, in early 1977 the accounting firms agreed with district court judge Malcolm Lucas to pay $39 million of the approximately $60 million to be paid to former shareholders of Equity Funding.[39] Other reports cite $43 million was to be paid by CPA firms. Another $4 million was to be available to shareholders at the end of bankruptcy proceedings. To high-income accounting firms, this payment was probably not crushing, but it may well have taught the accounting profession to expand the scope of audits to search for fraud.

The Looseness of Generally Accepted Accounting Principles

There has been a wide variety of cases in which companies have been able to change their methods of accounting, seriously deceive shareholders and others, and yet secure the signature of a CPA from a "Big Eight" accounting firm on its annual statements. Real-estate companies, selling land on small downpayments, were allowed to reflect the total cost of the contract as revenue. One such company alone recorded $44 million in sales in 1971.[40] Other major firms made "wash sales" of real estate between subsidiaries or with close associates to reflect gains of several million dollars on the year's profit-and-loss statements. In another case options to buy land were sold to a nonexistent equity. The development of conglomerates in the 1960s included many mergers in which the merged company's assets were put on the new company's accounts at a minimal book value in order to make the earnings of the new conglomerate look better.

To criticism that these accounting methods may be unethical Benston replies that the buyers of stock are not really fooled. He cites a number of surveys which conclude that the voluntarily chosen accounting alternatives do not affect prices of stocks.[41] He also comments that the accounting rules for treating stock purchased ín mergers were tightened substantially by the SEC, the AICPA, and the FASB.

On the other hand, Chatov believes that the "conglomerate mania" of the 1960s that helped bring about the "conglomerate recession" of 1969-1970 was largely a result of pooling-of-interest accounting techniques. He comments that interest-pooling permitted gains in earnings per share of the acquiring corporation since it recorded on its books only the under-valued assets of the acquired company. The profits were illusory because the acquiring company had paid for the assets, "perhaps even at above market value."[42]

If Chatov is right, the ethical purpose of accounting is not served by pooling of interest. It was designed to deceive buyers of the stock of the merged company into believing that actual earnings were increasing by natural means instead of by a temporary increase from the nature of the merger. Benston's answer would be that buyers are not deceived. But more importantly, buyers of shares may believe that they were deceived.

Generally accepted accounting principles allow corporations a wide freedom in handling revenues. The National Student Marketing Corpora-tion in 1969 accrued all revenues, without regard to the possibility of bad debts, resulting in heavy losses for many investors. Telex Corporation gave itself credit for revenues at full cost of manufacture for machinery leased only for a year. Four Seasons Nursing Centers recorded earnings on the basis of physical estimates of percentage of completion of buildings.[43] The phar-maceutical industry records expenses for research and information activities as incurred, thus understating its actual capital and showing a high rate of return on capital.[44] Accounting for inventories is also allowed to vary sharply. When commodity prices rose sharply in 1974, many businesses shifted from FIFO (first in, first out) to LIFO (last in, first out) inventory systems to reduce profits and taxes. Oil companies vary widely in how they capitalize exploration costs.

None of these actions are illegal, or formally outlawed by generally ac-cepted accounting principles. But changes in accounting methods should be fully disclosed. They may deceive the individual buyer of stock and thus be contrary to a two-thousand-year-old ethical tradition.

It is only fair to add that most large and medium-size American cor-porations have good internal-audit systems and receive careful objective audits from their accounting firms. Ethical problems remain in all account-ing systems. The cases described are perhaps not typical. Nevertheless, they contribute to public suspicion of American business. There is evidence to show that the accounting profession has made a series of mistakes. A Roper poll in 1978 showed 68 percent of the American public believed that business was far too often not honest with the public. In view of the efforts of IOS, Equity Funding, Penn-Central, Four Seasons, Vesco, and many others to deceive the public, often with annual statements reported by CPAs, the public can hardly be criticized for its attitude.

The numerous cases in which neither the ethics of the profession nor generally accepted accounting principles protected the investor or lender cannot be reviewed without the feeling that the profession of accounting needs some more ethical development. At least one study indicates a failure of CPAs to secure legal disclosures in small companies.[45] Was the fault solely in the laxity of standards? If so, should the accounting standards be made more rigid by a governmental agency? Chatov suggests a judicial remedy. Have CPAs assimilated some of the lack of concern about ethics observed in other parts of the business world? It seems so. Big accounting firms with large staffs to support did not want to lose large clients, even though those clients later proved to be engaged in fraud. Does some trace of *caveat emptor* or, "the public be damned" live on in this great profession?

Spokesmen for the status quo in the accounting profession maintain that uniform accounting principles would be unworkable. Companies vary within industries, and among industries; it is unthinkable to have uniform methods of charging depreciation, or of accounting for assets in mergers, or of recording installment sales. Such defenders may grant that in the meantime, individual investors may be fooled by a company's change in accounting method, but they claim that professional investment analysts will not be so deluded. It may be that more uniform accounting methods may at times damage one or another concern, unless adequate explanation is given; but it is hard to believe that the overwhelming Western tradition of truth-telling to customers should be overcome on this account. When the *Wall Street Journal* reports that Union Carbide has added $343 million to its 1980 earnings by changes in accounting methods such as extension of depreciation lives or a new method for valuing investment-tax credits, one wonders about the ethics involved.[46] There may be good business reasons for such practices. If comparative data on various accounting methods for several years are studied, the procedures may prove to be ethical.

Conclusion: The Courts Prescribe Accounting Ethics

The examples given of financial chicanery unopposed by some CPAs in the 1960s and 1970s have led to a more potent reform pressure—the suits against accounting firms brought by angry shareholders. Some of these suits have been successful and have cost the large accounting firms scores of millions of dollars. It is true that suits were often brought against the larger accounting firms because they had money, while the bankrupt corporations did not. Equity Funding cost the accounting firms almost $40 million. Another accounting firm lost $3 million because of its approval of Penn-Central misdoings. A federal court in 1981 awarded $80 million in damages against Arthur Andersen and Company because of a Fund of Funds transaction.[47] These multimillion-dollar awards show that the accounting firms failed in an important responsibility.

Were these suits a good means of enforcing more careful accounting standards? Most observers would have preferred to see standards set by the profession itself. But since the profession failed to do so, was not recourse to the courts reasonable? Many ethical standards have to be enforced by a governmental agency. For example, if parents, teachers, and ministers fail to teach standards to juvenile delinquents, the police or courts must do so. Perhaps the accountants will learn from these damage suits. Accountants are naturally trying to secure legislative limits on their liability.

It is only fair to add that most accountants probably wanted their profession to set proper standards. Three successive groups were established to do so—the Committee on Accounting Procedures, the Accounting Principles Board, and the Financial Accounting Standards Board. The first two failed perhaps because of the low ethical standards of the country.

Will the courts be able to establish adequate standards under the guidance of federal legislation? The Securities Act of 1933 clearly makes a CPA liable for false or misleading statements; so there is no doubt about the statutory basis of standards. The Securities and Exchange Commission Act of 1934 provided that it was unlawful to use any manipulative or deceptive device or continuance contrary to SEC rules. But judges can bring various legal doctrines into the discussion. One of the most prominent is whether public accountants could have foreseen that financial statements would be false or misleading. There were other factors: in the Bar Chris Construction Corporation case the court held a public accountant liable because he did not take all the steps his firm prescribed—he did not use adequate time, he was satisfied with glib answers.[48]

It may be that the courts, either alone or in tandem with the SEC, may succeed in broadening the CPAs' ethical conceptions. Several times in American history, legal action has started the development of a needed ethic. The accounting profession may thus be moving toward a more thorough form of auditing.

Notes

1. A.C. Littleton, *Accounting Evolution to 1900,* p. 29.
2. Basil L. Yamey, *Essays on the History of Accounting,* pp. 117-136.
3. Luca Paciolo, quoted in Yamey, *Essays on the History of Accounting,* p. 103.

4. Richard Brown, ed., *History of Accounting and Accountants,* p. 232.

5. Ibid., p. 319.

6. Ernest Cooper, "Chartered Accountants as Auditors of Companies," (1886) in Michael Chatfield, ed., *The English View of Accountant's Duties and Responsibilities,* pp. 30-36.

7. Brown, *History of Accounting and Accountants,* p. 272.

8. James D. Edwards, *History of Public Accounting.*

9. Saul Engelbourg, *Power and Morality,* pp. 123-129.

10. C.W. DeMond, *Price, Waterhouse and Co. in America,* pp. 60-61.

11. Edwards, *History of Public Accounting,* pp. 102-104.

12. Ibid., pp. 101-147.

13. Ibid., pp. 263-273.

14. John Brooks, *The Go Go Years,* p. 159.

15. Howard R. Bowen, *Investment in Learning,* pp. 120-123.

16. Brooks, *The Go Go Years,* p. 163.

17. Berryman, "Auditor Independence," in Stephen E. Loeb, ed., *Ethics in the Accounting Profession,* pp. 141-142 ff.

18. George J. Benston, *Corporate Financial Disclosure in the U.K. and the U.S.A.,* p. 188.

19. Loeb, *Ethics in the Accounting Profession,* pp. 101-102.

20. Ibid., pp. 343-372.

21. Abraham Briloff, *Unaccountable Accounting* and *More Debits than Credits;* Robert Chatov, *Corporate Financial Reporting.*

22. Chatov, *Corporate Financial Reporting,* p. 252.

23. John C. Burton, *Corporate Financial Reporting: Ethical and Other Problems.*

24. Chatov, *Corporate Financial Reporting,* pp. 274-277.

25. *Forbes Magazine,* March 15, 1977, pp. 37-43.

26. Chatov, *Corporate Financial Reporting,* p. 300.

27. *Business Week,* May 23, 1977, p. 94.

28. Charles Raw, Bruce Page, and Godfrey Hodson, *Do You Sincerely Want to be Rich?,* p. 85.

29. Ibid., pp. 275-276.

30. Ibid., pp. 301-309.

31. Briloff, *More Debits than Credits,* pp. 58-62.

32. Robert A. Hutchinson, *Vesco,* chap. 24.

33. *Wall Street Journal,* June 31, 1980.

34. *Wall Street Journal,* July 22, 1980.

35. Loeffler Report in J. Seidler, Frederick Andrews, and Marc J. Epstein, *The Equity Funding Papers,* pp. 131 ff.

36. Ibid., p. 171; pp. 271-275.

37. Benston, *Corporate Financial Disclosure in the U.K. and the U.S.A.,* p. 151.

38. William K. Frankena, *Ethics,* p. 68.

39. Seidler et al., *The Equity Funding Papers,* p. 577.

40. *Wall Street Journal,* June 21, 1971, cited in Briloff, *Unaccountable Accounting,* p. 166.

41. Benston, *Conglomerate Mergers,* pp. 8-9.

42. Chatov, *Corporate Financial Reporting,* pp. 207-209.

43. Briloff, *More Debits than Credits,* pp. 102-107.

44. Yale Brozen, ed., *Is Government the Source of Monopoly?,* p. 37.

45. Donald R. Dropp, "Professional Notes," pp. 80-87.

46. *Wall Street Journal,* January 25, 1980.

47. *Los Angeles Times,* November 6, 1981.

48. *Escott* v. *Bar Chris Construction Corporation,* 283F, Supp 643 SD NY, 1968.

12 The Pros and Cons of Advertising

Ethical Principles

America's business ethical heritage contains only a few fundamental principles about advertising. The general rule that sellers should tell buyers the truth about defects in products could apply to at least some advertising. This rule appeared in the Code of Hammurabi, the Old Testament, Greek and Roman law, and English common law, but was not followed in nineteenth-century British or American law. In the nineteenth century, the contrary doctrine of *caveat emptor* was followed, with disturbing effects on the ethics of advertising, as well as on sales in general. Later nineteenth-century decisions and laws modified the effect of *caveat emptor* but left the United States with a tradition (not a principle) which seemed to justify deception by sellers.

Another basic principle of Western ethics has some application to advertising—the rule of using property so that it does not damage others. Advertisements that damage competitors or customers can be the subjects of court action. There are also laws that forbid the use of advertisements to achieve criminal ends. William Blackstone cites two such laws. One stated that:

> even to advertise a reward for the return of things stolen with no questions asked, or words to the same purport, subjects the advertiser and the printer to a forfeiture of 50 pounds each.

Also, Statutes 33 Hen. VIII, c 1, 30 Geo 11, c.24 prescribe:

> if any man defrauds another of any valuable chattels by color of any false token, counterfeit letter, or false pretense—he shall suffer such punishment—as the court shall direct.[1]

Historical Background

Advertisements have existed for many centuries. In ancient Rome criers attracted customers to auctions, and auctioneers cried their wares.[2] Advertisements began to be more frequent in Britain and the colonies by the seventeenth century when they were printed for books, for coffee, for fabrics, for lost dogs, and for patent medicines—the latter with the inevitable claims of quackery. Coffee, tea, cloth, and dentifrices were soon publicized by newspapers and magazines. In the year of the Plague (1665) quack remedies were widely advertised on the posts of houses and corners of streets. There is no evidence of business or government rules to secure truth or factual bases for advertising; had there been rules, machinery of enforcement would have had to have been devised.[3]

Nor was there much improvement in the eighteenth century. An essay by Joseph Addison in *The Tatler* of September 14, 1710 comments that advertisements are of great use to the vulgar.[4] The ambitious may by advertisement place their names close to those of great men. Advertisements give opportunity for controversy between competitive products. They also inform the world about the necessaries of life. Advertisers try to catch the public eye through good writing. They are, however, subject to criticism for sometimes being "not at all proper to appear in the works of polite writers." An example are the *Carminative Wind-Expelling Pills*, which to be used clearly, should have been called "carminative" alone. Addison was of course prejudiced since he derived some income from advertising, but he seems to have foreseen one of the major arguments for advertising, as well as the desire for more informative advertisements, shown years later by the Federal Trade Commission.

The late eighteenth century was another time in which advertisements tended heavily toward quackery, like promises to cure stuttering by application of ointments, or to stimulate hair growth with magical combs. Sir Richard Steele in *The Spectator* described quacks who distributed bills at streetcorners as "Imposters and Murderers," but admitted some quackish advertisements into his own columns; some of these being advertisements that would not be allowed in the United States today.[5]

Caveat Emptor

The late Walton Hamilton of Yale and Ivan L. Preston of the University of Wisconsin give in their publications a picture of the historical development of one aspect of truth in advertising.[6] Hamilton points out that Thomas Aquinas wrote in the thirteenth century that a sale was rendered unlawful by a defect in the thing sold about which the seller failed to inform the buyer. If the seller did not know of the defect, he had not committed a sin, but he had to recompense the seller. A thirteenth-century parson denounced tricks of trade such as mixing hair with cloth, selling of rotten meat, and baking rotten corn; and noted many other deceptions that were strictly punished in ecclesiastical and temporal courts. Five centuries later, there were still complaints of abuses, frauds, and deceits in the woolen industry.

Beginning in the sixteenth century, the phrase *caveat emptor* ("buyer beware") was invented. It spread through use by lawyers and a few judges, although as late as the 1770s, Blackstone's *Commentaries on the Laws of England* followed Aquinas's doctrine that the seller should disclose defects.

In nineteenth-century America, the strictures of English common law were overturned in favor of the philosophy of *caveat emptor*. This was an unethical but understandable reaction in a new country where business activity was needed, and judges were trying to help business grow. Hamilton cites a leading case in New York in which the suit of a buyer who received a cargo of cheaper peachum wood although he had paid for a more expensive braziletto was dismissed on *caveat emptor* grounds.[7] Similar judgments prevailed in other state courts. The U.S. Supreme Court recognized the general acceptance of *caveat emptor* "where the common law prevails."[8] A California legislative committee in mid-century announced that *caveat emptor* was the common law.[9] In Massachusetts in 1843 in *Medbury* v. *Watson* the court stated:

> . . . in actions on the case for deceit, founded upon false affirmations, there has always existed the exception, that naked assertions, though known to be false, are not the ground of action, as between vendor and vendee.[10]

Perhaps a maximum use of *caveat emptor* came in *Brown* v. *Castles* in which the court said that the rule that misrepresentation by the seller beyond the observation of the recipient was fraud became inapplicable because it "is not applied to statements made by sellers, concerning the value of the thing sold, former offers for it, etc., it always having been understood, the world over, that such statements are to be distrusted."[11]

In the first half of the nineteenth century in Britain, E.S. Turner found material which he described as the "Blast of Puffery."[12] In both England and the United States the doctrine of *caveat emptor* had made it very difficult for a deceived buyer to bring action against a false advertisement.

In the United States the result of *caveat emptor* in the nineteenth century was a wide-open explosion of deceptive advertising. In the 1820s, P.T. Barnum had begun a career of deceptive advertisements and expositions of vastly overblown exhibits. The sign "This Way to the Egress" will long be remembered as a symbol of Barnum's ethics. Useless patent medicines were advertised in quite respectable papers. In the 1850s, petroleum from surface outcroppings was sold as a patent medicine under the name *Seneca Snake Oil*.

Some of the worst results of excessive emphasis on *caveat emptor* still existed at the turn of the century in America. Leading merchants like John Wanamaker of Philadelphia had made efforts to secure better standards, but the less reliable advertising included much misrepresentation of quality

and quantity of objects sold, including land and securities. Quacks and
charlatans had begun to advertise patent medicines heavily by the 1880s, at
a time when reputable businesses had not begun to advertise. The chief bar
to advertising swindling was the occasional exercise of the federal
postmaster general's authority to forbid the use of the mails to swindlers or
to ask the Department of Justice to prosecute them. A "complete sewing
machine for 25 cents" turned out to be a needle. A "steel engraving of
General Grant for 25 cents" turned out to be a 1-cent postage stamp. Sellers
of patent medicines offered extravagant claims.[13]

Some improvements in advertising were begun by Francis W. Ayer (of
the N.W. Ayer agency) and John E. Powers, an advertising consultant. Big
stores like Marshall Field, A.T. Stewart, Macy's, and Wanamaker's began
regular advertising in the 1870s. By the 1880s, *Scribner's, Harper's,
Munsey's,* the *Ladies Home Journal*, and the *Saturday Evening Post* were
setting some standards of advertising. However, much deceptive advertising
remained.

Hamilton expressed some broader results of *caveat emptor*: "For
decades the power of the state even over impure foods, if not lost, was inert
from disuse; for decades its negligent supervision took in little more than
milk and meat."[14] It was not legal to require that loaves of bread come
within two ounces of the announced weight or that shoddy material not be
used in bed coverings. Mere lies of sellers did not constitute fraud. The
federal government even issued pamphlets urging American merchants to
exaggerate the quality of their wares.[15] The general weakness of American
public administration in the nineteenth century also contributed to the
unhappy results recorded by Hamilton.

Even today when the principle of *caveat emptor* has been officially
eliminated in advertising by state law for seventy years, and by the U.S.
Congress for almost half a century, and when courts follow it only in
limited circumstances (like formal legal sales and cases where the seller does
not owe a duty of disclosure), the doctrine is still cited by New York City
court officials as a reason for not taking court action against obvious frauds
of lower-income people.[16] It has been suggested that juries fail to convict on
state criminal laws against deceptive advertising because they think the
crimes only "overzealous salesmanship."[17] Marshall B. Clinard in a study
of black-market sanctions in World War II suggests that *caveat emptor* and
laisser-faire interfered with the development of needed legal prohibitions
against a variety of business crimes.[18] E.T. Grether in 1966 wrote, "The
area of seemingly greatest misunderstanding and difficulty stems from the
legal doctrine of 'puffing' in advertising and sales promotion."[19]

The Slow Reform of Advertising

The American business and political reform movement that began in the
1890s affected advertising substantially. By 1900, a number of farm

magazines were guaranteeing their subscribers against loss from their advertisements. *Good Housekeeping* guaranteed protection of its readers and
established an institute to check into advertisers' claims, headed by Dr.
Harvey W. Wiley, father of the federal Pure Food and Drug law. In 1904, the
Ladies Home Journal and the *Saturday Evening Post* were supporting more
honest advertising. The muckrakers of the first decade of the nineteenth century wrote articles on fraudulent advertising of patent medicines, and on
frauds in retailing. So did editorial columns in the *Chicago Tribune,* the
Philadelphia North American, the *St. Louis Star,* the *Detroit Times,* and
others.[20]

Also, in the first decade of the twentieth century, advertisers themselves
began a movement for reform. The Associated Advertising Clubs of
America, formed in St. Louis in 1905 under a slightly different name, resolved to "expose fraudulent schemes and their perpetrators."[21] There were
only a score of these clubs in Midwestern cities. But by the 1911 Advertising
Federation meeting, there was a good deal of enthusiasm in the movement.
"The Ten Commandments of Advertising" advocated by the president of the
department of retail advertisers are a somewhat stilted imitation of the
decalogue, but worth quoting. It is interesting that the truth standard of these
advertising men was above that of Chief Justice Oliver Wendell Holmes in
Massachusetts Supreme Court cases of a few decades earlier.

1. Thou shalt have no other gods in advertising but Truth.
2. Thou shalt not make any graven image of wealth, or power, or station,
   and thou shalt not bow down thyself to them nor serve them except with
   honor.
3. Thou shalt not use the power of advertising in an unworthy cause or in
   behalf of unworthy goods.
4. Remember the working day to keep it holy.
5. Honor thy business and thy advertising, that they may honor thee, and
   thy days of usefulness may be long upon the land.
6. Thou shalt not kill fair competition from without, nor ambition from
   within thine organization.
7. Thou shalt not lie, misstate, exaggerate, misrepresent nor conceal; thou
   shalt not bear false witness to the public, but thou shalt be fair to thy
   merchandise.
8. Thou shalt not steal by false pretense in statements, spoken, written or
   printed.
9. Thou shalt not permit adulteration or substitution in advertised good.
10. Thou shalt not covet, nor imitate, nor run down thy neighbor's business;
    thou shalt not covet, nor imitate, nor run down thy neighbor's name, nor
    his fame, not his wares, nor his trade, nor anything that is thy
    neighbor's.[22]

Supporting the truth-in-advertising movement, the magazine *Printer's
Ink* featured the reform and carried a campaign for better advertising in its

columns for years. *Printer's Ink* recommended a model state statute penalizing fraudulent representations and false and misleading advertising. Most of enforcement responsibility was left to public officials and the courts. "Vigilance committees," which later became Better Business Bureaus, were formed in Boston and other cities. Advertisers adopted firm standards internationally at a Toronto meeting in June, 1914.

Newspaper delegates at a Chicago convention of the Associated Advertising Clubs in 1915 adopted a resolution against fraudulent advertising. In the same year the *New York Tribune* began to guarantee all its merchandise advertising.

The advertising clubs and Better Business Bureaus in 1915 worked-closely with the Federal Trade Commission established in 1914. Many cases came to the FTC from the National Better Business Bureau. Blocking of "blue-sky" security promoters became a part of the advertisers' work, supplemented chiefly by federal prosecution. Fraudulent oil-stock promoters were opposed by a similar grouping.

By 1921 Better Business Bureaus were at work in thirty-one cities, supported primarily by advertising groups. An epidemic of bucket-shop failures in 1921 secured broader business support for truth in advertising and some renewed federal prosecution of security swindlers. Better Business Bureaus tried to educate against fraudulent stock sellers. Swindles in land-sales advertising required special action in the 1920s.[23]

In the 1920s numerous businesses made exaggerated claims for their products, according to Carl Taeusch. One company advertised auto batteries that would last forever. Another company advertised rebuilt adding machines, which actually were simply used machines. Taeusch also decried testimonial advertising, especially of patent medicines. He found financial advertising was filled with undeserved superlatives; companies were "foremost" or "best." In fact, worthless securities were still being advertised by tipster sheets, put out by reputable banking establishments. The doctrine of *caveat emptor* was overused in this field.[24]

H.J. Kenner wrote of stock swindles and land frauds that were widely advertised in the 1920s.[25] The Julian Petroleum Corporation of Los Angeles, the Barbarino Motors Corporation, and the Arman Plate and Non-Shatterable Glass Corporation of New York were widely advertised for stock sale, with almost no assets. Publications of the Federal Trade Commission show a great deal of misrepresentation in advertising, by some well-established firms.[26] In the 1930s, as the Depression reduced the number of customers, some major retailers again became guilty of "baiting" and deceptive advertising. Better Business Bureaus worked with state and federal officials to end these frauds.

Style obsolescence was encouraged by television ads in the 1950s and 1960s; for example, new tinted refrigerators were devised. Advertising encouraged consumers to buy the latest styles in watches, hats, shirts, and ties. The Retail Furniture Association of California suggested that consumers needed a constant reminder that their furniture was getting old. Science was misused by advertisements; an amazing new drug was claimed to melt fat right off in spite of the luscious steaks, mashed potatoes, and pastries being eaten. Food and Drug Administration officials testified that overweight Americans were cheated out of $100 million a year in spurious diet aids and useless mechanical weight-loss devices. In 1958 television suffered from the price-rigging scandals. Ivan Preston reports a 1971 FTC action against a clear misstatement in a General Electric advertisement; *Advertising Age* supported the misstatement as "only puffery."[27]

As later sections on specific problems of advertising will indicate, the continued ethical problems of the industry were constantly criticized. A substantial consumer movement of the 1920s was critical of advertising excesses.[28] The reaction to the Depression in the 1930s continued those criticisms; in fact, the Wheeler-Lea Amendment of 1938 to the Federal Trade Commission Act empowered the Federal Trade Commission to compel truth in advertising, ending whatever legal status *caveat emptor* had at that time. Stricter enforcement of this provision came with the pressures exerted by the consumer movement of the late 1960s and the 1970s, headed by Ralph Nader and others. During the decades since 1900, an important sector of the advertising industry has attempted to maintain standards.

In less than two centuries the U.S. government has twice changed its policies about the legal basis of advertising—from the Western ethical tradition of truth-telling to the encouragement of lying under *caveat emptor,* and back to truth-telling again. It has also moved from no governmental regulation to fairly strict regulation, at least by the federal government. An ethical principle of two-thousand-years standing in the Western world was dropped for a century or more by the courts of fhe United States and Britain, two of the more progressive countries, both of which finally saw their mistake. American business ethics suffered substantially from this mistake.

Unfortunately, Better Business Bureau action and minimum governmental action did not improve the ethics of advertising adequately. Joseph Seldin gives a number of examples of low-quality of advertising in recent decades. Community leaders like the president of Columbia University, the former president of Brown University, the editor of the *Christian Science Monitor,* and Professor H.C. Commager of Columbia University found initial television advertising in the 1950s and early 1960s demoralizing, insulting, juvenile, antisocial, monotonous, obtrusive, trite, and repulsive. Interestingly, a survey of working-class and lower-middle-class people confirmed these negative judgments. Other examples of such advertising include: "Williams shaving cream placed a man—head and shoulders above the crowd"; "Florsheim Shoes put—smart good looks on feet"; "Vaseline

Hair Tonic—slicked hair for that look of success''; and "Del Monte canned spinach helped everyone—greet the morning with a smile.''[29] Within the last year, the *Wall Street Journal* ran an article on "sexual pitches" in a series of advertisements.

Is Advertising Necessary?

Many who have been reared in a work ethic, which emphasizes the value of productivity, naturally wonder if any expenditure on advertising is worthwhile. Why not save the constant annoyance and expense of billboards, electric signs, newspapers, and television cluttered with advertisements, and concentrate economic endeavors on production and distribution? Why not save the over $30 billion, which advertising costs the nation?

There are, however, powerful reasons for advertising, at least for advertising that gives information about products and opens up markets for new products. Even the Soviet Union recognizes the need to give the people exact information about goods and to create a demand for new products. Alfred Marshall, England's leading economist for decades, approved of informative advertising. David Ogilvy believes that informative advertising is the most useful. Neil Borden concluded after a lengthy study that the large scale of operations made possible by advertising has reduced costs.[30]

Robert Pitofsky, long an FTC administrator and commissioner, supported the point of advertising usefulness for new products with specific examples.

> . . . a recent massive advertising campaign by Schick on behalf of a new electric razor was probably the most efficient way to challenge the companies that dominated that industry . . .

> When Volvo, through extensive advertising, focused consumer concern on the durability of automobiles, it not only struck on a marketing strategy that facilitated its own entry into the American market but touched off a process whereby consumers could become knowledgeable about the relative durability of cars, and might eventually be offered more durable cars.

> Once advertising takes up nutritional content of cereals, low tar and nicotine levels in cigarettes, and safety characteristics in pesticides, it is predictable that research and development will be oriented towards improving those characteristics.[31]

Pitofsky demonstrated the undesirability of limits on persuasive advertising in cases where products differ from these examples. These examples also indicate why a free economy needs advertising. If advertising meets the requirement of economic usefulness, it becomes more ethical in our society.

There is still the possibility, indeed the probability, of unethical advertising. But the mere fact of the existence of advertising is not unethical, as some writers seem to imply.

Some economists believe that advertising makes the demand for products more elastic. Lee Benham has verified the point by a study of the effect of advertising on the price of eyeglasses. In states that forbade advertising of costs, the price of eyeglasses was twice as great as in states where advertising of costs was permitted.[32]

Objections to Advertising and Some Answers

A number of objections to advertising need to be considered on an ethical basis. Have Americans become slaves of the incessant advertising in most aspects of their lives? In *Antic Hay,* Aldous Huxley says:

> People don't know 'ow to entertain themselves now; they leave it to other people to do it for them. They swallow what's given them. They 'ave to swallow it, they like it or not. Cinemas, newspapers, gramophones, football matches, wireless, telephones—take them or leave them, if you want to amuse yourself. The ordinary man can't leave them. He takes and what's that but slavery.[33]

It certainly is true that incesant advertising is not always very pleasant. But to call it slavery is gross exaggeration. Most people can get away from it at home or at work. Publicly owned television gives a chance to escape advertising, as do the movies. Some people are able to read newspapers and magazines with almost no glances at the advertisements. Advertisements may be nuisances but Huxley's term "slavery" was too strong. There are things to be said for restriction of advertising in times or places, but few are enslaved by advertising.

A second charge is that advertising is in bad taste. The chairman of the FTC, Miles Kirkpatrick, on January 8, 1971, told the International Newspaper Advertising Executives convention that he found advertising to be insulting to good judgment and taste. Daniel Bell said that "advertising has concentrated on arousing the anxieties and manipulating the fears of consumers to coerce them into buying."[34] Examples are that *Listerine* forces consumers to worry about mouth odors; soap about body odors, *Serutan* about constipation. As noted, university presidents and other distinguished persons made similar charges about television advertising. Stephen A. Greyser of Harvard Business School, in general favoring advertising, grants there is a problem of "noisy attention-getting devices."[35] Martin Mayer rejects this charge on the ground that the product perhaps does help its users, psychologically if not physically. This kind of panic is not one of the serious ethical hazards of life, although it is annoying to have to listen to many objectional advertisements.

Another charge is that advertising forces conformity, a charge Mayer rejects by pointing out the wide variety of ways in which people entertain or instruct themselves. It is to be agreed that advertising's contribution to conformity is not a very malevolent feature of American life.

A criticism that advertising is forcing consumers into too-great consumer consciousness is made by Stuart Ewen in *Advertising and the Social Roots of the Consumer Culture*.[36] Ewen implies a deliberate effort on the part of business to invade family life and create consumer-consciousness. In a sense, of course, this is true. Many businesses are trying to make people conscious of, and indeed desirous of, their wares. But is this not the price of free business activity? Unless there really is a concerted effort to undermine the free thought of consumers, is it unethical? Ewen points out that advertising does not have the vast authority over the consumer which some critics assume.[37]

He alludes to a related attack on advertising, that of its impact on social values, but drops the point on the ground that there is not research adequate to justify a viewpoint. John A. Howard and Spencer F. Tinkham raise a similar point; the fear that advertising is shaping its prospective customers, by creating changes in the attitudes of the customer toward himself or other persons or toward possessions or other objects, or by changing the customer's belief structure.[38] It is probable that television and other modern media, in part through the advertising that finances them, and in part through their broadcasts, do have influence on many of the persons to whom they are directed. It may be that research is today adequate to support this criticism.[39] This is a very important problem, but since it involves freedom of expression, it should be left to churches, universities, and the schools, not the Federal Trade Commission, to attack. The author of this book and a colleague have written some suggestions about television.[40]

J. Kenneth Galbraith objects that advertising helps create demand for more consumer products than are needed, a "dependence effect" that exists at the cost of more worthwhile public expenditures.[41] Braybrooke somewhat agrees, arguing that corporate advertisers have instilled desire for their products into the public at the cost of a national value like that of the desire for safety. In fact, their sociological influence has been far-reaching. "The automobile companies (though certainly not these alone) have strenuously assisted in mixing us up about sex, making it more urgent, but also more diffuse, and commonly misdirected."[42]

Another opposes the Galbraith point with the argument that most wants are indeed created by seeing or otherwise learning that others are using the wanted commodity. All tastes are shaped by one's cultural environment. The fact that some people may be persuaded to spend unwisely does not mean that all their needs are satisfied.[43] In this day of nonconjugal domesticity, it is not certain that the automobile has had a prime role in the mix-up about sex relations.

There are objectionable features to advertising as it is currently used in America. There is an obvious environmental objection. Advertisements litter the landscapes, and clutter streets, streetcars, and other public places. Although Broadway's Great White Way has certain attractions, and some electric signs at night are interesting, advertising still raises problems of aesthetic ethics. To what extent should a business use advertisements that detract from the appearance of a street, or damage the business of a neighbor? *Sic utere tuo ut alienum non laedas,* the medieval Latin maxim to handle property only in ways that do not harm others, is often ignored in contemporary advertising.

More important than the ethics of advertising's low aesthetic standards is the problem of advertising's standards of veracity. Both the Judaic and the Christian ethical traditions set strict standards of truth in business representations. Immanuel Kant went even further and made an absolute value of truth, a position some of his fellow philosophers contested. Presentations in earlier chapters of this book demonstrated that nineteenth and early twentieth-century American advertising often violated the Judaic and Christian rules for truthful representation in business dealings. False statements were very numerous in advertisements from 1870 to 1910, and were rarely denounced by ministers or professors of ethics.

Despite the legal abandonment of the *caveat emptor* principle and statues requiring truthful advertising, a good deal of deception has continued. A relatively recent book lists the following questionable practices, some from FTC citations.

1. Spurious demonstrations. An ad for a window cleaner shows the window cleaned by it to be cleaner than the window cleaned by a competitive product; the latter window was cleaned less vigorously.
2. An identical ingredient is made to sound like something special. A large oil company advertised the miles secured by a car using its gas with a special ingredient, not mentioning that other major gasolines used the the same ingredient.
3. Visual misrepresentations were frequent. A soup company used colorless glass marbles at the bottom of bowls of soup to force the chunky parts up to where the television camera would catch it.
4. False authority. The use of celebrity testimonials is well known.
5. Health and nutrition claims. One bread claimed dietary advantages; it was merely sliced thinner.
6. Use of inadequate warranties of bargain prices to lure customers into buying.

7. Contests and games in which prizes are only partially awarded.
8. Corporate image advertising, which claims a philanthropic or conservative contribution that is exaggerated.[44]

Many smaller advertising devices are also described. The Federal Trade Commission has in recent years succeeded in banning most of these trickier ads, at least from nationwide media. But all these devices were attempts to deceive the buyer and thus were completely contrary to an age-old ethical principle.

Another objection to advertising is its effort to use emotional or snob appeal, usually for the sale of certain brands. Drug companies have been sharply criticized for the expensive brand names they publicize, rather than the simple chemical names of the drugs.[45] To what extent is it ethical for drug companies to use the market mechanism to increase greatly the cost of drugs to consumers? Many find these added costs a real economic burden. Up to 1965, a number of state laws and pharmaceutical regulations forbade advertising of retail prices for prescription drugs. The FTC opposed the regulations and a federal district court declared them unconstitutional.[46] The drug companies are now doing nothing illegal. But are they following the Western ethical tradition in their representation of expensive brand names to their customers?

Advertising can produce the impression of high social class. Expensive cars are pictured in front of country clubs or estate driveways—not in front of a middle-class store or service-station. Expensive clothes are pictured only if worn by expensively clothed people. Commander Schweppes looks distinguished, so people will buy *Bitter Lemon*. Countesses are portrayed because they use *Pond's Soap*.

Such advertisements are designed to make people believe that they will be associating with distinguished or famous individuals, or that they become famous or distinguished because they use the advertised product. This metamorphosis obviously does not happen, but is the suggestion an ethical deception? It probably is not a deception forbidden by Western ethics. Yet snob appeal is a kind of deception, the untrue suggestion that purchase of the advertised brand brings an introduction to the society of the wealthy and fashionable. Most view this deception as relatively harmless, but it must be admitted that many credulous people are damaged. Should such people be protected or is that protection too great an infringement on individual freedom?

Brand names of course relate to the world of advertising symbols, and the greater uncertainty as to what is ethical. The *Lucky Strike* ad "So round, so firm, so fully packed" was trying to secure a psychological appeal of oral satisfaction for that brand.[47] There is little in the Judaic-Christian tradition to judge if these actions are ethical. Perhaps they are mildly deceptive but should they be censored? The Maidenform brassiere ads raise a similar question.

It is true that the emotional or snob appeal of many brands tells little about the quality of the product. But is not a classroom lecture, a dramatic performance, or a political speech sold by emotional appeal? Should a higher standard be exacted of business than of drama or religion or other appeals to public emotion?

There are varying opinions as to the social, economic, or psychological values involved in each of the criticisms of advertising. But which practices are ethically wrong, so wrong that private or public regulation is needed to eliminate or greatly reduce the offensive action? Everyone is entitled to his own opinion, but ethical objections seem relevant only in four cases: any advertising which deliberately lies about its products is opposing an important ethical principle of the Western Judaic-Christian tradition; advertising that has the effect of inciting a substantial number of people to violence or crime against their fellows is objectionable, so is advertising that litters or clutters the landscape or public places; and advertising that encourages actions or attitudes inimical to societal cooperation.

Business is one of the chief victims if the advertising for which it pays is deceptive. Deceptive advertising does not spur competition as does true advertising. In the United States, with a well-educated population, deceptive advertisements soon become recognized as deceptive. Persons who recognize the deception tend to become angry; at least some portion of the constant criticism of business in the press comes from reaction against deceptive advertising. Ethics enforce themselves when a magazine like the *New Yorker,* with its finances based on expensive advertising, examines the advertisements in its own columns, becomes ashamed of them, and then adopts a self-limiting policy about advertisements. Similarly, politicians turn against business when they find it distrusted by most of their constituents. In 1971, the *Harvard Business Review* reported that only 30 percent of a sample of business executives believed that advertisements present a true picture; 42 percent thought the public's faith in advertising was very low.[48]

A number of critics have maintained that the role of advertising should be to inform, not to persuade. Some, like Stephen Greyser, doubt if this distinction can be made. Yet he suggests that more and better information be given to the consumer.[49] In a detailed study of techniques of advertising, John A. Howard and James Hulbert discuss the problem of how to reproduce a product. Clearly, mock-ups should be forbidden. There is some evidence that people accept claims, regardless of their illogicality.[50] A product may be advertised to appeal to a self-concept, but the standard of truth should remain.

Howard and Hurlbut's report points out the problem. When does the dramatic become deceptive? The report suggests that "puffery" should be restricted to product performance, where it must be substantiated. After a lengthy discussion of child development, Howard and Hulbert conclude that a goal for the FTC should be advertisements that help develop the child's judgment. They conclude that the poor and the disadvantaged have needs that are not well met by television advertising, which is directed toward more affluent people.

Advertisers also argue that their efforts give consumers greater freedom of choice, since advertising often helps launch new products or new industries. This argument is quite correct; however, it can be overused. Greyser testified, "The increasing diversity of our society and the vigorous affirmation of that diversity by subgroups in it make me think it unlikely we can reach strong consensus on what 'good ends' are."[51]

Greyser has overlooked the fact that American society, like most other societies, has reached agreement on many "good ends." If it were not agreed that murder, rape, stealing, and fraud were prohibited, the society would not survive. In fact the detailed procedural rights of individuals, the general policy of keeping the population fed and somewhat healthy, and other aspects of life are also agreed upon in American society.

Enforcement of Advertising Ethics

In the United States, a country that largely ignores basic ethical instruction, enforcement of rules and laws becomes a main means of introducing ethical standards. Such enforcement over advertising as exists seems to be a mixture of self-control by advertising agencies; control by firms that place advertising; control by newspapers and other media; and control by government agencies, chiefly the Federal Trade Commission but also the Federal Communications Commission and the Securities and Exchange Commission, sometimes by state "blue sky" laws and attorney-generals staffs, and occasionally by local prosecutors. Each of these mechanisms will be discussed to judge their effectiveness in ethical instruction as well as their record in punishing offenders. Self-control by industry is limited by basic legal forces. Any combination of merchants or advertising agencies which sought strict enforcement standards might find itself in violation of antitrust laws. As noted earlier, leading advertisers have supported advertising clubs and Better Business Bureaus through most of this century. Better Business Bureaus have had some success in persuading local retailers to refrain from "bait" advertising or untrue advertising.[52]

In 1971, three advertising agencies and the National Council of Better Business Bureaus established a national advertising division to hear complaints about national advertising. If the complaint could not be resolved by the advertising agency, it was referred to the review board, and then if necessary to the appropriate governmental agency. In the first year, 337 complaints were received; 112 were dismissed, 72 were found to be justified, and the advertiser agreed to withdraw or modify the ad. The other 153 were handled much more rapidly than under government procedures. In January 1972 the National Advertising Review Board announced that it would extend its consideration to areas of taste and social responsiblity.[53] In 1974 there were still substantial problems in connection with the program, but it was planned to establish similar local machinery.[54] The program is still vigorously developed.

The advertising-industry enforcement machinery is to be commended. Any substantial effort to lower the number of decisions made by the federal government is probably good. But the federal machinery continues, and probably has to do so, because of the impossibility of effective enforcement of the private judgments on all advertisers.

Newspapers also do some controlling of advertisements. As of November 1970, thirty-six newspapers had announced their intention of rejecting cigarette ads. *The New York Times* and other papers decided to require the Surgeon General's warning on every cigarette ad. However, the American Newspaper Publishers Association began a campaign to attract cigarette advertising. At least twenty-seven newspapers automatically reject all ads for X-rated movies.

Control by State and Local Governments

Controls of advertising by state and local governments vary greatly, but in general are quite weak. In one of the stronger states, California, the Department of Real Estate recently accused seventy-four mortgage-loan brokers of deceptive advertising, using desist-and-refrain orders.[55] Promises of large yields on trusts were the chief concern. In another recent action, the California attorney general's office and a county prosecutor's office have secured heavy legal damages from a firm that promised far too much in selling air conditioners. In New York State, the attorney general and some county prosecutors have taken similar actions. State and local governments are more effective against deceptive advertising than against business monopolies.

However, there is some evidence that state and local legislation against deceptive advertising is not very effective. In New York and California, a number of deceptive advertisements have gone unassailed for years.[56] In Ohio in 1971, an old law was reported ineffective, and the chances for a new one were questionable.[57]

A study of retail newspaper advertising in the major metropolitan area of Delaware in 1972 found a large proportion of the advertisements to be false, misleading, or deceptive. The standard used was that of a private agency, the Better Business Bureau of Delaware. The newspapers concerned belonged to a select group of newspapers which claimed to set standards for advertising. "In practice, however, the newspaper looks to government and the Better Business Bureau to take the lead in advertising regulation."[58] The investigators in charge of this study sent thirteen complaints to the Better Business Bureau. A report four months later indicated that five of the thirteen firms had explained the basis of their advertising or promised to try to prevent a recurrence. Eight firms did not respond, and no action was taken. Two complaints were then carried to the FTC and the Delaware Division of Consumer Affairs. The FTC bowed out of a case against a drugstore chain on jurisdictional grounds. The Delaware agency secured the chain's consent to publish manufacturers' list price rather than its own price before claiming sale deductions—a procedure that may have been better but was discouraged by both FTC and Better Business Bureau regulations.

Federal-Government Regulation

The Federal Trade Commission, the national agency most involved in advertising regulation, has been quite active, although its record through most of the 1960s was weakened by restraining court decisions, and by a not-always-brilliant bureaucracy. In 1972 *Business Week* noted that the FTC had proposed that three major drug concerns that spent $80 million a year to advertise *Bufferin*, *Anacin*, *Bayer Aspirin*, and other drugs had to spend 25 percent of their advertising budget to correct claims made in previous ads. FTC also ordered manufacturers of cough and cold remedies, toothpaste, televisions, tires, and other products to prove their advertising claims. It also moved to eliminate some $73 million in unnecessary advertising spending by cereal makers. The Federal Trade Commission was also reinterpreting the concept of unfair and deceptive ads to include ones that have claims not backed up by scientific data. However, supporting such data took a great deal of time of the FTC staff.[59]

The FTC now often requires published retractions of misleading advertisements in the magazine where the ad appears. As an example of the FTC procedure, Lorillard Tobacco in 1950 was called to account for quoting a *Reader's Digest* article as finding *Old Gold* cigarettes lowest in nicotine and in tars when the article really indicated that all brands were very close in these respects. The circuit court agreed with the FTC that this was a perversion of the article, a court viewpoint much different from the nineteenth-century Massachusetts and Maine cases of *caveat emptor.*[60]

The new activity of the Federal Trade Commission in the 1970s was in part a result of the consumer movement of the late 1960s and of Ralph

Nader's attacks on business and the Federal Trade Commission. In the 1970s the Federal Trade Commission questioned Unique Selling Propositions (that a product offers something no other offers and leads to purchase).[61] In 1971 the FTC began a requirement that advertising claims be substantiated, if necessary, by tests. It requires scientific tests which are "fairly extensive and well documented."[62] One test might be carried out on the road, another in the laboratory. Advertised claims for a battery additive must be fully supported by tests described in detail, with results given. Claims that imply uniqueness must be supported by tests. Obviously such requirements do not bode well for many Unique Selling Propositions.

Also as a part of the consumer movement, Congress in 1975 passed the Magnuson-Moss Warranty Act. There is a Uniform Commercial Code which operates in all states except Louisiana, and requires an implied warrant that a product is fit for the purpose for which it was sold, is properly packaged and labeled, and conforms to any promises or affirmations made on the label.[63] Such implied warranties, however, are difficult to enforce. Frequently even expressly printed warranties are not understood by customers because of the unwillingness of salesclerks to show the document, the obscurity of legal language, terms that remove the effective liability of the seller, or uncertainty as to who is responsible (manufacturer or dealer) for performance on the warranty. The 1975 act gives the FTC power to issue warranty regulations. It is directed to issue a rule requiring that the warrantor make the terms available to the buyer *before* the sale is completed. The remedy must be performed in reasonable time, or the buyer may elect either replacement or refund. There is an outright prohibition of disclaiming implied warranties. Where informal dispute settlements cannot be worked out, federal class-action suits are permitted under certain circumstances

Robert Pitofsky, who served as Director of the FTC's Bureau of Consumer Protection from 1970 to 1973, discusses some of the newer FTC positions in a way that permits ethical appraisal.[64] He does not believe that direct limitations on volume of advertising (for example to a specific percentage of sales) would be good since it might prevent entry into a new market or development of a new product. He grants that advertising could be used to exclude other products, and that such anticompetitive activity would probably be legally banned. In the Proctor and Gamble case the Supreme Court decided that the nation's largest consumer advertiser should not buy the largest liquid-bleach manufacturer; this being a market where product differentiation by advertising was very important.[65] Another case brought by the FTC opposed control of the ready-to-eat-cereal market by six manufacturers, who controlled 90 percent of it by 1960. Very high advertising expenditures were presumably keeping out competitors, as well as helping produce high prices and high profits. If ban of monopoly is an ethical precept, are not these FTC actions ethically reasonable?

Administration of statutory provisions against deceptive and unfair advertising has presented problems. Some people believe that consumers will pick out more satisfactory brands of products and disregard advertising. The FTC does not share that view, believing that consumers do not know enough to evaluate sophisticated modern products. The absence of data may also handicap the consumer. Many opportunities to purchase, for houses or swimming pools for example, are not repeated.

With these considerations in mind, the FTC has required the substantiation of advertising claims noted earlier. It has demanded higher standards of truth and relevance for susceptible audiences such as children or parents concerned about the growth of children, and substantiation of bases for advertising that a product is superior to others.

Believing that its cease-and-desist orders were too slow a change, the FTC has also ordered corrective advertising (discussed in a later section) and affirmative disclosures. The latter was illustrated by an order that a drug advertised as a marriage-saver should show its real content—the caffeine equivalent of two cups of coffee. Pitofsky concludes, as have other analysts of advertising, that presentation of more genuine product information is the best future for advertising. In a very long-run sense, ethics are accepted practice. It may be that the FTC and the advertisers will differ for some years before an established practice on deceptive advertising can be found. But if the advertisers continue to believe that they have a right to puffery, which includes deliberate deception, the standard will not be set. Standards should be set by the industry, but they cannot be standards that run counter to long-standing ethical traditions.

Criticisms of FTC Control of Advertising

There are sharp scholarly critics of the Federal Trade Commission's power. One of the most thoughtful is Richard Posner of the University of Chicago School of Law who has studied decisions made by the FTC in 1963 and 1968 and concluded that they were a spectacle "of misspent public resources." In fiscal year 1973 he found that of 215 deceptive practices, 76 did not involve serious deception, 92 were cases in which private remedies were adequate, 24 were criminal-fraud cases, and only 23 were appropriate cases for the FTC. In his analysis of cases for six months (July 1 to December 31, 1968) he found only 4 cases out of 123 were appropriate cases for the FTC.[66]

There is undoubtedly merit in Posner's attack. Some of his sample of "cases not involving serious deception" are persuasive. In one case a particular brand of tires claimed better traction but had proved their case only with respect to wet surfaces—a situation which seems unlikely to mislead consumers. He also does not believe that a candy endorsement by a group of athletes who were paid for the endorsement is something to worry about.

There are, however, difficulties in Posner's attack. His assumption that private remedies are adequate in a number of important cases overlooks the real difficulty most consumers would have in financing private legal remedies. One could also argue against some of his classifications of cases not involving serious deception. If the Old Testament—Thomas Aquinas—Blackstone standard of honesty in selling is returned to, a society of much greater honesty than we have today may result.

An attack somewhat similar to Posner's is made from the left. Edward F. Cox et al., criticize the FTC sharply for its incompetence, lack of energy, and reprehensible way of doing things.[67] Unfortunately, anyone who has worked long in the federal government knows that there is probably truth to these charges. However, if adequate private standards for enforcing morality cannot be worked out, it may be necessary to use the federal government.

A number of what *Business Week* called "admen" opposed more recent trends of the Federal Trade Commission. Undoubtedly these men were in part concerned about the lengthy bureaucratic procedures that seem to bog down many governmental procedures. But these admen did not acknowledge that the FTC was, in its perhaps clumsy way, trying to bring American advertising back into the main ethical traditions of the Western world.

Yale Brozen is concerned about the costs of the FTC requirement that advertisers replicate their proofs-of-advertising claims. He also does not want the FTC to issue complaints too hastily, or to worry too much about shared monopolies in concentrated industries, like the four firms that produce most cereals. He believes that their predominance is not a result of too much advertising, since advertising creates disloyalty to products.[68]

Most of these disputes are about ways and means of achieving truth in advertising. Coercive methods by which the government enforces truth should probably be kept to a minimum. But these problems of enforcement arise in part because some businessmen have forgotten or never learned that truth-telling is the only ethical way to conduct business. David M. Gardner, in a thoughtful article alludes to a main point of this chapter, that the sway of *caveat emptor* for a century kept the courts from developing a solid concept of deception of consumers.[69] The efforts of the FTC to force certain industries to document their claims for their products are designed to prevent deception. After reviewing several definitions, Gardner proposes that a deceptive advertisement is a false one that leaves the consumer with an impression different from what would normally be expected if the consumer had reasonable knowledge of the product. Gross lies about the product would clearly be deceptive. He suggests a multiattributable model in which deception would occur either by associating the product with an attitude or with a belief associated with a brand. Such product attributes may be either functional (for example wearing qualities) or nonfunctional (style). Consumer reactions need to be measured to determine if a deceptive picture of attributes has been created.

Gardner may be right. It is necessary to point out, however, that extensive studies of consumer attitudes about all sorts of products are probably beyond the financial capacity of the FTC. It may be that more careful analysis of the concept of deception may be as fruitful. What is the ethical result wished? What kind of FTC rules will help achieve that result?

A constructive criticism comes from Warren S. Grimes, an American lawyer who studied the control of advertising in Germany in 1972, leading him to wonder if the Germans did not have more effective control of advertising through private action. He notes that there are many advertisements which the FTC does not have time to consider. There is little chance for lower-income consumers to get their cases to the FTC. Only a very few states have effective controls of advertising in spite of the existence of laws against deceptive advertising in forty-four states, according to Grimes. Private remedies are rarely used at federal or state levels. Private regulations suffer from the antitrust difficulty mentioned earlier.

In Germany there appear to be adequate laws against deceptive advertising as a part of unfair competition. There are also federal laws controlling food packaging and advertising near federal highways. Injunctive relief may be secured in Germany, by consumer as well as business associations, against deceptive assertions on business matters. In 37 cases, Grimes found 22 individual businesses suing competitors; 12 trade or competition associations suing individual businesses; and 3 consumer associations suing individual businesses. German attorney acquaintances thought that this was perhaps a typical distribution. One association of businesses handled 3,000 cases in 1967, estimating that legal proceedings were necessary only in 5 percent of the cases. A consumer union formed in 1967 reported 544 cases of final action, a majority involving deceptive advertising in its first 3 years. In 200 cases relief was secured without resort to litigation; in 203 temporary injunctive relief was secured.

All disputes are handled by the commercial chambers of the civil courts, thus securing "expert and consistent administration." Mediation boards also handle a good many cases. German decisions appear to be rather similar to those in the United States. A claim that a coat was the "world's best coat" without proof was disallowed. Comparison advertising is forbidden, in partial disagreement with American practice. "Bait advertising" is unlawful in Germany as in the United States. Games of chance must have prior public approval. Unordered merchandise may be retained without payment. As yet there are no German bans on cigarette advertisements.[70]

Comparative generalizations are always dangerous. The Germans have generally been more law-abiding than Americans in this century. But

Grimes' account does make one wonder if America has used all the better methods of eliminating deceptive advertising.

Corrective Advertising

The chief authority of the FTC against deceptive advertising has been the securing of a cease-and-desist court order to which the offending advertiser must agree. There can be financial penalties for violation of this order but not for earlier violations of the law against deceptive advertising. Thus it may pay an advertiser to mislead until he is stopped by the cease-and-desist order. To prevent this form of evasion, the FTC has in recent years required corrective advertising. The corrective cease-and-desist order requires that the advertiser devote a fraction of his advertising budget for a period of time to correction of his previous error.

In 1971, the first FTC corrective order required Continental Baking Company to devote 25 percent of its media budget for one year to FTC-approved advertisements that its bread did not reduce weight as earlier advertisements had claimed. Ocean Spray, Inc. was required to devote 25 percent of its media budget to correct earlier possible misrepresentations as to the food energy of its cranberry juice as compared to orange or tomato juice.

FTC's weekly summary of September 14, 1979 indicates that STP Corporation, selling an oil additive, had agreed to spend $200,000 to advertise that tests conducted for the company cannot be relied on to support the oil-consumption-reduction claim made by STP. There was also a $500,000 civil penalty. A study by Thomas Kinnear indicated that the percentage of people aware that there was a problem in STP advertising rose from 12 percent to about 33 percent during the campaign. Also, a substantial number of people polled said they would not buy STP the next year.

Somewhat equivalent to corrective advertising was the counter-advertising in the antismoking commercials of 1968-1970. The authors of an FTC report found no evidence that these advertisements were an important deterrent.[71]

The FTC has also ordered corrective advertising in relatively small cases, for example, a Boise, Idaho Ford dealer who violated the Magnuson-Moss Warranty Act.[72] However, it rejected a suggestion that it require blanket corrective advertising in cases where health, safety, and nutrition advertising was false or misleading in a prolonged campaign.

The FTC also applied the "Fairness Doctrine" for regulation of broadcasters' opinions from political matters to cigarette advertisements. In January 1971 it asked the Federal Communications Commission to require counter-advertising, that is, regularly scheduled broadcasts of statements against broadcast advertisements. Although this doctrine did not prevail, it and corrective advertising have aroused serious objections. Counter-advertising is a broad term that includes at least some kinds of corrective advertising.

In 1972 Stephen Greyser reviewed the various problems that must be met by advertisers and their regulators. Most involve the exercise of discretion in an area where knowledge is far from complete. He correctly notes that the support of advertising is on economic grounds but the bulk of the criticism is on its social impacts.

Should the advertiser be forced to say things against his own product? Greyser doubts if he should. Efforts to ban ads that yield false impressions or raise problems of taste also worry him. Quite reasonably he points out that advertising may *reflect* as well as *create* values of society. Again, he correctly believes that the issue of truth or falsehood in advertising should be separate from whether this is good or bad. He concludes that advertising must be more sensitive about outside criticism, and learn to live in a world of critics. Too little is known about the effects of advertising.[73]

Greyser makes good points about the difficulty of outside judgments on the advertiser. But more than a century of substantial deception in advertising has left a mark on this country's morals that requires a change in attitudes of advertisers, which perhaps a limited amount of corrective advertising can help to bring about. Greyser worries about incorrect decisions from public or private reviewers of advertising. Indeed it would be good if the necessity for such review disppeared. But have not advertisers created the current necessity? Are more ethics being lost through false advertising than would be lost through a minor amount of correction?

A sharper critic of corrective advertising than Greyser is Lee Loevinger.[74] Loevinger's arguments are directed against counter-advertising. Only those points which are applicable to corrective advertising are discussed here.

Loevinger believes counter-advertising would cost the broadcasting industry heavily and reduce the quality of broadcasting and journalism; an argument which would not now apply to the small amount of corrective advertising in force. Counter-advertising would lead to confusion; consumers already have diverse sources of information. It would be unfair to honest advertisers, an argument which is presumably not applicable to the selected counter-advertising cases. He believes it would function against innovation, and would move government's role from simply stopping deceptive advertising to acting under pressure of small militant groups with political ends. This latter point seems to be applicable to corrective advertising; as government takes on more power to protect consumers, it may be creating ethical problems rather than correcting them.

Obviously, no exact judgment can be made about the number of customers misled by the deceptive advertising or the depth of this misinformation. So there is an ethical danger of overcorrection or undercorrection. The FTC staff is not adequate in size or training to conduct consumer surveys on each case. The method has been questioned.[75] Yet the fact of some correction may be better than no correction. An ethic has not yet been developed.

Comparative Advertising

For some time the FTC has been urging advertisements that compare the product with competitive products. A statement of policy was circulated in the FTC summary of August 3, 1979. The FTC hopes that comparative advertising will be a source of useful information to consumers, will encourage product improvement and innovation, and will lead to lower prices. The FTC does not object to disparaging statements if they are truthful. Comparative advertising may require a higher standard of substantiation.

In 1977 the FTC won a case in the District Court of Appeals supporting its decision that Warner-Lambert should spend $10 million to announce that there is no evidence that *Listerine* kills germs or cures sore throats.[76]

Comparative advertising can of course be misleading. Kroger Grocery Company was penalized for lack of support for data in comparative statements with a corrective advertising requirement, raising some question as to the desirability of comparative advertising.[77] However, a later *Business Week* story said that comparative advertising is flourishing in spite of some studies that seem to show its ineffectiveness.[78]

Comparative advertising raises new ethical problems. There is little tradition behind it; in fact, a number of industry codes expressly forbid critical comments about competitors. In most professions, it is difficult for practitioners to speak critically about competitors. The FTC may promote the new doctrine for the sake of the information to customers, but it will be difficult.

Conclusions

That portion of the Western ethical tradition which requires truth from seller to buyer is most seriously tried in advertising. Advertisers are paid only to produce more sales, so the pressure on them is tremendous. In fact, the tendency of advertisers to overstate their cases sometimes tries the temper of our whole society, and requires careful watching by those concerned with our future. It may take another half century before the ill effect of the *caveat emptor* doctrine disappears from American commercial ethics.

Review of intellectual analyses of advertising leaves little doubt that it has a useful place in our economic system, showing people what they can buy, where they can buy it, and how they can use it. Advertising makes costs more elastic, to use the economists' term. If truthful, it helps competition.

Criticisms of advertising begin with its incessant ubiquity and its frequent bad taste. These dangers are not really malevolent, merely annoying. Whether advertising is trying to change social values, making all of society into constant consumers, does not seem to be answered by current research, but does give cause for concern. Von Hayek points out that most wants are indeed determined by what fellow consumers want, so the rule of advertising may not be malevolent. Another charge is that advertising increases costs, principally through emphasis on brand names. If so, the answer should be market pushing of generic names.

This book is more seriously concerned with a possible negative effect of advertising on veracity, an important virtue in any society. In spite of the FTC's efforts, there are still many deceptive ads; do they help make deceptive people? There is agreement among most critics of advertising that it could usefully undertake to inform prospective buyers more about products, including the danger of misuse.

The advertising industry, some major newspapers, and Better Business Bureaus make efforts to raise the quality of advertising, with only partial success. The FTC has moved fairly effectively to reduce some kinds of deceptive advertising, but may have created too much business opposition in legislative channels. The FTC's enforcement program has been criticized as too detailed, as lacking in energy, and as too costly. Some critics wonder if it is possible for a governmental agency to ban deceptive advertising.

What is an ethical approach to advertising? All responsibility should not be left to the FTC. It should continue to regulate, but state and local governments as well as industry and private associations should work primarily for truth in advertising, but also to make advertising more informative. Corrective and comparative advertising both have an appropriate place. If these regulations are carried out with our ethical traditions in mind, advertising can be an important and useful part of the American economy.

Notes

1. William Blackstone, *Commentaries of the Laws of England*, vol. IV, pp. 133, 158.

2. Max Radin, *Manners and Morals of Business*, p. 186.

3. E.S. Turner, *The Shocking History of Advertising*, Ch. 1, pp. 21-30.

4. Joseph Addison, *The Tatler*, cited in Alexander Chalmers, ed., *The British Essayists*, pp. 67-69.

5. Turner, *The Shocking History of Advertising*, pp. 31-63.

6. Walton H. Hamilton, "The Ancient Maxim: Caveat Emptor," *Yale Law Journal*, pp. 1133-1187; and Ivan Preston, *The Great American Blow-Up*.

7. *Seixas and Seixas* v. *Woods*, 2 Caine R. 48, N.W., 1804.

8. Hamilton, "The Ancient Maxim," p. 1181.

9. Lawrence M. Friedman, *A History of American Law*, p. 233.

10. *Medbury* v. *Watson*, cited in Preston, *The Great American Blow-Up*, p. 100.

11. Cited in Preston, *The Great American Blow-Up*, p. 102.

12. Turner, *Shocking History*, pp. 64-99.

13. H.J. Kenner, *The Fight for Truth in Advertising*, pp. 3-16.

14. Hamilton, "The Ancient Maxim," p. 1184.

15. Ibid., p. 1185.

16. Philip G. Schrag, *Counsel for the Deceived*, p. 111.

17. Warren Y. Magnuson and Jean Carper, "Caveat Emptor" in John M. Johnson and Jack D. Douglas, *Crime at the Top*.

18. Marshall B. Clinard, *The Black Market*, p. 230.

19. E.T. Grether, "Sharp Practice in Merchandising and Advertising," *The Annals of the American Academy of Political and Social Sciences*, p. 115.

20. Kenner, *The Fight for Truth in Advertising*, p. 14.

21. Ibid., p. 18.

22. Ibid., pp. 23-24.

23. Ibid., pp. 26-112.

24. Carl Taeusch, *Policy and Ethics in Business*, pp. 484-485.

25. Kenner, *The Fight for Truth in Advertising*, pp. 113-126.

26. Stewart Chase and F.J. Schlink, *Your Money's Worth*, pp. 94-120.

27. Preston, *The Great American Blow-Up*, p. 290.

28. Chase and Schlink, *Your Money's Worth*, Chaps. 1-7.

29. Joseph Seldin, *The Golden Fleece*, pp. 3, 4, 29.

30. Cited in David Ogilvy, *Confessions of an Advertising Man*, pp. 132-145.

31. Robert Pitofsky, "Changing Focus in the Regulation of Advertising," in Yale Brozen, ed. *Advertising and Society*, p. 127.

32. Yale Brozen, "Is Advertising a Barrier to Entry?" in Yale Brozen, ed., *Advertising and Society*, p. 84.

33. Cited in Martin Mayer, *Madison Avenue, U.S.A.*, p. 308.

34. Ibid., p. 316.

35. Stephen A. Greyser, "Advertising Attacks and Counters," *Harvard Business Review*, March-April 1972, p. 145.

36. Victor Lebow, review of "Captains of Consciousness" by Stuart Ewen in *Challenge*, September-October 1976, pp. 41-43.

37. Greyser, "Advertising: Attacks and Counter Attacks," pp. 22 ff.

38. John A. Howard and Spencer F. Tinkham, "A Framework for Understanding Social Criticism of Advertising," *Journal of Marketing*, October 1971, pp. 2-7.

39. George Comstock, et al., *Television and Human Behavior*.

40. George C.S. Benson and Engeman, *Amoral America*.

41. John K. Galbraith, *The Affluent Society*.

42. David Braybrooke, "Skepticism of Wants and Certain Subversive Effects of Corporations on American Values," in Sidney Hook, ed., *Human Values and Economic Policy*, pp. 224-239.

43. Friedrich Von Hayek, "The Non-Sequiturs of the Dependence Effect," in Tom L. Beauchamp and Norman E. Bowie, *Ethical Theory and Business*, pp. 508 ff.

44. Edward Buxton, *Promise Them Anything*, pp. 1-22.

45. David Sanford, "Drugs on the Market" in Sanford, et al., *Hot War on the Consumer*, pp. 81-85.

46. Facts on File, *Consumer Protection*, p. 53.

47. Mayer, *Madison Avenue, U.S.A.*, p. 61; Buxton, *Promise Them Anything*, p. 213.

48. *National Journal*, August 7, 1971, p. 163.

49. Greyser, "Advertising: Attacks on Counters," pp. 22 ff.

50. John A. Howard and James Hulbert, "Report on Advertising and the Public Interest," pp. 50 ff.

51. J. Robert Moskins, *The Case for Advertising*, p. 32.

52. Kenner, *The Fight for Truth in Advertising*.

53. Greyser, "Advertising: Attacks on Counters," p. 144.

54. Howard H. Bell, "Self-Regulation by the Advertising Industry," *California Management Review*, Spring 1974, pp. 58-63.

55. *Los Angeles Times*, May 12, 1981.

56. Schrag, *Counsel for the Deceived*, Chap. 9.

57. James W. Carpenter, "Consumer Protection in Ohio Against False Advertising and Deceptive Trading" *Ohio State Law Journal* 32, pp. 1-15.

58. James R. Krum and Steven K. Keiser, "Regulation of Retail Newspaper Advertising," *Journal of Marketing*, 40, pp. 29-34.

59. *Business Week*, June 10, 1972, pp. 47-50.

60. Preston, *The Great American Blow-Up*, pp. 143-145.

61. Mayer, *Madison Avenue, U.S.A.*, pp. 49-52.

62. Robert E. Wilkes and James B. Wilcox, "Recent FTC Actions: Implications for the Advertising Strategist," *Journal of Marketing* 38, pp. 55-61.

63. Lawrence P. Feldman, "New Legislation and the Prospects for Real Warranty Reform," *Journal of Marketing* 40, pp. 41-47.

64. Yale Brozen, ed., *Advertising and Society*, pp. 125-147.

65. 386 U.S. 568, 1968.

66. Richard A. Posner, *Regulation of Advertising by the FTC.*

67. Edward F. Cox, et al. *Nader's Raiders.*

68. Yale Brozen, "The Impact of FTC Advertising Policies on Competition," in S.C. Divita, et., *Advertising and the Public Interest.*

69. David M. Gardner, "Deception in Advertising; A Conceptual Approach," *Journal of Marketing* 39 pp. 40-46.

70. Warren S. Grimes, "Control of Advertising in the United States and Germany: Volkswagen Has a Better Idea," *Harvard Law Review* 84:8, pp. 1769-1800.

71. *FTC News Summary*, Washington, D.C., September 28, 1979.

72. *FTC News Summary*, Washington, D.C., May 2, 1980.

73. Greyser, "Advertising Attacks and Counters," p. 22 ff.

74. Lee Loevinger, "The Politics of Advertising," in Divita, *Advertising and the Public Interest*, pp. 1-24.

75. Robert F. Dyer and Phillip G. Kuehl, "A Longitudinal Study of Corrective Advertising," *Journal of Marketing Research* 15 pp. 39-48.

76. *Access*, April 23, 1979, p. 2.

77. Stan Crock, "FTC is Told Its Charges Against Kroger's Survey Ads Could Contribute to Inflation," *Wall Street Journal*, March 1, 1979, p. 6.

78. *Business Week*, September 24, 1979, pp. 156, 161.

13 Product Liability and Related Problems

Ethical and Legal History

There are many historical examples of legal regulation of manufactured products, regulations designed to assure governmental purchase of quality products, or to assure the delivery of products that could command a continued market. The general Western rule of seller responsibility implies some kind of warranty of the quality of products sold. Both Roman law and the Pentateuch defined the ethical responsibility of some manufacturers. In the Middle Ages, guilds often set high standards for production. But in early nineteenth-century America *caveat-emptor* reigned. It was also generally the law that if a dealer sold a product to a customer and the product was unsatisfactory, the customer could sue only the dealer, not the manufacturer, who was legally two or three steps removed from the customer. A doctrine of *privity* excluded suit against a manufacturer with whom the customer had no contractual relationship. Since most dealers were not wealthy enough to pay any large damages, customers had no great possibility for compensation in case of serious defect in a product.

The liability of a manufacturer for defects in his products could be handled either by tortious action or by suit for breach of contract. Richard Posner writes that there is an economic logic for the common law in this field: the law's assignment of rights helps minimize transaction costs.[1] At a deeper level, the economic analysis rests upon the desire to secure an ethical result. The several-thousand-year-old desire to limit sales to products that are what they are said to be is reflected in either form of legal action.

Because of the situation in which some deserving people had no real legal recourse against defective products, the common law went through another of its great reversals; this time probably a move in an ethical direction. As in all such moves, many courts were involved and changes came slowly and uncertainly. Even today the law of manufacturers' liability for products varies in different jurisdictions; unjust damage may be done to some manufacturers, and to some consumers.

The process of change is worth examining as a case of legal development of an ethical principle, perhaps beyond a real ethic. In the last half of the nineteenth century, the doctrine of privity lost its effectiveness in cases involving hazardous products or products for intimate bodily use.[2] The case of *MacPherson* v. *Buick Motor Company* in 1916 led the New York Court of Appeals to decide that in spite of claims of privity, manufacturers were liable for injuries from a product if there was evidence of negligence in manufacture or assembly; in this case a wheel came off a car, causing bodily injury.[3] Such extensions of liability in cases of significant danger continued. Then the Uniform Commercial Code, adopted in all states but one by 1974, incorporated provisions about implied warranty (guarantee) that gave important opportunities for suing manufacturers; for example, Ford Motor Company advertised a shatter-proof windshield which a rock could break, implying a warranty that permitted suit against Ford.[4] A New Jersey case in 1960 held both manufacturer and dealer liable for personal injury when a car suddenly veered into a wall, a result of an implied warranty that completely eliminated the doctrine of privity.[5]

A claim against a manufacturer may now be based on breach of warranty. The warranty may be found in oral or written statements of the manufacturer or his representative, or may be implied from the law. Most usual is a warranty that the product is safe, usable, and fit for its reasonably intended purpose.[6] Advertising claims may be a basis for a suit of breach of implied warranty.[7] The best prevention of such suits is truthful advertising, a concept some businesses have found hard to accept.

An old legal doctrine that has become important in product liability is that of *res ipsa loquitur* ("the thing speaks for itself"). Injury resulting from an explosion could lead to use of this doctrine. It would establish a prima facie case of negligence, and could result in a summary judgment for the plaintiff or put the burden of proof on the defendant.

The strictness of laws and court decisions on liability of manufacturers has increased greatly in recent decades, perhaps to the point of unreasonableness. In 1963 the California Supreme Court, an enthusiastic advocate of consumer rights, decided that a manufacturer is strictly liable when an article he places on the market, knowing that it will be used without inspections, proves to have a defect that causes injury to a human being. No limitations of length of time of use or of alteration by owners were placed on this doctrine, which is now followed in thirty-five other states.[8]

By the 1960s the courts had also developed an opportunity for action in tort against manufacturers. The Restatement (Second) of Torts (state law) in 1965 held seller strictly liable if a product was in a defective condition unreasonably dangerous to the user, regardless of care exercised by the seller.[9] This doctrine of strict liability excluded defense on grounds of contributory negligence. It includes only serious and unusual defects.[10]

Thus negligence, express or implied warranty, or strict liability may be the bases of court actions. The publication, *Corpus juris secundum*, comments that the term *product liability* is often used interchangeably with the terms *implied warranty* and *strict liability*. A person may sue on the grounds of strict liability, or negligence, or both.[11]

In addition to these new court attitudes there is now a federal law on product safety that authorizes a Consumer Product Safety Commission to exercise powers over manufacturers to assure product safety.[12] Establishment of the Consumer Products Safety Commission in 1972 brought together a few earlier acts, and gave the commission broad powers to investigate, test, develop standards, ban products, require manufacturers or sales agencies to give public notice of deficient products, inspect plants, and conduct hearings. Previous acts on hazardous substances, toy safety and child protection, flammable fabrics, refrigeration safety, and poison prevention were all brought under the commission. Manufacturers must report to the Commission within twenty-four hours if they receive word of danger in any product. But the Consumer Products Safety Commission has been one of the least administratively successful of the new regulatory bodies. The difficulties lie in the legal complexity of the problem and in the internal administration of the commission. The Reagan administration and Congress may secure a cutback in the commission's program.

There are a number of cases in which judges and juries seem to have been unduly hard on manufacturers. A new doctrine that the manufacturer should foresee accidents is developing. The Kentucky Court of Appeals held a manufacturer of vacuum cleaners liable for an explosion when a cleaner designed for 115 volts and clearly labeled for 115-volt outlets only was plugged into a 220-volt outlet. The court's argument was that the label should have said that it would be bad to plug the machine into a larger outlet.[13] Personal injury damages were awarded in a tire-blowout case even though no defect was proven.[14]

A teenager poured some perfume over a lighted candle to scent it. The perfume burned, causing damage to a friend's neck. The manufacturer of the perfume was held liable.[15] A construction worker drove a forklift truck not equipped with a roll bar on a steep slope where it overturned and injured him. The California Supreme Court declared that the manufacturer must demonstrate that the forklift's benefits outweighed its dangers; surely a decision that the truck owner should make.

Some cases may be labeled nuisance or buy-off claims. Irwin Gray cites a 1973 study of nine product cases defended by one firm over two years. The plaintiffs in all nine cases sought almost $83 million, legal costs for defense were $40,000, and settlement of the cases cost only $43,000.[16]

Donald MacDonald's book on the auto industry adds other examples of the tremendous costs put on manufacturers by the strict liability doctrine or by decisions of the National Highway Traffic Safety Administration that trigger court suits. Two men who had been drinking rolled over in a Corvette. The roof collapsed and one man's hand was mangled. The victim sued General Motors on the grounds that rollover tests had not been conducted and won his case on the theory that the car's structure had not protected him.[17]

However, some courts have reasoned that the ethics of strict liability do not apply with universal extravagance. A $128-million jury judgment against Ford Motor Company because a young man was severely burned when another car struck a Ford Pinto was reduced to $3.8 million by judges.

The highly liberal California Supreme Court in May 1980 allowed a suit against several manufacturers when the mother of the plaintiff could not remember which drug she had taken twenty-six years earlier to prevent miscarriage.[18] The unknown drug was presumably linked to cancer in her daughter. The U.S. Supreme Court declined to review. Implications of such suits against several manufacturers may be tremendous.

The prospect is for great increase of product liability cases, with a corresponding increase in company expenditures for lawyers, computers, and research to help fight such suits. Plaintiff attorneys, having a taste of action, will be back for more filings.[19] The asbestos industry faces large costs.[20] Costs of products to consumers will rise.

These changes in the law have hit some firms rather hard. The number of claims filed annually has jumped from 50,000 in 1960 to more than 1 million in 1977, says the *U.S. News and World Report*.[21] However, *Consumer Reports* says the number of claims is less than 100,000.[22] Premiums for insurance were going up rapidly in 1973-1976, 200 to 1000 percent. Some juries have given amazingly large damage awards to some injured persons. Such verdicts inevitably lead to high insurance costs (estimated at $2.75 billion for product liability in 1978).[23] Some companies are having difficulty securing insurance; a few are being forced out of business. Product innovation is decreasing in pharmaceuticals and medical devices. Prices have been increased as a result of product liability but usually by less than 1 percent; 15 percent in the case of some sporting equipment is the estimate of a source biased for the consumer.[24]

This new liability of manufacturers goes well beyond the legal responsibilities of businesses at the beginning of the Republic, although the basic ethic of being responsible for making a good product is not completely changed. There is a parallelism between this change, the shift of laws about unions from repression to protection, and the change from *caveat emptor* to *caveat venditor* ("seller beware"). All three show a shift toward protection of persons of lesser means. Counsels for two business firms on product litigation agree that recent decisions support an increasing disinclination of the public to accept responsibility for its acts.[25]

It should be noted that England and other western European countries are moving toward tighter product-liability laws, following the American example.[26] Proposals for no-fault strict liability are being considered by the European Community's Commission in spite of concern about large costs.[27] However, since European courts do not have the tremendous power of American courts, it is doubtful if product liability will become as expensive across the Atlantic.[28] Some European companies in 1977 were paying ten times as much for insurance against liability for products sold in the United States as for products sold in Europe.[29] This difference may support the judgment that the United States has not yet found a generally acceptable ethic for product liability.

Did Business Deserve This?

Did the manufacturers deserve the difficulties imposed upon them by strict product liability? Any such general question is hard to answer in ethical terms. Conrad Berenson cited some reasons for the trend toward stricter liability:

1. Packaging techniques keep customers from inspecting contents.
2. Technological sophistication keeps customers from knowing enough to appraise products.
3. Advertising spending of $23 billion a year (now higher) overwhelms the customers with real and imagined information.
4. Growth of material-distribution networks has separated some manufacturers from a sense of legal and moral responsibility to customers.
5. Product planners have created an enormous number of new products that even sophisticated buyers cannot keep up with.
6. So many new products, often with radical new technology, are bound to have some honest errors.
7. Attorneys have found here a new field of exploitation.
8. The recent wave of consumerism (the third in this century) has put political pressure "on both executive and judicial branches of our government to impose greater responsibilities upon producers and distributors."
9. Today's citizen reacts to a presumed harmful product by calling his lawyer or writing his congressman.[30]

Are any of Berenson's reasons for strict liability a result of ethical fault on the part of the manufacturer or distributor? Do modern situations expand the historically accepted responsibility to turn out a good product? It seems that packaging, advertising, distributing networks, and the number of products have expanded the ethical liability of manufacturers. In each of these, the ethical question becomes involved. As packaging, technological, distribution, or other problems increase, the manufacturer develops an ethical responsibility to let the customer know more about the product. The manufacturer's monopoly of knowledge about use of the product adds to his liability. Product-liability statutes and court decisions have reinforced that new ethic.

This change in both courts and Congress from the *caveat emptor* doctrine of the nineteenth century to strict manufacturer responsibility for products was of course a great shock to business executives, many of whom were not thinking about the reasons underlying the shift. In a complex, industrial world faulty products are more likely to be disastrous. More consumers are better educated and thus better able to complain against unsatisfactory products. As Berenson suggests, new products are increasingly technical; often the manufacturer is the only party that could suggest a means of removing the difficulty. Better-educated employees are somewhat more likely to "blow the whistle" against unsatisfactory products. In short, manufacturing businesses have to face a much more critical world.

A problem that Berenson does not stress, perhaps included in his sixth point, is that many Americans question the quality of some American products. Automobiles come first to mind; Japanese-built autos, Volkswagens, and perhaps French cars seem to hold up better, and require fewer recalls. American automobile manufacturers may have changed styles annually for so many years that they have paid less attention to cost and quality of the product. International competition may change this attitude of American business but it may be too late to change the new ethic of strict product liability, if the new ethic should be changed.

It also is apparently true in some cases that manufacturers have attempted to avoid responsibility for their products. MacDonald, after considerable experience in the automobile industry, reports a number of cases in which manufacturers seem to have avoided paying for faulty construction.[31] The older law may have prevented legal responsibility but it did not eliminate ethical responsibility. A scholar who knows the auto industry well suggests that the development of a need for very large sales has put the salesmen and the finance men disproportionately on top in the industry; he doubts if engineer-executives would have been as irresponsible about customer safety. MacDonald believes that the effort of auto companies to ignore the one in ten thousand "lemons" has been bad for public relations; admission of fault and replacement would cost less in public esteem. If so, that ethical mistake parallels the mistakes of several businesses in failing to respond promptly to health dangers.

A word should be said in behalf of businesses. Strict liability of manufacturers is not always the highest ethic. It may prove to be one of the reasons for putting the American auto industry out of business. If there was adequate warning of how not to use the product, and that warning is disregarded, should the manufacturer really be responsible for all accidents or dangers? Is the government not adding unduly to the manufacturers' costs and encouraging customers not to follow directions?

A problem for manufacturers is the question of ignorance of the dangers of their products. Government scientists have sometimes been undecided as to the ill effect of products, so the slowness in banning a dangerous product may be the fault of government or due to simple lack of technical knowledge. Unfortunately, industry scientists often appear to present the point of view of an industry that wishes to continue selling its product. An ideal ethical sense should lead all scientists or engineers to come to similar conclusions about the dangers of a product, but the ideal ethical sense does not appear to be fully developed, or is perhaps overwhelmed by attitudes of superiors as suggested in earlier chapters of this book. More teaching of ethics to engineers is needed.[32]

The problem of falsification of product test records by intermediate officials involves a different ethical angle. Clearly what the falsifiers did was very wrong. But were they functioning according to the ethos of the corporations in which they worked? Had anyone told them that research reports must be strictly accurate? In the B.F. Goodrich Company, two managers who apparently ordered falsification of reports were subsequently promoted and the man who reported to the FBI was fired.[33] The company changed its products, but did not convince its staff that data about products must be accurate. Perhaps the ethical blame applies equally to those accused of falsification and the executives under whom they work. The same company received awards for its distinguished work in World War II and its development of the tubeless tire.

Business Resistance to New Ethics
of Product Liability

A few examples will indicate the substantial degree of business resistance to external pressures against unsatisfactory products. The initial resistance was often to ignore the ethical issue.

Ralph Nader's chief object of attack was first the auto industry. His book *Unsafe at any Speed* not unreasonably criticized the auto companies for lack of concern about safety measures, although traffic deaths were running close to 50,000 a year. Car bumpers had been made continually weaker, although costs for insurance against collision damage had been increasing. The rear-end motor Corvair was manufactured on an unsafe basis for several years, although design engineers probably had stabilizing techniques in mind. In the Comstock case, General Motors had produced a Roadmaster car with a faulty brake mechanism but was slow in letting dealers or buyers know about it. General Motors and other companies were said to be slow to introduce seat belts for fear that they would alert potential buyers to auto dangers. General Motors' response to Nader was an unjustified personal attack.

Nader cites a court hearing in which a Chevrolet service manager was queried about tire pressures needed to keep the Corvair stable. The manager indicated that such pressures were vital and critical, but no effort had been made by the manufacturer to inform the public or customers of that fact.[35]

In the early 1950s Supervisor Kenneth Hahn of Los Angeles County received answers of almost complete lack of interest from the auto companies when he communicated with them about the smog problem in the Los Angeles area caused by car motors.[36] Eventually, legislation compelled interest on the part of the auto companies.

Ernest Conine points out that Ford Motor Company spent months in legal maneuvering before it decided to change the gas-tank mounting on its 1971-1976 Pintos to reduce a well-proven fire hazard.[37] Similarly, Firestone recalled a line of tires only after many tire failures and federal government intervention. Admittedly the cost of change was great; but the slowness of action indicated to many people that these large corporations were not recognizing their ethical responsibility. This kind of ethical stolidity is very costly to the public image of some otherwise well-run corporations.

Fortune magazine ran an interesting article on how a big company can make its situation worse through belligerent denial of defects in products.[38] Firestone Tire and Rubber Company had manufactured the "500" series of radial tires which, according to federal authorities, were prone to blowouts, tread separations, and other deformities. The National Highway Traffic Safety Administration (NHTSA) after seven months of investigation ordered recall of the series, an order based on the number of consumer complaints, not on an exact knowledge of the defect. The company was, of course, plagued by loss of business and by court suits. The *Fortune* writer believes that Firestone exacerbated its difficulties. It held a clearance sale of "500" series radial tires in the Southeast in the spring of 1978, before the government investigation was well known, a sale the *Fortune* writer believes could be interpreted as a desperate effort to unload damaged goods.[39]

Firestone's vice president and general counsel, according to Fortune's writer, was aggressive in attacking the NHTSA official, taking equal action to try to suppress the results of a survey conducted by NHTSA, failing to answer an admittedly lengthy questionnaire from NHTSA, and its counsel arguing "like a lawyer, fighting a tough case" before the investigating House committee. Finally the NHTSA issued a recall order; Firestone had blown its case and "vividly demonstrated the wrong way of dealing with the government and the public." Chemical-manufacturing concerns for some time fought to maintain use of 2, 4, 5-T as a killer of brush in spite of evidence that 2, 4, 5-T is also destructive of human and animal life in the area where it is sprayed.[40]

In other cases faulty products have been completed because of poor testing pushed through by supervisors who were reluctant to admit their errors.[41] These included the falsification of test records on an airplane brake and the falsification of records as to the effect of a new drug on test animals. In both these cases the falsification was made by responsible but not top officials of the well-known companies involved.

Other companies have been slow to respond to criticisms of their products. In 1969 General Motors built some defective school buses, and GM representatives were very slow to recognize the faults or do much about getting the company to eliminate them. Some of the defects were dangerous for schoolchildren or passengers. They included a faulty brake-hose suspension, other brake troubles, burned-out clutches, and leaky gasoline tanks.[42]

Ford's difficulties with the Pinto seem to be another example of company policy that becomes a stubborn ignoring of public safety. This small car was brought out in 1971, although company documents showed that its gas tank could be ruptured by sharp rear-end collisions. The documents also included a cost-benefit analysis by a lower-ranking employee that showed that it would cost Ford $137 million to put a safer tank on the Pinto, which would have prevented 80 burn deaths, 80 burn injuries, and 2,100 burned vehicles, at a total benefit of $49.5 million, counting lives at $200,000 and injuries at $67,000. This somewhat callous appraisal agreed with the company's other thoughts about eliminating the Pinto problems earlier, but the available account does not indicate clearly that it was the basis of company policy. However, Ford opposed safety regulations that would have eliminated the danger. Finally a new safer gas tank was installed in models available in 1977.[43] Why did Ford delay action so long and encourage such bad public relations?

John De Lorean describes how engineering staffs at General Motors were convinced of the danger of the rear end of the Corvair as originally built and sold. The disastrous results flooded General Motors with lawsuits and resulted in death and injury, including children of General Motors executives. Finally Semon E. (Bunkie) Knudsen threatened to resign if the top officers would not agree to his proposal to make the Corvair safe.[44]

The Product Safety Commission has not been especially effective, and class-action damage suits against manufacturers or distributors or both have probably done more to make manufacturers responsible and careful about their products. However, either route to safety is unnecessarily cumbersome and expensive. The underlying (though not exclusive) answer should be an ethical education to teach manufacturers and distributors and their staffs to assume responsibility for the safety of their products. *Sic utere tuo, salus populi suprema lex,* and "love thy neighbor as thyself" are some of the ethical principles that could be cited.

The negative or slow reaction of many corporations to well-grounded public opinion or legal reactions against defective products is partly a result of factors internal to corporations, discussed in chapter 3. They are problems of serious concern that sometimes result in stringent legislative action. Corporations would be well advised to secure more attention from their staff for serious ethical charges. The corporation is more likely to survive as a useful element of society if it recognizes its ethical responsibilities to society.

Legal Resistance to New Ethical Standards

According to *Consumer Reports* the Department of Commerce stated that forty-two states were considering new product-liability laws; most of them designed to protect manufacturers from some of the crippling damage judgments.[45] A half-dozen states had already passed such laws and a few laws had been introduced in Congress. The bills frequently included three provisions:

1. A statute of limitations, dating the limitations from the time when the product was originally sold rather than a specific number of years, usually six to ten years after the accident. A six-year law would have excluded the famous Pinto case that occurred seven years after the car was sold. *Consumer Reports* prefers a provision that the jury may consider the age of the product.
2. A second feature is the state-of-the-art defense. If the product conformed with generally accepted standards of the industry at the time of manufacture, no suit would be possible. *Consumers Reports* opposes this provision on the ground that it will delay safety improvements.
3. The third feature is the alteration—or misuse—defense. The defendant would have no responsibility if he could prove that the product was misused or altered. *Consumers Reports* prefers a statute establishing comparative fault.

Why do legislatures consider laws restricting product liability so soon after the courts have extended it? The reason is not entirely ethical, although there may be some fraction of that. Primarily it is that businesses that feel threatened by large judgments in product-liability cases have told legislatures, "let's change the law or we will have to go out of business in your state." Threatened by the loss of jobs and of incomes, the legislatures respond more than do the courts. Perhaps the legislative reaction is a necessary part of the process of securing a fair ethic.

Consumers Reports opposes all these bills and predicts their downfall either in the legislature or the courts. It mentions as an alternative a no-fault system, suggested by Jeffrey O'Connell of the University of Illinois Law School. Under this scheme the victim would collect directly from the manufacturer's insurance company, thus avoiding expensive court proceedings, which are estimated to take two-thirds of awarded damages. The victim would have to show that the product caused injury but would collect only for verifiable losses such as medical expenses and income loss. The implementation of this idea seems some time off, but the current (1981) reaction against overregulation may speed up some variant of it.

The best solution to this problem goes beyond ethical rules to detailed problems of legal administration. The ethical person can hope, and perhaps work, for a solution that avoids huge legal fees, enables manufacturers to keep operating with a profit, but forces them to be as careful as possible, making use of experience and careful engineering research before marketing a product.

A Note on Repair of Complex Consumer Products

Vastly different from the problem of enforcing ethical conduct on the part of the manufacturer is the enforcement of ethical repair work. New complex consumer products require more complicated repairs, but repair work can be irresponsible. Garages and repair shops are too small to be disciplined by the expensive class-action suit, which seems to be prosecuted chiefly so that the law firm may receive its contingent fee. The federal government has almost no jurisdiction over repair work. Few states or cities have agencies that actively supervise this type of activity.

Unfortunately there is a good deal of evidence to indicate that these repairs are not always ethically handled. A recent Federal Trade Commission estimate is that $12 billion of $40 billion spent annually on auto repairs was for unnecessary work. A Dallas effort to regulate auto mechanics handled 10,000 complaints about auto-repair shops in three years' time. One hundred and ninety-one cases warranted prosecution; many were settled outside of court. The Dallas ordinance, somewhat similar to laws in one-third of the states, makes it unlawful to charge for unnecessary or imaginary repairs. It also requires a $50 license, written estimates, and detailed charges to be presented to consumers. The Dallas city officer, a mechanic of twenty years' experience, was surprised at the amount and extent of the frauds practiced by some repair shops.[46] The repair industry was unhappy about the ordinance, objecting particularly to a provision that forced repair shops to contact the customer if the job was to run 10 percent above estimates.

A 1975 study of twenty-four auto-repair shops in New York City and nearby Suffolk County found that eleven performed or recommended expensive work on the transmission or other unnecessary repairs.[47] *The New York Times* story went on to say that nationally, auto-repair complaints topped the list of consumer complaints. Senator Philip Hart in the early

1970s estimated in a Senate Antitrust and Monopoly Subcommittee that each year consumers paid $8 to $10 billion for repairs that were not needed, or were badly done.

A study reported by the Federal Trade Commission in 1975 found that consumers had a 20- to 50-percent chance of being defrauded on television-repair jobs. Half of twenty television-repair firms in Washington and another twenty in New Orleans were claimed to have replaced parts or tubes that did not need replacement. Such frauds occurred only four out of twenty times in San Francisco, where the state law licensing television-repair shops also provides for spot checks on the shops.[48] In New York City in the 1970s, a television-repair shop advertising citywide service took a TV set to repair, extracted a fee, took the set again when it didn't work, added another charge, and kept the set. More shocking than the fraudulent character of the advertised repair shop were the impossible obstacles presented to the New York City Department of Consumer Affairs by the New York City courts.[49]

Donald MacDonald believes the high cost of auto repairs stems from a desire to maintain convenience on the assembly line. Also auto companies are unwilling to give up heavy profits on sale of parts, masking some parts so they are expensive to change.[50]

It is difficult to avoid the conclusion that there are very genuine ethical problems in the business of repairing complex consumer products. Some of these problems come from the difficulty of securing effective legal action. Some system of licensing repair shops, as in California, may add a sanction which this economic area has not known. The threat of removing a license is real. But reform by pressure from the top is not as possible in the repair field as it is in large corporations.

Conclusions

The Western ethical tradition has all the needed ingredients to solve the problems of product liability, dealer relationships, and repair of complex consumer products. If the injunctions to tell the truth to buyers, to produce a worthwhile product, to protect the health and safety of the public, and to be fair to dealers, customers, and to other people with whom one is working are all followed, most of the problems in this chapter would be largely solved.

The serious problem is that manufacturers, dealers, and repair shops are often not willing to follow the ethical precepts listed above. The answer of all companies with product problems to the suggestions of this chapter is that competition forces them to avoid the expense of safety engineering. It is, however, totally wrong to allow an ethic of competitive costs to over-come an ethic of human life or well-being. The latter, according to Judaic-

Christian, Kantian, or other sources, ranks first in ethical values. Competitive disadvantage must be assumed in order to meet the more important ethical value of maintaining life.

Yet most Americans would like to retain an economic free market in manufacture, sale, and repair of these complex products. If the businesses are unwilling to conduct their operations in accord with the Western ethical tradition, it may become the task of government to nudge them into appropriate action, as has already been done in other aspects of industry like banking, and most aspects of security sales and retail sales. More regulation is to be regretted, but so is more ethical disturbance of the type too often encountered in some of the product lines discussed in this chapter.

Notes

1. Richard A. Posner, *Economic Analysis of Law,* p. 180.

2. Irwin Gray et al., *Product Liability,* p. 17.

3. *MacPherson* v. *Buick Motor Company,* 217 NY 283, III NE 1050.

4. Gray et al., *Product Liability,* p. 20.

5. *Henningson* v. *Bloomfield Motors, Inc.* 32 N.J. 358, 161 A 2d 69 1960.

6. Lawrence A. Bennigson and Arnold I. Bennigson, "Product Liability, Manufacturers Beware!" *Harvard Business Review,* May-June 1974, p. 123.

7. Fred W. Morgan, Jr., "The Products Liability Consequences of Advertising," *Journal of Advertising* 8:4, pp. 30-37.

8. Bennigson and Bennigson, "Product Liability," p. 123.

9. Gray et al., *Product Liability,* p. 22.

10. Conrad Berenson, "The Product Liability Revolution," *Business Horizons,* October 1972, pp. 75-78.

11. 72 Corpus Juris Secundum Supp., Products Liability, SS 2-3.

12. Gray et al., *Product Liability,* pp. 152-154.

13. Berenson, "The Product Liability Revolution", pp. 71-80.

14. *Collins* v. *Uniroyal Inc.* (New Jersey) cited in Gray et al., *Product Liability,* p. 19.

15. *Business Week*, February 12, 1979, p. 72.

16. Gray, *Product Liability,* p. 72.

17. Donald MacDonald, *Detroit 1985,* p. 112.

18. *Wall Street Journal,* December 30, 1980.

19. *Wall Street Journal,* June 16, 1981, p. 46.

20. *Business Week,* April 13, 1981, pp. 166, 169.

21. *U.S. News and World Report,* May 22, 1978, p. 93.

22. *Consumer Reports*, July 1978, p. 414.

23. *Business Week,* February 12, 1979, p. 72.

24. *Consumer Reports,* July 1978, p. 414.

25. *Business Week,* February 12, 1979, p. 72.

26. *Wall Street Journal,* September 21, 1979.

27. *Business Week, November 10, 1980.*

28. The Economist, July 1, 1978, p. 90; July 21, 1979, pp. 81-82; September 22, 1979, p. 57.

29. Thomas N. Gladwin and Ingo Walter, *Multinationals under Fire,* p. 344.

30. *Journal of Purchasing,* May 1973, pp. 5-11. Also "Product Liability Revolution," *Business Horizons,* October 1972, p. 71.

31. MacDonald, *Detroit 1985,* Chap. 13.

32. Edwin T. Layton, Jr., *The Revolt of the Engineers.*

33. Robert L. Heilbroner et al., *In the Name of Profit,* p. 3031.

34. Ralph Nader, *Unsafe at any Speed.*

35. James Bishop, Jr., Henry W. Hubbard, *Let the Seller Beware,* pp. 90-91.

36. Correspondence between Hahn and the presidents of GM, Ford, and Chrysler on controlling air pollution, Los Angeles, 1953 and 1972.

37. *Los Angeles Times,* August 27, 1979, part 2, p. 5.

38. *Fortune,* August 28, 1979, p. 78.

39. Ibid., p. 46.

40. Harrison Wellford, *Sowing the Wind,* pp. 187-218.

41. Heilbroner, *In the Name of Profit,* chapters 1 and 4.

42. Colman McCarthy, "Deciding to Cheapen the Product," in Heilbroner et al., *In the Name of Profit,* pp. 32-59.

43. Mark Darvie, "Pinto Madness," *Mother Jones,* September–October 1977, reprinted in Robert J. Baum, ed., *Ethical Problems in Engineering,* vol. 2, pp. 167-174.

44. J. Patrick Wright, *On a Clear Day,* pp. 65-68.

45. *Consumer Reports,* July 1978, pp. 412-416.

46. John M. Johnson and Jack D. Douglas, *Crime at the Top,* pp. 319-322.

47. Frances Cerra, "11 of 24 Auto Repair Shops Pass a Test on Honesty," *The New York Times,* December 8, 1975, pp. 1, 50.

48. *The New York Times,* January 13, 1975, p. 56.

49. Philip Schrag, *Counsel for the Deceived,* pp. 72-96.

50. MacDonald, *Detroit 1985,* pp. 198-212.

14 The Ethics of International Corporations

In recent decades multinational corporations have become a major part of the world of commerce. The *multinational corporation* (MNC) is a corporation that produces and sells its products in several countries. Ford Motor Company, for example, received over half its 1979 income from foreign investments. In 1975 multinationals produced over 25 percent of the world's goods and services.[1] Scores of major companies operate in one or more countries. Some multinational companies, operating in less-developed countries (LDCs) may find their local plants to be the larger and more remunerative institutions of the countries in which they are operating. Multinational corporations in such LDCs may begin with praise, but may also find themselves sharply criticized when economic conditions or managerial mistakes force retrenchment. Much of this chapter is devoted to the ethical problems of MNCs in less-developed countries.

Ninety-five percent of the multinational companies have headquarters and do three-quarters of their business and earn profits in eight countries: the United States, the United Kingdom, the Federal Republic of Germany (West Germany), the Netherlands, France, Japan, Sweden, and Switzerland. The economic importance of the MNCs is in the home countries of other MNCs; MNCs are also important to developing countries because they bring those countries into the world economy.[2]

MNCs, if properly conducted, could help the economic status of many LDCs tremendously. They can teach new technologies to LDC nationals, pay higher wages, increase the countries' gross national product (GNP) and help move them forward economically. It may be true that multinational corporations are the greatest hope of bringing the population of the free world into cooperative relationships; it is hoped that multinationals might also be helpful to some collectivist economies.[3]

A host of ethical problems are raised when economic entities of one or more highly developed countries start operating in an LDC. Will the LDC's financial and accounting laws be adequate and fair? Will the multinationals decide to withdraw for economic reasons, thus raising great employment problems in the LDC? Will the higher salaries paid by the multinational upset the economy of the LDC? Will the government of the LDC permit the multinational to operate freely?

The modern multinational corporation that conducts extensive sales or manufacturing operation began mostly with American corporations. Ford

Motor company started assembling cars in Great Britain in 1911, and was a major producer in both Great Britain and Germany by the 1920s. General Motors started operations in Europe in the 1920s. The "Seven Sisters"—British Petroleum, Exxon, Gulf Oil, Mobil, Royal Dutch Shell, Standard of California, and Texaco—have operated widely over the world for several decades. International Business Machines (IBM) sells its computers in most of the developed world. Sears, Roebuck, and Company, the world's largest retailer, operates only in the New World.

These companies vary in method of operation. Sometimes they do business directly, sometimes through national subsidiaries, sometimes in forced partnership with local governments or local economic interests. Despite the advantages of MNCs to host countries, they are often viewed with suspicion or hostility, and several times their property has been expropriated or they have been forced to quit operations.

Ethical Background of Multinational Corporations

The Judaic-Christian ethical background of the Western world has not furnished any special ethical principle for multinational corporations. The basic proscriptions against stealing, deceiving, bribing, or bearing false witness remain. But there has been no religious code dealing with the ethics of corporations or multinational corporations. The *law merchant* was a special body of doctrine developed by merchant communities in various countries but acknowledged by the courts of most countries in which it was found. Hugo Grotius (1583-1645), a distinguished student of international law, thought it was generally agreed by mankind that the privileges granted to the subjects of foreign countries were the common rights of all. It was, however, lawful for a nation to agree to a monopoly on certain products. But this should not be allowed as a means of enhancing prices. Treaties that provide for rights of hospitality and commerce fell under the law of nations.[4] The philosopher Immanuel Kant wrote extensively on international relations and in his writing foresaw an ethic of international relations. In his essay on perpetual peace, he said that the independent existence of each state should be preserved. There should be a right to hospitality in each country. Commercial interchange would help further peace.

The doctrine of "love thy neighbor as thyself," vague and unenforceable as it sometimes appears to be, may be of particular importance when skilled Western businessmen in multinationals deal with unskilled natives of less-developed countries.

None of these earlier efforts probably went so far as to forbid bribery in international commercial relations. Yet most advanced countries forbid it of their own citizens, so it is reasonable to suppose that an international obligation also exists. Bribery of public officials has long been a crime in the Western ethical tradition. It is forbidden in the Code of Hammurabi and in the Pentateuch. William Blackstone notes that it may be allowed in the East or in despotic countries, but notes that in Roman law it was severely punished (strangely, magistrates were allowed to receive small presents). In England in Blackstone's time fines and imprisonment were levied on inferior officers and on those who offered bribes but penalties were more severe on judges. One chief justice was hanged for accepting bribes.[5]

Bribes or Extortion

Most MNCs are large, reputable corporations that need substantial capital and important connections to start large-scale operations in other countries. Hence it was a surprise when the Securities and Exchange Commission (SEC) learned of extensive corporate payments to foreign government officials or to foreign political parties. In May 1976, the SEC brought injunctive action against twenty-two companies, all of which made consent settlements to avoid court battles; the number who made such settlements later rose to 300. The SEC was operating on the theory that such payments were material information, which under the Securities and Exchange Act of 1945 should be disclosed to shareholders, though the payments were generally very small percentages of the corporations' income. The Internal Revenue Service later contended that funds produced from bribes were "denied foreign tax credits, tax deferral or tax benefits."[6] For example, Ashland Oil paid $150,000 to the president of Gabon in 1972, $100,000 to a Libyan "consultant" in 1971, and $50,000 to several Dominican Republic businessmen including its ambassador-at-large to Europe in 1967 and 1968. Del Monte Corporation paid $500,000 in 1975 to an agent who helped the corporation to buy a plantation from the Guatemalan government. Both Exxon and General Motors made large contributions to Canadian political parties, which were perfectly legal under Canadian law, but illegal in the United States. Gulf Oil in 1975 told the Senate Foreign Relations Committee of $5 million in illegal contributions in South Korea, Bolivia, Lebanon, and elsewhere. In 1975 Lockheed reported having paid $22 million in commissions to Saudi Arabia, mostly to a single businessman. United Brands paid $1.25 million to the minister of economics of Honduras to receive a tax reduction on banana exports.

Such payments are in general demanded and expected of MNCs. English, French, and German competitors met such demands without complaint except in the "zone of nonbribery" (Western Europe). Governments in all of the countries in which they were operating could stop their work completely by refusing visas for company personnel, permits to build plants, authorization for oil rigs to enter territorial waters, police protection when needed, or by repatriating capital. The U.S. State Department would give no help to a business that found host-country governments extorting substantial payments for normal governmental actions. In the Middle East, political payment to do business has been traditional for centuries. In Africa, business corruption has been almost universal. In India most officials demand personal payments. In Southeast Asia, smuggling has led to general political corruption. In Latin America, political corruption is universal. Even in western Europe it sometimes occurs.[7]

Payments have also been made in the Netherlands and Japan, two countries in which extortion or bribery has not been a universal custom. In the Netherlands, Lockheed was apparently asked to make a $4 million contribution to Prince Consort Bernhard, and contributed at least $1,100,000 in its efforts to sell L-1011 Tri-Star jets. In Japan, Lockheed paid over $7 million to a right-wing militarist; $2.8 million presumably went to high-ranking officers. Both countries felt substantial political impact after these payments, more extortions than bribes, were publicized. Both are countries in which bribes have been offered or extortion demanded but not countries in which this has been a common practice; so Lockheed could not justify its action by the moral standards of the countries. The great care taken to conceal bribes in other cases shows that most companies were aware that bribery was wrong, even if there were excuses.[8] In some Middle Eastern countries, the law required that sales be made through a sales agent who collected large sums before securing approval of a major contract.

All multinational companies reimburse their employees to pay *cumshaw* or *baksheesh*, small bribes required to travel or work in less-developed countries. The U.S. government now admits this and in the Proxmire Act of December 1977 forbids major payments to officials or political figures but allows these smaller payments. The distinction is hard for company lawyers to make. The real ethical problem is that of the larger payment, specifically forbidden by the Proxmire Act since 1978. If Judaic-Christian principles are followed enough to believe that all men are brothers, it might reasonably follow that we should not bribe the officials of other nations when we would consider it illegal to bribe our own. American bribes in the Netherlands or Japan seem morally offensive since these countries have at least as high a general sense of political rectitude as the United States. But do Americans have the right to forbid bribes or extortion payments that may be standard practice in other countries? Apparently no other country has legislated as the United States did in the Proxmire Act. Paradoxically, some of the other homes of multinationals like England, Switzerland, and Sweden have more nearly honest governments. Are these countries immoral to not ban such payments by their corporations or are they merely paying respect to the customs of the countries in which their corporations are working?[9]

There have been several efforts at international guidelines. The Organization for Economic Cooperation and Development (OECD) (twenty-seven more-industrialized countries) has recommended voluntary guidelines for MNCs which ban bribes and contributions to public officials and illegal contributions to political parties. This portion of the guidelines was *not* attacked at a workshop sponsored by the Chamber of Commerce of the United States, the National Association of Manufacturers, and the U.S. Council of the International Chamber of Commerce.

The board of directors of the United States Chamber of Commerce in 1977 condemned any improper practices by MNCs but believed that public disclosure of payments could be adequate punishment. The permanent council of the Organization of American States in 1975 condemned any act of bribery or illegal payment by MNC. The United Nations has established a commission to work on problems of conduct of multinational companies; the International Chamber of Commerce has expressed a wish that such a code be voluntary.

The Proxmire Act is more potent than any of these voluntary guidelines. It has sharp penalties for both corporations and responsible executives. There is evidence that some public as well as corporate officers believe the act to be unworkable. Since it comes from a country with proportionately more political corruption than any other MNC home country, it is a surprising example of American idealism, as well as of an American propensity to pass laws that will be difficult to enforce. Although Neil H. Jacoby et al. assert that America is guided by the New England Puritans' concept of an ideal society, there is much evidence that most American states have been dominated by different ideologies.[10] But it is good if quixotic that the Puritan ethical heritage does occasionally appear in national policy.

Since the passage of the Proxmire Act, there have been conflicting reports of its effect. Some American multinationals have reported loss of business; others have felt no loss. It may be that the age-old ban against bribes will now receive some partial degree of enforcement in countries around the world because of the American impact on world trade through multinationals.

A study by the Chamber of Commerce of the United States indicates much difficulty with interpretation of the Proxmire Act.[11] The line between permissible payments that are common practice in many countries and illegal corporate bribes is hard to determine. The SEC and the Department of Justice differ on this issue. The Proxmire Act has been used as a means of extorting payments from American companies.

Changes will probably be made in some provisions of the act in the current (1981) Congress, but it will survive in some form. The OECD guidelines plus the International Chamber of Commerce advice, plus the underdeveloped nations' desire to make the guidelines into law, plus the Proxmire Act, all seem to indicate there is a new ethic against bribes by multinationals. Is it truly an ethic?

If present pressures are indicative, there will be an ethic for multinational corporations in developed countries, and if less-developed countries appear to agree, that is a start. Firms from less-developed countries may hesitate to report bribery when they look at the outward consequences. Yerachmiel Kugel and Gladys Gruenberg list some retaliatory actions in host countries: the president of Honduras was ousted; Bolivia jailed a Gulf Oil executive; the Soviet Union executed an official; the Prince Consort of the Netherlands was "dropped from the advisory council of the Queen."[12] In the home country from which the American bribes came, there was a strong negative reaction when they were discovered. Such unpleasant experiences may not create an ethic but they start it. It needs starting; one estimate is that only a dozen countries in the world frown on bribery, although almost all nations have laws against it.[13] Kugel and Gruenberg also give the results of several surveys, most of them discussed in chapter 2, which indicate that managerial groups view bribes, at least domestic ones, as undesirable.[14]

Fred T. Allen, chairman and president of Pitney-Bowes, Inc. is quoted by U.S. News and World Report of April 12, 1976: "It's necessary for American business to conduct itself as ethically as possible in order to increase its credibility with the United States public."[15] Allen's comments should be extended to indicate that MNCs should conduct themselves as ethically as possible to increase their credibility with the publics of a wide variety of nations.

What Do International Bribes Tell Us about American Business Ethics?

The problem of multinational bribery sheds some light on the general ethics of American business. Most of the bribing businesses were well-known, reputable companies, a fact that tends to confirm the uncertainties about ethics of American businessmen discussed in chapter 2. Thomas N. Gladwin and Ingo Walter point out that views on business morality differ widely among individuals in senior management positions, and this difference inevitably affects their firms.[16] They quote Anthony Sampson's remark that former Lockheed chief executive officer Dan Houghton's drive and impatience pressed his staff to use hard-sell methods including bribery.

Multinationals, say Gladwin and Walter, are more likely to make dubious payments. The bribes are small in relation to their firms' revenues and resources, and their internationality makes it easier to hide such transactions. They believe that multinationals are more likely to bribe if their operation is partly owned by the host country, although the device of shared ownership is recognized as desirable for international-relations purposes. Dow Chemical's bribes, for example, were mostly made by foreign affiliates.

The firms most subject to government regulation were the ones pressed hardest for illegal contributions. Pharmaceutical and health-care companies, oil companies, or beverage companies may be such firms. Half the disclosure of bribes were in the aerospace and petroleum industries.

Gladwin and Walter note that the customary watchdogs, (legal counsel, directors, and accountants) did little to stop the bribery. A few lawyers aided in the illegal process. One outside accounting firm actually transmitted money to a foreign tax official. Others were aware of the transaction but did nothing to report them. There is also evidence that American governmental agencies were aware of illegal payments but did little to stop them; in fact, they themselves make clandestine payments to secure information.

American Unions and Multinational Corporations

In 1975 the Industrial Union Department of the AFL-CIO in its quarterly *Viewpoint* issued vehement criticisms of multinational corporations[17] The charge was that multinational corporations were lowering labor standards in the United States by shifting American technology to plants in foreign countries where much lower wages were paid. The federal government was assisting this antiunion movement with legislation that made effective tax rates lower on income earned abroad than on income earned in the United States, claimed the article. America was losing its technology and its jobs; a situation only partially ameliorated by the sterling performance of international trade secretariats. The tendency of multinationals to invest in countries like Spain, South Africa, Brazil, South Korea, or the Republic of China (Taiwan) where union rights are curtailed or nonexistent exacerbates the difficulty.

The American economy is not self-sufficient; it must import many metals and some technology. As the leading nation of the free world, the United States also has some responsibility to help other countries move themselves forward. The United States cannot withdraw from international competition in order to guarantee the wage levels of the less than 20 percent of the work force in Industrial Union Department unions. The United Auto Workers union is currently asking Japan to build auto plants in the United States so that American workers may be employed. How can the union then maintain that American Companies should not build plants in other countries, except to imply that the welfare of their members is more important than the welfare of workers elsewhere? There is also considerable employment generated in the United States through the processing and selling of imported goods.

The argument that American technology should not be exported is not very reasonable; technology is bound to get into the hands of people who wish to use it sooner or later. It would be extremely difficult at this stage of world economic development to create an isolated economic "Fortress America."

Labor Abroad and Multinational Corporations

Unions and other labor groups naturally have grave concern over the operations of large industrial firms, especially foreign firms. A multinational decision could upset long-established employer-employee relations, or could put a substantial fraction of the population out of work. The guidelines appended to the OECD declaration of 1976 provide rules for handling such problems. They include the following responsibilities of multinational businesses:

1. They should respect the rights of their employees to be represented by unions or other employee organizations and to engage in negotiations.
2. They should provide facilities and information needed for such negotiations.
3. They should provide information so that employees may have a fair view of the performance of the national subsidiary or if necessary of the multinational corporation as a whole.
4. They should observe standards of employment and industrial relations not less favorable than those of comparable corporations operating in the host country.
5. They should utilize, train, and prepare for upgrading their employees in connection with the employee organizations and governmental bodies of the host country.
6. In the event of changes regarding layoffs or dismissals, MNCs should cooperate with employee representatives or governmental authorities to mitigate adverse effects as far as possible.
7. Personnel policies should eliminate discrimination unless it is in accord with governmental policy designed to secure equality of employment opportunity.
8. In negotiations, multinationals should not use the threat of withdrawing from the host country to influence negotiations unfairly.
9. Multinationals should enable authorized representatives of employees to conduct negotiations on collective bargaining or labor arrangements.

This group of proposed labor provisions, even though voluntary, raised serious questions from American multinational corporations. Most American MNCs had worked with unions at home and abroad, and often found them irresponsible or unethical. One company referred to a country where the "legal authorized representative" of labor spoke for only 80 out of 240 employees, but the company was forced to deal with him, and neither the other employees nor the employer was allowed to testify at a hearing. In some countries in Central America and the Far East, between 7 and 20 signatures are enough to secure recognition of a union. Chase Manhattan had a branch that had been unprofitable for 8 years; the union demanded 4 years' pay for each of several hundred employees in the event of a shutdown.[18] Ford Motor Company was concerned that managerial employees were not excluded from such union negotiations. Ford also was concerned that unions wanted to conduct international negotiations with parent companies rather than to conduct national or local negotiations in host countries. Ford was quite willing to consult on investment decisions on an in-country basis. Other companies were worried about the loose language of the OECD guidelines.

What are the ethical values in these points? As seen in an earlier chapter, the ethics of union relationships are not yet clear in America. Perhaps those who wanted to be sure that all negotiations were conducted in the host country, both management and unions having the power to decide at the bargaining table, were ethically right. Perhaps there was reason for ethical concern about the easy decision to form unions where host-country laws were favorable. But overall there is still some ethical value to the slogan "When in Rome, do as the Romans do," or at least to "When in Rome, follow the Roman law." Multinational corporations should be law-abiding in each country where they operate; the alternative is not to operate.

Economic Ethics of Multinational Corporations

Several economic questions regarding multinationals have been raised by the OECD guidelines. The variety of opinions on some of these provisions reflect the differing economic outlooks of different countries and different groups within countries. Many of these are subjects on which ethics have not yet fully developed.

The OECD guidelines reflect some of the spirit of the American antitrust laws discussed in chapter 7. They ask enterprise to refrain from participating in actions that would "adversely affect competition" such as (a) anticompetitive acquisitions, (b) predatory behavior toward competitors, (c) unreasonable refusal to conduct business, (d) anticompetitive abuse of industrial property rights, and (e) discriminatory pricing or using transfer pricing within the enterprise as a means of discriminating against outside competitors.

Few of these provisions were difficult for American businessmen, because of the ninety-year American tradition of antitrust laws. It is, however, hard to guess whether collectivist countries (as many LDCs say they are) will seriously try to enforce provisions like these. Nor can one guess how cartel-influenced industrial nations will take to these provisions.

The guidelines call for similar treatment of multinational and domestic enterprises. This will be very difficult; even as advanced a country as Canada has been unable to give equal treatment to American enterprises operating in its borders. Equal treatment of foreigners in trade will not be an ethic in most countries for a long time to come. Less-developed countries have difficulty in realizing the value of multinationals, that they have more to gain from MNCs than vice versa.

The voluntary guidelines also say that multinationals should give due consideration to the economic and social planning of the host countries, including industrial and regional development, protection of the environment, the promotion of innovation, and the transfer of technology. Most of these are policies that broadminded corporations would follow at home and should follow in host countries. If a corporation is to be a good citizen of a host country, it should be attentive to that country's goals. It is easy to see, however, how an ultranationalist or collectivist regime of a host country would use these guidelines to persecute a multinational corporation. If so, perhaps the only answer is operation of economic laws. If a multinational withdraws and other multinationals do not come in, the host country will lose in economic development.

The guidelines also provide that multinationals shall allow their component entities (subsidiaries in the host country) freedom to develop activities and to exploit the competitive advantage in domestic and foreign markets, "consistent with the need for special action and sound commercial practice." This is a more difficult ethic to establish, especially if the multinational established the subsidiary only because it fit into the production processes of the parent corporation. It is economically desirable in some cases to have autonomous subsidiaries but the clause about need for specialization perhaps excludes this provision from being a future ethical rule.

Paragraph six of the guidelines says that enterprises should fill responsible posts in each country without discrimination as to nationality. This effort to persuade treatment of individual employees as equals is in accord with the Judaic-Christian tradition. The practical problem is one of execution of the policy. How is the relative efficiency of potential administrators determined in spite of differences of language or national characteristics? This is obviously a case in which ethical considerations are reinforced by practical ones. If more managers are hired from the host country, the multinational is less likely to be viewed as an intruding foreigner. Peter Drucker advocates sending host-country employees to secure training in MNC operations in other countries.

The International Chamber of Commerce has also made some suggestions for solution of these international economic problems. It, like OECD, recommends a voluntary code. Its working commission agrees that corrupt practices should be outlawed. However, such recommendations should apply not only to multinationals, but also to national companies and state agencies.

Particular attention should be paid to OECD's (Organization for Economic Cooperation and Development) recommendations on the transfer of technology in connection with attitudes of American unions. It shares the desire that technology be transferred to the developing countries but suggests this be done by voluntary action, not by a legally binding code. Technology is more likely to be transferred if there is assurance of mutual benefit to both parties. It is more likely to be transferred by enterprises than by government edicts. This is especially true of proprietary technology. Government and business together may make plans for an educational infrastructure and new technology. Businesses would like to discuss means of transferring patents. Thus the ethics of mutual international helpfulness may best come not from rules but from processes.

The developing countries have proposed a very different approach to technology. They ask that national personnel be trained in appropriate technology, including operation and management techniques. All improvements in techniques shall be made known to the LDC operation during the lifetime of the arrangement. Necessary parts shall be furnished. Government of the technology-receiving country may require:

> that technology be adequate
>
> that local consultancy shall be fully utilized
>
> that there be continuous exploration for local inputs into materials, equipment, and spare parts
>
> favorable terms to one recipient shall be granted to other recipients in the host country
>
> that the parties make full use of any technology located in the host countries
>
> the achievement of a predetermined volume of exports
>
> that personnel of the host country be involved in all aspects of technology transfer[19]

Proposals like these not yet ratified by the home countries of the MNCs, arouse a good deal of sympathy. LDCs would naturally like to learn the technology of manufacture. On the other hand, the multinationals probably view their hard-earned technology as one of the things they have to sell; Appendix B of the OECD Draft Codes authorizes host-country governments to order MNCs to turn over their technology to the host country. This one-sided agreement is not likely to encourage multinationals to operate in such host countries.

Drucker notes that multinationals make less money in LDCs than elsewhere. He believes developing countries can develop capital if they can develop the means of using their resources, human and otherwise. The objective is to recruit local capital. The host country will be better off if local industry is integrated into the world economy by multinational corporations. It would also be good if the personnel of the host country worked with the MNC in other countries, so its host-company personnel could learn from the operations somewhere else. Integration into the world economy will be of greater use.

Balance-of-Trade Problems

Some LDCs maintain that MNCs do not help them economically. Louis Turner writes that parts of the Third World will be paying back to the developed countries more than they receive in aid. Much aid is in the form of loans. LDCs frequently find themselves short of foreign exchange because of interest on such loans, dividend and management payments on MNC-owned businesses, and possible imprudence on the part of the LDCs.[20] Such a situation, if true, is in marked contrast to nineteenth-century America, which built its economy in part on British capital, or to Japan and West Germany which rebuilt themselves after World War II in part on American capital.

Today some countries may be benefited by multinationals while others may not. Turner's comments in 1973 may still be true today: "Acceptance of multinational investment may provide growth for countries like Taiwan, Brazil, South Korea, or Iran, but it will also create decrees of inequality, which the governments of Cuba, Tanzania, and China are trying to avoid."[21]

There seems to be an ethical responsibility of an MNC not to start economic operations or other transactions that will damage the host country. The same sense of ethical responsibility for one's fellow men under the "love thy neighbor" principle should lead an MNC not to pull completely out of an LDC with disastrous economic results unless the economic plight of the MNC is as great as that of the LDC. The more economic development occurs in LDCs, the less urgent is this obligation.

Mixing Politics and Economics

American or western European multinationals operating in a less-developed Asian, African, or Latin American countries are always subject to the charge of mixing politics and economics. Are their purposes purely ecomomic or partly political? Will their home support be economic or political? In Chile, International Telephone and Telegraph Corp. (ITT) wanted the U.S. government to intervene against the near-communist Allende government. The Hickenlooper Amendment would forbid foreign aid to a country that nationalizes property of an American corporation without just compensation. OPEC has always promoted Arab political goals. Can politics and economics be kept separate? If not, where does one find basic ethical principles?

Where domestic economic strength exists, these questions are usually not very important; but in LDC, they may have great political and hence ethical importance. Are international charters and regulations needed to keep a multinational from disturbing local politics? In an era when most modern industrial countries have forsworn territorial aggrandizement, are MNCs a veiled economic substitute for imperialism? Richard Barnet and Ronald E. Muller have written a book with this thesis.[22] However, the evidence does not seem very convincing.

Five Latin American countries agreed in 1976 on an "Andean Investment Code" that required foreign firms to form joint ventures or to offer at least 51 percent of their shares for purchase by national investors. Though U.S. investors viewed this with suspicion, Raymond J. Waldman reported in 1980 that there was not yet a decline in U.S. investments. The divestment procedure acts as a safety valve against all-out expropriation.[23]

Ethical attitudes toward this problem are likely to reflect what the Germans call *weltanschauung* (world viewpoint). If, like Jacoby et al. and others, one believes that progress for all is more likely to come through a relatively free economic system, the LDCs should be urged to deregulate their economies so undue controls will not cause corruption or burden the economy.[24] If, like Barnet and Müller one believes that large corporations are evil and government is good, stronger governments in the LDCs should be opted for. If, like C. Fred Bergsten, one thinks in terms of economy-directing institutions, and international institution to control MNCs is the total answer.[25]

The tremendous price-raising by OPEC is generally agreed to have been one of the reasons for the unhealthy inflation since 1979. To what extent did the multinational oil companies cause this inflation because of their tendency to treat the oil-producing LDCs a little cavalierly? Perhaps multinationals have become an economic mechanism with tremendous political impact. If so, is there not an ethical obligation on the oil countries to win more confidence from the host countries?[26]

If politics and economics must be mixed, and the less it is done, the better off we are, an unusual degree of ethical restraint on both sides is required.

Conclusions

The United States has expressed considerable confidence in MNCs. It has legislated ahead of the rest of the world in forbidding MNC bribery or acquiescence in extortion. It has provided some payments for expropriated properties. It has given some diplomatic assistance. Clearly the U.S. public has accepted "trade, not aid" as one means of helping Asian, African, and Latin American nations.

But there are still many problems. Should LDCs be urged to form unions, when U.S unions are concerned only with a fairly small minority of the work force? Should MNCs be required to inform their host countries more fully of their accounting situations? Should MNC economic policy be directed to temper the economic influences on LDCs?

Several commentators advocate further governmental action on our part. David Rockefeller and others have urged multinational ownership of stock, and employee profit-sharing schemes.[27] Some want international licensing of MNCs. The suitability of such international machinery, however, is doubtful. Part of the problem of United Nations' control of multinationals is that the United Nations has become a one-sided body in its view of international economic problems. But it is clear that MNCs need to give a greater impression of ethics and compassion to LDCs.

Extension of the American economy to other lands through multinational corporations is attractive to American businessmen for one or more of several economic reasons: a new market, cheaper labor, or opportunity to use technical know-how. Americans who would like to see a more peaceable, happier world share in the hope that multinationals can bring more modern economic methods and a better standard of living to some of the world's poorer populations. Our national ethical code, including individualism and humanitarianism, fits the economic development of LDCs far better than it does military or colonial development.

The big problem is that the LDCs have their own ethical codes and their own governmental ways of doing things. Under present nationalist doctrines, any LDC may expropriate an American corporation's property or create untenable conditions of economic operation. Proposed United Nations regulations would make this situation worse. Social and political mistakes have been made by some Americans much like a few characters in *The Ugly American*. But more important than our mistakes has been the inability of LDC officials to recognize what they can and cannot gain from a multinational corporation. Multinational corporations should be attentive to the effect of their policies on wage levels, on foreign-exchange positions, on employment, and on educational policies in LDCs. Now, under the Proxmire Act, they must distinguish between the lesser bribes they have to pay and the larger bribes which will get them into serious legal problems at home. The OECD guidelines or other international codes may also cause difficulties. Some corporations may withdraw from overseas activity. But if negotiators can devise other codes which are acceptable to LDCs and MNCs, a new international ethic may bring the whole world closer to decent living standards and to world peace.

Notes

1. Raymond J. Waldman, *Regulating International Business through Codes of Conduct*, p. 6.

2. Peter Drucker, "Multinationals and Developing Countries," in Drucker, *Towards the Next Economics and Other Essays,* p. 64.

3. Richard Eells, *Global Corporations,* pp. 80, 172.

4. Hugo Grotius, *The Rights of War and Peace,* pp. 152, 168-179.

5. Blackstone, *Commentaries on the Laws of England,* vol. 4, p. 139.

6. Neil H. Jacoby et al., *Bribery and Extortion in World Business,* p. 72.

7. Ibid., chap. 1.

8. John J. McCoy et al., *The Great Gulf Oil Spill,* pp. 285-295; and Thomas N. Gladwin and Ingo Walter, *Multinationals under Fire,* pp. 298-299.

9. Jacoby et al., *Bribery and Extortion in World Business,* chap. 6.

10. Daniel Elazar, *American Federalism: A View from the States,* chap. 4.

11. Howard I. Weisberg and Eric Reichenberg, *The Price of Ambiguity,* pp. 1-30.

12. Yerachmiel Kugel and Gladys Gruenberg, *International Payoffs,* pp. 134-135.

13. Lord Shawcross, quoted in Thomas N. Gladwin and Ingo N. Walter, *Multinationals under Fire,* p. 306.

14. Kugel and Gruenberg, *International Payoffs,* pp. 28-29.

15. *U.S., News and World Report,* April 12, 1976, pp. 33-34.

16. Gladwin and Walter, *Thinking about Overseas Corporate Payoffs,* p. 31.

17. "Trading U.S. Jobs for Corporate Profit," *Viewpoint* 5:4 (Washington, D.C.: Industrial Union Department AFL-CIO, 1975), pp. 1-35.

18. OECD, *Guidelines,* Workshop of June 1976 (Paris: Organization for Economic Cooperation and Development, 1976), p. 116.

19. Waldman, *Regulating International Business through Codes of Conduct,* Appendix B, pp. 101-111.

20. Louis Turner, *Multinational Companies and the Third World,* pp. 56-62.

21. Ibid., pp. 72-73.

22. Barnet and Müller, *Global Reach.*

23. *Waldman, Regulating International Business,* pp. 28-38.

24. Jacoby et al., *Bribery and Extortion in World Business,* p. 244.

25. C. Fred Bergsten, *A New U.S. Policy Center for Transnational Corporations.*

26. Anthony Sampson, *The Seven Sisters.*

27. Barnet and Müller, *Global Reach,* pp. 105-210.

15 Conclusions

At the beginning of the Republic, the United States was inferior to England in business operations and business ethics. But the situation soon changed. The Industrial Revolution was beginning in England and ingenious Yankee traders and manufacturers soon found ways of getting English manufacturing techniques to America. The American farm population was willing to help build an American economy, although they were suspicious of banks and other Eastern urban institutions. American professional classes encouraged the development of business, presumably to help the whole population move forward economically. By the end of the civil War in the 1860s, the United States had become an important economic power.

However, some of the ethics of American business moved forward less slowly, and in a few cases moved backward. Indeed, our British ancestors who gave us the important traditions of judicial independence and the beginnings of legislative and executive democracy gave us little of the mechanism of business ethics. English law provided almost no workable laws on commercial corporations, which took over a majority of the U.S. economy in the first six decades of the nineteenth century. The restrictive legal notions of how to handle workers and associations of workers that the British followed were contrary to the ethical aspiration for the rights of men, and were certain not to survive in the new democracy based on human rights. British mercantilist notions of how to develop markets for investment in land, commodities, or securities required major legislative and judicial changes in a partly *laissez-faire* nineteenth-century America. The government regulation of transportation rates or prices which the British passed on to the United States were a hodge-podge of ill-thought-out, rigid legal controls. Britain had made as much or more progress in accounting as most European nations, but in 1776 the uses of this important ethical tool were rudimentary in both England and her colonies. Both countries had advertising but neither had much notion of how to use it for constructive economic purposes or how to keep it within the Western tradition of truth-telling. Britain, in its common-law courts, had some traces of antimonopoly tradition but did not recognize that tradition much in national economic matters; Adam Smith's *Wealth of Nations* was not published until 1776. Britain's notions of controlling overseas trade included most of the follies of mercantilism.

It is true that by 1900 Britain had established some ethical institutions considerably fairer than ours. Her police were better trained, her courts were fairer, her lawyers were more conscious of searching for the right. Her accountants were a half-century ahead of ours in securing governmental and business respect. Her corporations were required by national law to report annually to shareholders seventy years before ours. Her banking system was much more stable. America learned lessons from Britain on many of these points but they were not part of our original ethical heritage.

The unsophisticated American economy grew and painfully built its ethics as it grew. Our businessmen had some ethics from church-going, although nineteenth-century clerics were very slow to pay much attention to detailed problems of business ethics; they preached primarily Calvinist or Arminian viewpoints. Some business ethics grew out of the work situations; people no longer wanted to deal with deceitful or tricky business partners. Courts and legislatures helped a little with new recognition of rights of labor, of the fixing of contracts, and the need for responsibility of corporations.

It must be conceded that there was in mid-nineteenth-century America an ethical retrogression that did not begin to be remedied until the business and political reform movement began about 1890. Indeed some results of mid-nineteenth-century low business ethics have lasted to the present time.

The major American economic mechanism, the commercial corporation, has been regulated by legislatures and courts for many, many decades with some limited success. The most flagrant conflicts of interest by directors and executives occurred before 1900, but have now been largely eliminated by statutes, court decisions, and a slowly growing ethic among businessmen against such conflicts. Major corporations must now report regularly to their shareholders, even if the CPAs at times allow confusing changes of accounting methods by corporate management deeply concerned about profits and stock prices. There are still fields in which corporate practice is wrong but the present trend seems to be good.

The rights of labor or labor associations in early American common law were limited. But the doctrine of natural rights and other philosophic acceptances of the value of the individual influenced American courts and legislators very much. By the first half of the twentieth century, laws allowing cheating of laborers, common-law restrictions on labor associations, and similar antilabor precepts had disappeared. In the twentieth century, organized labor was given some legal privileges that were not accorded to any other economic group. Although organized labor is losing some percentage of the work force and participative management may take its place in new high-technology industries, the ethic of labor-management relations needs much careful consideration if the American economy is going to withstand the new international competition. Unfortunately the internal ethics of many unions leaves much to be desired.

More determined efforts have been made to create an antimonopoly ethic in the United States than in any other free-market country, although the United Kingdom, Canada, and West Germany have made some efforts, and the European Common Market is experimenting with it. Congress passed the Sherman Act almost unanimously in 1890; no general effort to repeal it has ever been made, yet antimonopoly policy has not become an accepted ethic. This may be partly the fault of Congress, which has passed some contradictory legislation; it may be partly the fault of "big business," which is accused by some of never really wanting antitrust policies; it may be partly the fault of the courts for legalistic and noneconomic interpretations of the law. Antitrust ethics came nearest to failing in 1933 when the National Recovery Administration approved industrial codes that reduced competition. Today the general tendency is to support an antimonopoly ethic. In the near future, worldwide competition may supersede our national laws in some industries, but there are signs of some international cooperation against monopoly.

Many Americans think of government regulation of industry as an alternative to the antitrust laws. In monopolistic industries like telephones or electricity or gas retail use, one supplier seems to be the cheapest way, prices should be regulated to avoid monopoly overcharges. Some types of government regulation go back to the clumsy mercantilism which the British administered in the eighteenth century and which helped lead to the American Revolution. Government regulation of public transportation lasted all through the *laissez-faire* era of the nineteenth and early twentieth centuries. Somehow such regulation has rarely been effective or generally satisfactory. The Interstate Commerce Commission in almost a century of effort managed to reduce the usefulness of the railroads. Petroleum-price controls were used to make OPEC's price increases worse in their long-range results. The fault in the regulatory situation lies in part with business, which has rarely tried to secure statesmanlike members on the important regulatory commissions or to work with them in a constructive way, but also with the regulatory failure to understand businesses. The susceptibility of our government to economic and geographic pressure groups has also made regulation less useful. A majority of economists today would like to see regulatory matters handled by the marketplace as much as possible, but some regulatory ethics will remain.

The twentieth century has brought much reform in business ethics but also a whole new series of reproaches against business. Consumer problems, the ethics of advertising, the social responsibility of corporations, product liability, the immense problems of employee theft and kickbacks, and finally the ethics of multinational corporations will be discussed.

The consumer has always been an important person; without him, no business would flourish. However, little was done to protect him from the sometimes evil practices of our partly *laissez-faire* economy in the nine-teenth century. Antitrust and railroad-regulation laws were passed as much for the benefit of small businesses as for consumers. Consumers were mer-cilessly exploited by con artists and lower-level businessmen in the last half of the nineteenth century. The only consumer protection was offered by postal inspectors who prosecuted some persons for use of the mails to defraud. However, at least three important consumer movements in this century have altered the consumer's picture. The muckrakers and the pro-gressives secured a federal food and drug act after the publication of Upton Sinclair's *The Jungle* in 1906. Another movement in the late 1920s merged in part with the various groups concerned about the Great Depression of the 1930s. A third movement came to its greatest importance in the late 1960s, with Ralph Nader and his colleagues at its head.

From these movements have come changes in the attitudes of retailers, several business groups that try to help disgruntled consumers, and a fair amount of government regulation in favor of the consumer. Too much of the government work has been concentrated in the Federal Trade Commis-sion, and the ineffective machinery of all levels of government is as much to blame as is business for wrongs to consumers. But American business is slowly beginning to recognize an ethic of treating the consumer fairly—the opposite of *caveat emptor,* although some abuses continue.

Advertising has been a major ethical problem of American business for over a century. In the last three decades of the nineteenth century and the first decade of this century, deceptive advertisements were regularly run in outstanding newspapers and magazines. Patent medicines were shamelessly sold by nationwide retailers. "Bucket shops" advertised their fraudulent wares in reputable journals. Leaders of the advertising profession at the turn of the century pressed for higher standards, with the truth-in-advertising movement. These business reformers also pressed for state "blue-sky laws" around 1910 and for Federal Trade Commission establish-ment in 1914. Thus both business and government worked toward a better ethic of truth in advertising. Unfortunately, perhaps because of the linger-ing influence of *caveat emptor,* everything was not accomplished and drives of government and business against false advertising continue to appear. Advertising is still not the economic tool of giving useful information to potential buyers which it could be.

There have long been occasional examples of corporate social respon-sibility. Mr. Pullman was proud of his model suburb of Chicago in the first decade of this century. At about the same time John D. Rockefeller, Jr. tried to improve the life of the workers of Colorado Fuel and Iron. But the larger business assumption of social responsibility began in the 1920s when the Internal Revenue Act permitted corporations to give up to 5 percent of their net income to charities. Today the average is only slightly above 1 per-cent, but the possible percentage of income has been raised to 10 percent.

Corporate giving covers a broad area of social activities, some related to the corporations' needs, some to the communities' needs, and some to the needs of civilization. This social response is coming slowly but in certain corporations it is carefully considered.

It is not generally known that America has the highest violent-crime rate and perhaps the highest overall crime rate of modern industrial democracies. Business suffers from a large share of this crime; shoplifting, employee thefts, kickbacks, and other white-collar crime are nearing $50 billion a year. For public relations and other reasons, many businesses do not try to find or secure conviction of all these criminals. American business needs to do harder ethical thinking about crime in business.

A major new ethical problem has come to many manufacturers because of a relatively sudden change in court decisions that has made manufacturers liable for accidents growing out of the use of their products. Some important changes in methods of delivering products and the fact that the manufacturer is the best central information point seem to justify this change in the law. It has a profound effect on many manufacturers and it is uncertain that the new ethic of product liability will remain unqualified. Putting manufacturers out of business so lawyers can receive large contingent fees is not necessarily the most ethical way to run an economy.

Finally, the multinational corporation, in which America was a leader after World War II, shows much hope for progress of less-developed countries, but also raises a host of ethical problems. The United States has unilaterally tried to settle one problem with the Proxmire Act, forbidding bribery of foreign officials. Questions of wage policy, effect of corporate policy on balance of trade, exchange of technology, and others all require a new world ethic. The UN and OECD, U.S. and International Chambers of Commerce have worked on such ethical codes, but it is not yet clear what the outcome will be.

For those who prefer to read their history in tabular form, the following table lists briefly in the first column the business ethical principles which were generally accepted at the beginning of the Republic and in the second column the major changes in the use of those principles since that time.

Principles and Their Acceptance in 1776	Subsequent Changes in Principles or or Acceptance Thereof
Overall Obligations	
Salus populi suprema lex was accepted as an abstraction but frequently not allowed.	The principle probably was less observed in the last half of the nineteenth century but is today nearer acceptance than at the beginning of the Republic.

Sic utere tuo was a common-law principle which may often have been forgotten.

The principle was sometimes overruled by the courts in the nineteenth century, but is today more generally followed than ever before.

Manufacturers and artisans should maintain the quality of their products; a fairly generally accepted principle in the colonies.

Especially in the latter half of the nineteenth century, this principle was often ignored by both manufacturer and law-enforcement officials. In the twentieth century it has been accepted more by manufacturers and in recent decades severely enforced by some officials.

Prices may be controlled by government.

Laissez-faire philosophy has largely eliminated this precept, except for relatively short-term war and emergency conditions.

A generally accepted currency was not available at the time of the American Revolution.

America has slowly moved toward a more stable and adequate currency with major political interruptions.

"Love thy neighbor as thyself" was an aspiration with occasional results. The rights of individual workers have received increasing respect.

The pursuit of this principle has continued to be sporadic, but greater wealth has increased the occasional uses.

A responsibility for charitable giving was recognized at times, especially in New England.

An ethic of some charitable giving by business is recognized by law and slowly being accepted by business.

The law was obeyed except where unreasonable rules encouraged large-scale smuggling.

In the later nineteenth century, there was a real drop in respect for law; it is still lower than in other modern industrial countries.

Commercial Obligations

Stealing was forbidden; enforcement was spotty.

Stealing is still forbidden; enforcement may be less effective.

No deception in commercial transactions was accepted as a principle, although often ignored in practice.

With judicial acceptance of *caveat emptor* the principle was not followed in the nineteenth century; it is slowly returning to effect in the twentieth.

Weights and measures were well recognized in Revolutionary times; accounting was not much used as a check on honesty.

Weights and measures continued to be accepted; accounting began to be important at the end of the nineteenth century and is more so today.

Obligation of contracts was respected with legal queries.

Obligation of contracts became more respected in law and practice.

Interest was recognized as legal.

Interest was legal but regulations of the amount of it varied in accordance with politics during the nineteenth and twentieth century.

Trusts were little developed.

Trusts have become much more important.

Leasing and hiring were often used.

Leasing and hiring have become major means of doing business.

The consumer's needs are paramount.

In the late nineteenth century, the consumer was often misled and cheated. He still is sometimes the victim of fraudulent enterprises.

Business Operations

The right to hold property was well recognized, although the distribution of public lands was often a matter of patronage by royal governors.

The right to hold property continued to be recognized, though the development of business and government led to increasing use of eminent domain.

Employee rights were few and restricted under common law.

In the nineteenth century, employee associations were greatly extended; in the twentieth century, employee associations were given a legal control of much of economic life.

In colonial times a real work ethic was necessary for existence.

In the nineteenth century an intellectual work ethic was encouraged; it weakened during the twentieth century.

Corporations were limited to a few hundred, mostly public-utility operations.

By the 1890s, corporations were doing three-quarters of American business. There had been many experiments in legal regulation of them, most only partially successful.

Conflicts of interest existed but little attention was paid to them, except for public officials.	As conflicts began to be uncovered stricter rules against some kinds were devised; most of the new ethic was developed in the twentieth century.
Laws against monopoly were illegal under common law.	In 1890 the United States adopted a rigorous law against monopoly. Enforcement has been only partly successful. An ethic against business monopoly is partly recognized.
Patents were recognized under British law.	Patents have become a major economic matter, and sometimes help contribute to monopoly.

This table seems to tell us a bit about ethics in America. Ethics can change for better or worse. American democratic individualism probably helped raise our ethics in treatment of labor and in efforts to avoid monopoly. The spread of *caveat emptor* in the nineteenth century helped lower American ethical standards in a fundamental respect which carried over into neglect of consumer interests—a mistake that has now been mostly repaired. New ethics had to be developed in the areas of the commercial corporation, the problem of large monopolies, conflicts, of interest within and outside corporations, and the need for fuller and fairer business records; they came slowly from governmental pressures and from business desires.

Business ethics, like political ethics, reflect the ethics of the society of which they are a part. Reports of major scandals within businesses rarely indicate the work of professional criminals; rather it is of men and women whose own ethical instruction was too weak to resist business pressures. When business corrupts a governmental agency, the onlooker often cannot be sure whether the money is a bribe or an extortion. We would all like to have top business executives who resist unethical pressures, but we are not likely to have such persons until society develops an appropriate ethical education for them.

The one serious charge to be made against business is that it has often failed to realize its responsibility for better laws and better governmental control machinery. The crimes of those who have preyed on consumers are not designed or made by big, responsible executives, but the latter have not shown much interest in developing the quality of governmental machinery to reduce or eliminate consumer crime. Perhaps the large-corporation executives have not realized that some critical persons are going to blame big business for the crimes of the smaller operators. Perhaps they have not realized that high-quality appointments to regulatory commissions would result in better or less expensive regulation. Whether we like it or not, government is an essential part of modern life, and business leaders should recognize that fact.

One other admonition. In chapter after chapter of this book, a major point has been that better education of individuals to have a reasonable regard for the rights of others would eliminate much of business unfairness. Parents, teachers, priests, pastors, rabbis, and writers who shy away from teaching ethics to young and old fellow Americans bear much of the blame for the ethical lapses of businesses described here.

Bibliography

Ackerman, Robert, and Bauer, Raymond. *Corporate Social Responsiveness: The Modern Dilemma*. Reston, Va.: Reston, 1976.

Adams, Charles Francis, Jr., and Adams, Henry. *Chapters of Erie*. Ithaca, N.Y.: Cornell University Press, 1963.

Addams, Jane. *Twenty Years at Hull House*. New York: Macmillan, 1910.

Addison, Joseph. *The Tatler* 224 (September 14, 1710). In *The British Essayists*, vol. 5, pp. 66-70. Edited by Alexander Chalmers. London: Nichols, 1808.

Allen, Frederick Lewis. *The Lords of Creation*. New York: Quadrangle/The New York Times Book Co., 1935.

Aristotle. *Nichomachean Ethics*. Translated by Martin Ostwald. Indianapolis: Bobbs-Merrill, 1962.

Austin, Robert W. "Code of Conduct for Executives." *Harvard Business Review* 39 (1961):19-27.

Baer, Walter E. *Grievance Handling*. New York: American Management Association, 1970.

Baer, Walter E. *Strikes*. New York: Amacom, 1975.

Balfour, Campbell, ed. *Participation in Industry*. Totowa, N.J.: Roman and Littlefield, 1973.

Ball, Harry V. and Friedman, Lawrence M. "The Use of Criminal Sanctions in the Enforcement of Economic Legislation." *Stanford Law Review* 197 (1965).

Barnard, Chester I. *The Functions of the Executive*. Cambridge, Mass.: Harvard University Press, 1945.

Barnet, Richard and Müller, Ronald E. *Global Reach*. New York: Simon and Schuster, 1974.

Baruch, Hurd. *Wall Street—A Security Risk*. Baltimore: Penguin, 1972.

Baum, Robert J., ed. *Ethical Problems in Engineering*. 2d ed. vol. 2. Troy, N.Y.: Rensselaer Polytechnic Institute, 1980.

Baumhart, Raymond. *Ethics in Business*. New York: Holt, Rinehart, 1968.

Beauchamp, Tom L., and Bowie, Norman E. *Ethical Theory and Business*. Englewood Cliffs, N.J.: Prentice-Hall, 1979.

Beaver, William H. "Current Trends in Corporate Disclosure." *The Journal of Accountancy*, 145 (1978):44-52.

Bell, Howard H. "Self Regulation by the Advertising Industry." *California Management Review* 16 (1974):58-63.

Bennigson, Lawrence A., and Bennigson, Arnold I. "Product Liability: Manufacturers Beware!" *Harvard Business Review* 52 (1974):122-1320.

Benson, George C.S., and Engeman, Thomas. *Amoral America*. Stanford, Cal.: Hoover Institution Press, 1975.

Benson, George C.S.; Heslop, Alan; and Maaranen, Steven. *Political Corruption in America*. Lexington, Mass.: LexingtonBooks, 1978.

Benston, George J. *Corporate Financial Disclosure in the U.K. and the U.S.A.* Hampshire, England: Saxon House, Teakfield Ltd., 1978.

_____ . *Conglomerate Mergers*. Washington, D.C.: American Enterprise Institute, 1980.

Berenson, Conrad. "The Product Liability Revolution." *Business Horisons* 15 (1972):71-80.

Bergsten, C. Fred. *A New U.S. Policy Center for Transnational Corporations*. Carnegie Center for Transnational Studies. New York: 1976.

Berle, Adolf A. *The 20th Century Capitalist Revolution*. New York: Harcourt Brace, 1954.

Berle, Adolf A., and Means, Gardiner C. *The Modern Corporation and Private Property*. New York: Macmillan, 1950.

Bishop, James, Jr., and Hubbard, Henry W. *Let the Seller Beware*. Washington, D.C.: The National Press, 1969.

Black, Hillel. *The Watchdogs of Wall Street*. New York: Morrow, 1962.

Blackstone, William. *Commentaries on the Laws of England*. Chicago: University of Chicago Press, 1979.

Bonbright, James C., and Means, Gardiner C. *The Holding Company*. New York: McGraw-Hill, 1932.

Bork, Robert H. *The Antitrust Paradox*. New York: Basic Books, 1978.

Bowen, Howard R. *Investment in Learning: The Individual and Social Value of American Higher Education*. San Francisco: Jossey-Bass, 1977.

Bradshaw, Thornton, and Vogel, David. *Corporations and Their Critics*. New York: McGraw-Hill, 1981.

Brenner, Steven N., and Molander, Earl A. "Is the Ethics of Business Changing?" *Harvard Business Review* 55 (1977):57-71.

Briloff, Abraham. *More Debits than Credits*. New York: Harper & Row, 1976.

_____ . *Unaccountable Accounting*. New York: Harper & Row, 1972.

Brooks, John. *The Autobiography of American Business*. Garden City, N.Y.: Anchor Books, 1975.

_____ . *The Go Go Years*. New York: Weybright and Talley, 1973.

Brown, Richard, ed. *A History of Accounting and Accountants*. Edinburgh: T.C. and E.C. Jack, 1905.

Brozen, Yale, ed. *Advertising and Society*. New York: New York University Press, 1974.

Brozen, Yale, ed. *Is Government the Source of Monopoly?* San Francisco: Cato Institute, 1980.

Burns, James MacGregor. *Leadership*. New York: Harper Colophon, 1978.

Burns, Joseph M. *A Treatise on Markets*. Washington, D.C.: American Enterprise Institute, 1979.

Burton, John C. *Corporate Financial Reporting: Ethical and Other Problems*. New York: American Institute of Certified Public Accountants, 1971.

Buxton, Edward. *Promise Them Anything*. New York: Stein and Day, 1972.

Caplovitz, David. *Consumers in Trouble*. New York: Free Press, 1974.

Carosso, Vincent P. *Investment Banking in America*. Cambridge, Mass.: Harvard University Press, 1970.

Carpenter, James W. "Consumer Protection in Ohio against False Advertising and Deceptive Trading." *Ohio State Law Journal* 32 (1971).

Carper, Jean. *Not with a Gun*. New York: Grossman Publishers, 1973.

Chase, Stewart, and Schlink, F.J. *Your Money's Worth*. New York: Macmillan, 1927.

Chatfield, Michael, ed. *The English View of Accountants' Duties and Responsibilities*. New York: Arno Press, 1978.

Chatov, Robert. *Corporate Financial Reporting*. New York: Free Press, 1975.

Clarey, Robert I. "The Prosecution of Consumer Fraud: New York's New Approach." *Criminal Law Bulletin* 14 (1978):197-201.

Clark, John W. *Religion and the Moral Standards of American Businessmen*. Cincinnati: Southwestern, 1966.

Clark, Timothy B.; Kosters, Marvin H.; and Miller, James C., III. *Reforming Regulation*. Washington, D.C.: American Enterprise Institute for Public Policy Research, 1980.

Clews, Henry. *Fifty Years on Wall Street*. New York: Arno, 1973.

Clinard, Marshall B. *The Black Market*. Montclair, N.J.: Patterson Smith, 1972.

_____ . *Cities with Little Crime*. Cambridge: Cambridge University Press, 1978.

Cochran, Thomas C. *Railroad Leaders*. New York: Russell & Russell, 1965.

Cole, Robert E. *Work, Mobility and Participation*. Berkeley and Los Angeles: University of California Press, 1980.

Commerce Clearing House Federal Securities Law Reporter. Chicago: Commerce Clearing House, 1961, p. 76803.

Comstock, George; Chaffee, Steven; Katzman, Natan; McCombs, Maxwell; and Roberts, Donald. *Television and Human Behavior*. New York: Columbia University Press, 1978.

Conklin, John E. *Illegal But Not Criminal*. Englewood Cliffs, N.J.: Prentice-Hall, 1977.

Cox, Edward F.; Fellmeth, Robert C.; and Schulz, Robert E. *Nader's Raiders*. New York: Grove, 1969.

Cressey, Donald R. *Other People's Money*. Glencoe, Ill.: Free Press, 1953.

Crozier, Michel. *The Bureaucratic Phenomenon*. Chicago: University of Chicago Press, 1964.

Dalton, Melville. *Men Who Manage*. New York: Wiley, 1958.

Darvie, Mark. "Pinto Madness." *Mother Jones*, September/October 1977.

Daughen, Joseph R., and Binzen, Peter. *The Wreck of the Penn Central*. New York: New American Library, 1973.

De George, Richard T., and Pichler, Joseph A. eds. *Ethics, Free Enterprise and Public Policy*. New York: Oxford University Press, 1978.

DeMond, C.W. *Price, Waterhouse and Co. in America*. New York: 1951. Reprint. New York: Arno Press, 1981.

Derber, Milton; Chalmers, W.E.; and Edelman, Milton T. *Plant Union-Management Relations: From Practice to Theory*. Urbana: University of Illinois, 1965.

Divita, S.C., ed. *Advertising in the Public Interest*. Chicago: American Market Association, 1974.

Donaldson, Thomas, and Werhane, Patricia H. *Ethical Issues in Business*. Englewood Cliffs, N.J.: Prentice-Hall, 1979.

Dropp, Donald R. "Professional Notes." *Journal of Accountancy*. January 1979:80-87.

Drucker, Peter. *Towards the Next Economics and Other Essays*. New York: Harper & Row, 1981.

──────. "What is Business Ethics?" *The Public Interest* 63 (1981):18-36.

Dyer, Robert F., and Kuehl, Phillip G. "A Longitudinal Study of Corrective Advertising." *Journal of Marketing Research* 15 (1978):39-48.

Editorial Research Reports. *Consumer Protection Gains and Setbacks*. Washington, D.C.: Congressional Quarterly, Inc., 1978.

Edwards, James D. *History of Public Accounting*. East Lansing, Mich.: Bureau of Business Research, Michigan State University, 1960.

Edwards, P.K. *Strikes in the United States 1881-1974*. Oxford, England: Basil Blackwell, 1981.

Eells, Richard. *Global Corporations*. New York: The Free Press, 1972.

Elazar, Daniel. *American Federalism: A View from the States*. New York: Crowell, 1966.

Elias, Christopher. *The Dollar Barons*. New York: Macmillan, 1973.

──────. *Fleecing the Lambs*. Chicago: Regnery, 1971.

Engelbourg, Saul. *Power and Morality*. Westport, Conn.: Greenwood Press, 1980.

Epstein, Edwin M. *The Corporation in American Politics*. Englewood Cliffs, N.J.: Prentice-Hall, 1969.

Ewing, David. *Freedom inside the Organization*. New York: Dutton, 1977.

Facts on File. *Corruption in Business*. New York: Facts on File, 1977.

──────. *Consumer Protection*. New York: Facts on File, 1976.

Feldman, Lawrence P. "New Legislation and the Prospects for Real Warranty Reform." *Journal of Marketing* 40 (1976):41-47.

Fellmeth, Robert C. *The Interstate Commerce Commission.* New York: Grossman, 1970.

Fendrock, John J. "Crisis in Conscience at Quasar." *Harvard Business Review* 46 (1968):2-10.

Ferber, Nat. *I Found Out.* New York: Dial, 1939.

Finn, David. *The Corporate Oligarch.* New York: Simon and Schuster, 1969.

Flores, Albert, ed. *Ethical Problems in Engineering.* 2d ed., vol. 1. Troy, N.Y.: Rensselaer Polytechnic Institute, 1980.

Fortune Magazine, eds. *The Conglomerate Commotion.* New York: Viking, 1970.

Frankena, William K. *Ethics.* Englewood Cliffs, N.J.: Prentice-Hall, 1973.

Friedman, Lawrence M. *A History of American Law.* New York: Simon and Schuster, 1973.

Friedman, Milton. *Capitalism and Freedom.* Chicago: University of Chicago Press, 1962.

Freund, Ernst. *Administrative Powers over Persons and Property.* Chicago: University of Chicago Press, 1928.

Fuller, John. *The Gentlemen Conspirators.* New York: Grove, 1962.

Galambos, Louis. *The Public Image of Big Business in America 1880-1940.* Baltimore: Johns Hopkins University Press, 1975.

Galbraith, John K. *The Affluent Society.* Boston: Houghton-Mifflin, 1976.

Gardiner, Alan. *Egypt of the Pharaohs.* London: Oxford University Press, 1961.

Gardner, David M. "Deception in Advertising: A Conceptual Approach." *Journal of Marketing* 39 (1975):40-46.

Geis, Gilbert, and Meier, Robert F. *White Collar Crime.* New York: Free Press, 1977.

Gentry, Curt. *The Vulnerable Americans.* New York: Doubleday, 1966.

Gewirth, Alan. *Reason and Morality.* Chicago: University of Chicago Press, 1978.

Gladwin, Thomas N., and Walter, Ingo. *Multinationals under Fire.* New York: Wiley, 1980.

_____. *Thinking about Overseas Corporate Payoffs.* New York: New York University Graduate School of Business Administration, 1977.

Goodman, Walter. *All Honorable Men.* Boston: Little, Brown, 1963.

Graham, Benjamin, and Dodd, David. *Security Analysis.* New York: McGraw-Hill, 1940.

Gray, Irwin, et al. *Product Liability: A Management Response.* New York: Amacom, 1975.

Green, Mark J.; Moore, Beverly C., Jr.; and Wasserstein, Bruce. *The Closed Enterprise System.* New York: Grossman, 1972.

Green, Mark J., ed. *The Monopoly Makers.* New York: Grosssman, 1973.

Grether, E.T. "Sharp Practice in Merchandising and Advertising." *The Annals of the American Academy of Political and Social Science* 363 (1966):108-116.

Greyser, Stephen A. "Advertising Attacks and Counters." *Harvard Business Review* 50 (1972):22-28, 140-146.

Grimes, Warren S. "Control of Advertising in the United States and Germany: Volkswagen Has a Better Idea." *Harvard Law Review* 84:8 (1971):1769-1800.

Grotius, Hugo. *The Rights of War and Peace.* New York: M. Walter Dunne, 1901.

Hackman, J. Richard, and Suttle, J. Lloyd, eds. *Improving Life at Work.* Santa Monica, Cal.: Goodyear, 1977.

Hahn, Kenneth. "Record of Correspondence between Kenneth Hahn, L.A. County Supervisor, and the presidents of General Motors, Ford, and Chrysler on Controlling Air Pollution." Los Angeles, 1953-1972. Mimeographed.

Hall, Burton H., ed. *Autocracy and Insurgency in Organized Labor.* New Brunswick, N.J.: Transaction, 1972.

Hamilton, Walton H. "The Ancient Maxim: Caveat Emptor." *Yale Law Journal* (1931):1133-1187.

Hammaker, Paul M.; Horniman, Alexander B.; and Rader, Louis T. *Standards of Conduct in Business.* Charlottesville, Va.: Center for the Study of Applied Ethics, copy undated (1978 ed.).

Hartz, Louis. *The Liberal Tradition in America.* New York: Harcourt Brace Jovanovich, 1955.

Heermance, Edgar L. *The Ethics of Business.* New York: Harper, 1926.

———. *Code of Ethics, A Handbook.* Burlington, Vt.: Free Press Printing Co., 1924.

Heilbroner, Robert L., et al. *In the Name of Profit.* Garden City, N.Y.: Doubleday, 1972.

Herford, R. Travers, ed. and trans. *The Ethics of the Talmud: Sayings of the Fathers.* New York: Schocken, 1974.

Herling, John. *The Great Price Conspiracy.* Washington, D.C.: Luce, 1962.

Hessen, Robert. "Corporate Legitimacy and Social Responsibility." International Institute for Economic Research reprint paper 13 (March 1978).

Hill, Ivan. ed. *The Ethical Basis of Economic Freedom.* Chapel Hill, N.C.: American Viewpoint, 1976.

Hoffman, W. Michael, and Wyly, Thomas J. *The Work Ethic in Business.* Cambridge, Mass.: Oelgeschlager, Gunn, and Hain, 1981.

Hook, Sidney, ed. *Human Values and Economic Policy.* New York: New York University Press, 1967.

Horwitz, Morton J. *The Transformation of American Law*. Cambridge, Mass.: Harvard University Press, 1977.

Howard, John A., and Hulbert, James. "Report on Advertising and the Public Interest: A Staff Report to the Federal Trade Commission." Chicago: Crain Communications, 1973.

Howard, John A., and Tinkham, Spencer F. "A Framework for Understanding Social Criticism of Advertising." *Journal of Marketing* 35 (1971):2-7.

Hunter, Louis C. *Steamboats on the Western Rivers: An Economic and Technological History*. Cambridge, Mass.: Harvard University Press, 1949.

Hurst, J. Willard *Law and the Conditions of Freedom in the Nineteenth Century*. Madison: University of Wisconsin Press, 1976.

Hutchinson, John. *The Imperfect Union*. New York: Dutton, 1972.

Hutchinson, Robert A. *Vesco*. New York: Avon, 1974.

Jacoby, Neil H.; Nehemkis, Peter; and Eells, Richard. *Bribery and Extortion in World Business*. New York: Macmillan, 1977.

Jaspan, Norman. *Mind Your Own Business*. Englewood Cliffs, N.J.: Prentice-Hall, 1974.

Jaspan, Norman, and Black, Hillel. *The Thief in the White Collar*. Philadelphia: Lippincott, 1960.

Johnson, John M., and Douglas, Jack D. *Crime at the Top*. Philadelphia: Lippincott, 1978.

Kanter, Rosabeth Moss. *Men and Women of the Corporation*. New York: Basic Books, 1976.

Kassalow, Everett M. *Trade Unions and Industrial Relations*. New York: Random House, 1969.

Kenner, H.J. *The Fight for Truth in Advertising*. New York: Round Table Press, 1936.

Kirkland, Edward Chase. *Dream and Thought in American Business*. Ithaca, N.Y.: Cornell University Press, 1956.

Kohlmeier, Louis M., Jr. *The Regulators*. New York: Harper & Row, 1969.

Krum, James R., and Keiser, Stephen K. "Regulation of Retail Newspaper Advertising." *Journal of Marketing*. 40 (1976):29-34.

Kugel, Yerachmiel, and Gruenberg, Gladys W. *International Payoffs*. Lexington, Mass.: LexingtonBooks, 1977.

Kwitney, Jonathan. *Vicious Circles*. New York: Norton, 1979.

Ladd, John. "Morality and the Idea of Rationality in Formal Organizations." *The Monist* 54 (1970):488-512.

Lane, Robert E. *The Regulation of Businessmen*. New Haven: Yale University Press, 1954.

_____ . "Why Businessmen Violate the Law." In Geis and Meyer, *White Collar Crime*, pp. 102-116.

Layton, Edwin T., Jr. *The Revolt of the Engineers.* Cleveland: Case Western Reserve Press, 1972.

Levy, Leslie. "Reforming Board Reform." *Harvard Business Review* 59 (1981):166-172.

Leys, Wayne A.E. *Ethics for Policy Decisions.* New York: Greenwood, 1968.

Likert, Rensis. *The Human Organization.* New York: McGraw-Hill, 1967.

Lipman, Mark. *Stealing.* New York: Harper's Magazine Press, 1973.

Lipset, Seymour Martin. *The First New Nation.* New York: Basic Books, 1963.

Littleton, A.C. *Accounting Evolution to 1900.* New York: Russell & Russell, 1933.

Loeb, Stephen E., ed. *Ethics in the Accounting Profession.* New York: Wiley, 1978.

Luthans, Fred, and Hodgetts, Richard M., eds. *Social Issues in Business.* 2d ed. New York: Macmillan, 1976.

Maccoby, Michael. *The Gamesman.* New York: Simon and Schuster, 1976.

MacDonald, Donald. *Detroit 1985.* New York: Doubleday, 1980.

MacPherson v. *Buick Motor Co.* 1916, 217 New York 283 III NE 1050.

Manne, Henry G. *Insider Trading and the Stock Market.* New York: Free Press, 1966.

March, James G., and Simon, Herbert A. *Organizations.* New York: Wiley, 1958.

Mayer, Martin. *Madison Avenue, U.S.A.* New York: Harper, 1958.

McCloy, John J., et al. *The Great Gulf Oil Spill.* New York: Chelsea, 1976.

McGregor, Douglas. *The Human Side of Enterprise.* New York: McGraw-Hill, 1960.

Messick, Hank. *The Politics of Prosecution: Jim Thompson, Richard Nixon, Marje Everett and the Trial of Otto Kerner.* Ottowa, Ill.: Carolina House Books, 1978.

Miller, James C., III, and Yandle, Bruce, eds. *Benefit and Cost Analyses of Social Regulations.* Washington, D.C.: American Enterprise Institute, 1979.

Mintzberg, Henry. "Organization Design, Fashion or Fit." *Harvard Business Review* 59 (1981):111 ff.

Moffitt, Donald, ed. *Swindled.* Princeton, N.J.: Dow-Jones Books, 1976.

Morgan Fred W., Jr., "The Products Liability Consequences of Advertising." *Journal of Advertising* 8:4 (1979):30-37.

Moskins, J. Robert, ed. *The Case for Advertising.* New York: American Association of Advertising Agencies, 1973.

Nader, Laura, ed. *No Access to Law.* New York: Academic Press, 1980.

Nader, Ralph. *Unsafe at Any Speed.* New York: Grossman, 1972.

Nader, Ralph; Green, Mark; and Seligman, Joel. *Taming the Giant Corporation.* New York: W.W. Norton, 1976.

Newman, Donald J. "Public Attitudes toward a Form of White Collar Crime." *Social Problems* 4 (1954): 228-232.

Ogilvy, David. *Confessions of an Advertising Man.* New York: Ballantine, 1963.

Origo, Iris. *The Merchant of Prato.* London: Jonathan Cape, 1957.

Ouchi, William. *Theory Z.* Reading, Mass.: Addison-Wesley, 1981.

Parker, Don B. *Crime by Computer.* New York: Scribner's, 1976.

Pascale, Richard Tanner, and Athos, Anthony G. *The Art of Japanese Management.* New York: Simon & Schuster, 1981.

Peck, Sidney. *The Rank and File Leader.* New Haven, Conn.: College and University Press, 1963.

Pilon, Roger. "Corporations and Rights on Treating Corporate People Justly." *Georgia Law Review* 13:4 (1979):1245-1370.

Posner, Richard A. *Antitrust Law.* Chicago: University of Chicago Press, 1976.

_____ . *Economic Analysis of Law.* Boston: Little, Brown, 1977.

_____ . *Regulation of Advertising by the FTC.* Washington, D.C.: American Enterprise Institute, 1973.

Post, James E. *Corporate Behavior and Social Change.* Reston, Va.: Reston, 1978.

Preston, Ivan. *The Great American Blow-Up.* Madison: University of Wisconsin Press, 1975.

Purcell, Theodore V., and Cavanaugh, Gerald F. *Blacks in the Industrial World: Issues for the Manager.* New York: Free Press, 1972.

Radin, Max. *Manners and Morals of Business.* Indianapolis: Bobbs-Merrill, 1939.

Randall, Willard S., and Solomon, Stephan D. *Building 6.* Boston: Little, Brown, 1975.

Raw, Charles; Page, Bruce; and Hodson, Godfrey. *Do You Sincerely Want to be Rich?* New York: Viking, 1971.

Rodgers, Daniel T. *The Work Ethic in Industrial America, 1850-1920.* Chicago: University of Chicago Press, 1978.

Rothschild, Donald P., and Throne, Bruce C. "Criminal Consumer Fraud: A Victim Oriented Analysis." *Michigan Law Review* 74 (1976): 661-675.

Rottenberg, Simon, ed. *Occupational Licensing and Regulation.* Washington, D.C.: American Enterprise Institute for Public Policy Research, 1967.

Sakolski, Aaron M. *The Great American Land Bubble.* New York: Harper, 1932.

Sampson, Anthony. *The Seven Sisters.* New York: Bantam Books, 1976.

Sanford, David; Nader, Ralph; Ridgeway, James, et al. *Hot War on the Consumer.* New York: Pitman, 1969.

Schotland, Roy A. "Unsafe at Any Price." *Virginia Law Review* 53 (1967): 1475-1478.

Schrag, Philip G. *Counsel for the Deceived*. New York: Pantheon, 1972.

Scott, S.P., ed. and trans., *The Code of Justinian*. New York: AMS, 1973.

Seidler, J.; Andrews, Frederick; and Epstein, Marc J. *The Equity Funding Papers*. Santa Barbara, Cal.: Wiley, 1977.

Seldin, Joseph. *The Golden Fleece*. New York: Macmillan, 1963.

Selekman, Benjamin. "Cynicism and Managerial Morality." *Harvard Business Review* 36 (1958).

Selekman, Benjamin, and Selekman, Sylvia. *Power and Morality in a Business Society*. New York: McGraw-Hill, 1956.

Sethi, S. Prakash, ed. *The Unstable Ground: Corporate Social Policy in a Dynamic Society*. Los Angeles: Melville, 1974.

Shore, Barry. "A Framework for Procurement Decisions Dominated by Environmental Constraints." *Journal of Purchasing* 8 (1972):46-53.

Smigel, Erwin O., and Ross, H. Lawrence. *Crimes against Bureaucracy*. New York: Van Nostrand, 1970.

Smith, Adam. *The Wealth of Nations*. New York: E.P. Dutton, 1927. Originally published 1776.

Smith, Richard Austin. *Corporations in Crisis*. Garden City, N.Y.: Doubleday-Anchor, 1966.

Smyth, Richard C., and Murphy, M.J. *Bargaining with Organized Labor*. New York: Funk and Wagnalls, 1948.

Sobel, Lester A., ed. *Consumer Protection*. New York: Facts on File, 1976.

Thomas Aquinas. *Summa Theologiae*. Vol. 37. New York: McGraw-Hill.

Steele, Eric H. "Fraud, Dispute and the Consumer: Responding to Consumer Complaints." *University of Pennsylvania Law Review* 123 (1975):1107-1186.

Stevenson, Russell B., Jr. "The S.E.C. and the New Disclosure." *Cornell Law Review* 62 (1976):50-93.

Stone, Christopher. *Where the Law Ends*. New York: Harper Colophon, 1976.

Sultan, Paul. *The Disenchanted Unionist*. New York: Harper, 1963.

Taeusch, Carl. *Policy and Ethics in Business*. New York: McGraw-Hill, 1931.

Thimm, Alfred L. *The False Promise of Codetermination*. Lexington, Mass.: LexingtonBooks, D.C. Heath, 1980.

Thomas, Dana L. *The Plungers and the Peacocks*. New York: Putnam, 1967.

Thorelli, Hans B. *The Federal Antitrust Policy*. Baltimore: Johns Hopkins Press, 1955.

Trebing, Harry M. *The Corporation in the American Economy*. Chicago: Quadrangle Books, 1970.

Turner, E.S. *The Shocking History of Advertising*. New York: Dutton, 1953.

Turner, Louis. *Multinational Companies and the Third World.* New York: Hill and Wang, 1973.

Twentieth Century Fund. *Abuse on Wall Street.* Westport, Conn.: Quorum Books, 1980.

U.S., Senate Committee on Banking, Housing, and Urban Affairs. *Hearing on Foreign Corrupt Practices,* Washington, D.C.: Government Printing Office, 1977, pp. 98-99.

Waldman, Raymond J. *Regulating International Business through Codes of Conduct.* Washington, D.C.: American Enterprise Institute, 1980.

"Weber and Bakke." *Wayne Law Review* 26 (1980):1309.

Weidenbaum, Murray L. *The Future of Business Regulation.* New York: Amacom, 1980.

Weisband, Edward, and Frank, Thomas M. *Resignation in Protest.* New York: Penguin Books, 1976.

Weisberg, Howard I., and Reichenberg, Eric. *Research Reports. The Price of Ambiguity: More Than Three Years under the Foreign Corrupt Practices Act.* Washington, D.C.: International Division, U.S. Chamber of Commerce, 1981.

Wellford, Harrison. *Sowing the Wind.* New York: Grossman, 1972.

Welles, Chris. *The Last Days of the Club.* New York: Dutton, 1975.

Westin, Alan F. *Whistle Blowing.* New York: McGraw-Hill, 1981.

Whitney, Simon N. *Antitrust Policies.* Vol. 2. New York: The Twentieth Century Fund, 1956.

Wiebe, Roger H. *Businessmen and Reform.* Chicago: Quadrangle Books, 1968.

Wilkes, Robert E., and Wilcox, James B. "Recent FTC Actions: Implications for the Advertising Strategist." *Journal of Marketing* 38 (1974): 55-61.

Wilson, James Q., ed. *Politics of Regulation.* New York: Basic Books, 1980.

Wilson, Robert A. "Barriers to Trust Busting: 'Efficiency' Myths and Timid Trustbusters." *Antitrust Law and Economics Review* 9:3 (1977):19-39.

Winter, Ralph K., Jr., "State Law, Shareholder Protection and the Theory of the Corporation." *The Journal of Legal Studies* 6:2 (1977):278 ff.

Wright, J. Patrick. *On A Clear Day You Can See General Motors.* New York: Avon, 1980.

Wylie, Irvin G. *The Self-Made Man in America: The Myth of Rags to Riches.* New Brunswick, N.J.: Rutgers University Press, 1954.

Yamey, Basil L. *Essays on the History of Accounting.* New York: Arno, 1978.

Index

Accounting: accounting procedures, 195; development of, 190-192; history of, 189

Accounting standards, 193; courts and accounting ethics, 201-202; failures of, 196-199; history, 189-202; looseness of accounting principles, 199-201; real-estate accounting, 199; reporting revenue and income, 200

Accounting Principles Board, 194-195, 202

Ackerman, Robert, 53

Adams, Charles Francis, Jr., 38

Adams, Henry, 38

Addison, Joseph, 206

Adler, Peter and Patricia, 17, 25

Advertising, 205; *Caveat emptor*, 206-208; does advertising create dependence effect, 214-215; historical background, 205-206; quality of advertising, 215; snob appeal, 216; truth in advertising movement, 208-210; usefulness of advertising, 212-213

Advertising ethical standards: business self-regulation, 218-219; comparative advertising, 227; corrective advertising, 225-227; enforcement of, 218; Federal Trade Commission, 220-223; state and local government, 219-220

Aetna Insurance Company, 99

Affirmative action, 92-95; methods of securing integration, 93-94; prevention of psychological harassment, 95-97

Airlines Traffic Association, 174

Allen, Frederick Lewis, 40

Altheide, David and Duane, 17, 25

Amalgamated Meat Cutters and Butcher Workmen, 66

American Association of Public Accountants, 191

American Institute of Certified Public Accountants (AICPA), 192-193

American Petrofina (Dallas), 32, 57

American Society of Newspaper Editors, 46

American Stock Exchange, 9, 138, 198

American Sugar Refining Company, 108

AMK conglomerate, 166

Andrews, Frederick, 199

Antitrust laws: administration of, 159-160; antitrust in politics, 160-163; electrical manufacturers case, 156-159; English and American history of, 151-156; Federal antitrust law, 153-154; Jewish and Roman law, 151

Anyon, James T., 191

Aquinas, St. Thomas, 1, 28, 51, 101, 107; honesty sales 206

Aristotle, 1, 89, 93

Arman Plate and Non-Shatterable Glass Corporation of New York, 210

Arthur Andersen and Company, 196, 202

Associated Advertising Clubs of America, 209

Association of Chartered Accountants, 190

Association theory of crime applied to business crime, 16

Athos, Anthony G., 84

Atlantic Richfield Company (ARCO), 56

Austin, Robert W., 13

Auto-repair industry and government regulation, 243

Baer, Walter E., 79

Barbarino Motors Corporation, 210

Bar Chris Construction Corp., 202

Barnard, Chester I., 30

Barnet, Richard, 259

Baruch, Bernard, xvi, 139

Baruch, Hurd, 139

Bauer, Raymond, 53

Baum, Robert J., 241

Baumhart, Raymond, 5, 6, 18, 159

Beauchamp, Tom L., 41

Beaver, William H., 143

Bell, Howard H., 219

Bennigson, Arnold I., 234

Bennigson, Lawrence A., 234
Benston, George J., 144, 164, 193, 198
Berenson, Conrad: reasons for stricter
    product liability, 234, 238
Beresford, Dennis R., 103
Bergsten, C. Fred, 259
Berle, Adolf A., 28, 57
Bethlehem Steel, 32
Better Business Bureau, 115; influence
    on advertising, 210
Bevan, David C., 40
Binzen, Peter, 40
Bitter Lemon, 216
Black, Hillel, 138
Blackstone, William T., 28
Blue Sky laws, 210
Bonbright, James C., 135
Borden, Neil H., 212
Bork, Robert A., 154, 162
Boulware, Lemuel R., 62
Bowie, Norman E., 41
Bradshaw, Thornton, 56, 58, 92, 127
Brenner, Steven N., 7
Bribery, 37, 249; corporate payments
    to foreign officials, 249; payments
    by multinational corporations,
    250-252; Proxmire Act of 1977, 250-
    251
Briloff, Abraham, 46
Brokerage firms, ethics of, 132
Brooks, John, 17, 193
Brown, Richard, 190
Brozen, Yale, 213
"Bucket shops", 132
Burns, James MacGregor, 31
Burns, Joseph M., 132
Burton, John C., 194
Business ethics: American heritage of,
    1; definition of, xiv; literature
    described, xiii; relation to general
    ethics, xiv-xv; religion and, 22-23
Business firms: ethical background, 89-
    90; social responsibility, 89-104;
    responsibility for health and safety
    of employees, 69-72
Business persons: effect of age on
    ethics, 17-18; effect of education
    on, 21-22; higher education and
    pressures of competition on, 21-22;
    effect of religion on, 22-23; studies
    of ethics, 5

Business social standards, insurance
    policies, 102; redlining, 102; social
    betterment of employees and under-
    privileged groups, 102-104; violence
    on television, 101
Buxton, Edward, 215-216

California Contractors' State License
    Board, 121
Canteen Corporation, 161
Caplovitz, David, 118
Carnegie, Andrew, 131
Carosso, Vincent P., 134, 137
Carpenter, James W., 219
Carper, Jean, 120, 208
Carpet and Rug Industry Consumer
    Action Panel, 115
Carroll, Archie B., 8
Cavanaugh, Gerald F., 96
Caveat emptor, xvi, xvii, 110, 118; de-
    cline of, 208; in nineteenth century,
    3; in nineteenth-century advertising,
    205-207; in twentieth-century adver-
    tising, 209
Celler-Kefauver Act, 156
Central States Pension Fund, 66
Cerra, Frances, 243
Chandler, Alfred D., Jr., 172
Charitable obligations of corporations,
    91
Chase National Bank, 40
Chase, Stuart, 109
Chatfield, Michael, 190
Chatov, Robert, 195, 200-201
Chemicals: cancer, 70; Rohm and Haas
    Company, 70-72
Chesapeake and Ohio Railroad, 28
Chicago, Burlington, and Quincy Rail-
    road, 39
Chicago Stock Exchange, 192
Chicago Tribune, 209
Chief Executive Officer (CEO), 30;
    role in ethical education, 30-31
Chrysler Corporation, 14, 40, 79, 123
Churches and ethical education, 22
Citibank, 198
Civil Aeronautics Board (CAB), 176-
    178
Civil Rights Act of 1964, 95
Clarey, Robert I., 122
Clark, Timothy B., 7, 8

Class-action suits, 241
Clayton Act of 1914, 39, 155-156
Clean Air Act of 1970, 179
Clews, Henry, 133-134, 136
Clinard, Marshall B., 10, 15, 21, 30
Coal mines, mining-safety laws, 70
Cochran, Thomas C., 38
Cohen, Nathan H., 120
Cole, Robert E., 174
Collective bargaining, 60-65
Committee on Accounting Procedures, 202
Common law, 1; ethical traditions in, 51; restrictions on labor, 52; restrictions on restraint of trade, 152
Compensation, ethics of, 52-54
Computer crime, 18
Comstock, George, 101
Conflict of interest: in corporate development, 37-41; in the securities business, 140-143
Conglomerate mergers: AMK and United Fruit, 166; the case against and for conglomerates, 164-166
Conklin, John E., 16
Consolidated Edison, 32
Consolidated Oil and Gas, 196; King Resources, 196
Consumers, 107-124; auto safety, 109; business actions to protect, 115-116; business responsibility for consumer health, 109-112; fraud against, 112-113, 121; improvement of law to protect, 122-123; legal problems of poorer consumers, 116-122; state and local regulation in behalf of, 116-122
Consumer Products Safety, 21, 124, 179; Commission Act of 1972, 235
Continental Baking Company, 225
Continental Oil Company, 39
Contracts, obligations of, 2
Control Data Corporation, 56
Cooper, Ernest, 190
Coopers and Lybrand, 196-197; Lybrand, Ross Brothers, and Montgomery, 196
Cordiner, Ralph, 58
Corporations: affirmative action, 92; corporate codes, 42-44; effect on individual, 31-33; employee loyalty to, 30-31; environment, 97; ethical codes, 42; ethical history of, 27-30; industry-wide code of ethics, 44; legal action against, 35-36; legal rights, 33-34; morality of, 30-31; political powers of, 36-37; responsibility for health and safety standards, 34-35; social responsibility and, 34-36; stealing from, 16-17
Cornfeld, Bernard, 196-197
Cresap, Mark, president of Westinghouse: involvement in antitrust violations, 158
Cressey, Donald, R., 13, 22
Crime, association theory of, 15
Crock, Stan, 227
Crozier, Michael, 87

Daley, Robert, 21
Dalton, Melville, 16, 63
Darvie, Mark: comments on Pinto car, 241
Darwinism, social, xviii, 2
Daughen, Joseph R., 40
De George, Richard T., 46
Delta Air Lines, 56
De Lorean, John, 30, 31, 41, 61, 103, 241
DeMond, C.W., 191
Department of Health, Education, and Welfare (HEW), 111
Department of Justice, 100, 161
Derber, Milton, 61
Detroit Times, 209
Direct Selling Association, 46
Disclosure of information, corporate accounting, 143-145
Disposable containers, 100
Division of Consumer Fraud and Protection, Illinois State Attorney General, 116
Divita, S.C., 223
Dodd, David, 135
Douglas, Jack D., 8
Dow Chemical Company, 56, 70
Dowdy, John, 121
Drew, Daniel, 38, 131
Dropp, Donald R., 201
Drotning, Philip T., 94
Drucker, Peter, 64, 85, 256
Duber, Kenneth, 19

Durant, William C., 131
Dyer, Robert F., 227

East India Company, 33
Eaton, Marian, 116
Eckert, Ross, 177-178
Edwards, James D., 191
Edwards, Paul, 80
Edwards, P.K., 68-69
Edwards, Sarah, 80
European Economic Community
    (EEC), 236
Eells, Richard, 247
E.I. Du Pont de Nemours and Co.,
    123-160
Electrical Workers' Union, 68
Elias, Christopher, 139
Embezzlers, 13
Employee Retirement Income Security
    Act of 1974 (ERISA), 102, 124,
    141-142
Employees: affirmative action, 92;
    business responsibility for health
    and safety of, 69-72; ethical rela-
    tions with business, 51-52; grievance
    management of, 79-80; history of
    employee rights, 62-63; loyalty to
    the corporation, 84-86; rights of in
    multinational corporations, 253-255;
    supervision of, 77-87
Employee theft, reduction of, 18-20;
    white-collar theft, 58-60
Engelbourg, Saul, 39
Engeman, Thomas E., 17
Engineering Council for Professional
    Development, 47
Environment, business responsibility
    concerning, 97-100
Environmental Protection Agency, 21,
    111, 175, 179
Epstein, Edwin M., 36
Epstein, Marc J., 199
Equal Employment Opportunity Com-
    mission, 179
Equity Funding Company of America
    (EFCA), 18, 29, 32, 35, 54, 197;
    Equity Funding Life Insurance
    Company, 197
Erie Railroad, 38
Ethical codes: America's initial, 1;
    present-day codes, 267-270

Ethical education, 20-22; of corporate
    executives, 21; role of the CEO, 22
Ethics, xiv; legal approach, xvii-xviii.
    See also Business ethics
Ewen, Stuart, 214
Ewing, David, 56-58
Exxon, payments to foreign officials,
    249

Facts on File, 29
Federal Communications Commission,
    176-178, 182
Federal Department of Transportation,
    55
Federal Energy Administration, indict-
    ments of oil refiners, 160
Federal Power Commission, 176
Federal Reserve Act of 1914, 134
Federal Trade Commission, 29, 46-47,
    111-112, 156, 164, 173, 179; action
    on fraud against consumers,
    123-124; Bureau of Consumer Pro-
    tection, 221; charges of misrepresen-
    tation made against Anacin,
    Bufferin, and Bayer Aspirin, 110,
    220; issue of warranty regulations,
    221
Feldman, Lawrence P., 221
Fellmeth, Robert C., 18
Fendrock, John J., 31
Ferber, Nat, 133
Financial Accounting Standards Board
    (FASB), 195, 202
Financial Analysts Federation, 194
Financial Executives Institute, 194
Finn, David, 32, 103, 175
Firestone Tire and Rubber Company,
    240
Fisk, Jim, 38
Flores, Albert, 47
Food and Drug Administration, 32,
    211; action against drug manufac-
    turers, 111; more inspectors needed
    in the food industry, 110
Foolproof Protection, Inc., 118
Ford, Henry, 53
Ford Motor Company, 123; involve-
    ment in auto-safety standards, 234
Four Seasons Nursing Center, 200
Frank, Thomas M., 55
Frankena, William K., 199

Franklin, Ben A., 70
Franklin National Bank, 35
Freedman, Eric, 114
Free enterprise, excuse for illegality, 111
Freund, Ernst, 172
Friedman, Lawrence M., 27,29
Friedman, Milton, 91-92
Fuller, John, 13
Fund of Funds, 196
Furniture Industry Consumer Action Panel, 115

Galambos, Louis N., 153
Galbraith, John K., 214
Gardiner, Alan, 51
Gardner, David M., 223
Gas Products Association, 45
General Electric Company, 13-14, 56-57, 62, 100; antitrust violations, 158
General Motors, 30-31, 34, 61, 123, 163; payments to candidates, 249; product safety, 235
Gentry, Curt, 35
Germany, control of unfair competition, 224
Gewirth, Alan, 34
Gladwin, Thomas N., 252
Golden Rule, 5
Goldman Sachs, 41, 135, 142, 166
Good Housekeeping, 209
Goodrich Company, B.F., 32, 34
Gould, Jay, 38
Government regulation: business, 171-186; detailed regulations of specific industries, 176-179; excessive regulations, 179-183; history of, 171-172; problem of enforcement, 179-185; steps toward more workable regulation, 183-186
Graham, Benjamin, 135
Gray, Irwin: product liability suits, 235
Great Crash of 1929, 29, 135
Greek law, 51
Green, Mark J., 156, 159
Greenberg, David I., 115
Grether, E.T., 208
Greyser, Stephen A., 213, 217
Grimes, Warren S., 224
Grotius, Hugo, 248

Gruenberg, Gladys, 252
Gulf and Western Industries, Inc., 167
Gulf Oil, 10, 21; payments to foreign officials, 248

Hackman, J. Richard, 82
Hahn, Kenneth, 99, 109, 240
Hall, Burton H., 60
Hamilton, Walton H., 206
Hammacher, Paul M., 42
Hammurabi, Code of, 1, 89, 205
Harris, Louis, 90
Harvard Business Review, 5, 217
Haskins and Sells, 198
Health and safety, 90; responsibility of corporations for, 90; Rohm and Haas Company and chemical safety, 70
Heermance, Edgar L., 44, 46-47
Heilbroner, Robert L., 54
Helffrich, Stanton, 47
Hepburn Act of 1906, 191
Herling, John, 158
Herman, Edward B., 141
Hessen, Robert, 34
Hewlett-Packard Corporation, 62, 82
Hill, Ivan, 46-47
Hodgetts, Richard M., 90, 107
Hodson, Godfrey, 196
Hoffman, W. Michael, 82
Holding companies, 28
Homestead Act of 1863, 127
Horning, Donald N.M., 17
Horwitz, Morton J., 132
Howard, John A., 217-218
Hubbard, Henry W., 112
Huge, Harry, 174
Hulbert, James, 217-218
Hunter, Louis C., 172
Hurst, J. Willard, 172
Hutchinson, John, 61
Hutchinson, Robert A., 197

Industry codes, 44-48
Inland Steel Corporation, 103
Insider information, 145-147; "the wall," 148
Insull Utility Investments, 134-135
Insurance industry, 102, 191
Interest on loans, 128
International Business Machines (IBM), 62, 82, 248

International Telephone and Telegraph
   Corp. (ITT), 161
Interstate Commerce Commission Act
   of 1870, 123, 176, 178-179, 182
Interstate Investment Trust (IIT), 196
Investment Bankers Association (IBA),
   137
Investment Company Act of 1940, 129
Investors Overseas Service, 54, 137,
   196
Iowa Beef Packing Company, 66-67
Iowa Hotel Association, 46

Jacobs, Leslie W., 41
Jacoby, Neil, 103
Japanese management methods, 82-85
Jaspan, Norman, 8, 12-20
Johnson, John M., 8
Joint Stock Companies Act of 1856,
   190
Judaic-Christian ethics, 51, 78, 89-90,
   92, 151, 174
Julian Petroleum Corporation of Los
   Angeles, 210

Kaiser Aluminum Company, 161
Kant, Immanuel, 51, 55, 90
Kanter, Rosabeth Moss, 12, 33, 95
Karikas, Angela, 116
Kassalow, Everett M., 52, 68
Katzenbach, Nicholas, 161
Kefauver Committee, 11, 158
Keiser, Steven K., 220
Kelman, Steven, 181
Kenner, H.J., 132, 209-210
Kerner, Governor Otto, 15
Kintner, Earl W., 46
Kirkland, Edward Chase, 22
Kohlmeier, Louis M., Jr., 176, 182
Kristol, Irving, 33
Krum, James R., 220
Kuehl, Phillip G., 227
Kugel, Yerachmiel, 252
Kwitney, Jonathan 65-67

Labeling Act of 1960, 179
Labor, 52-54, 60-64; ethical codes con-
   cerning, 52-52
Ladd, John, 30
Ladies Home Journal, 208
laissez-faire doctrine, 172

Lake Shore Associates, 196
Land sales, history of 127-128; real-
   estate investment trusts, 128-130;
   boom and bust cycles, 128
Land speculation, 128
Lane, Robert E., 15, 21, 183
Law and ethics, xvii
Lawler, Edward E., III, 82
Layton, Edwin T., Jr., 239
Leasing and hiring, 2
Lebow, Victor, 214
Lehman Brothers, 41
Lesser-developed countries, 247
Levin, Michael, 181
Leviticus, 134, 139
Levy, Leslie, 36
Leys, Wayne A.E., 52
Likert, Rensis, 86
Lincoln Securities, 137
Lincoln Stores, 41
Lipman, Mark, 15, 17-18
Lipset, Seymour Martin, 61
Littleton, A.C., 189
Lockheed Corporation, 103
Loeb, Stephen E., 193
Loevinger, Lee, 226
Lorillard Tobacco, 220
Los Angeles County, 57; Department
   of Consumer Affairs, 121
Loyola University, Chicago, 5
Lucas, Malcolm, 199
Luthans, Fred, 90, 107

Maccoby, Michael, 11-12, 82
MacDonald, Donald, 113
Macy's Department Store, 208
Magnuson, Senator Warren G., 124
Magnuson-Moss Warranty Act, 124,
   221, 225
Maimonides, Moses, 89
Major Appliance Consumer Panel, 115
Mammana, Nicholas, 107
Management, 77-87; authoritarian su-
   pervision at middle-management
   level, 78; participative, 80-81
Manne, Henry G., 146
March, James G., 86
Maritime Commission (Shipping Act,
   1916), 177
Marshall Field, 208
Massachusetts Supreme Court, 41, 132

Matsushita, 84
May, Marvin, 165
Mayer, Martin, 142, 213-214, 216, 221
McAvoy, Paul W., 180
McCarthy, Colman, 241
McCloy, John J., 250
McDonald's Corporation, 56
McGregor, Douglas, 85
Means, Gardiner C., 28, 135
Mecom, John, 196
Merrill-Lynch, 41
Mexico Oil Company, 39
Middle West Utilities Company, 135
Mill, John Stuart, xv
Miller, James C., III, 180
Miller-Tydings Act (1937), 156, 183
Mills, C. Wright, 16
Mintzberg, Henry, 31
Molander, Earl A., 7
Monarch Corporation, 120
Monopoly, control of, 151-152, 154
Morgan, Fred W., Jr., 234
Morgan, House of, 133
Mosaic Law, ethical traditions in, xiv,
    xvi, xvii
Moskins, J. Robert, 218
Moskowitz, Milton, 95
Motor Vehicle Manufacturers Associa-
    tion, 109
"Muckraking," 153
Muller, Ronald E., 259
Multinational corporations, 247-260;
    American unions, 253; disclosure
    of information, 254; economic
    ethics of, 255-258; employee rights
    and industrial relations, 254; ethical
    background, 248-249; involvement
    in bribery and extortion, 249-252;
    involvement in lesser-developed
    countries, 256-259
Munsey's, 208
Murphy, M.J., 63

Nader, Ralph, 33, 36, 54, 109-110, 114,
    166; business resistance toward
    greater auto-pollution standards,
    109; food industry, 109-110; safety
    and the auto industry, 239;
    "whistle-blowing," 54-56
National Academy of Science, National
    Research Council, 111

National Advertising Review Board,
    219; Automotive Trade Association
    managers, 115
National Association for Advancement
    of Colored Peoples (NAACP), 117
National Association of Broadcasters, 47
National Association of Home Build-
    ers, Home Owners' Warranty Pro-
    gram, 115
National Association of Ice Cream
    Manufacturers, 45
National Association of Manufactur-
    ers, 52, 90
National Association of Retail Cloth-
    iers, 45
National Association of Securities
    Dealers, 46
National Commission on Product
    Safety, 111
National Council of Churches of
    Christ in America, 22
National Highway Traffic Safety Ad-
    ministration, 235
National Institute of Occupational
    Safety and Health, 71
National Maritime Council, 177
National Recovery Act, 137
National Retail Merchants Association,
    115
National Student Marketing Corpora-
    tion, 200
National Traffic & Motor Vehicle
    Safety Act of 1966, 175
Natural rights, influence in American
    life, xv
New Jersey Bell Telephone Company, 30
Newman, Donald J., 59
Newton, Lauren K., 144
New York Central Railroad, 38, 134
New Yorker, 217
New York Life Insurance Company, 39
New York Stock Exchange, 9, 36, 134,
    136, 138-139, 192, 198
New York Times, 219
New York Tribune, 210
Northrop Corporation, 11
Noxious Products Act of 1976, 179

Occupational Safety and Health Ad-
    ministration (OSHA), 21, 29, 81,
    175, 179, 181

Ocean Spray, Inc., 225
Offen, Neil H., 46
Office of Price Administration, 10
Ogilvy, David, 212
Opinion Research Center, 44, 47
Organized crime: involvement in business, 65; connection with unions, 65-67
Origo, Iris, 89
Ouchi, William, 54

Paciolo, Luca, 189
Page, Bruce, 196
Parke-Davis and Company, 161
Parker, Don B., 18, 20
Participative management, 80-81; in Japan, 82-84
Pascale, Richard Tanner, 84
Penn-Central Corporation, 9, 34, 40
Penn-Central Railroad, 141
Pennphil, 40
Perkins, George W., 39
Philadelphia North American, 209
Pichler, Joseph A., 46
Pilon, Roger, 34
Pinkerton's Inc., 60
Pinto car, 236, 241
Pitney Bowes, Inc., 56
Pitofsky, Robert, 212
Plumbing Fixtures Manufacturing Association, 159
Polaroid Corporation, 96
Pond's soap, 216
Posner, Richard A., xvii, 162, 233
Post, James E., 96
Prairie Oil and Gas, 39
Preston, Ivan L., 206-207
Price, Waterhouse and Company, 17, 191, 192, 196
Price cutting, Robinson Patman Act, 156
Printer's Ink, 209
Private pension funds, 141
Product liability, 29, 233-245; business resistance to liability, 239-242; the Corvair, 240; ethical and legal history, 233-237; new liability, 234-235; the Pinto, 240; responsibility of business, 237-239
Product Safety Commission, 124
Profit sharing, 61
Property, right of holding, 2
Proxmire, Senator William, 10

Proxmire Act of 1977, 250-251; forbidding major payments to officials and political figures, 251
Public Relations Society of America, 46
Public Utility Holding Company Act, 135
Pujo Committee, 134
Purcell, Theodore V., 96
Pure Food and Drugs Act, 179

Quaker Oats Company, 35
Quality of Working Life (QWL), 81

Radin, Max, 205
Rae, John, 173
Randall, Willard J., 70-72
Ranger National Life, 199
Ransom, Roger, XVII
Raw, Charles, 196
Real Estate Investment Trusts (REIT), 128-130
Redlining, 102
Reed-Bulwinkle Act of 1948, 156
Reich, Robert B., 173
Reichenberg, Eric, 251
Religion and business ethics, 7, 22-23
Repair of complex products, 243-244
Reserve Mining Corporation, dumping of used iron ore into Lake Superior, 99
Retail Furniture Association of California, 211
Richardson-Merrell Corporation, 32, 35, 111
RKO, 58
Robert Morris Associates, 194
Robin, Gerald D., 59
Robinson Patman Act of 1936, 156
Rockefeller, John D., Jr., 39-40
Rodgers, Daniel T., 77
Rohm and Haas Company, 70
Rosenwasser, Rena, 116
Ross, H. Lawrence, 17
Rothschild, Donald P., 122
Rottenberg, Simon, 124

Sakolski, Aaron M., 128
Salt Lake City Tribune, 161
Salus populi suprema lex, 56, 108, 110, 174
Sampson, Anthony, 252, 259

Sanford, David, 110
Saturday Evening Post, 208
Schlink, F.J., 109
Schotland, Roy A., 128, 146
Schrag, Philip G., 117
Schwab, Charles M., 39
Scotch Institutes of Accountants, 190
Scott, S.P. 151
Scribner's, 208
Sears, Roebuck and Company, 248
Securities: "bucket shops," 132-133; disclosure, 143-145; fraud, 138
Securities Act of 1933, 192, 202
Securities and Exchange Commission Act of 1934, 36, 46, 136-137, 145-146, 191, 192; investigation of corporate payments to officials and politicians, 249-252
Security sales, 130-132; boiler rooms, 137-138; brokerage houses, 138; conflict of interest, 140-143; corners and bears, 131, 136; fraudulent sales, 138; holding companies, 134-136; legislative control, 136-137; speculative securities, 132; usefulness of security markets, 132-133; watered stock, 133-134
Seidler, J., 199
Seldin, Joseph, 212
Selekman, Benjamin, 62, 74
Selekman, Sylvia, 62, 74
Seligman, Daniel, 94
Senate Antitrust and Monopoly Subcommittee, 244
Servants, a master's responsibility for actions of, 77
Shawana Development Corporation, 138
Shawcross, Lord, 252
Sherman Antitrust Law of 1890, 151-153, 163, 168
Sheth, Jagdish N., 107
Shore, Barry, 98
Sicilian Mafia, 65
Sic utere tuo ut alienum non laedas, 1, 56, 69, 90, 99-100, 174
Simon, Herbert A., 31, 86
Sinclair Crude Purchasing, 39
Singer Company, 56
Slaves, treatment of in ancient Athens, 51

Sloan-Kettering Institute for Cancer Research, 71
Smigel, Erwin O., 17
Smith, Adam, 51, 172
Smith, Line, and French Company, 103
Smith, Richard Austin, 14, 32, 159
Smyth, Richard C., 63
Sobel, Lester A., 111
Social Gospel Movement, 77
SOHIO, 98
Solomon, Stephan D., 70-72
Sowell, Thomas, 95
Standard Magazine Service, 117-118
Standard Oil of Indiana, 39-40, 152
Stanton, Thomas H., 115
Starkman, Ernest S., 99
Stealing, prohibition under various ethical codes, 2; valid if from corporations, 16-17
Steele, Eric H., 116
Steele, Sir Richard, 206
Steinman, Moe, 66
Stevenson, Russell B., Jr., 145
Stewart, A.T., 208
Stewart, Robert W., 39
St. Louis Star, 209
Stone, Christopher, 35
Strikes, 68-69
Sultan, Paul, 64
Supervision, ethics of, 77-78; participative management, 80-87; grievance handling, 79-80
Sutherland, Edwin H., 13, 30
Suttle, J. Lloyd, 82

Taeusch, Carl, 210
Teamster's Union, 61, 66-67; Central States Pension Fund, 66
Television, 101
Telex Corporation, 200
"Ten Commandments of Advertising," 209
Texas Gulf Sulphur, 35
Theory Y, 85
Thimm, Alfred L., 79
Thomas, Dana L., 135
Thorelli, Hans B., 154
Throne, Bruce C., 122
Tinkham, Spencer F., 214
Tobias, Andrew, 18

Toxic Substances Control Act of 1977, 175
Traffic Safety Administration, 175
Trane Home Comfort Center, 120
Trans World Airlines, (TWA), 58
Trebing, Harry H., 75, 282
Trusts, 152-153
Truth in Lending Act of 1968, 29, 124, 179
Truth in Packaging Act of 1966, 179
Turner, E.S., 207
Turner, Louis, 258

Ungar, Sanford J., 111
Uniform Commercial Code, 234
Union Carbide, 201
Unions, 60-69; attitude toward supervision, 63-64; closed shop, 65; multinational corporations and unions, 253-254; unions in politics, 64-65
United Auto Workers, 79
United Fruit Company, 166
United Mine Workers, 141
United States Department of Labor, 60, 66, 181
United States National Bank of San Diego, 29
University of Virginia, 42
U.S. Chamber of Commerce, 8
U.S. Fidelity & Guaranty Company, 20
U.S. Senate Banking and Currency Committee, Pecora Committee, 136
U.S. Steel Corporation, 32, 39, 52, 160; Federal Steel, 191

Vanderbilt, Cornelius, 38, 108, 134
Vanderbilt, William Henry, 32
Vesco, Robert L., 196-197
Virginia Center for Study of Ethics, 43-44
Vogel, David, 95, 127
Von Hayek, Friedrich, XVI, 228

Waldman, Raymond J., 247, 257, 259
Walter, Ingo, 252
Wanamaker's 208

Warner-Lambert Company, 161, 227
Warranties and product liability, 234
Watergate, 11
Weaver, Suzanne, 154
Webb-Pomerene Act of 1916, 156
Weidenbaum, Murray L., 180, 185
Weights and measures, ethical codes supporting, 2
Weisband, Edward, 55
Weisberg, Howard I., 251
Welles, Chris, 9, 166
Wellford, Harrison, 110
Wells Fargo, 198
Westin, Alan F., 54, 56
Westinghouse Corporation, 14, 158; antitrust violations, 156-159
Wheeler-Lea Amendment of 1938, 211
"Whistle Blowing", 54-56
White-collar crime, 18
Whitney, Richard, 9
Whitney, Simon N., 160
Whyte, William H., Jr., 11
Wiebe, Roger H., 90, 153
Wiggin, Albert H., 40
Wilcox, James B., 221
Wiley, Harvey W., 209
Wilkes, Robert E., 221
Wilson, Ian H., 100
Wilson, James Q., 154, 181
Wilson, Robert A., 163
Winter, Ralph K., Jr., 41
Wolfson, Nicholas, 142
Wolfson, Weiner, 197
Women's rights, 92-96
Workers, rights of, 41-42; 51-52
Wright, J. Patrick, 30-31, 34, 41, 61, 103, 241
Wylie, Irvin G., 131
Wyly, Thomas J., 82

Xerox Corporation, 62, 82

Yamey, Basil S., 189
Yandle, Bruce, 22
Youthful morals, 17-18

Zapola Norness, Inc., 166

About the Author

George C.S. Benson received the B.A. in 1928 from Pomona College, the M.A. in 1929 from the University of Illinois, and the M.A. in 1930 from Harvard University. He received the Ph.D. from Harvard University and has several honorary degrees. He has had a distinguished career of lecturing and teaching positions at several major universities, as well as a position as deputy assistant secretary of defense (education) from 1969-1972. Dr. Benson is currently president emeritus, Claremont McKenna College, and director of the Salvatori Center for the Study of Individual Freedom in the Modern World. In addition, he has held numerous consulting and public service positions, including: member, California Coordinating Council on Higher Education (1967-1969); president, Western College Association (1958-1962); and member, Board of Foreign Scholarships, U.S. Department of State (1956-1960). In addition to numerous articles on political science and ethical matters, Dr. Benson has published several books including *Political Corruption in America* (Lexington Books (1978), *Amoral America* (1975), *The Politics of Urbanism* (1972), *The New Centralization* (1941), *Civil Service in Massachusetts* (1935), and *Financial Control and Integration* (1933).